AMERICA'S TENTH LEGION

AMERICA'S TENTH LEGION

X Corps in Korea, 1950

Shelby L. Stanton

PRESIDIO

Published by Presidio Press
31 Pamaron Way, Novato CA 94949

Library of Congress Cataloging-in-Publication Data

Stanton, Shelby L., 1948–
    America's Tenth Legion: X Corps in Korea, 1950/Shelby L.
Stanton.
      p. cm.
    Bibliography: p. 333
    Includes index.
    ISBN 0–89141–258–1
    1. Korean War, 1950–1953—Regimental histories—United States.
2. United States. Army. Corps, 10th—History. 3. Almond, Edward
M. (Edward Mallory), 1892–1979. I. Title.
DS919.S72   1989
951.904'2—dc20   89–8835
                                                                      CIP

Printed in the United States of America

CONTENTS

FOREWORD

The campaign of X Corps in the first year of the Korean war, from its amphibious invasion behind enemy lines at Inch'on through its drive to the Yalu River and final evacuation of Hungnam, remains one of the most remarkable battlefield episodes of modern United States military history.

During 1950, X Corps existed as a uniquely independent organization directly under General Douglas MacArthur's command. The separate status of this corps offered an excellent opportunity to depict operational combat at corps level involving joint and multinational forces in both offensive and defensive roles, unfettered by higher field Army headquarters complications.

The concept for this book was proposed by my publisher, Robert V. Kane, and represents an outgrowth of my previous work, *Anatomy of a Division*. In that work I analyzed the wartime roles and functioning of a division-sized formation, using the 1st Cavalry Division in Vietnam as the critique vehicle. Shortly after completing the research for the division volume, I was selected by the Department of Defense to compile the official Army order of battle for the Korean War. My reorientation from Vietnam studies toward the Korean conflict, and from division to the corps spectrum, confirmed my feeling that X Corps would serve as a valuable example of modern wartime operations at the next higher plane of military decision.

The X Corps record also demonstrated the vital impact of leadership and personality in shaping a military structure and determining its fate in the combat arena. The success or failure of X Corps hinged on the attributes of its commanding general, Edward M. Almond. Colonel Rod Paschall, the director of the U.S. Army Military History Institute at Carlisle, Pennsylvania, graciously permitted me access to the Almond papers and senior officer debriefings which ultimately shaped my appraisal of this officer.

As the X Corps story unfolded, it became imperative to address two dominant themes of internal corps relations that affected all operational considerations. The first aspect was the crucial Army-Marine relationship, and I was indeed fortunate that Marine Brig. Gen. Edward H. Simmons—a combat veteran of the X Corps campaign and the director of the U.S. Marine Corps Historical Center—shared both his own objective wisdom and accumulated documents pertaining to this sensitive topic. The other critical feature of X Corps operations involved the prejudices and limitations of a segregated Army, and I sincerely thank Morris J. MacGregor of the U.S. Army Center of Military History—a nationally recognized expert in this field—for his published works and personal advice on these matters.

Numerous other veterans and officials helped immensely with this project. I appreciate the insights and assistance of all those who corresponded or met with me in this regard. Three persons deserve particular mention. Richard L. Boylan of the National Archives rendered invaluable assistance, and performed a masterful job of locating even the most obscure official references needed for the book. Adele Horwitz at Presidio Press continued to provide me with the finest editorial assistance. My wife, Kathryn, gave me the constant support and encouragement that made the book possible.

The X Corps campaign in Korea during 1950 is both exciting and tragic, and underscores many lessons valid today. My hope is that this book adds to our understanding of that important military endeavor.

Shelby L. Stanton
Bethesda, Maryland
May 15, 1989

PROLOGUE

THE MAN

The Korean campaign of the United States X Corps in 1950 begins with the life of its commander, Maj. Gen. Edward Mallory Almond. He resurrected the corps as the spearhead of a mid-twentieth-century counterattack into northeastern Asia, but the corps and its creator were shaped by events within the rolling mountain valleys of Virginia almost a hundred years earlier.

On December 12, 1892 Edward ("Ned") Mallory Almond was born at Luray near the South Fork of the Shenandoah River, nestled in the midst of one of the richest farming regions of nineteenth-century agricultural America. The wealth of its fields and orchards was deeply scarred by the living memories of a ruthless campaign waged to deprive Confederate forces of the valley's bountiful foodstuffs during the Civil War. The entirety of Ned's childhood was dominated by familial bonds, reverence for the soil, and the chivalric legacy of Confederate resistance, which once summoned local boys to fight and die alongside their elders. This sacred blood consecrated Ned's homeland and molded his ambitions.

Wartime defeat had impoverished many Shenandoah families, but financial comfort was always secondary to pride of origin. The propriety of the family remained the bedrock of Southern society at the turn of

1

the century. In this aspect, Ned was considered fortunate. Although his parents were staunch, religious, and normally educated by the standards of the day (both having the equivalent of high school educations), he also benefitted immensely from their background and connections.

Ned's father, Walter C. Almond, was a descendant of the French Allemonde family from Meaux, his forebears having arrived in the United States during the Napoleonic period. This line was not socially distinguished, either by early property ownership within Virginia or Civil War service, but the senior Almond gained the long Virginia association of the prestigious Mallorys and Pophams by marrying Grace (the daughter of Confederate rifle company commander Capt. Thomas Popham) in 1890.

Walter Almond was a businessman who sold heavy farm machinery throughout the Page and Rappahannock County areas of the lower valley. As a young boy, Ned sometimes accompanied his father on his horse-and-buggy business trips across the Blue Ridge to take orders for binders, mowers, rakes, and fertilizer spreaders from regional farmers. Ned spent the summers on his grandfather's farm along Hawksbill Creek near Luray. Some of his fondest memories of the farm were the evening stories told by his grandmother, whom everyone called Aunt Matt. Just before bedtime, she would gather the family around the porch and relate her experiences as a thirteen-year-old girl during the Civil War in 1863 and 1864.

Hour after hour, Ned, along with his younger brother Malcolm and sister Judy, listened intently as the distant mountains receded in the gathering twilight and Union cavalrymen again scoured the Shenandoah for food, especially fine Virginia hams. In many episodes, the crafty valley farmers would outwit the blue-garbed intruders, but occasionally Confederate skirmishers would challenge the foraging parties. Such breathless clashes usually combined humor and dashing bravery, and the Union raiders were often humiliated despite their numbers and hungry intent.

While the rituals of church and school played significant roles in molding Ned's youth, another Virginia custom of the period formed a lasting impression that greatly influenced his entire life. On the last Monday of each May, he accompanied solemn communal processions to lay flowers among the graves of Confederate dead. This annual ceremony reinforced Ned's belief in the intimate relationship between God and state, and the ultimate worthiness of the soldier's sacrifice.

Ned grew to realize that these small cemetery plots contained only a fraction of the remains of Shenandoah's gray-clad youth who answered Virginia's increasingly urgent call to arms. Most boys marched or rode away down dusty turnpikes and never returned, their bodies vanishing in the upturned soil of unknown battlefields. To Ned, these men remained truly lost. With a boy's clear vision of elder fears, he grasped the town's unspoken dismay about the fate of the missing. No flowers could be sprinkled truthfully over absent bones, and false markers never quite properly marked empty graves. The assurance of final peace came only by burial in native soil, close to the relatives, friends, and neighbors of one's youth.

Seeking better business opportunities, Walter Almond moved the family to Culpeper in 1906. The next year, Ned and a high school friend visited Washington, D.C. This was Ned's first trip beyond rural Virginia. The beautiful white marble monuments and massive government buildings of the nation's capital created an indelible impact on the fifteen-year-old youth. He sensed the pulse of a great nation which far exceeded the importance of any Virginia township, and he longed to serve in defense of such a worthy establishment.

Ned's attraction to military service was reinforced by his close association with Dr. Fred Amos. When Ned was eight years old, Doctor Amos—the neighborhood physician who lived across the street—presented him with four shiny brass buttons taken off his Virginia Military Institute (V.M.I.) uniform coat. Young Ned considered the buttons a priceless treasure and a tangible link to the state's Civil War service, especially the valiant charge of the V.M.I. boy cadets against Federal cannon near New Market.

Ned's desire to attend Virginia Military Institute, the "West Point of the South," originated with his four brass buttons, the stories of Dr. Fred Amos, and the deeds related by Aunt Matt. The family's limited financial assets, however, appeared to preclude this option. As Ned entered his last year of high school, he continued to express interest in applying to the college. His mother Grace, as the daughter and niece of two esteemed Virginia captains, used her society influence to arrange an interview with an old acquaintance, state senator George Browning of the Orange district.

Senator Browning was impressed with Grace's recounting of her son's background and ambitions, and offered him a State Cadetship to the Virginia Military Institute. This was a Virginia-sponsored scholarship that covered full board and clothing at the school. The arrangement made it financially possible for the family to send Ned to the academy, and Ned was notified of his appointment to V.M.I. during the winter of his senior year in high school.

Unfortunately, Ned suffered a drastic appendicitis attack in the spring which developed into peritonitis. He was rushed to the hospital at Charlottesville where surgeons performed four different operations in ten days to save his life. Ned entered the Virginia Military Institute as a sophomore and his weakened condition exempted him from all first-year hazing activities. As a result, he was tagged a "third class rat."

Ned concentrated on his studies in the school's electrical (engineering) course and developed an uncompromising faith in his own ability and resolve. He was taught to revere the memory of the institute's Confederate hero, Stonewall Jackson. The school yearbook described Ned as a daring and handsome youth, and teased his womanizing potential, "Sic 'em, Ned!" Ned graduated third in his 190-member class of 1915.

After graduation, Almond became an instructor of military science at Marion Institute, a fashionable junior college in central Alabama. The school held dances and social events with nearby Judson College, a women's Baptist institution with an equally prestigious antebellum heritage. At one of these occasions, Ned met Margaret Cook, a Judson College student from Anniston, and their engagement was announced in 1916.

The advent of American participation in World War I and passage of the National Defense Act offered Ned the chance for active military service. He turned down a commission in the Marine Corps, choosing to take the examination for an Army officer's appointment at Fort Myer, Virginia. After completing a three-month officer candidate course he was commissioned a lieutenant on March 17, 1917. In June, he took command of a machine-gun company in the 4th Division.

Lieutenant Almond used his first extended leave to marry Margaret on August 4. When he returned to the division, preparations for overseas deployment were intensifying. On March 28, 1918, he was promoted to captain. The 4th Division sailed to France in June.

In the predawn hours of August 4, on his first wedding anniversary, the 4th Division was ordered to relieve the 42d "Rainbow" Division on the Vesle River front near Rheims. Although the 4th was composed of regulars, they were fresh troops led by combat-inexperienced officers. The German artillery massed fire on the bunched columns, and Captain

Almond spent an exhausting day driving his company forward through the pouring rain to support the advance.

After midnight, Almond grabbed his first bite to eat, a quick supper of hardtack with ham and corn willy. He had just opened the can of corn willy when a "whiz-bang" high-explosive shell detonated close by and sent a piece of shrapnel tearing through his steel helmet. The metal creased his scalp, causing profuse bleeding, and knocked him unconscious. The young captain was carried to an aid station where he joined hundreds of other division soldiers wounded in the first twenty-four hours of combat.

Almond was recuperating in a hospital at Biarritz when he received a letter from his former machine gun commander, who had been recently promoted to lead the regiment. He promised Ned command of the machine gun battalion if he could get back to the front in time. The division was already engaged in the Meuse-Argonne offensive, the final drive of the war.

Captain Almond headed north on top of a boxcar, was stricken with influenza, but finally received command of the 12th Machine Gun Battalion at the end of September. During the next few weeks, the 4th Division attacked the Cunel heights and battered through the shell-splintered forests in a series of costly attacks. On October 20, Almond was promoted to temporary major, and the war ended less than a month later.

Almond's combat service sharpened several characteristics that dominated his army career. Controlling machine guns required a high degree of technical mastery and intimate knowledge of all friendly troop movements within the battle zone. Weapon sites required painstaking selection, and their various fire plans required constant checking and rechecking.

An ardent disciple of Civil War leadership by personal example, Almond exhibited relentless zeal in moving among his scattered machine gun positions to exercise direct command. This technical supervision over the guns had to be maintained so they could be adjusted to rapidly changing situations. His presence also prevented control and straggler problems which undermined attacking units. He often courageously displaced weapons forward, and his personal bravery during such efforts earned him the Silver Star.

The machine gun command also quickened his rigid intolerance of contrary behavior in subordinates. This trait manifested itself in his low flash point to anger, which was always preceded by a chilling glare from his blue eyes. There was little margin for error in directing machine gun fire close to the men it supported, and Almond witnessed adverse episodes where specific orders were not followed. The need to keep machine guns moving in offensive situations heightened his impatience at any perceived slow response.

Almond reverted to his permanent rank of captain and returned to the United States in 1919. He volunteered for the Army's postwar education plan, and was detailed to Marion Institute as director of its Reserve Officers' Training Corps (ROTC) program.

The next four years at Marion Institute comprised the happiest period of Ned's life. The president of the school was a close personal friend and the school provided every accommodation possible, even to the extent of building a special cottage as the Almond residence. Their Margaret ("Peggy"), was born in Anniston on September 1, 1920, and their son, Edward Mallory Almond Junior, was born at Marion on December 7, 1921. Young Ned was the male heir and primary lifeline of the family in Southern society.

During 1923, Captain Almond was ordered to Fort Benning, Georgia, to attend the advanced infantry course. His scholarship and crisp staff reports impressed superior officers and he became an instructor of infantry officers. This duty reestablished him in the main Army routine. The Army had reached an inter-war low of only 11,655 commissioned officers, and the remaining few gained an extra edge in perfecting staff work and becoming acquainted with fellow members.

The handful of officer-instructors at Fort Benning was keenly aware that their small "broomstick army" would have to form the nucleus of any mobilization in case of national emergency. The debates about manpower utilization invariably introduced the question of the employment of blacks in future wartime situations. The testimony of World War I commanders and traditional public sentiment, especially in the South, judged black capability to be substandard.

Almond considered the poor wartime record of the 92d Division (Colored) enough proof that blacks were better off in labor units "utilizing Negro personnel in areas that did not require exposure, decision of individuals, and bravery in offensive operations. The Negro is a useful individual; he is an American citizen, and he should be employed in the defense of this nation. But to expect him to exercise characteristics abnormal to his race is too much and not recommended by me."[1]

During 1928, Almond submitted a proposal for realistic night exercises to the infantry school's assistant commandant, a fellow V.M.I. graduate Lt. Col. George C. Marshall (Class of 1901). Marshall was extremely pleased with this suggestion because his own fame resulted from planning and supervising the First Army's successful night movement from St. Mihiel to the Meuse-Argonne front. His favorable response assured Almond's career advancement. That fall he was selected to attend the Fort Leavenworth Command and General Staff School and on August 13, 1928, he was promoted to major.

Almond graduated in 1930 and was posted to the Philippine Department, becoming a battalion commander of the Philippine Scouts. The native scouts fell neatly within the ambit of Major Almond's expectations. His colonial officer life-style along the tree-lined parade grounds of Fort William McKinley was in splendid contrast to Depression-gripped United States.

Almond enjoyed golfing excursions in the mountain pine forests of Baguio. He was known to fellow officers as a stern and well-polished Army professional who expressed a courtly, convivial and sentimental personality off-duty. He was also a devoted family man. Almond had given up tobacco five years before but had a celebrated partiality for an old-fashioned before dinner. When a host once served only sherry, Almond frowned and then quipped, "Well, I guess I'll have to have an old-fashioned sherry."

In 1933, Major Almond received orders to the Army War College in Washington, D.C., with a three-month interval between assignments. In June, the Almonds left Manila and spent two months on a journey through the Far East. They visited the British Crown Colony of Hong Kong, and then crossed the water forty miles west to Portuguese Macau. Ned's own family had never been able to afford the luxury of travel, and he viewed this trip as an invaluable learning experience for his son.

From Macau, the Almonds travelled by steamer up the Pearl River to the bustling port of Canton (Guangzhou), the largest city in southern China. As tourists, they were unaware of the bloody communist uprising in the city five years earlier, a rebellion partially sparked by the articles and teaching of Mao Zedong in Canton during 1925 and 1926. Two decades later, the same Mao Zedong—as chairman of the Chinese Communist Party—would send his armies into the northern Korean peninsula with orders to destroy Almond's X Corps command.

The Almonds lived in Washington, D.C., for the next five years.

Major Almond was assigned to the War Department General Staff, where he solidified his status as a superb staff officer. Among his close friends was Charles W. Ryder, who headed the "China desk." The family budget was tightened to permit young Ned's attendance at Millard's Preparatory School, a private academy specializing in service academy orientation.

Major Almond's service in Washington convinced him of the need to have naval and aerial warfare credentials. On September 6, 1938, he was promoted to lieutenant colonel and attended the Army Air Corps tactical school at Maxwell Field, Alabama. The following year, Almond attended the Naval War College at Newport, Rhode Island, and young Ned was accepted into the United States Military Academy. At the beginning of 1941, Almond secured an operations staff job in VI Corps under Colonel Ryder. When Ryder was promoted, Almond replaced him as corps chief of staff. He was promoted to full colonel on October 18.

Less than two months later, the United States entered World War II. The nation's mobilization created several black divisions and a sudden need for suitable officers to lead them. The political sensitivity of the race issue caused Gen. George C. Marshall, now Army Chief of Staff, to carefully select candidates for this delicate task.

Almond's steadfast loyalty to Army policy, Southern background, instructional experience, and uncompromising discipline harmonized with the qualities Marshall wanted for leaders of black units. Furthermore, Almond's previous acceptance on ROTC duty in Alabama affirmed his ability to win the confidence of Southern communities, which Marshall considered vital. He knew that large black formations might be placed near Southern communities during training, and wanted commanders who could defuse any resulting problems.

Ironically, the Army also viewed Southern regional philosophy as a crucial ingredient in successful black unit leadership. The Army believed "the white officers chosen should have some acquaintance with Negroes; therefore it was often assumed that, since few individuals from other parts of the country had come into frequent contact with Negroes, they should be Southerners."[2]

Colonel Almond met Marshall's peculiar criterion for black unit command, but he lacked the troop-leading experience normally considered essential for division-level appointment. Almond had spent twenty-one of his twenty-four years of military service in staff and school positions, and his field portfolio was remarkably slim. Company command experience was limited to several months stateside and one day in combat, and battalion command totalled just over a month in combat and a few months' Philippine constabulary duty. He had never served at regimental or brigade levels.

This notable command deficiency was secondary, however, in a segregated army anxious to fill the largely unwanted high command vacancies for black units. Almond acknowledged the Army's logic in his selection for general, "I think that General Marshall felt that General Hall, who was in command of the 93d Division when I was assistant commander and was from Mississippi, understood the characteristics of the Negro and his habits and inclinations. The artilleryman of that time (within the division) was General William Spence from North Carolina, as I recall, who also had that understanding. I, being from Virginia, had an understanding of Southern customs and Negro capabilities, and the attitudes of Negroes in relationship thereto. I think that my selection for the 93d and 92d Divisions was of the same character."[3]

On March 14, 1942, Edward Mallory Almond was promoted to brigadier general and became assistant division commander of the 93d Infantry Division (Colored) at Fort Huachuca, Arizona. He stayed long enough to organize a cadre. On September 23, General Almond received his second star and was tossed the hottest potato in the Army; command of the 92d Infantry Division (Colored)—an outfit that had "failed" in World War I and was destined for equal controversy in World War II. Almond approached his difficult chore with determination and dogged persistence, but expressed continual exasperation with the quality of his officers and soldiers.

In the meantime, Ned Junior became close friends with a fellow cadet, Thomas Taylor Galloway, at West Point. Tom married Peggy Almond upon his graduation from the academy in 1942. Tom transferred to the Air Corps in May and received his pilot's rating in December. General Almond was very pleased with Peggy's new husband. The Galloways were an esteemed Maryland family of unequivocal Southern heritage; prior to the Civil War they had been the second largest slave-owning family in the state. Ned Junior graduated from the academy in 1943 in the upper bracket of his class.

Despite Almond's happy family news, his infantry division was experiencing serious difficulties. There were several adverse incidents, including the attempted murder of a white officer and the stoning of several others. During the summer of 1943, the Army investigated the formation.

Brig. Gen. Benjamin O. Davis, the Army's first black general, headed the inspection team and concluded,

> General Almond has, in the opinion of the inspector general, overlooked the human element in the training of this division. Great stress has been placed upon the mechanical perfection in the execution of training missions. Apparently not enough consideration has been given to the maintenance of a racial understanding between white and colored officers and men. The execution of ceremonies with smartness and precision, and perfunctory performance of military duties is taken as an indication of high morale. This is not true with the colored soldier. He can be driven to perform without necessarily having a high morale.[4]

General Almond stated General Davis's report was unfair to him, but never filed an official rejoinder. He briefed Maj. Gen. Virgil L. Peterson, the Army's inspector general, that agitators were trying to foster resentment within the division by emphasizing insignificant incidents. He argued that most division members enjoyed high morale, citing as proof the "champion basketball team and topnotch band featuring Sergeant Bobby Plater who composed 'Jersey Bounce.' "

Despite General Almond's assertions, the division flunked its operational readiness test at the end of 1943. Almond excused this shocking lack of preparation by claiming most of his men were marginal learners with below-average literacy. Training delays were caused, in Almond's words, "because it took longer for instructors to secure a sink-in result in any instruction we offered."[5]

While Almond's division struggled to pass muster for overseas deployment, his own son and son-in-law were being called into action. Tom Galloway, Peggy's husband, was promoted to captain in the 436th Fighter Squadron and was sent to England during April 1944. Within a month the squadron's P-38 Lightnings were strafing German positions across the Channel in preparation for D-Day. Ned Junior was a lieutenant in the 63d Infantry Division undergoing final training in Mississippi.

The 92d Infantry Division (Colored) was judged ready for combat deployment at the end of its Louisiana exercises in June. In Europe, the Allied drives in both Italy and France were under way. The German defenses were crumbling in northwest France, and American forces were preparing for the breakout in Operation COBRA. On July 24, 1944, a day marked by low clouds and rainstorms, the aerial onslaught which preceded the ground attack phase of COBRA commenced. Most flights were postponed because of weather, but twenty-four-year-old Major Galloway went aloft to engage targets selected for aerial destruction. Just beyond St. Lo, his P-38 Lightning spiraled out of control fifteen thousand feet into the Foret du Preche north of Tournouvre. French resistance fighters recovered the pilot's body and secretly buried it in the woods.

Tom's death was a great personal tragedy for the Almond family, and General Almond felt the loss very deeply. His daughter Peggy had just given birth to young Tommy Galloway. But officer losses were escalating throughout Europe, and increased casualties created an urgent demand for replacement lieutenants. Ned Junior was ordered to the European theater of operations in August and joined the 45th Infantry Division fighting in southern France.

General Almond's 92d Infantry Division (Colored) received orders to the Mediterranean theater of operations. The formation was given a lukewarm sendoff by the commander of Army ground forces, Gen. Lesley J. McNair, who remarked, "My own estimate of the value of these troops has risen as they emerge from the painfully slow process of drumming things into them. They are, I believe, a better outfit than the 93d when it left this country [for the Pacific], and their future will be a most interesting contribution as to the value of the Negro soldier."[6]

The division arrived in Italy throughout the month of October 1944, and was assigned the mission of anchoring the coastal Ligurian section of the Allied line across the Italian peninsula. The division would contest this narrow band of coastal plain and adjoining mountains for the next six months with scant progress. Almond attributed the division's spiritless performance on the failure of his "best" regiment to seize Mount Cauala during the first weeks of battle. This, he claimed, lowered morale and forced the division on the defensive. Starting in late October, after a small group of men refused to advance, he ordered regimental commanders to disarm and arrest "substandard" platoons. Almond later expanded this punishment to dispose of entire regiments.

Almond conducted energetic daily sojourns to the front line and constantly checked the division's zone. He often visited forward outposts and listening posts to personally scout farm houses or road crossings. Almond moved so rapidly through the division that staff members often lost track of his whereabouts. He derived great pleasure from complicating efforts to log his movements accurately in the daily command journal. Back at headquarters in the company of his trusted lieges, he relaxed with a drink and recounted funny incidents. His fellow senior officers remembered that he had a good sense of humor and a flair for mimicry.

One of his favorite episodes involved a forward post south of La Spezia, where he came under intermittent automatic weapons fire. It was obvious to Almond that the Germans had advanced a light machine gun forward and were pestering the mountain slope. Almond grew tired of the weapon going unchallenged and turned to the sergeant. "Go out and smash that machine gun!" he ordered, meaning for the sergeant to silence the weapon by eliminating its crew. After a while the sergeant came back. "Well," General Almond demanded, "did you find that machine gun?" The soldier replied simply, "Yes, sir." Almond persisted, "Did you destroy it?" The sergeant shook his head slowly, "No sir, General, that gun was in use."

Discouraged by the performance of his men, General Almond applied most of his energy toward detailed staff supervision. The pulse of the entire division revolved in strict conformity to the two daily situation briefings, held at 7:45 A.M. and 5 P.M. sharp. The morning briefing was followed by an extensive planning session under the direction of the operations officer. Almond approved plans at 5 P.M. and units spent the next hour in hectic response to his rigid timetable. Once approved, the plans became orders and were transmitted to subordinate elements as compartmentalized instructions. The instructed units had to telephone or send staff personnel to Almond to check if there were oral modifications. All plans had to be ready by 6 P.M.

The overall division plan was kept so secret that no one but General Almond and his operations officer, Lt. Col. William J. McCaffrey, had any idea what it entailed. Participating units were usually given instructions covering every detail, down to assigning individual soldiers to different tanks, and it was not unusual for Almond to prescribe the movement of every platoon and sometimes every man. Yet subordinate units went into battle unaware of any larger objectives or tasks assigned to other units around them. Alternative plans were unknown.

In November, a separate black infantry regiment was attached to Almond's division. He did not appreciate the reinforcement because this particular unit was an experimental unit with black officers in field-grade positions (above the rank of captain). He launched a formal investigation when elements of the regiment were defeated in a heavy fire fight. Almond badgered the regimental commander until he requested relief, "before I break under the present strain as I am now physically and mentally exhausted."[7]

On December 26, 1944, the Germans launched a full-scale attack against the 92d Division in freezing winter conditions. The division's lines were rapidly driven back, except for a resolute stand made by a battalion in Sommocolonia. The defenders forced the Austrian mountaineers to fight house-to-house for possession of the town. Black Lt. John Fox and his group of artillery observers adjusted shellfire on the attackers until their small farmhouse was close-assaulted. As the enemy troops moved closer, Fox phoned for artillery fire directly on the building. An astonished artilleryman phoned back, "Is it safe to fire?" Fox replied, "Fire it. There's more of them than there are of us." The bodies of these heroic black troops were later found in the demolished farmhouse.

Despite such incidents of bravery, the Germans soon caused several division units to withdraw precipitately. Almond blamed his black troops "because they saw safety in going back to the area they knew, and they had a tendency to be flighty at night."[8] In actual fact, unit flanks were exposed by undestroyed bridges left standing for lack of demolitions, and Almond's orders to dig in were impossible to execute because the men lacked intrenching tools. One entire battalion was destroyed and several others were decimated, forcing British Maj. Gen. Dudley Russell's 8th Indian Division to take over the sector.

On January 10, 1945, the division was returned to the front. During this time, Almond carefully monitored news of the heavy fighting on the Franco-German frontier, where Ned Junior was serving with the 45th Infantry Division. A German artillery shell wounded his son on January 16. Almond was dismayed at the news but he was relieved that his son was safely hospitalized, perhaps for the duration of the war.

In early February, Almond drafted elaborate plans for a renewed division offensive. He even raised a specially trained raider force to stage diversionary attacks. The division pushed through the Italian defenses in the mountains but its gains were eradicated quickly by German counterattacks. On February 8, Almond directed a renewed assault across the coastal plain. Fifth Army commander Gen. Lucian K. Truscott joined Almond and other senior dignitaries to witness this attack from a special hillside observation post.

Despite air support and artillery barrages, the division was cut up by mine fields and German defensive fire along the Cinquale Canal. The entire fate of the division as an effective fighting organization was now at stake. Almond recalled, "They were very impatient of the results obtained by the 92d Division, but they were patient with me, personally, because they understood our problems and the ineffectiveness of the offensive capability of the troops which made the attack."[9]

General Marshall, the Army chief of staff, was in Italy during the division's last attack. Its offensive failure confirmed his long-held belief that blacks lacked initiative and aggressiveness, and should not be concentrated into large formations. The Army's inherent animosity against racial minorities, coupled with serious handicaps imposed on the division both in training and combat service, were actually responsible for the division's failure on the battlefield.

Marshall conferred with the senior Allied commander in Italy, Gen. Mark W. Clark of Fifteenth Army, who ordered two of the division's black regiments converted into engineer labor units and replaced by white and Japanese-American regiments. The 1945 reorganization of the 92d Infantry Division (Colored) gutted the formation in such a drastic fashion that it became obvious the Army retained no more faith in the black unit's fighting ability.

The most surprising result of the 92d's overhaul in the first months of 1945 was the fact that the commanding general's own leadership qualities were never questioned. Almond remained completely unscathed by its poor performance record. Priding himself as the Confederate Jacksonian model of righteousness, he remained confident of his own infinite patience and fairness in leading the division—blaming his men instead for combat losses and morale difficulties. The ingrained prewar army conviction that only Southerners could handle black troops was so strong that all of Almond's superiors echoed his sentiments. In their opinion, if Almond couldn't wet-nurse the blacks into action, no one else could have made a better effort.

The black press in the United States was appalled by the 92d Infantry Division situation. On March 24, the *Chicago Defender* protested that their soldiers, who had fought bravely and valiantly in all American wars, now had to fight "Nazis *and* Dixie race haters." The March 31 edition of the *Baltimore Afro-American* clamored for a new commander in its editorial, "Remove General Almond." The newspaper stated, "The *Afro* advises all soldiers overseas to fight the enemy and let us at home battle the segregation. It is plain that the 92d doesn't take our advice. It had no intention of fighting for General Almond and his lily-white staff and clubhouses. General Almond should be removed, quickly."

General Marshall expressed continued confidence in Almond's capability and ignored any calls for his dismissal. As the calendar turned to the month of March 1945, Almond began to believe that he had survived the worst that the war could dish out. The inevitable collapse of the German Reich on both the Rhine front, where his son was hospitalized and being promoted to captain, and on the Italian front, where he prepared to command a revitalized combat formation, was certainly not far away.

During March on the main European front, the 45th Infantry Division remained deadlocked in its struggle to break through the fortified West Wall guarding the German border. Capt. Edward M. Almond, Jr., rejoined the unit after recovering from his shrapnel wounds and was given command of Company L, 157th Infantry. The division was preparing for a major attack against the maze of enemy strong-points, but frontal assault was suicidal. Routes of advance required careful reconnaissance to mark enemy positions nestled in the barren brown fields and deep ravines dotted with patches of stark, leafless trees.

On the night of March 19, 1945, twenty-three-year-old Captain Almond led a handpicked team of men to reconnoiter the German sector. He hoped that the cold overcast night would assist their dangerous venture. The small American patrol moved cautiously past the forward listening posts and into the darkness near Uttweiler, a small German farming community next to the border. A German sharpshooter from the 17th SS Panzergrenadier Division *Gotz von Berlichingen* watched the small patrol advance near his hidden position. The sniper raised his telescopic-sighted rifle and fired through the chilling damp air. Young Ned dropped, mortally wounded.

The death of his son left Edward Almond shaken and embittered. While he had always felt that an officer's death on the field of battle was the noblest sacrifice possible, his deep-rooted Southern beliefs were embedded in the sanctity and continuity of the family. The loss of the sole male heir was a family tragedy of unspeakable consequences, because it terminated the blood line. While many officers seconded their families to career aspirations, Almond considered the family an essential foundation of society. Young Ned's death tore a massively irreplaceable part out of Almond's heart.

The communal fraternity of generals realized the terrible anguish that occasioned the death of a son in combat. Many of them also had sons, several of them West Point-educated officers like Almond's boy, fighting in the war. Although such tragic events were not unknown, they were extremely rare. Generals Clark and Truscott compassionately accepted Almond's assurances that he was better off busy leading his division, and kept him in command. Almond, however, conducted the final campaign in Italy with subdued resignation that barely disguised his great emptiness.

At the conclusion of European hostilities, Almond was summoned back to the United States to take over the 2d Infantry Division for the invasion of Japan. This selection resulted from the fact that his wartime Italian service amounted to less than a year overseas, considerably less time than many other generals. The termination of World War II, however, cancelled movement into the Pacific. In April 1946, Almond moved the garrison division to Fort Lewis, Washington.

On May 1, Maj. Gen. David G. Barr telephoned Almond from the Pentagon and offered him the important position of military attache to the Soviet Union. Almond rejected the opportunity with the blunt explanation that he had never admired the Russians, the communist takeover, or the manner in which Soviet forces had behaved during World War II. Barr reminded Almond that unless he took the Moscow assignment, he would have to fill one of the general officer vacancies in the Pacific. Almond acknowledged the situation, but refused to change his mind.

General Almond received orders later that month transferring him to Japan. Almond realized that his command of a wartime black division and refusal to go to Russia had derailed his career, perhaps permanently. He did not know Gen. Douglas MacArthur, the Supreme Commander for the Allied Powers (SCAP), but he was good friends with his chief of staff, Maj. Gen. Paul J. Mueller. General Mueller appointed Almond as G1 in charge of personnel for MacArthur's headquarters in Tokyo.

Almond was initially an outsider to MacArthur's inner circle, but his close friendship with Mueller and unabashed admiration for the supreme commander slowly gained him a SCAP reputation for dependability. His prewar Philippine service in the 1930s helped to offset his lack of previous service under MacArthur, who divided officers into Pacific-friendly and European-alien circles. During November, Almond was promoted to deputy chief of staff for the Far East Command and earned a privileged place in the inner sanctum of the supreme command. He referred to MacArthur as "the greatest man alive."[10]

General MacArthur once strolled into Almond's office and bantered about the hard working conditions that might disturb some people. Almond said, "General MacArthur, nothing you could do would disturb me emotionally." MacArthur smiled and asked, "Why is that?" Almond answered frankly, "Because once I commanded the 92d Infantry Division."[11]

The Almond family had resided in Japan since August. The nearness of his wife Margaret, daughter Peggy, and grandson Tommy brightened his duty. He often drove home from his Dai-ichi office building for a light lunch and forty-five minutes on his garden's nine-hole putting course. During long weekends with his family in the mountains at Karuizawa he played thirty-six holes of golf daily, with scores in the middle 80s.

When enjoying cocktails with close friends, Almond's tough professional character was replaced by a sociable and even jovial temperament. His fondness for baked Virginia ham never waned, and he recounted how a soldier once lost a Virginia ham being delivered to him. The soldier bought another ham from the local butcher and tried to pass it off as a genuine Old Dominion product. Almond detected the fake and made the soldier write twenty-five differences between ham and Virginia ham.

Throughout 1947, General Almond dedicated most of his energy to the burial plots of young Ned and Tom Galloway. He was convinced that their interment in temporary cemeteries on foreign soil was unacceptable. He remembered paying homage at unfilled tombs during the Confederate Day ceremonies of his youth, and how their terrible emptiness echoed the perpetual solitude of unfortunate souls fallen on distant battlefields. During the summer, Almond flew to Virginia and arranged for suitable adjoining burial plots at Arlington National Cemetery.[12]

On February 18, 1949, General Almond replaced Mueller as MacArthur's chief of staff. The supreme commander's style of command imposed great demands on this position, because MacArthur customarily dealt with subordinates exclusively through his chief of staff. Almond had to be thoroughly informed on every aspect of the vast SCAP empire, and every important staff matter went through him before reaching MacArthur. The chief of staff even represented MacArthur at most official social functions, and their offices were attached through a mutually shared map and conference room. Almond adopted MacArthur's long office hours and seven-day work routine, but subordinates noted the souring of Almond's temper as their hard-driving chief became engrossed in carrying out MacArthur's dictates.

One of the backwater trouble spots in MacArthur's realm was Korea. The country had posed a serious dilemma to United States foreign policy ever since the peninsula had been arbitrarily divided in half at the 38th

Parallel. Military observers patrolled the uneasy border between the separated Korean states, but the U.S. Army had withdrawn its units from South Korea in June 1949. By the spring of 1950, however, ominous intelligence began reaching MacArthur's headquarters about well-equipped North Korean troops massing along the border. General MacArthur dismissed the enemy buildup as mere communist bluffing.

The North Korean invasion of the south was launched in the predawn darkness of Sunday, June 25, 1950. Just before daybreak, General MacArthur was phoned by a duty officer at the Dai-ichi headquarters: "General, we have just received a dispatch from Seoul, advising that the North Koreans have struck in great strength south across the 38th Parallel at four o'clock this morning." MacArthur was momentarily dazed by the news. He believed himself to be asleep and dreaming, overwhelmed by recollections of the Japanese invasion of the Philippines at the start of World War II. Reality returned quickly when he heard the crisp, calm voice of "his fine chief of staff," General Almond, who queried him with precisely the right words, "Any orders, General?"[13]

The Korean war had begun.

Notes

1. U.S. Army Military History Institute, *Senior Officer Debriefing Program of Lt. Gen. Almond by Capt. Thomas G. Fergusson,* dtd 25 March 1975, p. I-39. Hereafter cited as USAMHI Interview. The papers of General Almond, retained by the Military History Institute, constitute the main source of this prologue.
2. Ulysses Lee, *The Employment of Negro Troops,* Department of the Army, 1966, p. 180.
3. USAMHI Interview, p. II-80.
4. Davis Memorandum for The Inspector General, dtd 7 August 1943, quoted in Lee, p. 334.
5. USAMHI Interview, p. II-82.
6. Lee, p. 496.
7. Letter from Cdr 366th Inf Regt to CG Fifth Army, dtd 11 December 1944, quoted in Lee, p. 559.
8. USAMHI Interview, p. III-17.
9. USAMHI Interview, p. III-20.
10. William Manchester, *American Caesar,* Little, Brown, & Company, 1978, p. 496.
11. USAMHI Interview, p. III-68.
12. Capt. Edward M. Almond, Jr., was originally buried at the St. Avold temporary U.S. Military Cemetery, twenty-eight miles east of Metz, France. Maj. Thomas T. Galloway's remains had been removed from his first grave site near the crash site, and reburied at the St. Andre-De-Eure temporary U.S. Military Cemetery, fifty miles west of Paris and midway between Everaux and Dreux.
13. Manchester, p. 548.

CHAPTER 1

THE FOUNDATION FOR X CORPS

1. Six Days in June

On June 25, 1950, North Korea achieved complete strategic surprise against its southern neighbor. An intensive early morning bombardment deluged the border in a withering firestorm of high-explosive artillery and heavy mortar shells. The landscape was smothered in billowing clouds of smoke and flame that demolished Republic of Korean (ROK) outposts and communications networks. Before many of the stunned defensive garrisons could react, divisions of tank-escorted North Korean *People's Army* (*NKPA*) troops rolled across the boundary on a broad front. The mechanized onslaught overwhelmed the dazed South Koreans in classic blitzkrieg style and the invaders marched rapidly south.

The disorganized ROK army began to disperse and disintegrate almost immediately. Meaningful resistance was fragmentary and pushed quickly aside. The small number of United States military personnel in Korea who served as members of the Korean Military Advisory Group (KMAG) was unable to influence the course of battle. At the main ROK headquarters in Seoul, inked-over wall charts and frantic telephone calls reflected the near meltdown at the front. North Korean jet fighters strafed the city and nearby Kimpo airfield.

In Japan, the Sunday tranquility of Far East Command and its peace-time garrison soldiers was shattered by news of the communist assault. The military attache in Seoul contacted MacArthur shortly after Kaesong city fell to enemy forces, confirming the full-scale nature of the North Korean intervention. This message concluded optimistically, "No evidence of panic among South Korean troops," but the bleak reports that followed described a worsening situation. General MacArthur contacted higher officials in the United States immediately, alerting them to the seriousness of the event and expressing outrage over North Korea's brazen act of war.[1]

The interim commander of KMAG, Col. William H. Sterling Wright, was in Japan for the weekend, sending his family home to the United States. He was already on orders to America and had become the temporary leader of KMAG following the previous commander's departure ten days earlier. Colonel Wright was attending church in Tokyo when a messenger scurried down the aisle and breathlessly whispered to Wright that he was needed back in Korea at once. The colonel packed hastily and returned to Korea, confident that U.S. advisory personnel would be summoned out of the war zone at the earliest opportunity.

In Korea, American ambassador John J. Muccio took charge of operations. In the absence of higher directives, his foremost concern was the safety of U.S. family members in Seoul. Muccio ordered all American women and children sent to the nearby port of Inch'on, where a Norwegian vessel was commandeered and filled with evacuees and their hastily gathered belongings. He briefly considered gathering other Americans in the embassy and declaring diplomatic immunity if the North Koreans entered the capital, but the military advisors saw this only as a last resort. They realized the *NKPA* showed scant concern for normal diplomatic conventions.

South Korean president Syngman Rhee conferred with Muccio and insisted more ammunition was required for a successful defense, blaming deteriorating ROK army performance on lack of fighting material. Muccio demanded emergency deliveries, stating that "it would be catastrophic for the United States to permit the South Koreans to succumb for lack of ammunition."[2] MacArthur told Maj. Gen. Edward M. Almond, his hard-pressed chief of staff, to dispatch two munitions ships from Yokohama immediately. Aircraft from the Far East Command were dispatched to cover these ships as well as the evacuation of American dependents from the Seoul area.

The Far East Command, previously concerned with routine occupation duty in Japan, was thrust suddenly into a full-scale wartime crisis. General Almond, anxious to get a firsthand account of the situation, managed to ram through a late-evening telephone call from Tokyo to Seoul. The correspondent of *Time* magazine related that a near-hysterical Korean operator broke into the call and wailed, "Oh, save us, save us, General Almond!" Tart-tongued in moments of exasperation, the chief of staff answered, "What in the hell do you think we're trying to do? Whose planes do you think were flying over Seoul today?"[3]

In Korea, the North Korean advance continued largely unchecked, and the American mission in Seoul destroyed its embassy radio station. On the morning of June 27, Muccio's staff withdrew to Suwon, and non-essential personnel of both government agencies and KMAG were ordered to leave the country. The precipitous flight of the ROK high command from the capital left South Korean forces north of Seoul without communications or orders. Colonel Wright and his KMAG party chased the Korean leaders in a small convoy of trucks and jeeps and caught up with them halfway to Suwon.

During this trip, the KMAG mobile long-range radio (an SCR-399 mounted in a truck) received several messages from MacArthur's supreme headquarters urging "good cheer" because "momentous decisions were pending."[4] Wright used these dispatches to convince the ROK military leaders to return to Seoul, and dispatched a courier to Suwon to recall all KMAG personnel still at the airport. In Seoul, however, the uneasy population was thoroughly alarmed by the sudden departure of both Korean and American command center personnel, and their meek return did not calm the unsettled atmosphere.

On the same afternoon, the Far East Command sent a group of senior officers under Brig. Gen. John H. Church to assess Korean requirements. En route the plane was diverted from Seoul to Suwon, and Church was radioed that his team would form MacArthur's advance command post in Korea. Upon landing, they were confronted by the hectic departure of dozens of missionaries, foreign dignitaries, and embassy staffers on shuttle flights leaving the country. Ambassador Muccio met Church at planeside and told him the latest tidings: North Korean armor, apparently unstoppable, was rumbling toward the national capital a scant thirty miles away.

Enemy tanks were viewed as the biggest threat to South Korean army cohesion because they appeared impervious to antitank fire. The

North Korean People's Army tank fleet consisted exclusively of 120 Russian-built T34s with 85mm cannon. The armored fighting vehicles were no longer the strongest machines in the Soviet arsenal, but they were extremely powerful and had broken the back of the German army during World War II. The T34s featured highly sloped frontal armor plating and excellent protection, and these tanks seemed invincible as they clanked inexorably closer to Seoul.

Two hours after midnight on June 28, Wright awakened to learn that ROK troops were retreating through the city and their high command had retired in disorderly haste. Soon afterwards, the main Han River bridge was demolished in a spectacular explosion that sent thousands of refugees to their deaths in the darkened river below. The loss of this bridge, which constituted the primary escape route for ROK units still defending the north side of town, removed all hope of continued defense. Panicked soldiers abandoned their positions and the pandemonium of the fleeing mobs intensified as they sought other means of escape.

General Church radioed MacArthur from his command post near Suwon and warned that the chaotic military situation might become irreversible. Throughout the day, a steady stream of exhausted advisors and ROK army personnel trickled into Church's compound. One KMAG radioman was so fatigued that he transcribed a message by filling in the form with scrawling waves of meaningless lines instead of letters. There was doubt whether anyone could hold on much longer.

MacArthur responded with characteristic force, deciding to fly into Korea and get a firsthand impression. He knew that his personal presence would also help stabilize the jittery South Korean leaders. Maj. Gen. Edward M. Almond, the supreme commander's loyal chief of staff, urged MacArthur to fly into Pusan on the southern coast because of uncertain security and bad weather throughout the country. MacArthur was undeterred in his desire to visit the battle zone, however, and insisted on flying directly into Suwon. Almond obediently gathered the selected headquarters officers and reporters for the flight.

On June 29, MacArthur's C-54 long-range transport plane *Bataan*, escorted by four P-51 Mustang fighters, approached Suwon through the drizzling clouds. The airfield was littered with smoldering plane wreckage from recent strafing by North Korean Yak aircraft. One enemy fighter made a feeble attempt to intercept the *Bataan*, but MacArthur's personal pilot Lt. Col. Anthony F. Story, USAF, landed the Douglas Skymaster safely. These circumstances underscored the seriousness of South Korea's predicament.

At Suwon, MacArthur was briefed on the dismal status of the ROK army by General Church, in concert with Ambassador Muccio and President Rhee. Church stated that only eight thousand of the one hundred thousand South Korean soldiers could be accounted for, although he hoped straggler interception points might round up a few thousand more. The depressing atmosphere disgruntled MacArthur, who ended the meeting abruptly and announced he wanted to see the front at Seoul. A few dilapidated civilian cars were secured and MacArthur and Almond squeezed into a black Dodge, escorted by several jeeps.

The vehicular caravan followed the winding dirt road north to the shabby industrial town of Yongdungp'o, just across the Han River from Seoul. Throngs of terrified Korean soldiers and civilians, intermixed with ambulances and carts, milled around them. MacArthur took out his pipe and, pointing it at a small hill, turned to Almond, "What do you say we push up there, Ned?" A little farther on, the entourage stopped.

Almond got out of the car as the loud din of concentrated communist artillery fire reverberated through the earth and air. Columns of black smoke hovered over the burning capital. The river was awash in the wreckage of toppled bridges, clusters of rafts and trees, and the flotsam of urban ruin. Only one refugee-clogged railroad bridge still spanned the water. Almond viewed the scene as one of utter defeat.

General MacArthur walked alone across the trampled earth and stood on the rise of ground, gazing solemnly across the Han River at Seoul silhouetted against the fiery backdrop of smoke-laden sky. He assumed a typical pose, standing erect with his hands in his rear pants pockets and clamping his corncob pipe tightly in his mouth. He seemed oblivious to the scores of bodies on the river bank below or the multitudes of people passing behind him. He returned to the car and issued only one order, referring to the last intact bridge offering enemy access to the near side, "Take it out."[5]

Unknown to the other participants at the time, General MacArthur was not merely gazing at a destroyed city. He saw that Seoul was lost, but silently envisaged a master plan for its recovery. He reached a momentous decision that would profoundly affect the future life of Almond and tens of thousands of young men destined to fill the ranks of X Corps. He secretly decided—if American intervention was allowed—to fight the *NKPA* to a standstill and then make a victorious amphibious landing behind North Korean lines to conclude the war.

MacArthur was silent during most of the twenty-five-mile trip to and from the Han River. Almond gazed sullenly out the window of the Dodge with contempt. The fleeing masses of Korean soldiers reinforced his low regard for troops "melting away." Most seemed to have weapons and gear, and many were grinning at him as they streamed by. Some waved happy salutes. Almond never remembered seeing any wounded, and his overall impression was that nobody was bothering to fight. He reported to the Joint Chiefs of Staff that the South Korean soldiers were "all smiling, all with rifles, all with bandoleers of ammunition, all saluting."[6]

General MacArthur had also seen enough. They flew out of Suwon as the first American combat unit in Korea was setting up four M55 antiaircraft machine guns along the airstrip. He was adamant that enemy aircraft would no longer have "free shots" strafing undefended airfields. When MacArthur returned to Tokyo he went right to business, in Almond's opinion, with the calm conviction of a resolute leader determined to check an unprovoked enemy assault. At 7 P.M., he fired off a message to the Pentagon, describing the plight of the ROK forces and urging authorization for a U.S. infantry regiment to reinforce Pusan. With Pusan secured, two divisions could begin landing from Japan to launch an early counteroffensive.

Both MacArthur and Almond in Tokyo were linked into Washington, D.C., and the Pentagon's Joint Chiefs of Staff via teletype machines. An urgent conference was arranged between MacArthur and Gen. J. Lawton Collins, the Army chief of staff, to hammer out an appropriate course of action. General Almond was among five senior staff officers gathered around MacArthur in the Dai-ichi building's tele-conference room. He was cognizant of the event's utmost importance, and treasured it as a rare opportunity to witness a "great commander making the right decision under pressure."[7]

General Collins stated that permission only existed for one regimental combat team in Pusan. MacArthur responded that this provided him insufficient latitude for militarily efficient operations. Collins objected that any decision to do more was a presidential matter and reminded his Japan-based audience it was only 3 A.M., Washington time. MacArthur replied with a finality that implied waking the president, "Time is of the essence and a clear-cut decision without delay is essential."[8]

Almond delighted in envisioning the triumphant MacArthurian clarion call slicing through the indecisive, procrastinating Washington mentality. His judgments were affirmed when, on June 30, General MacArthur received President Truman's permission to use two divisions to ensure retention of the Pusan area, and employ naval and air forces against targets throughout most of Korea. At the same time, Truman informed the United Nations of the American response to the Korean crisis.

2. Almond and Emergency Response

At the outbreak of the Korean war, the major component of the Far East Command was the Eighth Army under Lt. Gen. Walton H. Walker. The army was an emaciated, peacetime garrison force stationed in Japan. Although the organization had four divisions on paper (1st Cavalry, 7th, 24th, and 25th Infantry), these were far below strength and ill-suited for active operations. The divisions were short of manpower and shy on training, and there was insufficient materiel in Japan's FEC logistical depots for sustained warfare.

The North Korean assault, however, steadily squeezed the remnants of the faltering South Korean army into a shrinking corner of southeastern Korea. The Far East commander realized it was imperative to deliver a riposte while enough territory for maneuverability still remained under friendly control. MacArthur's decision to hasten American elements into Korea—and commit them piecemeal as they arrived—was not the most orderly procedure recommended by military textbooks, but it represented the only hope to save the situation. To block the complete fall of South Korea, MacArthur was compelled to expedite U.S. troops there, regardless of their battle readiness, by every means of transport available.

The Far East commander's chief of staff, General Almond, faced awesome, almost overwhelming, responsibilities as overseer of MacArthur's emergency response. He was expected to coordinate and ride herd on the overnight transformation of the Eighth Army pacification constabulary into a combatant organization, and then supervise the myriad mix of motor, rail, sea, and aerial transportation required to move it into battle.

Putting the divisions on a war footing was the most urgent of Almond's tasks. Units scattered in widely separated posts throughout the Japanese islands had to be reassembled, stripped of nondeployable personnel and refilled with combat-qualified soldiers, and equipped with the necessary tanks, artillery, communications equipment, bridging, and other implements of war. The divisions had to be moved from installations in Japan to ports and airfields for ship and aircraft transport to Korea.

On July 24, Almond added another hat to his multifaceted job when he assumed the additional role of chief of staff for the United Nations Command upon MacArthur's elevation to that post. Without hesitation, Almond fulfilled the expanded duties of this dual position, serving as a critical conduit and buffer between the commander and his larger staff.

MacArthur placed great dependence on his chief of staff, and Almond's intimate knowledge of the complexities of the Far East Command domain was phenomenal. Almond served as trusted counsel to the commander and they were in and out of each other's offices constantly. Almond was one of MacArthur's most fervent disciples and never shrank from the most difficult assignments. Almond's keen intellect and closeness to the throne of General MacArthur made him one of the most powerful and controversial generals in the Far East.

Almond was fifty-eight. His silvery hair and squarish face emphasized his stern, gruff countenance and piercing blue eyes. His energy and alertness were revealed in the rapid movement of his head and eyes, which relentlessly scanned his environs with unceasing scrutiny. As chief of staff, he often wore a tropical-worsted officer's service cap. Its stiff russet-leather visor cut straight across his forehead, just above his iron-gray eyebrows, and hardened the features of his furrowed forehead and penetrating glare.

Almond's imposing presence demanded attention. He gave the appearance of a large man despite his medium stature, just two inches shy of six feet. His hard-driving, all-business generalship was accentuated by the open collar of his khaki shirt (no tie was worn). The loose-fitting shirt also disguised the slight stoop of his shoulders. His only insignia were two diminutive metal stars on one collar and a small general staff emblem pinned through the other. His rank was clearly manifested, however, by the oversized general's gold-plated circular buckle on his wide leather belt.

Almond was feared and obeyed throughout the Far East Command. His all-consuming obedience to MacArthur was combined with an impassioned love of work molded in his spartan college years at the Virginia Military Institute. He drove himself hard and he demanded the same degree of hard-driving loyalty from his subordinates. Known as a "whip-cracking" chief, underlings quivered when he scowled at them, prefacing his low flash point to anger. Higher placed officers were not so intimidated, but they knew Almond's instructions carried the weight of MacArthurian directives.

The major concern now occupying most of Almond's waking thoughts involved MacArthur's private revelation of his grand strategic plan to win the war. Within days after their late June visit to Korea, MacArthur shared his tentative idea for a seaborne thrust to turn the enemy's flank. While witnessing the destruction of Seoul, MacArthur said, he had shaped the image of returning by sea. He was confident that military success hinged on stopping the North Koreans and locking them in place, followed by a surprise amphibious attack to sever their supply lines in the rear. The envelopment would isolate the *NKPA* and force their surrender. Throughout the frantic initial weeks of the Korean conflict, the strategic plan for repulsing the North Korean invasion was always uppermost in both generals' minds.

MacArthur had employed strategic amphibious movement throughout his New Guinea and Philippine operations in World War II. Almond also understood the effect of such grand turning movements in warfare. His schooling in Civil War history emphasized Confederate General Robert E. Lee's use of Stonewall Jackson to accomplish such a feat at Chancellorsville, a lesson he later taught during lectures at Marion Institute and Fort Benning. Almond, an ardent MacArthur believer, endorsed the idea with great enthusiasm.

MacArthur specified that Almond consider an invasion locale near Seoul, so a strike could be made directly into the center of the *NKPA* communications and supply network. On July 4, this idea was discussed at a special Far East Command meeting between MacArthur, Almond, and representatives of the combined services in the Far East Command. The United States Marine Corps existed as the nation's primary amphibious assault force, but there were few available Marine troops for the task. As a result, Marine Col. Edward H. Forney was selected to begin working on invasion plans, using the 1st Cavalry Division as the potential basis of the landing. The operation was coded secretly, BLUEHEARTS.

The first task was to stop and pin the main North Korean attackers. MacArthur instructed Almond to formulate complete and accurate estimates of the minimum American force required to accomplish this mission. Once this information was tabulated MacArthur could determine what reserves could be spared for the second, amphibious envelopment stage. Almond believed his attempts to reach a viable estimate for MacArthur were undercut constantly by Eighth Army exaggerations of the enemy threat (in order to secure more men and equipment) and the fluidity of the Korean battlefield itself. Almond was forced to continually reevaluate his estimates, which prevented MacArthur from reaching a firm conclusion on the size or composition of the invasion force.

The Far East Command staff was forced to set aside internal assets for an amphibian strike because the Pentagon was unable to release the needed manpower. General Almond's old 2d Infantry Division, stationed at Fort Lewis on the American west coast, was an early candidate in reinforcement requests. The division was alerted for overseas duty on July 9, but such reinforcement offered only a partial remedy. More replacements were needed to replace casualties in units already sent to the front.

On July 7, 1950, MacArthur alerted the Joint Chiefs of Staff that he needed thirty thousand more men—in units ranging from full divisions to parachute regiments and armored groups—in order to stop the North Koreans and conduct an amphibious maneuver around them. Because of the inability of the Eighth Army to stop the North Korean invaders, however, the original scheduled invasion date of July 22 was abandoned on July 10.[9]

3. Eighth Army in the Pocket

On the Korean front itself, the early confidence that U.S. troops could easily stop the North Korean opponents disappeared. Standard 2.36-inch bazooka shells bounced off T34 tanks as they crashed through the Eighth Army lines. Waves of well-disciplined North Korean infantrymen firing submachine guns surged past American rifle-firing companies short of experienced leaders, training, and ammunition.

In two hot dusty days of confused fighting, lasting July 11–12, the 24th Infantry Division was defeated at Choch'iwon and retreated across the Kum River. On the following day, General Walker officially assumed command of ground forces in Korea. The elements of the 24th were not alone in their retreat. Both the 25th Infantry and 1st Cavalry Divisions also yielded ground to the North Korean onslaught in disastrous engagements at Sangju and Yongdong. These events prompted an emergency appeal from General Walker, asking for two additional battalions from Okinawa. Both units were moved quickly to Korea in response, but their subsequent slaughter in the Korean maelstrom cut into the scant resources still remaining in the Far East Command for amphibious flexibility.

The Allied situation continued to deteriorate. Reports reached Almond that many combat withdrawals were unjustified, disorderly, and out of control. Almond's mind instantly flashed with visions of panic along the front, mixed with vivid recollections of past disasters in Italy. He was incensed at this ignominious behavior and its effect of front stabilization, the first ingredient in MacArthur's recipe for eventual success.

One of Almond's numerous high-echelon functions for General MacArthur was the interception and transmission of calls to and from the field generals. Although this service was a duty imposed by the supreme commander, Almond's intercession generated open enmity with General Walker of the Eighth Army. Walker's own loyal staff members believed that Almond was deliberately undermining and isolating their commander from MacArthur at every opportunity. They sneered that Almond's cozy Japanese war room was distant from events sweeping southern Korea. The relationship between Almond and Walker, which was never good to begin with, eroded as their mutual animosity intensified.

On July 26, Walker issued an Eighth Army directive announcing future withdrawals to prepared positions. He called Far East Command for authority to withdraw his own headquarters from Taegu to Pusan, but Almond intercepted the call. Almond was aghast at the request. He had a clear vision of MacArthur's strategic purpose that Walker lacked, and realized the importance of containing the enemy advance. Almond bristled at any mention of further withdrawal because none of MacArthur's amphibian plans could be activated until the *NKPA* was stopped first. He could not divulge this information to Walker, however, over telephonic circuits.

The resulting conversation was full of fireworks. Almond bristled at mentions of further withdrawal, and Walker became enraged that his arguments for retrograde movement (to safeguard vital equipment and build a stronger line along the Naktong River) were rejected out of hand. Almond promised to relay Walker's message to MacArthur with his own strong disagreements. Lecturing Walker that his own role model, Confederate General Stonewall Jackson, would have obviously held firm, Almond pleaded for steadfast action. He concluded that moving the army headquarters to Pusan was such a backward step that it "might be the forerunner of a general debacle."[10]

As soon as Almond hung up the phone, he alerted MacArthur that Walker might be wavering and recommended a flight to Taegu at once to confront the Eighth Army commander about the gravity of the situation.

Within the half hour, MacArthur directed Almond to arrange for a flight to Korea in the morning and a session with Walker.

MacArthur's personal aircraft *Bataan* landed at Taegu on July 27, and the supreme commander conferred privately with Walker at the forward headquarters. The only other person present at the session was Almond, who related that MacArthur stated flatly that further withdrawals must cease. With curious irony—in view of the future fate of X Corps—MacArthur announced there would be no Korean evacuation similar to World War II's Dunkirk. Walker reassured his commander that he certainly harbored no intention of abandoning Korea. Two days later, Walker issued an order to the Eighth Army that it would, in the words of the press, "stand or die."[11]

In the meantime, despite the cancellation of BLUEHEARTS, Brig. Gen. Edwin K. Wright's Far East Command Joint Strategic Plans and Operations Group kept devising new recommendations for an amphibian envelopment. On July 23, a new concept for the amphibious counterstroke was devised and coded Operation CHROMITE. Several prospective Korean landing sites were investigated. These included a landing midway up the western coast at Inch'on, in close proximity to Seoul. Other likely intrusion points were also detailed, such as a west coast landing further south at Kunsan (enabling an offensive toward Taejon) or an east coast landing at Chumunjin, across the peninsula from Seoul.

All the alternative invasion areas were presented to MacArthur for his final determination. He decided that a quick thrust at the Seoul chokepoint still offered the best chance of rapidly strangling the *NKPA* zone of communication southward and ending the war. After reaching this conclusion, MacArthur notified Pentagon officials that he was scheduling an amphibian assault by the 5th Marines and 2d Infantry Division. These formations, according to MacArthur, would land behind North Korean lines in conjunction with a general offensive by the Eighth Army from the south.

Even as these plans were being finalized, a renewed *NKPA* offensive sliced through the Eighth Army. The North Korean troops seized the Koch'ang approach to the Naktong River and captured Chinju. The Eighth Army was again forced to retreat. On July 29, MacArthur lamented to the Joint Chiefs of Staff, "In Korea, the hopes that I had entertained to hold out the 1st Marine Division['s brigade] and the 2d Infantry Division for the enveloping counterblow have not been fulfilled, and it will be necessary to commit these units to Korea on the south line rather than . . . their subsequent commitment along a separate axis in mid-September. . . . I now plan to commit my sole reserve in Japan, the 7th Infantry Division, as soon as it can be brought to an approximate combat strength."[12]

Almond's brooding ill-humor worsened with these negative developments. Still insistent on a staunch defensive backbone as the key element in securing ultimate victory, he became livid when he heard—via common wire service (United Press)—that the Air Force had abandoned another airfield. Yonil Air Base was evacuated on August 13, after the North Koreans surged across the mountains in the east.

By the end of August the enemy had completely outflanked General Walker's Eighth Army in the west and forced it back across the Naktong River. Compressed into a small pocket of southeastern Korea, Walker's troops dug in for their final stand along the Pusan perimeter. The adverse tactical situation, coupled with Pentagon difficulty mustering reinforcements for the Far East Command, seemed to terminate all realistic hope of an amphibious maneuver behind the North Korean lines.

MacArthur remained undaunted. Both the supreme commander and his chief of staff were confident of CHROMITE's viability, but questioned operational execution because of the unavailability of needed manpower.

Notes

1. James F. Schnabel, *U.S. Army in the Korean War, Policy and Direction: The First Year,* Department of the Army, 1972, p. 65.
2. USMILAT Message to CINCFE, dtd 250530Z June 1950, cited in Maj. Robert K. Sawyer, *Military Advisors in Korea: KMAG in Peace and War,* Department of the Army, 1962, p. 120.
3. "Command," *Time Magazine,* October 23, 1950, p. 27.
4. Sawyer, p. 125.
5. William Manchester, *American Caesar,* Little Brown and Company, 1978, p. 555.
6. Joseph C. Goulden, *Korea: The Untold Story of the War,* Times Books, New York, 1982, p. 95.
7. USAMHI Interview, p. IV-15.
8. Roy E. Appleman, *South to the Naktong, North to the Yalu,* Department of the Army, 1961, p. 47.
9. Schnabel, pp. 83, 140.
10. Appleman, p. 206, 207. General Walker did not survive the Korean war, and his senior staff contested Almond's recounting of the conversation. Contrary to Almond's recollection of the call, these officers indicated that Walker would not have asked to retreat his headquarters to Pusan. Because the conversation was private between Almond and Walker, the exact telephone exchange will never be known.
11. Appleman, p. 205.
12. Appleman, p. 489.

CHAPTER 2

SHAPING X CORPS

1. The Amphibious Gamble

The reality of MacArthur's amphibious strike behind North Korean lines was first given substance after Lt. Gen. Lemuel C. Shepherd, Jr., arrived at the Far East Command from his Hawaiian headquarters on July 7. Shepherd, as commander of Fleet Marine Force Pacific, was coordinating the introduction of the 1st Provisional Marine Brigade into Korean combat.

Relations between the Army and Marines were at a very low ebb. Just months previously, on October 17, 1949, Commandant of the Marine Corps, Gen. Clifton B. Cates had charged that the Army general staff was attempting to "destroy" the Marine Corps.[1] The entire corps totalled only 74,279 men at the end of June 1950 and was facing drastic budget cuts. The Marines spent most of June demonstrating their combat proficiency for President Truman at Quantico, Virginia. It was no secret that the U.S. Marine Corps was striving for survival when the war in Korea erupted on June 25.

On July 10, General Shepherd attended a conference with MacArthur at the Dai-ichi building in Tokyo. The Marine general stopped by General Almond's desk to extend courtesies before going into MacArthur's office.

Shepherd was a 1917 graduate of Virginia Military Institute where Almond had graduated two years earlier. Almond informed him that MacArthur was keenly interested in mounting a major amphibious attack in Korea, but that the War Department had turned down all requests for more troops.

Shepherd instantly grasped the potential of Almond's remarks. The chance to execute a quintessential Marine mission would demonstrate the readiness of the Corps as a valuable instrument of national power. He asked Almond why MacArthur didn't ask for Marines.

Almond replied, "We have done so repeatedly. We have asked for any kind of troops that will fight, and we were told that there were none available." He recited that a request made eight days previously only netted the possibility of one regiment, a force insufficient for the task. Shepherd responded, "We could get enough Marines together throughout the world to provide a division." Almond was delighted, "Well, if you believe that, go in and tell General MacArthur."

During the conference MacArthur expressed his desire for amphibious attack capability and, recalling past glories in World War II, lamented the absence of a Marine division under present circumstances. Shepherd suggested that the 1st Marine Division could be made combat ready. He knew that this formation had just been gutted to field the Korea-bound provisional brigade, but reasoned that it could be rebuilt swiftly by using reserves and rapid transfers. MacArthur asked if the Marines could be ready by mid-September. Shepherd replied affirmatively.

At that point, MacArthur instructed Shepherd to sit down at his desk and formulate a suitable dispatch recommending that a division of Marines be sent to the Far East. After the message was composed, MacArthur walked over to Almond's desk and told him to send a telegram to the Joint Chiefs of Staff, "I understand that a force of division strength can be assembled by the Marines in a matter of six weeks and be in Japan. I hereby make that request at the present time."[2]

MacArthur's request for a full-strength Marine division with appropriate air support was justified on the basis that a strong Marine spearhead could open a second front in Korea amphibiously, entrapping the *NKPA* between it and Eighth Army, but he refrained from disclosing the intended invasion point. Nevertheless, the Joint Chiefs of Staff approved the Marine reinforcement for MacArthur's command, and CHROMITE assumed new vitality.

On July 25, General Cates directed that the 1st Marine Division be brought to full wartime strength within three weeks, even though it required approximately the same number of marines as existed in the entire Fleet Marine Force. Mobilized reserves would have to fill the gaps. Cates was also insistent that the Marine Division would have its own brand of close air support. He ordered Marine aviation in the Far East increased from a single group to a full aviation wing.

All Marine facilities were ruthlessly combed to expand Maj. Gen. Oliver P. Smith's 1st Marine Division from a skeletal shadow (having just fielded a brigade for Korean duty) to a solid phalanx at Camp Pendleton, California. By the end of the month, the first reservists were flooding in. They were bolstered by more than nine thousand Marines from Camp Lejeune, North Carolina (most of the 2d Marine Division) to form the rejuvenated 1st Marines, the division's first regiment.

The 7th Marines became the division's second regiment and was formed by augmenting two weakened battalions of the 6th Marines with more regulars and reservists. The division relied on units overseas for completion: the last battalion of the 7th Marines was derived from the Sixth Fleet landing force steaming to Japan from the Mediterranean Sea, and the division's third regiment, the 5th Marines, was already in Korea as the basis of the Marine brigade fighting on the Eighth Army front.[3]

While the Marine division was being assembled, Far East Command was trying to pull together an Army formation, the 7th Infantry Division in Japan. Ironically, this was the same division that had guarded Korea's 38th Parallel boundary as late as December 1948 (only eighteen months earlier) before returning to Japan. Unfortunately, the Korean emergency had cut through the ranks of this division like an ax, ruthlessly swiping sergeants, technical specialists, and fit riflemen for sister divisions ordered into battle. The 7th Division was so depleted and scattered by these incessant demands that it was hardly more than a flag on MacArthur's wall chart.

The 7th Infantry Division was dispersed throughout the Japanese islands providing garrison security for installations vacated by other occupation forces dispatched to Korea. The division was also a cadre outfit instructing recruits arriving in Japan with some elemental training before being sent to Korea as replacements. It was known lazily as the "Hourglass Division" because its shoulder sleeve insignia was a red circular patch with two black sevens inverted against each other (forming a stylistic hourglass), but its hour was up.

MacArthur ordered the division reassembled in the Mount Fuji maneuver area and filled up the only way possible—by soaking off all incoming replacements bound for the Eighth Army. He also took care of the passive Hourglass and coded the revised formation "Bayonet." The 7th Infantry Division was known proudly as the "Bayonet Division" for the duration of its Korean service.[4]

Artillery, the king of battle, was the big bone of contention between General Walker and the Far East Command. He needed it desperately, and knew MacArthur had a full group tucked away in Japan. The 5th Field Artillery Group was a triple-threat outfit with a mobile antiaircraft battalion (50th), a regular howitzer battalion (96th), and a fully tracked, self-propelled howitzer battalion (92d). Such guns could mean the difference between life and death in the Pusan perimeter, according to Walker, but Almond had better ideas for their employment—giving rapid fire support on a hostile beach. He put the group under the wing of the 7th Infantry Division and kept it in Japan for invasion purposes.[5]

As Marine and Army muscle was added to the bones of the Far East Command, MacArthur was still pondering the choices for invasion. He wanted to land at Inch'on port because it was close to the capital of Seoul, but he knew the dangers of this option. Indeed, the invasion faced catastrophe at the water's edge. Any landing force would have to negotiate drastic tidal shifts, a narrow dead-end channel, fortified islands, and bottomless mud flats. The troops would land directly into a built-up and very defensible city.

There were alternatives, but MacArthur considered them less appealing in their overall effect on the war. Nights on end, Almond and Wright hashed over the choices with their supreme commander. They could land on the east coast at Wonsan and cross the peninsula to reach Seoul, but the march across the hinterland faced a 125-mile ordeal over mountains and through blocking units while the enemy fortified the capital. They could land on the west coast farther south at Kunsan, but its feasibility was too obvious. The enemy could contain an amphibious turning maneuver by quick response from their nearby main front, and success would only gain a small extension for Eighth Army.[6]

The sole significant strategic option that could break the Korean stalemate was a daring amphibian thrust at Inch'on on the middle western coast. The city of Seoul, a crucial political target and a main *NKPA* nerve center of its logistical lifeline, was only eighteen miles farther inland. The only natural military barrier between Inch'on and Seoul was the Han River. A rapid Allied conquest of this critical region would regain South Korea's capital and sever enemy supply arteries before the North Koreans could react, isolating the enemy divisions facing Walker's beleaguered troops. MacArthur resolved to win the war at Inch'on.

2. The Creation of X Corps

Operation CHROMITE, the amphibious invasion of Inch'on, formally commenced on August 15. MacArthur directed Almond to establish the embryonic planning group that would become the nucleus of CHROMITE's actual operational headquarters. The entire scheme was cloaked in absolute secrecy and known to insiders as Force X.

To outsiders, the small band of members was known only as the Special Planning Staff of general headquarters, Far East Command. They worked in clandestine isolation at the musty bomb shelter of an old airplane hangar in the Far East Command's downtown Tokyo motor pool. The motor pool military clerks and gas pumpers sweated under the hot Japanese sun unloading truckloads of rolled charts, furniture, and paper into the dank hangar. They didn't know what section had been assigned these forsaken quarters, but it was clear to them that MacArthur's colossal staff had finally run out of decent office space.

On August 6, General MacArthur summoned Maj. Gen. Clark L. Ruffner to serve as Force X chief of staff. Ruffner was a trusted MacArthur staff genius from World War II days who was chief of the legislative and liaison division of the Army special staff in Washington. Almond did not know this powerful general, but he was delighted to discover that Ruffner was a fellow V.M.I. graduate (class of 1924). Marine Col. Edward A. Forney, the previous commander of an elite Pacific Fleet troop training unit in Japan, was added as the Force X deputy chief of staff to lend amphibious expertise.

Other top Force X slots were filled with a mix of MacArthur and Almond favorites. Lt. Col. John H. Chiles, Almond's secretary of the general staff, became the crucial G3 operations chief (earlier he had been a regimental commander under Almond in the 2d Infantry Division). Col. Aubrey D. Smith, who was married to retired Gen. Walter Krueger's daughter (General Krueger had commanded MacArthur's Sixth Army in World War II) was given the demanding job of logistics chief. The

G2 intelligence chief was Lt. Col. William W. Quinn. A few Army, Navy, and Marine officers were detailed for specialized assistance and rounded out each section.[7]

Force X worked feverishly on its highly classified mission. Inside their secluded hangar, the minuscule staff completed preliminary arrangements for a seaborne assault involving seventy thousand troops—the mightiest amphibious endeavor since World War II. Although there were many difficulties, one of the most frustrating was the lack of suitable maps. Maddeningly, the Army had been in the Inch'on-Seoul area for nearly five years, and its engineers had built a massive array of complexes, yet accurate charts were virtually non-existent. Almond relied on a specially prepared raised relief map for his master planning, but the model was very deficient in terrain details.[8]

The plan for Operation CHROMITE envisioned a successful invasion, resulting in a rapid link-up between the invading force and the Eighth Army advancing from the south. If this junction failed to occur, however, the invasion force would be forced to operate by itself. This possibility led to the accumulation of extra quantities of essential materiel. Almond later received much criticism for the extravagant amount of corps baggage carried into Korea, but MacArthur authorized abnormally high equipment levels because success was never guaranteed. A stranded corps-sized force on a hostile shore was not a pleasant thought, but that eventuality had to be prepared for.

Bureaucratic entanglements soon produced barriers to invasion just as menacing as rows of enemy antitank mines. The logisticians of Force X discovered that the straitjacketed army logistical system filled requisitions according to exact organizational levels. There were apparently no "back-channel" stockpiles in Truman's tightly budgeted Pentagon. Department of the Army officials demanded to know what authority existed for such urgent deliveries, as well as unit compositions involved, before the requests could be honored. The supply orders sent from Far East Command were rejected because "Force X" was not referenced as a proper organization anywhere in Army manuals.[9]

This supply stalemate required Almond to approach MacArthur about upgrading the ad hoc status of Force X. Almond stated that the projected force was larger than a division and therefore should be designated a corps, as the next higher echelon in the Army chain of command. MacArthur asked him to recommend a suitable corps designation. The first number that entered Almond's mind was the Roman numeral ten, because the staff operating in the motor pool was called Force X. He suggested, "Why not call it the X Corps?"

MacArthur was delighted with the choice, "That's a good idea. The X Corps fought in the Pacific campaign and I will approve of that." He knew that X Corps (raised at Sherman, Texas, on May 15, 1942) had moved overseas to New Guinea during July 1944 and invaded the Philippines at Leyte Island in October. He was familiar with its excellent campaign record under his command, when the corps secured Leyte and Samar, cleared the Vizayen passages, and conquered Mindanao. Many people in the Far East Command remembered it because the X Corps had performed a brief stint of occupation duty in Japan before being inactivated on January 31, 1946. Furthermore, the corps' association with the Eighth Army dated from December 26, 1944.

After General MacArthur approved X Corps as the title, Almond asked him who would command it. Almond was aware that Army protocol required MacArthur to coordinate with the Pentagon for a commander of such an important unit. Leadership of a corps in combat was a plum assignment reserved for the War Department's inner clique of favored generals. Almond reminded MacArthur that, regardless of where the new leader came from, his prompt selection would allow participation in the planning stages. The corps commander needed to become rapidly familiar with operational demands because of the proximate invasion date. MacArthur nodded, "I will let you know this afternoon."

General Almond entered MacArthur's office late in the day to receive the commander's nomination. Almond stated quietly, "I came in for the name of the person that you selected to command this force for the Inch'on landing." MacArthur looked up, "It's you." Almond was shocked. He realized intuitively that MacArthur had made the choice himself, without consulting the War Department. Almond was well aware of General Collins's dislike for him, and knew that the Army chief of staff would never have approved the choice.

General Almond was also worried about the status of his chief of staff position, because it was a crucial adjunct to MacArthur's command. He surmised that the great responsibility of leading X Corps would automatically prevent his continuation in that capacity. Almond said, "This surprises me greatly and changes the position of the chief of staff. I cannot hold two jobs at once."

MacArthur announced another surprise: Almond would continue as his chief of staff. MacArthur explained that the brevity of the operation allowed Almond to assume corps command with an additional duty as staff chief. The Inch'on landing would be a short operation and the Eighth Army would take control as soon as the port area was captured and the link-up achieved. Almond would then be able to resume his role of full-time chief of staff. MacArthur promised Almond his choice of extra assistants to cope with the enlarged workload and conveyed his optimism, "We'll all be home by Christmas."[10]

After the supply snafu almost stalled CHROMITE, MacArthur determined that his invasion corps would not be derailed again by outside influences. To insure independence of action, regardless of circumstances, MacArthur arranged for X Corps to serve directly under his own Far East Command. Almond's corps not only enjoyed separate status but it was lavished with extra components, being reinforced from normal corps size to the strength of a virtual field army.

X Corps had two reinforced divisions, its own tactical air command, and a complete artillery group despite the paucity of artillery assets in Korea itself. The 2d Engineer Special Brigade at Yokosuka was assigned for amphibian and port service, and a host of engineer units was furnished for combat and construction. A reinforced signal battalion was tailored for both normal corps-level and Tokyo-link communications.

The corps service support structure was geared for absolute corps independence. A range of ordnance ammunition and maintenance support organizations was gathered at Atsugi and placed under control of the 60th Ordnance Group headquarters. To coordinate services ranging from laundries to rations, the 6th Quartermaster Group was added from Yokohama. A corps medical establishment was raised at the same port that included field, surgical, and evacuation hospitals. Three transportation battalions were also included in its massive support apparatus.

Dozens of miscellaneous elements, extending from chemical smoke generator battalions to base post offices, were gathered from all over Japan. These included a water supply company from Tokorozawa, a veterinary food inspection detachment from Tokyo, an ordnance explosive disposal squad from Kushi, a bakery company from Camp Zama south of Tokyo, and a graves registration company from Yokohama. This massive support structure would enable the corps to operate freely on a self-sustaining basis which, Almond opined, befitted an expeditionary force.[11]

General Collins at the Pentagon was astonished. He knew that X Corps was a miniature army and the message was clear; it could avoid any reliance on Eighth Army. He believed that MacArthur had conjured up such a cumbersome and irregular arrangement as a deviation to permit Almond's avoidance of service under Walker. To Collins, the extensive size of X Corps was merely a contrivance that undercut Eighth Army by draining it of many critical specialty units. In his opinion, the separate status of the corps outside Eighth Army jurisdiction violated one of the most elementary principles of war: unity of command.

As Almond had foreseen, the Joint Chiefs of Staff were perturbed that MacArthur chose him as corps commander without consulting them. Navy officials were angered that Marine generals with proven combat amphibious experience were never considered. Several outstanding Marines with the right rank and credentials were readily available, including Lieutenant General Shepherd, who commanded the Fleet Marine Force, Pacific. The War Department viewed MacArthur's high-handed manner as a manifestation of the Far East commander's uncontrollable shogun tendencies.

General Collins was particularly incensed over the choice of Almond as X Corps commander. Their mutual dislike caused, in Almond's own words, "a stormy relationship."[12] Although Almond was a senior major general, he was one star below the customary rank of corps command and had no prior knowledge of amphibious operations. Collins believed that MacArthur displayed little grasp over operational demands by keeping General Almond on as chief of staff, with corps command as extra duty. The very fact that Almond would acquiesce to such a situation, in Collins's opinion, confirmed his bad judgment.

General MacArthur elevated Almond to the command of X Corps for one simple reason: loyalty. MacArthur knew the inherent difficulties of the plan, and wanted the invasion force commanded by a man who would not shrink before the apparent impossibility of the task. Almond exhibited the unswerving personal allegiance and tough resolve that could keep X Corps moving in conformity with MacArthur's dictates. The supreme commander wanted a loyal subordinate who would faithfully adhere to his guidance with unquestioning exactitude.

The unspoken but ultimate reward for Almond's dutiful performance as corps commander would be a probable third star. General Collins may have believed that MacArthur (or Almond) was engaging in subterfuge of normal promotional procedures, because otherwise Almond would remain a major general. This would have further angered Collins against the choice.[13]

3. Decision to Invade

While X Corps was taking shape, the Operation CHROMITE planning group continued to assess the invasion's feasibility. One problem was proper determination of the enemy's capability to oppose such an invasion with their own ground forces. MacArthur's intelligence officer, Gen. Charles Willoughby, estimated that a relatively low number of North Korean troops were in the Seoul-Inch'on area. The *9th* and *18th NKPA Divisions* were suspected of guarding the capital with a total of eight thousand soldiers. Except for a small number of 76mm artillery pieces, which planners expected to eliminate or scatter by naval and air bombardment, no cannon capable of challenging the invasion armada was emplaced.

In reality, the North Korean People's Army indeed committed a grave blunder in neglecting to adequately garrison the Inch'on-Seoul district. The Inch'on port complex was defended by the newly conscripted and poorly trained *226th NKPA Marine Regiment*, with about two thousand men, and bolstered by a smattering of 76mm guns from the *918th NKPA Coast Artillery Regiment* overlooking the harbor approaches. The enemy obviously placed great faith in the natural geographical obstacles to bar invasion attempts.

The only enemy division-sized formation in the area was the *18th NKPA Division* "Seoul Defense Division." This division had been raised by upgrading an independent brigade near Chorwon in early August to ten thousand men, and it was relocated to Seoul shortly thereafter. The *9th NKPA Division* (formed at Kaesong on July 9 by expanding a border constabulary brigade) was situated in Seoul until August 12, but was then called to the Taegu front, leaving only the two thousand-man *87th Regiment* behind at Yongdungp'o. Other forces were tentatively available, such as the *105th NKPA Tank Division,* from regions within a few days' march of the capital, but the enemy underrated the hardships of such travel under the UN air supremacy.

One mystery concerning intelligence assessments of the enemy order of battle was the exact whereabouts and strength of the *105th NKPA Tank Division.* This was the only divisional tank organization in the North Korean arsenal and its T34 tanks posed a serious threat to any projected offensive. Allied planners knew that the division usually operated by splitting its regiments in frontline support, and assumed that the organization would only be encountered on a fragmentary basis. In actuality, on September 10, the full division reassembled at Kumch'on to regroup with fresh equipment and replacements. This divisional reconsolidation was capped by the newly assigned *849th NKPA Antitank Regiment.*[14]

On a tactical level, planners worried about the effectiveness of predominantly Soviet-equipped North Korean People's Army weapons against American arms. One of the prime factors considered in pursuing an invasion alternative was the reluctance of the Soviet Union to equip her North Korean ally with modern tools of war. Equipment was usually given to the North Koreans only if it was in some stage of obsolescence, and the bulk of *NKPA* military hardware obviously came from outmoded Soviet surplus stocks.

The North Korean military possessed no heavier field artillery than the old 1931/37-style 122mm corps gun, no larger mortar than the 1938-type 120mm mortar, and no later tank than the T34. Only the lighter versions of the truly excellent Soviet series of antitank guns were present. These factors lessened the effectiveness of the North Koreans immeasurably against the modern U.S. weapons systems fielded in time for the Inch'on invasion. The planners, keenly aware of the fate of the understrength and underequipped American units first sent into combat, were intent on preventing North Korean units from ever trading blows with X Corps elements on equal terms.

The planners were able to partially discount the severity of the enemy mobile threat, even if portions of the *105th Tank Division* appeared on the battlefield, because of lessons being learned along the Pusan perimeter. The SU76 self-propelled gun was found to be simply a lengthened version of an obsolete Russian tank chassis, on which a 1942-style 76.2mm gun was mounted. It was typical of the generally inferior equipment supplied to North Korea by the USSR. The open-topped fighting compartment presented a glaring weakness that made the vehicle extremely susceptible to ground attack. Standard Soviet self-propelled guns had covered fighting compartments and featured impressive 85mm, 100mm, and even 122mm guns.[15]

The once-unstoppable T34 tank, which had caused such wide consternation during the initial weeks of the conflict, was no longer an insoluble dilemma. Early tank-to-tank combat with U.S. forces proved that American 76mm and 90mm tank guns could penetrate and destroy T34s at any reasonable battle ranges, and they were countered successfully by M46 Patton and M4A3 late-model Sherman tanks. The enemy tank still posed a serious danger to infantrymen, but X Corps was outfitted with liberal amounts of new 3.5-inch rocket launchers found capable of destroying T34 armor (the production of 3.5-inch rocket shells had just begun in mid-June, two weeks before the Korea war). With these weapons, planners hoped that even T34s lying in ambush would be unable to fire off more than the first round.

The chances of success might have been far different if the North Korean arsenal had included more modern Soviet weapons. For example, no Allied armored fighting vehicle was capable of engaging the mammoth JS-III with its superlative armored protection and powerful 122mm gun. Fortunately, first-rate Soviet armament systems—such as 152mm howitzers, the Joseph Stalin series of heavy tanks, or very heavy artillery—were never turned over to the North Koreans (there were periodic reports of JS-III sightings, but none were ever encountered on the Korean battlefield).

The geographic obstacles at Inch'on, however, seemed to present insurmountable obstacles to an amphibious landing regardless of enemy opposition. The Inch'on tidal cycles were far more treacherous than expected, with extremes of almost thirty-two feet. At low tide Inch'on was surrounded by immense mud flats. The landing had to coincide with peak tides, when the sea poured over the mud with enough depth for maneuvering amphibious vessels to the seawalls that encased the port city.

The only passage into Inch'on from the Yellow Sea was through Flying Fish Channel, a narrow lane of deep water containing islands and obstructions on both sides. Wolmi-do Island jutted into this channel near the southern tip of Inch'on. The island's extent of fortification was unknown, but it offered an ideal battery position to deter seaborne attack. The harbor area of Inch'on was divided and Wolmi-do governed all approaches. Even at high tide, the port area was hemmed in by breakwaters, tidal basins, and salt pans. The dock area was fronted by a 15-foot-high concrete and rock seawall.

The absolute necessity for favorable tide periods mandated a landing on either September 15, September 27, or October 11. If this was not accomplished, winter ice would force operational postponement until the next year. MacArthur considered surprise essential for success and wanted speed of execution to help insure this vital element. The earliest invasion date would also be the most beneficial in relieving enemy pressure against the Eighth Army's southern front. Therefore, MacArthur insisted that September 15 was the "must" target date.

Navy liaison officers in the planning group became distraught as Almond's team continued to crank out attack plans at dizzying speed. They surmised that the naval textbook on amphibious operations, gleaned from proven World War II combat experience, was apparently being thrown out the window. This "military bible" recommended 160 days. for readying a landing of such magnitude, but Almond was determined to do it in thirty days—from the inception of planning to the first wave of Marines storming the beaches. Loading and target dates remained fixed, even as new landing hazards were uncovered.

Navy officials were dismayed at the seeming recipe for disaster being cooked up by Almond's Army-heavy staff. The fearsome tides, lack of ship maneuver space in the channel, and other landing barriers were compounded by dangerous seasonal storm patterns. The Navy's meteorological service revealed a sinister brood of typhoons in the South China Sea. These storms were predicted to race north through the Pacific's typhoon alley past Taiwan, and then spin off unpredictably in one of three directions. A left turn could shunt a typhoon around Korea to savage the path of an invasion fleet, while a straight northern track would let it pass over Japan to smash out-loading efforts. Only one chance out of three, a right turn, would hurl a typhoon into the deep expanse of the North Pacific and out of harm's way.

The Far East Command's Navy staff was composed of staunch veterans of the successful wartime Pacific amphibious onslaught. They expressed open concern that Almond possessed little understanding of amphibian operations and less inclination to begin learning. Many senior naval officers were eye-witnesses to typhoon destruction, and some had served in the Third Fleet during the December 1944 typhoon that buckled cruiser frames and sank destroyers. These naval experts viewed the entire Inch'on scheme as incredibly reckless.[16]

Adm. Arleigh A. Burke, the deputy chief of staff to Commander Naval Forces Far East, was distressed about the impact of a typhoon on a convoy of troop ships. Burke was no stranger to bold risks; the legendary exploits of his Destroyer Division 45 "Little Beavers" off the Solomon Islands had solidified his reputation as one of the Navy's bravest skippers. He also knew that steering into the teeth of possible typhoon weather was foolhardy seamanship, and he was determined not to let the Navy get stampeded into such a possibility by Almond's impetuous scheduling.

Almond was worried justifiably that this Navy reaction would only stifle CHROMITE development. He hurriedly prepared a favorable staff report on typhoons that discounted the threat. His report challenged Navy objections by claiming most typhoons within the past twenty-five years turned east into the Sea of Japan. The conclusion was patently aimed to please MacArthur: in all these years only one typhoon struck the Straits of Tsushima between Korea and Japan, and the likelihood of typhoon damage was very slight.

When Admiral Burke attempted to express his objections to MacArthur, he was waylaid by Almond. Almond stated that he would transmit any message to MacArthur. "No," Burke countered, "because somebody has to make a decision; I've got to talk to MacArthur myself." Almond suggested that he see General Wright and Burke objected again, "I have to see the boss man. I think it's important." Almond urged Burke to speak with him, but Burke replied, "Well, I'm sorry, but I can't do that. I'll go back to my office."[17]

Almond seized his special report on typhoons and tides and rushed it into MacArthur's office. By the time Burke returned to his office, a message was waiting that he could see MacArthur. Almond was confident that his report allowed MacArthur to outmaneuver naval reservations. Burke discussed the situation with MacArthur and explained that the typhoon's potential track would force the invasion fleet to sail much earlier than originally projected. The admiral then handed the movement orders directly to MacArthur because he no longer trusted Almond to arrange it.

Rear Adm. James H. Doyle, the Navy attack force commander, was also acutely aware of the tidal and typhoon hazards of the area and protested immediately to his boss, Vice Adm. Charles Turner Joy, the commander of U.S. Naval Forces, Far East. Turner Joy relayed MacArthur's choice of landing sites to the Joint Chiefs of Staff, along with his reservations about the project's haste and disregard of dangers.

The Joint Chiefs of Staff were thoroughly roused by the Army-Navy bickering at Far East Command and unsure of MacArthur's exact plans. The JCS sent General Collins, its Executive Agent for the Far East, and Adm. Forrest P. Sherman, the service chief most directly involved with amphibious operations, to Tokyo. They would confer with MacArthur personally and review the situation for final JCS approval. The meeting that decided the fate of Operation CHROMITE was held in the Dai-ichi building's conference room on the sixth floor at 5:30 P.M., August 23, 1950.

General MacArthur gave a brief introduction that opened the conference. He was followed by General Wright, his operations officer, who outlined the basic two-punch landing plan. The dominating island of Wolmi-do would be seized at first high tide in the morning. The main Marine assault would take place on the evening tide and conquer the docks and port city seawall. The meeting was then turned over to the Navy for comment.

The Navy representatives presented an intensive briefing on the problems of invading Inch'on. The difficulties of such an attempt were stressed, including the danger of navigating a highly perilous and possibly mined channel; the unfavorable sea and weather conditions that hampered naval gunfire and air support; the hazard of a Marine assault against high-walled dockyards; the menace that strong currents presented to congested boat traffic carrying men and supplies; and the scanty intelligence on enemy defenses, including artillery that might engage shipping trapped in restricted waters. Admiral Doyle concluded, "The operation is not impossible, but I do not recommend it."[18]

There was a hushed pause as General MacArthur rose to speak and refilled his pipe. Almond stirred uneasily in his chair. Then MacArthur addressed the conference members in a low, deep voice that heralded a dramatic discourse. He stated that the unsuitability of Inch'on masked it as a target, and the very reasons against such an attack gave it the vital surprise he desired. He reminded his listeners how British General Wolfe had climbed the steep cliffs of Quebec against the unsuspecting French to achieve a surprise victory in 1759.

MacArthur moved to the large wall map behind him and pointed to the southern Pusan region where the Eighth Army was pressed against the sea, comparing it to the more central location of Inch'on and Seoul along the Korean coastline. He proclaimed that retaking the capital would not only seize the imagination of all Asia and win support for the United Nations cause, but also control the territory to the rear of the main North Korean army. Inch'on was described as an anvil on which General Walker could hammer the *NKPA* from the south.

MacArthur summarized the alternatives. He brushed off General Collins's favorite target, Kunsan, as merely a logical alternative with limited scope and not a decisive envelopment. He spoke of amphibious attack as a powerful military device if used to strike hard and achieve strategic surprise with crushing results. MacArthur noted that, without Inch'on secured, Walker's Eighth Army would be committed to a long winter campaign as it fought northward at a tragic cost in lives.

MacArthur remarked that "the Navy has never let me down," but promised that he would withdraw the landing force if enemy opposition proved too tough. Admiral Doyle cried out, "No, General, we don't know how to do that. Once we start ashore we'll keep going!" Someone commented that enemy guns might cover the channel, only to be silenced by a mesmerized Admiral Sherman, "I wouldn't hesitate to take a ship in there!" MacArthur congratulated him, "Spoken like a Farragut!"[19]

He continued speaking for a few more minutes, but Sherman's support of MacArthur effectively ended the conference. The Joint Chiefs of Staff were convinced of the merits of landing at Inch'on and cleared Operation CHROMITE to proceed as scheduled.

The Marine generals who would have to conduct the actual assault were far from happy over the situation. General Smith of the 1st Marine Division had met Almond at the Dai-ichi building on the previous day, and they had clashed immediately. Almond had informed Smith bluntly, "the proposed operation *would* involve his division's participation as the principal landing unit and that this invasion would occur about the 15th of September." Smith answered that the Marines required more time in accordance with amphibious doctrine. Almond was stung and stated flatly, "this was not our idea of responsiveness."

Almond later remarked of this first meeting, "I got the impression that General Smith always had excuses for not performing at the required time the tasks he was requested to do."[20] Both Marine Generals Shepherd and Smith were excluded from the conference, despite their obvious crucial roles in the upcoming operation, and were chagrined when they heard the results. They pleaded their case with higher officials and soon Admiral Sherman expressed second thoughts as well. All three went to see MacArthur the very next day about shifting the landing site thirty miles south, to Posung-Moon near Osan, where the water was deeper.

Almond intercepted them at the door. He was adamant that the plans could not be changed, and began to display his most unpleasant characteristic. The compulsion of being inherently correct, mixed with Jacksonian stubbornness and insular intolerance, came across as rudely disagreeable and overbearing. Almond described the amphibious operation as a mechanical exercise, an angry outburst that raised uncertain Marine highbrows even higher. Shepherd and Smith were now extremely annoyed and insisted on seeing MacArthur directly. Almond relented and the supreme commander met the visitors, but he was in no mood to modify the landing either.[21]

4. Launching CHROMITE

Operation CHROMITE had the green light, and General Almond was anxious to round out his corps staff. Many key positions were filled directly by Force X personnel, and MacArthur had promised Almond his choice of other assistants. In response to MacArthur's suggestion, General Collins stopped by Almond's office as he departed the Dai-ichi building for his return to Washington.

Collins inquired, "Is there any other thing that I could do to aid you in this operation?" Almond opened his top desk drawer and pulled out a list of thirty officers and presented it to Collins, stating he wanted them transferred to X Corps. Almond delighted in watching General Collins's reaction. "He almost had heart failure."

General Collins was enraged at the list. He retorted about the difficulties of transferring such important officers. When Almond asked for Lt. Col. William J. McCaffrey (his former 92d Infantry Division chief of staff and a close friend of proven loyalty) for X Corps deputy chief of staff, Collins replied that McCaffrey was already slated for a crucial infantry school assignment. Almond rejoined that his corps was an active combat command that took precedence over training institutions, and "with this kind of persuasion imposed on General Collins, I got about a third of my staff list."[22]

McCaffrey became one of six former 92d officers added to X Corps within the month. Almond's artillery chief was Col. William P. Ennis, Jr., who provided artillery support to Almond's 92d Infantry Division and joined it at the conclusion of hostilities in Italy. Col. Edward L. Rowny, his former 92d Infantry Division engineer, became corps chief engineer. Lt. Col. William T. Campbell, his 92d Infantry Division headquarters commandant, became corps provost marshall. Almond also selected officers from his former command of the 2d Infantry Division, such as Lt. Col. Frank T. Mildred who became the deputy G3 officer in charge of plans.

On August 26, 1950, Gen. Edward M. Almond's X Corps was formally activated by Far East Command General Order 24. All units of GHQ Reserve were immediately transferred under control of the new corps. On the last day of August, the corps was formally mustered with its Army and Marine divisions, Col. James K. Wilson Jr.'s 5th Artillery Group, Col. Joseph J. Twitty's amphibian 2d Engineer Special Brigade, and a gargantuan host of supporting units. Eight days into

September, the unprecedented creation of an independent "corps air force" was accomplished when the X Corps Tactical Air Command was activated from Maj. Gen. Field Harris's 1st Marine Aircraft Wing at Itami Air Base.

The availability of the 5th Marines, scheduled as the combat-experienced core element of the invasion, was threatened by a last-minute Korean emergency. The 1st Provisional Marine Brigade (composed of the 5th Marines) was being employed on the Eighth Army front to shoulder its defensive perimeter against renewed North Korean attacks. The frontline situation worsened and Walker insisted on retaining the Marines as his only mobile reserve to counter enemy breakthrough. Fortunately, the fighting stabilized and, following a flurry of top staff conferences, Almond was able to substitute a regiment of the 7th Infantry Division as a "floating reserve" for Eighth Army. These ships would be capable of sailing quickly to Inch'on.

The 1st Marine Division was finally assembled. The 1st Marines arrived at Kobe from San Diego on September 2. At midnight on September 5, the 5th Marines were disengaged from active combat west of Yongsan and moved to Pusan for future reconsolidation with the division. On September 9, the former Sixth Fleet landing force arrived at Pusan, via the Suez Canal, from its last Mediterranean port in Crete. This unit was redesignated as the 3d Battalion, 7th Marines. The rest of the 7th Marines landed at Kobe on September 17, completing the division.[23]

The 1st Marine Division was known as the "Guadalcanal" division, an honor bestowed by Gen. Alexander A. Vandegrift (its first World War II combat commander), who had stitched the island's name in white letters down the elongated red numeral of its blue diamond-shaped shoulder patch. Following the bitterly fought, six-month campaign to wrest Guadalcanal from Japanese control, the division had stormed eastern New Guinea, New Britain, Peleliu, and Okinawa. The premier division was well endowed traditionally to spearhead MacArthur's amphibious assault at Inch'on.[24]

General Smith, the division commander, and Almond were completely opposite in almost every quality except one, extreme pride, which doomed both men to dislike each other. This friction caused the worst working relationship between American generals of the Korean war. Temperamentally, Almond was brash and dictatorial; Smith was refined and polite. Physically, Almond was of medium husky build with a squarish face; Smith was tall and slender with graceful features. Almond was a proud Virginian who relished his regal position under General of the Army MacArthur; Smith was a proud Texas Marine who resented Army overlordship.

The 7th Infantry Division was shaping up, but not as fast as hoped. The formation had absorbed ten thousand soldiers in the past few weeks, but more were needed. To complete its ranks, another expedient measure was introduced during the last week of August. The division received 8,637 raw Korean recruits, dumped into the assembly area just three weeks shy of D-Day Inch'on.

Lt. Col. Charles R. Scherer, the assistant S4 officer of the division, recalled, "The Koreans we received looked as though they had been herded together to get them off the streets of Pusan. They spent their first week in Japan in quarantine, since they had to be deloused and cleaned. Then we had to equip them completely. Japan Logistical Command did a wonderful job in getting the articles of clothing and equipment to us, but it was a real problem to teach the Koreans how to live in a camp. They could not speak in English and we had few interpreters. Our instruction was given primarily in sign language and making simple motions for them to watch and imitate. We had a long way to go in two weeks. These men had no idea of sanitation, let alone the more complicated activities of military life. . . . The Koreans have not lived as we have, and our easy-going discipline did not work with them. In their own army discipline was strict, arbitrary, and often brutal. They had been reared under such discipline and seemed to understand no other kind. The integration of Koreans was unsatisfactory. They ate our rations, rode our trucks, used our supplies. But except for menial tasks, they were a performance cipher."[25]

The division was commanded by Maj. Gen. David G. Barr, the same man who telephoned Almond offering a Moscow assignment in 1946, and then transferred him to the Pacific after he refused the position. Almond knew Barr as a fellow Southern officer from Alabama since their days as captains together after World War I. Barr had spent most of his World War II combat service as chief of staff to Gen. Jacob L. Devers, who commanded the Sixth Army Group in southern France and Germany (the same army group in which Ned Junior was killed).

General Barr was considered a "China hand" and had acquired valuable firsthand knowledge of communist Chinese tactics while in charge of the Army mission to China. He was serving in this capacity when Chiang Kai-shek was expelled from the mainland in December

1949. Previously the Eighth Army chief of staff (where he had experienced several bristling encounters with Almond), he received command of the 7th Infantry Division because of seniority.

Despite their pre-World War II friendship, Almond and Barr were not on amiable terms. Almond viewed Barr as a ''junior'' officer because Barr's rank as major general dated from February 23, 1944—almost two years behind his own. He also considered Barr to be quite lean in command experience. In actuality, Barr was only slightly junior to Almond in total commissioned service and his qualifications to lead a division were probably superior to Almond's own when selected for the 92d.

Although hidden by their opposite personalities, both men shared the same capabilities: strong staffers with much Southern heritage, but marginal experience in command. Almond was brash and forceful, and Barr was polite to a fault and much meeker. General Almond could disguise any leadership weaknesses by an intense dynamism, which invariably placed the blame for delay or failure on vacillating subordinates. Barr was an easy target for such abuse because he visibly lacked self-confidence and was too honest to deny problems with his command.

The personality conflicts between corps and division commanders seemed minor compared to the magnitude of the invasion task at hand. Almond's anxiety to capture Kimpo airfield just off the beach, which would assure land-based air coverage, led him to form a commando unit for that purpose. Almond's scheme stemmed from his infatuation with the exploits of Virginia partisan ranger John Singleton Mosby. Almond had formed raider forces on several occasions during his Italian campaign, most notably as a diversion for the Cinquale Canal attack of February 1945 (which failed miserably). Col. Louis B. Ely's provisional raider company of the Special Activities Group (later designated the 8245th and 8227th Army Units, respectively) was an American-Korean strike element reliant on individual skill and cunning for success in surprise raids. Colonel Ely believed it could take Kimpo field from its expected defenders, the ragtag *107th NKPA Security Regiment*.

Almond asked for Marine reinforcement of the enterprise, but General Smith rejected the idea as foolish. The concept called for paddling rubber boats three miles against a strong eight-knot tidal current and then crossing the muddy wasteland, on foot and out of radio range, to reach Kimpo by dawn. General Shepherd seconded Smith's objections, and the Navy considered the raid cancelled for lack of Marine participation.

In the meantime, larger questions about the whole invasion scheme were being raised. During the first week of September, Operation CHROMITE again fell into disfavor at the War Department level. The Joint Chiefs of Staff expressed renewed doubts about the wisdom of the venture and sent messages to MacArthur urging reconsideration of the effort. General Almond blamed this latest apprehension on General Smith's conveyance of exaggerated fears to Admiral Joy.

General MacArthur was not distracted by Pentagon misgivings. On September 8, he replied that his final assessment of the operation remained positive, repeating his convictions that CHROMITE would deliver a decisive blow by envelopment. The message closed by reciting that the embarkation was proceeding according to schedule, a clear signal that MacArthur was committed and not backing down.

During the last days prior to embarkation, the deputy chief of staff at Far East Command, Maj. Gen. Doyle O. Hickey, took over most of Almond's Japan-related responsibilities. Hickey and Almond were on good terms, and they used the few remaining mornings to work feverishly through reams of reports and coordination meetings. On September 12, Hickey became the acting chief of staff for all three of MacArthur's commands: Far East, United Nations, and SCAP (forces in occupied Japan).

With the mornings preoccupied by Hickey, Almond only had the afternoon hours to check corps units as they prepared for movement in their final staging areas. He visited the troop locations repeatedly, observing "the men's fitness and attitude for battle" and inquiring into embarkation details. This Almond flair for mobile excursions was ingrained from World War I, when wide sector responsibilities mandated constant movement among his scattered machine guns. Although Almond viewed these visits as an expression of vigorous command presence, many subordinate units resented his dictatorial scrutiny over minor technicalities and noticed the superficiality of his brief visits. They felt the overall embarkation process was not being monitored sufficiently.

Almond's remaining time was devoted to reshaping his headquarters into a conveyable command post. He realized that battlefield mobility would be a rude awakening for staff sections complacent in their well-furnished, placid Japan offices. He fretted over adjusting staffing measures under various movement contingencies. His passion for complex planning culminated in an exhaustive three-day "map exercise" to test staff procedure alternatives. He insisted on speed in paperwork, and demanded that an operational order be written, stenciled, and back on his desk within twenty minutes after oral issuance. Almond also mandated it not be longer than one foolscap page, quipping, "Then maybe someone will read it."[26]

While Almond was juggling to acquaint Hickey with his new multi-faceted job, inspecting the troops readying to sail, and dallying with functional control over staff work for his mobile headquarters, Col. Aubrey Smith was coping with the major X Corps headache: the supply quandary. The corps was forced to beg, steal, and emergency-requisition just about every item needed for the invasion. The CHROMITE logistical plan was so hopelessly complex and overloaded with projected niceties that Colonel Smith's section was swamped in frantic orders for materiel. The urgent pressure that attended most requisitions added to the difficulty of securing authorization and actually finding the items.

The tight security surrounding the impending corps movement hampered requisitioning and planning, but reflected Almond's predilection for absolute secrecy. All corps plans and staff sections were strictly compartmentalized and no one except the top officers had any idea of CHROMITE's magnitude. The inability or failure to share information created an understandable failure on the part of supplying agencies to appreciate the exigency of the situation.

The invasion troops were isolated in their embarkation camps and informed that destinations would be released only after they were at sea. Despite these precautions, it was obvious that a large amphibious enterprise was brewing. Thousands of Marines were pouring into Japan and entire shiploads of young Korean males were being dumped into the 7th Infantry Division training areas. The press dubbed the operation "Common Knowledge," but the exact landing site was kept secret. Most observers guessed it was Kunsan.[27]

General MacArthur and Almond remained at the Far East Command's Dai-ichi headquarters building to the last minute in an effort to forestall enemy forecasting of the invasion time bracket. On September 13, typhoon Kezia was raging between Iwo Jima and southern Japan. Generals MacArthur and Almond flew from Tokyo on the commander's new personal Constellation *Scap*, but typhoon winds forced them to land at Itazuki and travel the last eighty-six miles over winding, unpaved Japanese roads to reach the port of Sasebo. That night the generals boarded the amphibious force flagship AGC-7 USS *Mount McKinley* for the voyage to Inch'on.

In accordance with his predilection for secrecy, General Almond never confided any knowledge about Operation CHROMITE to his wife. When the naval task force departed Japan, Margaret was unaware that he would be leading a reinforced corps into the most perilous attack of the Korean War.

Notes

1. U.S. Marine Corps Historical Division, *A Chronology of the United States Marine Corps, 1947–1964,* Vol. III, p. 10.
2. USAMHI interview, p. IV-25.
3. Lynn Montross and Capt. Nicholas A. Canzona, *U.S. Marine Operations in Korea: 1950–1953,* Vol. II, U.S. Marine Corps, 1955, Ch. 2.
4. 7th Infantry Division, *Annual Unit Histories,* 1949 and 1950.
5. Eighth Army History Section Order of Battle Section, *5th Artillery Group 1950,* Office of the Center of Military History, File No. 8-5.1A.
6. X Corps Commanding General H 314.7 File, *Special Reports,* dtd 14 May 1953.
7. Background from Almond's papers, except for Colonel Smith, from Blair, p. 408.
8. Lt. Col. James F. Schnabel, General Headquarters, Far East Command, *FEC GHQ Support and Participation in the Korean War.*
9. X Corps, *Operation Chromite,* Book IV, G-4 Summary, 15 August–30 September 1950.
10. USAMHI interview, p. IV-29.
11. See Appendix II.
12. USAMHI interview, p. V-64.
13. Clay Blair, *The Forgotten War,* Times Books, New York, 1987, p. 229. Blair carefully records this hypothesis as: "Collins may have believed that the appointment of Almond to command X Corps, which would operate at Inchon under MacArthur's direct control like a separate army, was a devious device, conceived by MacArthur or Almond to get Almond promoted to three stars. Collins had consistently opposed promoting Almond, but a successful Inchon landing could build such pressure to promote Almond that he could not reasonably continue in opposition."
14. Far East Command General Staff Military Intelligence Section, *History of the North Korean Army,* dtd 31 July 1952.
15. First Lt. Bevin R. Alexander, Eighth Army Historical Section, *History of the Korean War: Enemy Materiel,* Vol. III, Pt. 13.
16. Commander Joint Task Force Seven and Seventh Fleet, *Inch'on Report.*
17. Donald Knox, *The Korean War: Pusan to Chosen, An Oral History,* Harcourt Brace Jovanovich, New York, 1985, p. 201.
18. Appleman, p. 493.
19. Manchester, p. 576.
20. USAMHI interview, pp. IV-34 and 36.
21. Goulden, p. 196.
22. USAMHI interview, p. IV-43.
23. Montross and Canzona, Vol. II, Ch. 4.
24. Marine Corps History and Museums Division, *The 1st Marine Division and its Regiments,* U.S. Marine Corps, 1981.

25. 7th Infantry Division, *Annual Narrative History,* 1950, and Lt. Col. Charles R. Scherer interview in Westover, pp. 184, 185.
26. "Command," *Time,* 23 October 1950, p. 28.
27. Robert Leckie, *Conflict: The History of the Korean War, 1950–53,* G. P. Putnam's Sons, New York, 1962, p. 131.

CHAPTER 3

THE INVASION

1. The Armada Sails

From its inception X Corps was a mystery corps born in haste and secrecy, and destined for a role in Korea as exceptional and compelling as its appellation, "Big X." At the beginning of September 1950, General Almond's organization was the preeminent corps in the United States military, poised on the threshold of a major invasion with global implications. Its success would cut the logistical ribbon sustaining the North Korean armies, break the back of the communist offensive in southern Korea, and insure the viability of the United Nations cause and American presence in the Far East. Failure was inconceivable.

The strength of the seventy thousand-man X Corps on the eve of combat, however, was apparent only on paper. The corps was not massed in any single assembly area and its whole might was not easily discerned. It was still a collection of written directives and radio transmissions binding a host of fragmented and largely untried units, and these statistics were classified to everyone except a few top officers. General Almond understood the intrinsic power of X Corps and remarked to MacArthur that it possessed over twice the manpower available to General Lee's

Army of Northern Virginia defending Richmond. Even more telling, X Corps contained more men than the entire U.S. Army around the turn of the century.[1]

Against this modern phalanx, estimates of *NKPA* strength in the Seoul-Inch'on area remained fixed at eight thousand North Koreans from the *9th* and *18th NKPA Divisions*. Most of these were in the capital and only a thousand troops were posted to Inch'on. The bulk of this manpower consisted of service troops or trainees, and they possessed no significant artillery or air support. If these intelligence appraisals were correct, Almond realized that his X Corps sledgehammer might overwhelm the beachhead, strike inland, and take Seoul before the advance could be checked by enemy reinforcements rushed in from other areas.[2]

For these reasons, the invasion force needed to swiftly consolidate the beachhead and capture the Inch'on-Seoul area. General MacArthur's ultimate invasion goal for X Corps, however, was only partially related to military necessity. He wanted to capture Seoul quickly and re-install South Korean president Syngman Rhee in the capital exactly three months to the day after the war had started. MacArthur believed that the "oriental mind" placed great emphasis on signs connected with calendrical events, and that such an accomplishment would overawe both his Chinese and North Korean enemies.

MacArthur might have disclosed this motive to Almond, but other senior commanders were not fully informed of this priority. General Smith and other leaders premised their objectives at Seoul on military logic: to seal off the capital and prevent enemy escape from the region. Almond was anxious to wrest the city from enemy hands at the earliest opportunity, even in a pitched battle, but his subordinate division commanders—either unaware, or scornful of, MacArthur's political target timing—wanted to surround Seoul and avoid a difficult urban battle inside the city itself.

General Almond treated MacArthur's desires as obligatory and he viewed the tide-enforced invasion date of September 15 as providential. Upon landing, X Corps would have ten days to recapture the nearby South Korean capital in coincidence with the quarterly anniversary of the communist attack on the Republic of Korea. Yet the logistical hurdles still facing X Corps threatened to ensnare its movement before it could even reach Korea.

Almond conceived Operation CHROMITE as an amphibious strike force sailing on hundreds of attack transports, fast cargo ships, and amphibious specialty vessels built in the recent Pacific war years. Unfortunately, the Navy could not produce a fraction of its once-proud support fleet. Commercial merchant ships incapable of amphibious operations were substituted. These vessels were built for regular pierside freight discharges and lacked the crew training and mechanical gear for ship-to-shore operations using landing craft. Several merchant ships experienced mechanical failure even during routine transit service.

The Far East Command had transferred units from Japan to Korea since June, but these movements were rather haphazard. Operation CHROMITE confronted the command with the necessity of staging an organized seaborne enterprise. Four embarkation echelons—Able, Baker, Charlie, and Dog—were used to corral the multitude of components being redirected into port assembly areas from their training camps all over Japan. Another unnamed embarkation echelon, consisting of the 5th Marines at Pusan, was in Korea and scheduled to rendezvous with the main invasion fleet at sea.

The naval base of Kobe was used to embark the 1st Marine Division and Army 2d Engineer Special Brigade, which comprised Able echelon. A major typhoon roared through the port on September 3, with wind gusts of 110 miles per hour and forty-foot-high waves. The harbor was left in shambles, several large vessels almost capsized, and numerous harbor craft were sunk. Port authorities and dock workers performed a miracle as they replaced material, repaired ships, and embarked the Marine division on schedule.

Other corps elements embarked at Yokohama. Of these, the most important was Baker echelon, which consisted of the 7th Infantry Division and most Army support forces slated for the invasion. While a typhoon did not strike Yokohama, the out-loading of Baker echelon fell into such disarray that cargo losses and movement delays surpassed difficulties caused by the storm damage at Kobe. As a result, most of the 7th Infantry Division, including its precious medium and heavy artillery, was shifted to late-sailing ships of Charlie echelon. This setback might be disastrous if the Marines needed reinforcing ground artillery or infantry assistance early in their drive to clear Inch'on.[3]

On September 10–12, 1950, the X Corps invasion elements embarked on a multinational flotilla of 261 warships and transports from Australia, Britain, Canada, France, Holland, New Zealand, and the United States. Many of the latter vessels were piloted and manned completely by Japanese who, just five years earlier, had been fighting the Americans. Japanese sailors manned thirty-seven of the forty-seven LSTs (Landing Ship, Tank) ferrying the Marines. Hundreds of Japanese stevedores were also recruited to provide labor at Inch'on port, in case the Korean population was hostile. They were issued one blanket each and slept on the open decks of the transports carrying X Corps into battle.[4]

Control over Operation CHROMITE was no longer in Almond's hands. When the troops embarked on transports, the corps commander relinquished authority to the amphibious commander, Rear Admiral Doyle. Doyle took his instructions from the Seventh Fleet commander, Vice Adm. Arthur D. Struble. These men governed the voyage and the first stages of the assault, while ammunition and initial supplies were unloaded and the troops proceeded inland. The X Corps commander would assume command after his men were put ashore and whenever control could be exercised more efficiently from an inshore location, and only after the safety of the beachhead was assured.

These time-honored arrangements reduced Almond to the temporary status of a high-ranking passenger. The invasion plans were set and Admiral Struble was in charge of the attack until X Corps was ashore. Almond visited MacArthur's cabin every morning and afternoon and inquired if he had any requirements. MacArthur replied ''no'' on every occasion and Almond responded each time, ''I will see you on the fifteenth.''[5]

The *Mount McKinley* was packed with dignitaries and lack of space allowed only Almond's aides to accompany him on the command ship. General Ruffner and the rest of the X Corps staff were aboard another transport. Before leaving Japan, Almond worked out an elaborate plan to receive dispatches regardless of Struble's imposition of strict radio silence. Aircraft would deliver bags of important Far East Command paperwork to the *Mount McKinley* at sea. The effort failed ingloriously on the first day's attempt when the bag dropped into the ocean, causing Almond to remain disgruntled most of the trip.[6]

The ships plowed through rough seas churned by the backlash of another severe storm, typhoon Kezia, as they rounded Japan. Black waves thrashed the decks and hatch covers of merchant ships wallowing in the deep swells. Rigging parted and cargo broke loose, damaging precious military equipment both in holds and topside. Much of the vital corps communications gear, assembled painstakingly by Col. Alvin R. Marcy, was rendered unserviceable as radio tubes smashed. Vital bridging components needed by corps engineer Colonel Rowny for the planned Han River crossing were washed overboard.[7]

The Marine and Army servicemen in the convoy were locked below decks, penned in crowded bunk compartments. Many were miserably seasick. Others listened apprehensively to the overworked reciprocating steam engines, diesels, and turbines laboring to propel their rolling ships. The shimmering groan of ship plates was considered an ominous portent for the upcoming invasion.

The carrier *Boxer* (CV-21), racing to join the invasion fleet from California, bucked the storm all night, depending on triple-tight lashings and deflated landing wheels to bring 110 aircraft safely through the raging seas. Fortune still smiled on Almond, however, because the invasion fleet's course was behind the storm. If the typhoon and fleet had actually crossed, the endeavors of X Corps might have ended well short of the Korean peninsula.[8]

As carriers and transports pitched in the typhoon-tossed ocean, other Navy warships brazenly sailed up Flying Fish Channel in sight of Inch'on. Seven destroyers passed a field of moored mines and dashed close to Wolmi-do Island, drawing fire and revealing enemy shore batteries for spotter aircraft overhead.

Well-camouflaged North Korean guns scored several hits on the destroyers. The *Collett* (DD-730), which had evaded a swarm of Japanese planes and torpedoes during a fast carrier raid off Luzon in November 1944, was not so lucky in this new war. She suffered five hits which mauled her superstructure and knocked out her armament directional control. The destroyers withdrew under the hail of enemy fire, their mission accomplished. The *NKPA* batteries were worked over and destroyed by bomb strikes and naval shelling.[9]

On September 13, while Wolmi-do was being blistered by incessant air strikes and cruiser/destroyer gunfire, the invasion fleet rounded Korea and entered calmer waters in the Yellow Sea. General Smith's 1st Marine Division used the short voyage as its only opportunity to give specific invasion briefings. Col. Raymond L. Murray's 5th Marines would land a battalion on Green Beach at Wolmi-do Island on the first morning tide, and the other two battalions on Red Beach at the tip of the city on the evening tide. The 5th Marines were chosen for the critical opening assault because they were combat veterans of the hard Naktong River battles at Masan and No-name Ridge and were seasoned warriors who knew *NKPA* tactics firsthand. Col. Lewis B. "Chesty" Puller's 1st Marines would land at Blue Beach against the southeastern factory district.[10]

Most Marine officers within the division believed the whole invasion plan was improvised too quickly, allowing no time for simulated landing drills or amphibious tractor (amtrac) rehearsals. The Marine riflemen were told that scaling ladders to climb the seawall was like attacking a fort in the movies, but many remembered films where stockade defenders pushed the ladders down. The Marine staffs studied the aerial photographs apprehensively. The pier extensions and other obstacles duplicated scenes of Tarawa atoll. They memorized the maps coded with the standard trio of beach colors (Red, Green, Blue) while learning the call-signs for high ground: Radio Hill, Observatory Hill, and the foreboding Cemetery Hill.

Along both Korean coasts, the Navy and special operations forces commenced diversionary bombardments and other feints to draw attention away from the Inch'on vicinity. Colonel Ely's X Corps provisional raider company of 124 troops, specially trained by Navy mobile training teams in demolitions and amphibious techniques, embarked on the British frigate *Whitesand Bay* at Kobe. After sunset on September 12, the raider company conducted a classic commando assault at Kunsan on the lower west coast. The daring raiders struck a number of targets, but their shotguns, submachine guns, and carbines were outclassed by enemy machine gun emplacements and mortar batteries. Ely's men left the burning shoreline while naval warships pounded the area with heavy gunfire to reinforce the deception.[11]

Invasion threats failed to worry the North Korean high command, which confidently ascribed such efforts as a probable feint to siphon troops from the main Pusan front. *NKPA* senior commanders callously disregarded rear areas subject to attack and remained oblivious of X Corps' actual size and status right up to the moment of amphibious attack. North of Seoul at Kumch'on, however, North Korean Lt. Col. Lee Chui Kun of the reinforced five thousand-man *27th NKPA Brigade,* reported to an urgent conference where both commander Brig. Gen. Kang Yon Kol and assistant Col. Shin Ri Bon emphasized rumors that the "U.S. forces would make a landing at Wonsan, Inchon, or Mokpo in the very near future." His excellent brigade was braced to reinforce the battlefield in case of such an eventuality.[12]

2. Seizure of Wolmi-do

The invasion commenced as scheduled at 2 A.M. on September 15. The first unit to storm the enemy beaches was Lt. Col. Robert D. Taplett's

3d Battalion of the 5th Marines, tasked to take the key island of Wolmi-do on the first high tide. The fast, turbulent current of the incoming morning tide rushed the high-speed transports down Flying Fish Channel. The nimble modified destroyers used special radar to probe the predawn darkness and find their stations. The ships were followed by the huge 4500-ton dock-landing ship *Fort Marion* (LSD-22), which carried the mailed fist of Taplett's shock force: nine Marine M26 flame-throwing and dozer-equipped tanks designed to bury bunkers and seal island caves. The attack group anchored against the swirling water a mile offshore.

The naval gunfire support group lowered its triple- and twin-mounted guns at Wolmi-do Island. The eight-inch guns of the heavy cruisers *Rochester* and *Toledo* began firing in concert with the six-inch guns of the British light cruisers *Jamaica* and *Kenya*.

The naval bombardment ceased as a faint blush of pink dawned in the overcast sky. Carrier-based aircraft were striking the smoking island and its causeway with bombs and strafing cannon fire. Marine Corsairs demolished an armored car trying to cross this raised road linking the island to the mainland. The low-flying aircraft continuously raked the island's 335-foot-high fortified height, Radio Hill, and the island's summit was smothered in multiple fiery explosions.[13]

The amphibious flagship *Mount McKinley* was positioned to oversee the landing. A throng of senior commanders and reporters, garbed in oversized helmets and inflated life vests, crowded the ship's bridge and watched the pre-invasion bombardment and air strikes. General MacArthur joined them at 6:25 A.M. and sat in the admiral's swivel chair. Almond focused his binoculars past the ship's 40mm gun pedestals but could only see pillars of smoke masking the island's outline in the grayish light.[14]

The landing craft full of Marines circled tightly in classic World War II holding patterns. Forty-five minutes before sunrise, Admiral Doyle ordered the flag hoists raised on the flagship: "Land the Landing Force." Three LSMRs (Landing Ship, Medium, Rocket) closed within yards of the smoking shoreline and unleashed salvoes of clustered five-inch rockets into the thousand-yard-wide island. The landing craft straightened out and crossed the line of departure as dawn streaked across the horizon. The final rocket fire suddenly ceased. The landing craft disappeared into the thick pall of smoke and dust covering the shore.

At 6:33 A.M., the first wave of Marines landed unopposed on Wolmi-do's stony Green Beach. They charged past the tangle of toppled telephone

Inch'on Invasion

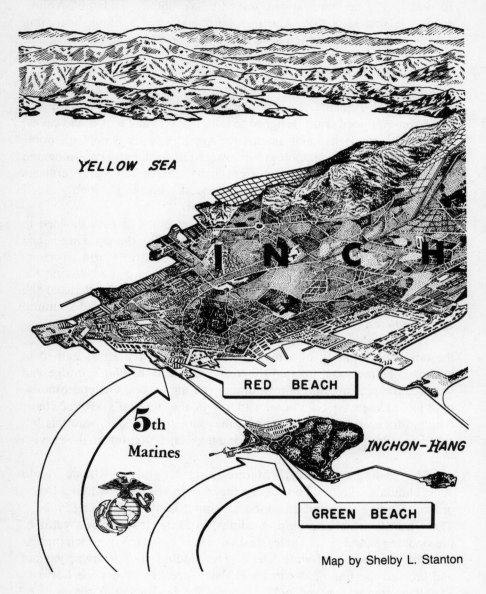

YELLOW SEA

INCH

RED BEACH

5th
Marines

INCHON-HANG

GREEN BEACH

Map by Shelby L. Stanton

BLUE BEACH

1st Marines

Map Scale in miles
                                          2

X CORPS

poles and wire and raced up the sandy scrub and pine thickets of shell-splintered Radio Hill. Although the island was honeycombed with caves, trenches, and gun positions, enemy opposition was light. The Marines hurried past sandbagged bunkers built with overhead cover so thick that the deafening pre-invasion bombardment had only blown away the camouflage netting. The barrels of intact Soviet-made 76mm cannon protruded from beneath the cross-beamed caverns, their distinctive double-baffle muzzle brakes silhouetted starkly against the leaden skies. But the pits were empty and the four hundred dazed North Koreans of the *3d Battalion, 226th NKPA Marine Regiment* were in no mood to fight.

Within a few minutes the second wave landed, and the tanks rumbled ashore next. The tanks moved up the slopes and cranked their tubular steel dozer-blade arms flush to the ground. They pushed heavy sand and dirt into cave entrances to entomb North Koreans who refused to surrender. Within thirty minutes of the landing, a Marine sergeant raised an American flag on the summit of Wolmi-do. General Almond spotted the cloth waving in the distance and knew Operation CHROMITE's first hurdle was cleared.

Lieutenant Colonel Taplett's Marines systematically cleared the rest of the island, cordoned off the causeway, and posted a squad at the tip of the island's lighthouse extension at Sowolmi-do. A final group of North Koreans were machine gunned trying to swim to the mainland. Taplett's request to charge across the causeway into Inch'on itself was denied. The Marines dug in their weapons, to render enfilade fire for the main afternoon assault. There was little left to do but wait as the tide receded and surrounded Wolmi-do with an impenetrable swath of mud. Rain began falling from the overcast mantle of clouds.[15]

Almond and MacArthur boarded a barge and tried to reach the island, but the ebbing water flowed out too quickly and they turned back to the *Mount McKinley*. Both generals were elated with the morning events. The Marines reported finding extensive foundations for future fortified construction everywhere. Within months Wolmi-do would have been transformed into an impregnable redoubt. By attacking on September 15, a single Marine battalion captured the island at a cost of only seventeen wounded. MacArthur remarked that more people were injured in everyday traffic accidents, and sent a message, "The Navy and Marines have never shone more brightly than this morning."[16]

The Americans were powerless to conduct further offensive activity against Inch'on until the next tidal surge in the late afternoon. A steady rain fell as carrier-based fighters flew past the fleet and disappeared over the ridge line behind Inch'on. The umbrella of aircraft was designed to intercept enemy reinforcements trying to reach the port within a thirty-mile arc of air interdiction. Almond hoped that this isolation could be enforced despite the bad weather.

3. Red and Blue Beaches

At 3:30 P.M., the main two-pronged assault against Inch'on began. Marines loaded with weapons and combat gear clambered down sagging cargo nets into the landing craft as the naval bombardment intensified and LSMRs blasted the landing areas with repeated rocket salvos. Burning buildings and oil towers emitted thick pillars of smoke that mixed with low-hanging clouds and framed the harbor in a pall of destruction. A mix of dirty smoke and misting rain began to blot out portions of the shoreline. Scores of landing craft and amphibious tractors passed the patrol vessel marking the final departure line.

At Red Beach fronting the main city, the lead boats of the 5th Marines slammed against the mile-wide seawall at 5:33 P.M. Some boats managed to land directly through holes blasted in the wall by cruiser gunfire, but most Marines clambered over the seawall on ladders while grappling hooks or lines secured their landing craft close by.

On Blue Beach in the industrial complex area of southeastern Inch'on, the smoke-filled twilight severely limited visibility. The unforeseen strength of swirling tide currents began scattering the neatly arranged waves of landing craft and complicated a situation made worse by crew inexperience, lack of compasses, and no radios. Navy guide boats escorted the first tractor waves to the shore. Some amtracs of the Army's 56th Amphibious Tank and Tractor Battalion bogged down in the mud before reaching the beach but others reached the shore and delivered Marines directly through the cruiser-blasted gaps in the wall. But, like Red Beach, most Marines were forced to use ladders to scale the fifteen-foot-high seawall in front of the beach.

Heavy rain squalls and dense smoke blotted out Blue Beach to all but the first three waves of landing craft. Succeeding waves were reduced to clusters of boats struggling to reach beaches obscured by smoke and rain. The attack became disordered as Marine units were fragmented and landing craft slammed into wrecks offshore or deposited men in the wrong places.

The boats carrying the regimental reserve went astray when they followed a control ship searchlight that pointed them erroneously toward the salt-pan retaining wall to the left of the actual beach. The mistake was realized quickly after the first Marines scrambled over the obstacle. The Marines were ordered off the wall and back into their landing craft, a process that became rather jumbled because some empty boats had already strayed away. The battalion, except for one stranded platoon, finally pulled away from the wall. The isolated men showed up the next morning after marching overland around the salt-pan overland with a respectable number of dispirited captives.[17]

These hazards on Blue Beach proper were complicated by a deep drainage ditch extending the far side of the seawall, which was invisible in the darkened haze of evening battle. Numerous casualties were incurred as men fell or jumped into this trench, which also claimed several amtracs. The North Koreans were so stunned by the onslaught, however, that they could offer only scattered resistance from towers and blazing ruins.

Struble brought his personal launch alongside the *Mount McKinley* to invite Shepherd, Doyle, and Almond to see the amphibious landing firsthand. Almond stated, "I felt that it was sufficiently safe for me and anybody who desired to accompany me to take a small admiral's gig and go ashore and see the situation for myself."[18]

The third-wave boats were jumbled next to the seawall landing marines weighted down by bazookas, machine guns, and munitions. Struble's admiralty barge suddenly appeared in the midst of these landing craft. One Marine sergeant was preparing demolitions to blast a portion of the seawall barrier. Just prior to setting off the charge, he looked up in amazement to see Struble's slim flag-studded boat. He yelled out, "Boat there! Get the hell out of here!" The gig's coxswain promptly backed the boat around as the sergeant's charge sent a cloud of powder and chunks of rocks flying over the water.[19]

The darkness, seawall obstacles, and misdirection of many units combined to create havoc on the beach. No one expected the situation to be so hectic, although Struble later claimed he was using the opportunity to show Almond the complications of a seaborne assault. The four senior officers threaded their way past charging Marines, shore control parties, bomb-tossed debris, and boulders for about an hour. General Almond was impressed with the aggressive spirit of the Marines. As dusk faded into darkness, searchlights were turned on to assist unloading, and Struble's party returned to the *Mount McKinley*.

The disorganized North Korean defenders, still in shock from the bombardment and fury of the landing, were unable to form a coherent defense. On Blue Beach, the 1st Marines encountered negligible fire from factory towers and warehouses at the water's edge and passed many abandoned gun positions. Colonel Puller's Marines moved through the lightly defended outskirts of Inch'on and crossed the Inch'on-Seoul highway, one mile inland, an hour after midnight. The Marines used the remainder of the night to consolidate blocking positions across the road.

In the Red Beach sector of downtown Inch'on, the foothold of the 5th Marines was confined to a small area dominated by the steep cliffs of Cemetery Hill. Sharp skirmishes and fallen Marine flamethrowers marked individual struggles for possession of seaside bunkers. One Marine lieutenant, Baldomero Lopez, died trying to knock out a key bunker system. After being wounded severely, causing his hand grenade to drop in the midst of an attack, he smothered the blast with his own body—an act later recognized with the Medal of Honor. Another Marine platoon under Lt. Francis W. Muetzel neutralized the enemy strong-point at the Asahi Brewery building and then reversed direction, conquering Cemetery Hill from its gentler sloping landward side. Lieutenant Muetzel's men captured a stunned North Korean mortar company that had lost its will to continue fighting.[20]

The intermixing of Marine companies and communications mishaps created confusion in seizing Observatory Hill, which overlooked the beach farther inland. The Marines, however, pushed through scattered enemy opposition and secured the heights. By midnight all three enemy strong-points at Cemetery Hill, Observatory Hill, and the Asahi Brewery building were under control of the 5th Marines. With a third of Inch'on city in their possession and the main heights secured, Colonel Murray's Marines halted to reorganize and sent out patrols to safeguard their front line. Flares illuminated the pitch-black night, and naval gunfire lashed out periodically at the unseen hills in the distance.

The invasion's only adverse incident occurred on Red Beach at 6:30 P.M., while Almond was still inspecting Blue Beach. Navy Lt. Cdr. James C. Wilson's eight LSTs, loaded with special "assault packets" of fighting materiel, lumbered toward Red Beach to line up on the evening tide. This approach right on the heels of the invading Marines brought Wilson's ships under enemy machine gun and mortar fire within two hundred yards of Red Beach. An automatic weapons burst laced several ammunition trucks jammed together on one LST deck and started a fire, but sailors and Marine transportation personnel managed to extinguish it quickly.

Several LSTs returned fire with bow-mounted 40mm antiaircraft guns which peppered both Marine and enemy-held territory. One series of rounds chased a group of Marines right into the firing range of an enemy machine gun nest and then neatly eliminated the enemy weapon—all quite by accident.

The LSTs were deliberately stranded on the mud flats for the night-long chore of disgorging ammunition, gasoline, emergency supplies, and combat equipment. Engineer dozers were rushed off the ships first and leveled the unloading area as Wilson's "Large Slow Targets," beached as "Large Stationary Targets," were pelted with more North Korean machine gun fire and mortar rounds. Mountains of gas and oil drums lashed to the upper decks were hit by shrapnel and bullets, but no fires resulted—even though gasoline poured over one LST deck and spilled into its hull compartments.

The nervous Navy gunners immediately returned fire with automatic antiaircraft guns leveled into the city, apparently making little or no attempt to ascertain targets or properly aim their weapons. This indiscriminate naval gunfire hit several Marine units and stopped, according to some witnesses, only after the 5th Marines threatened the LST crewmen with retaliatory fire. The incident killed one marine and wounded twenty-three, and increased the total Marine casualties during the invasion to twenty killed, one missing, and one hundred seventy-four wounded.

The periodic enemy fire did not stop the Marine 1st Shore Battalion workers, who were keenly aware that unloading time was compressed by tidal considerations. They labored under the glare of floodlights as vehicles were rolled out and goods dumped everywhere possible. The LST enterprise was instrumental in keeping the initial Marine drive supplied, and Wilson was later pinned with the Silver Star for "determined action under heavy enemy fire" in the "unswerving use of his LSTs as counter-battery platforms and as decoys diverting enemy fire from the Marine landing craft" while en route to the shore.[21]

Almond enjoyed a late evening dinner with MacArthur and Doyle on the amphibious flagship. He, too, was honored for the day's actions with a Silver Star (his second oak-leaf cluster).

Major General Edward M. Almond, 04666, United States Army, displayed conspicuous gallantry, aggressiveness, and leadership as Commanding

General of the X Corps during the eminent invasion of Inchon on 15 September 1950. General Almond was charged with the execution of Operation Chromite which involved the seizure initially of Inchon. He visited the front line units, and by personal example and fearless leadership, encouraged them to seize assigned objectives with the minimum of delay. His keen tactical judgment, initiative, and unremitting devotion to duty in coordinating all tactical elements ashore during the initial phases of the operation have materially contributed to the success of our Arms.[22]

Almond recalled that the assembly was almost festive: "We could already see the landing had been successful the first day, which was really the critical point. Once ashore, we had no fear of being able to take care of any enemy that might meet us eventually."[23] The bold gamble at Inch'on had worked, X Corps was firmly ashore, and Almond basked in the afterglow of MacArthur's great triumph.

Notes

1. In 1902 the U.S. Army totalled 59,866 personnel. Department of the Army General Orders No. 108, 1902.
2. X Corps, *Operation Chromite*, Book II, G2 Summary, 15 August–30 September 1950.
3. Japan Logistical Command Historical Section, *Logistical Problems and Their Solutions: 25 August 1950–31 August 1951*, dated 15 February 1952, p. 70; Japan Logistical Command, *Activities Report*, 25 August–30 September 1950.
4. Japan Logistical Command, *JLCM Summary*, September 1950.
5. USAMHI Interview, pp. IV-44, 45.
6. Max Hastings, *The Korean War*, Simon and Schuster, New York, 1987, p. 105.
7. X Corps, *Operation Chromite*, Book IV, G4 Summary, 15 August–30 September 1950.
8. Naval Joint Task Force Seven, *Inch'on Report*.
9. Knox, pp. 217–220. World War II battle action from Samuel Eliot Morison, *History of United States Naval Operations in World War II*, Little Brown & Company, Boston, 1963, Vol. XII, p. 356.
10. Marine Corps Historical Reference Pamphlet, *A Brief History of the First Marines*, U.S. Marine Corps, 1962. Colonel Puller had previously taken the 1st Marines into the maelstrom of Peleliu on September 15, 1944, and fearlessly led the regiment past Japanese shore guns which destroyed scores of Marine-laden amphibious tractors and DUKWs at the water's edge. Puller assumed command of the reactivated 1st Marines on August 5, 1950. Uncannily, the attack date against Inch'on marked the exact sixth anniversary of the deadly Peleliu assault.
11. Montross and Canzona, Vol. II, p. 144.
12. Statement of Prisoner Lee Chui Kun, Lt. Col., 27th Brigade, in X Corps Special Report: War Diary Summary, 30 September 1950.
13. Appleman, p. 505.
14. Manchester, p. 579.
15. Montross and Canzona, Vol. II, pp. 88–96.
16. Manchester, p. 579.
17. Montross and Canzona, Vol. II, Ch. 6.
18. USAMHI Interview, p. IV-46.
19. Robert Leckie, *Conflict: The History of the Korean War, 1950–1953*, G. P. Putnam's Sons, New York, 1962, p. 142.
20. Montross and Canzona, p. 107.
21. GHQ Far East Command General Orders, 1950.
22. Citation confirmed in GHQ Far East Command General Orders No. 32, dtd 27 September 1950.
23. USAMHI Interview, p. IV-47.

CHAPTER 4

EXPANDING THE BEACHHEAD

1. Marines Clear the Way

Before dawn on September 16, the X Corps provisional raider company transferred from its British frigate to a South Korean picket boat offshore near Kimpo airfield. General Almond planned to capture the air base at dawn using a surprise commando raid. He was so confident of the venture's probable success that he issued advanced orders to his personal pilot, Capt. Charles Keleman, to fly the corps L-5 light utility plane off its escort carrier that morning and meet him at the airstrip. Unfortunately, the commando raid was cancelled at the last minute because the North Koreans were fully alerted by the main invasion and the vital element of surprise was lost to the commandoes.

In the meantime, General Almond's L-5 *Blue Goose* took off from the carrier *Badoeng Strait* (CVE-116) and circled vainly over the enemy-held airfield. The *Blue Goose* was a tiny artillery spotter plane, capable of landing on short airstrips, which had been hastily drafted for Almond's use in Operation CHROMITE. The aircraft was painted navy blue during its voyage to Korea because there was not even enough time to repaint her metallic silver fabrication before leaving Japan. When it became apparent that the Kimpo raid had failed, Keleman was forced to fly the *Blue Goose* back to the carrier and attempt a landing.

Keleman approached the ship as it steamed into the wind at thirty knots. The landing signal officer waved his flag to cut speed, but failed to reckon with the slow landing power of the light Army aircraft. As the carrier plowed ahead, Keleman's L-5 slowed up and the aircraft barely connected with the end of the flight deck. The landing wheels made contact but the tail wheel caught on the deck's edge and was ripped from the plane. The landing was less than ideal, but the *Blue Goose* began her legendary X Corps career as the first Army aircraft to land on an aircraft carrier in the Korean war.[1]

The Marine and Navy carrier aircraft produced much better results as they ranged in front of the battle line throughout the day. This close air support began at first light when Corsairs from the escort carrier *Sicily* (CVE-118) bombed and napalmed six North Korean T34 tanks moving up the Seoul highway toward Inch'on with infantry riding aboard. Marine M26 Pershing tanks reached the site later in the morning and promptly destroyed the surviving T34 armor.

The X Corps offensive against Inch'on continued as its Marine spearhead concentrated on gaining ground, clearing the main city streets, and widening the beachhead in order to distance the port from North Korean counterattacks. The Marines suppressed intermittent sniper fire and secured the urban flanks of this headlong advance. The attached 1st ROK Marine Regiment was employed to eradicate the last pockets of resistance. The logistical lifeline from Japan to Inch'on port was so tenuous that X Corps could not afford communist infiltrators or saboteurs behind the lines.

During the day's fighting on the main front, the Marine regiments brushed past light opposition as they advanced on both sides of the east-west highway leading to Seoul. By nightfall the Marines had seized a line of steep hills six miles from the coast at Inch'on, placing the beaches beyond the range of North Korean cannon. At 6 P.M., General Smith formally took control of the 1st Marine Division at his forward command post east of the port. General Almond followed the Marine progress on a large battle map taped to the forward bulkhead on the *Mount McKinley*.

In the predawn darkness of September 17, a North Korean tank-escorted infantry force meandered down the main Seoul-Inch'on highway, oblivious to the location of the Marine front line. The six enemy T34 tanks and two hundred soldiers moved past Ascom City and through a winding pass in the hills southwest of town as the first morning light glowed faintly behind them. The Marines ambushed the column from forward positions overlooking the defile with automatic weapons and rocket launchers. Corp. Okey J. Douglas slithered down the hillside, stalked one T34 with his rocket launcher and destroyed it at close range, and then reloaded and scored a hit against another T34.

The detonations signalled Marine Pershing tanks and recoilless rifle crews to fire from main positions hidden on the night-shrouded hills to the south. The darkness suddenly erupted into a blazing vortex of exploding fireballs, detonating shells, and brilliant lines of criss-crossing machine gun tracers. The startled enemy force tried desperately to maneuver out of the pass. Marine rocket launcher teams, armed with their new powerful weapons, crawled forward to take the T34s under point-blank fire. Direct 90mm pounding from Marine tankers blasted the North Korean armor into smoking hulks. The accompanying *NKPA* infantrymen were also annihilated, with only one marine wounded in exchange.[2]

Later that morning, MacArthur and his entourage paid a visit to the battlefield. They stopped briefly for a situation updating at General Smith's division headquarters, where helmeted marines in battle fatigues pointed out the front line on crude map boards. Almond sat beside MacArthur and other prominent officers in a row of folding chairs as field phones on the otherwise bare wooden table rang with urgent situation updates. The stark Marine building and combat-attired occupants contrasted sharply with the visiting delegation dressed in khaki uniforms and service caps.

MacArthur was impatient to see the battlefield. Generals Shepherd and Smith felt responsibility for the supreme commander's safety in the Marine zone, but they knew his reckless tendency to visit dangerous forward positions. They arranged for his jeep motorcade to see the tanks eliminated by aircraft on the previous day. MacArthur and Almond gloated over the wrecks. To Shepherd's consternation, Colonel Murray suddenly blurted out that if MacArthur liked knocked-out enemy tanks, more were just down the road. At that time, "down the road" was the leading edge of the battle line.

General MacArthur insisted on proceeding up the road and climbed a small ridge with Almond. From its summit, they surveyed the burning wreckage of the ambushed enemy tank column. MacArthur ignored sounds of sniper fire around them, commenting that the *NKPA* marksmen were second-rate troops. The carnage vividly underscored Operation CHRO-MITE's overwhelming success, and reporters took several pictures. These spoils of victory miffed Almond, who suddenly suspected a Marine publicity ploy. He snapped at Shepherd, "You damned Marines! You always seem to be in the right spot at the right time. Hell, we [might have] been fighting this battle with Army troops but MacArthur would arrive just as the Marines had knocked out six enemy tanks."[3]

Almond resented the news spotlight on Smith's Marines as conquerors of Inch'on, because he felt slighted that his role as corps commander of the great offensive was being ignored. As far as Almond was concerned, the Marines had balked during the planning stages and were now grabbing all the glory. He became convinced that the only way to focus media attention on X Corps and the Army participation in the campaign was to rush Barr's 7th Infantry Division on line, thus ending the exclusive Marine claim to the fighting front.

2. Sustaining the Front

Throughout September 17, the Marines widened the American foothold at Inch'on. In the southern sector, Colonel Puller's 1st Marines ran into heavy resistance late in the day from elements of the *18th NKPA Division,* which had dug in along the hills guarding the road into Yong-dungp'o. The Marines made slim progress against the entrenched enemy defenders outside Sosa. Marine tank-escorted riflemen were counter-attacked in a narrow gorge outside the town and pushed back.

One of the leading M26 tanks under Lt. Bryan J. Cummings stalled out as North Korean infantrymen stormed over the vehicle. The tank crew members locked their hatches, but dense chemical fumes inside forced them to crank open the pistol port for fresh air. An enemy hand grenade was pitched through this opening and exploded inside the confines of the hull. The lung-searing blast sent shrapnel tearing through the crew, and they all prepared to die. At that instant, however, another Marine Pershing clanked around the bend and raked the trapped tank with machine gun fire, dusting the enemy soldiers off its sides and turrets. Low-flying aircraft blistered the hills on either side of the highway and Marine infantry soon reclaimed the lost ground, securing Lieutenant Cummings's vehicle and crew from further harm.[4]

In the northern sector, Colonel Murray's 5th Marines brushed aside enemy resistance in Ascom City, and advanced seven miles across rice paddies and fields of tall corn to reach the edge of Kimpo airfield just after sunset. Advancing in concert with tanks, the Marines skirmished through two hours of scattered fighting to secure the lower runway. The enemy defenders were so surprised by the speed of the Marine advance that they never mined the airstrip. Several disconnected North Korean counterattacks were made during the predawn darkness of September 18. At 5 A.M., Marine riflemen and tank cannoneers annihilated the last enemy charge and Kimpo airfield was in American hands.[5]

The first aircraft to land at Kimpo was a dark green four-passenger Sikorsky S-51 Marine helicopter. Wearing his slouched fatigue cap, Lieutenant General Shepherd stepped out and sprightly tapped the solid concrete with his sharp-pointed walking stick. He knew, like Almond, that capturing Kimpo's six thousand-foot runway and facilities transformed the temporary division beachhead into a permanent corps front. The first fighter-bombers of Marine Air Group 33 flew in from Japan before sunset to give continual air support to advancing ground troops. Aerial replenishment of supplies was also assured. By the end of September, the Far East Air Forces Combat Cargo Command would fly 10,505 tons into Kimpo to sustain X Corps.[6]

Although Kimpo provided X Corps with an important airdrome, the seaport of Inch'on was the logistical key to Operation CHROMITE and the liberation of Seoul. Colonel Twitty's 2d Engineer Special Brigade laid the crucial foundation for port operations. Over three thousand Army engineers and support troops, Navy beachmasters, and Marine shore party controllers working with hundreds of Japanese stevedores, hatch-gang laborers, and dragooned Korean workers, repaired port damage, cleared the docks, and pressed the harbor into functional service.

Ironically, the pre-invasion bombardment had created the most extensive damage to the port area. Only one finger pier of the original eight was left standing. Every warehouse along the tidal basin was gutted by bombs, with one exception. Rows of tall industrial chimneys, blackened by fire, pointed eerily into the sky where walls had collapsed into heaps of rubble and blocked roadways. The most serious handicap was the inoperable lock-gate at the entrance to the Inch'on harbor basin. Water depth within the basin was sufficient only for small craft.

Until technicians repaired the gateway, the "Maru-class" transports could not unload normally. The ships relayed cargo ashore through landing craft which shuttled all over the harbor within fourteen hours of the

Blue and Red Beach landings. This ferrying system was inefficient and time-consuming because regular transports were designed for direct harbor discharge. Floating pontoon piers were built to replace the demolished regular piers.

LSTs proved invaluable workhorses because they could be unloaded over the mud, and X Corps owed much of its success to these ships. Actual lighterage was needed urgently, but all that could be spared from Japan was a motley collection of ninety-seven Japanese powered cargo barges. None of the barges had radios or navigational instruments and only one interpreter was present.

Port authorities implemented control over the Japanese lighters by giving dispatch tickets written in English and Japanese to the barges as they passed through the tidal basin locks to get more cargo from ships offshore. The barge skippers often ignored the written instructions and proceeded according to verbal requests from Japanese merchant officers. The few radio-equipped patrol boats and tugs plied the inner and outer harbors, guiding errant barges to their proper destinations.

Ammunition for X Corps was in critically short supply. Fortunately, a munitions crisis was avoided unexpectedly by Marines advancing through the Ascom city depot, just outside Inch'on. They uncovered more than two thousand tons of American ordnance captured by the North Koreans in their initial offensive. The ammunition was still packed in pristine condition. Trucks to haul cargo were so scarce, however, that they were operated around the clock and filled so full they had to be pulled by bulldozers. Inch'on port operations were a critical part of the X Corps effort, and the dedicated service troops at the harbor and nearby Kimpo airfield kept the supplies flowing.[7]

3. Objective: Han River

On the combat front, progress was slowing and enemy resistance steadily mounted as X Corps moved closer to Seoul. Aerial observers and fighter pilots reported long enemy troop columns advancing along the twisting mountain roads. Every day the North Koreans shoved more units into the capital, and each passing hour decreased the chances of meeting MacArthur's liberation timetable.

During September 18, the 1st Marines roared past roadblocks and entered Sosa and the hills beyond. The Marines charged through grass fires on the smoking heights and captured them, but the enemy retaliated by shelling the Marine victors with 120mm heavy mortars, causing heavy casualties. It was evident that the North Koreans had recovered from the shock of invasion and were beginning to fight tenaciously.

On the afternoon of the same day, the 5th Marines captured the high ground overlooking the industrial suburb of Yongdungp'o. This was the same town that MacArthur and Almond had visited in June during the North Korean offensive against the South Korean capital. The Marines peered across the muddied Han River toward Seoul, as Colonel Murray prepared attacking orders under the dim lanterns of his command post at Kimpo airfield.

General Almond was now most anxious to get Army infantry ashore and cancel the Marine sole claim to the battle. He insisted that Admiral Doyle rearrange port unloading priorities to stop Marine supply discharges and get General Barr's 7th Infantry Division into Inch'on. The division lacked one-third of its infantry strength—the entire 17th Infantry off Pusan—and half its artillery and support because of shipping complications in CHROMITE's Baker and Charlie sea transit echelons. Almond realized, however, that at least one divisional regiment could secure the Marine right flank, and Doyle obediently landed Col. Charles E. Beauchamp's 32d Infantry on September 18.[8]

The men of the 7th Infantry Division expected a tough fight ahead and were uneasy with the large numbers of ill-trained Korean "augmentation troops" dumped in their ranks. Every third soldier within the 32d Infantry was a Korean draftee (upon landing the regiment contained 3,241 Americans and 1,873 South Koreans). The 7th Infantry Division quartermaster, Lt. Col. Kenneth O. Schellberg, revealed the expected intensity of the upcoming combat, "I loaded rations enough for thirty days. Anticipating that water might be short until we captured Inch'on [and ensured potable water supply], I included thirty gallons of water per man. On pure guess I included three loads of insecticides, and burial supplies for five thousand."[9]

The 32d Infantry was known as "The Queen's Own," stemming from its nineteenth-century Hawaiian predecessor that Queen Liliuokalani had distinguished as her personal infantry guard. The 32d Infantry had been part of the Far East Command since its reactivation in Japan during March 1949 (from elements of the 12th Cavalry, 31st Infantry, and 511th Parachute Infantry). The organization was given a solid foundation by its first commander, Col. Allen D. MacLean, and Colonel Beauchamp insured the retention of high standards when he took over three months before the Korean war erupted.[10]

Like most X Corps Army soldiers, the riflemen of the 32d Infantry had been issued generous amounts of clothing and equipment for the invasion. The soldiers had filled their cargo and combat packs to bursting and crammed the rest into duffel bags before putting everything aboard ship. The infantrymen were ordered to shake down to mission-essential loads before landing, but most were reluctant to leave any gear behind. As a result, like other green units, the 32d Infantry marched into positions south of Sosa overburdened with extra equipment. This gear was discarded during later advances and a trail of abandoned materiel marked the regiment's advance along the front.

The very next day, September 19, the 7th Infantry Division's second available regiment, the 31st Infantry, marched down LST ramps and went to the front. The 31st Infantry had been commanded by Col. Richard P. Ovenshine since February 6, 1950. It was officially known as the "Polar Bears" because of its two-year stint of duty guarding the Trans-Siberian railway during the U.S. intervention in the Russian civil war.

General Almond considered the 31st Infantry to be inferior in training and leadership to Beauchamp's men, and its previous station of Sapporo (on the northernmost island of Japan, Hokkaido) had isolated it from the rest of the division. As Barr filled up the 7th Infantry Division on the main island of Honshu, the remote 31st Infantry often received the last pick of troops or was overlooked altogether. Caustically nicknamed "Foreign Legion of the United States"[11] because the 31st was the only regiment never to serve in America, the unit had surrendered at Bataan in 1942. Although Capt. George A. Sansep had gallantly burned the unit colors and standards to keep them from falling into Japanese hands, many military officers believed the 31st was stained by the dishonor of defeat.

The 19th Engineer Combat Group also landed during the day and was sent to reconnoiter bridge and ferry sites over the Han River. Colonel Murray's 5th Marines had battled their way to the river in a series of sharp skirmishes. The Marines repulsed an enemy counterattack in the rice fields outside Kimpo in the morning, and then bombarded the ridgeline and hills barring approaches to the river. The available Marine firepower included artillery, air strikes, and naval gunfire from the powerful sixteen-inch guns of the battleship *Missouri* (BB-63).

The 5th Marines charged the high ground overlooking the Han River and took the Hill 118 hill mass and Hills 80 and 85. The more easterly heights of the latter dominated the junction of the Han River with Kal-ch'on Creek, a large stream in front of Yongdungp'o. The Marines remained in possession of Hills 80 and 85 until evening, when boundaries between the 5th and 1st Marines were adjusted in preparation for the Han River crossings. The battalion that moved off the hills was not replaced because of an unfortunate oversight, leaving both summits unoccupied.[12]

During September 19, the 1st Marines continued their drive east along the main Seoul-Inch'on highway. The armored spearhead plowed into a field of wooden shoebox mines blocking both the roadway and its shoulders. The leading Pershing tank was disabled by a mine and the Marine riflemen were pinned down by concentrated enemy automatic weapons fire. A rolling barrage of Marine howitzer shelling and fighter-bombers plastered the mined field, but failed to clear the area for tank passage.

The tops of the crudely designed box mines could be spotted in the roads, and Marine tanks firing with bow machine guns tried to set them off. When this tactic failed, Lt. George A. Babe's determined Marine combat engineers dashed forward across the bullet-swept roadway, packed explosive compound around the boxes, and then raced back to safety in order to set off their charges. Enough mines were eliminated in this fashion to clear a narrow lane for the Marine tanks to continue their assault.[13]

By the end of the day, General Smith's Marine division was lined up on the Han River from the vicinity of Kimpo to Kal-ch'on Creek west of Yongdungp'o. General Barr's infantry division assumed control of the zone south of the Seoul-Inch'on highway on the Marine right flank. Almond and MacArthur were optimistic that the Han River represented the enemy's last formidable barrier before Seoul, and that breaching the river line might undercut further resistance.

That night, the 5th Marines decided to cross the Han River and gain a surprise foothold on the far bank. Capt. Kenneth J. Houghton crossed the river with a selected reconnaissance team. The Marines did not draw enemy fire and, at 9 P.M., radioed for the amphibious tractors to cross. The nine amtracs took over an hour to reach the site and the noisy whine of their engines pierced the night air. If the North Koreans had been asleep, they were awake now.

The enemy waited in ambush until the amtracs were in midstream and peppered them with intense machine gun and mortar fire. The amtracs retreated as the harsh amber light of exploding flare clusters and red tracers colored the sky. The patrol members swam back to their lines, but four of the amtracs became bogged down in the muddy bottom. Frantic efforts to move the mired machines succeeded in extricating two of the stalled vehicles by dawn, but a pair of amtracs had to be left where they had grounded in the water.

The 5th Marines were ordered to commence the next river assault with the full weight of the regiment. At 6:45 A.M. on September 20, the Marines began crossing the Han River at the Haengju ferry site. This point in the river's course offered the most ideal place to cross, but enemy defenders were entrenched on Hill 125 covering the river with machine guns and mortars.

The amphibious tractors carrying the 5th Marines churned across the sandy bottom land of the Han River and waded into the thickly muddied river current. The amtracs were bracketed by splashes from North Korean fire but reached the far shore. Their thick armored plating protected the Marines inside, although the first wave took over two hundred direct hits from 14.5mm antitank projectiles, high-explosive rifle shells, and machine gun bullets. The amtracs dismounted their Marines, and fired point-blank into enemy-held dwellings. The Marines captured the hill after a sharp battle in the smoking haze of shell-splintered trees.[14]

Once the crossing site was secured, further movement became routine. The lines of amtracs soon turned the water's edge into a muddy, track-imprinted paste as they continued to rumble across the river. DUKWs scurried across the Han River with meshing strapped to the tops of their frames. The mesh was laid over the soil to prevent vehicles bogging in the mud. The Marine engineers floated tanks and heavy equipment across the water on field-expedient ferries, pontoon rafts tied together and overlaid with bridging sections.

The amtrac column reached the railroad paralleling the river a mile from its shore. The double-tracked rail lines were raised on an embankment to prevent flooding. This wide dirt causeway ran southeast into Seoul. The railroad's elevation offered the amtrac crews and riders a sweeping panorama of the Han River and its estuaries, the flat rice-paddy lowlands partitioned by dikes, and the low mountains on the distant horizon. By nightfall the 5th Marines, 2d ROK Marine Battalion, and twelve tanks were on the far side of the river and heading towards Seoul.

4. Battle for the Approaches

Fighting intensified along the Yongdungp'o front. The North Koreans counterattacked the Hill 118 vicinity in the early morning darkness, but were repulsed. South of the hill fight, the Marine roadblock on the Inch'on highway was subjected to another mechanized assault. The poorly executed *NKPA* predawn mechanized drive disintegrated under heavy Marine defensive fire. The enemy infantrymen became disorganized and were decimated by combined infantry, artillery, and mortar fire. An ammunition truck at the head of the enemy column exploded in a brilliant fireball of flame and munitions, illuminating the whole scene of destruction. Pfc. Walter C. Monegan, Jr., grabbed his 3.5-inch rocket launcher and charged down a hillside, destroying two T34s silhouetted against the sky before being killed by an enemy machine gun burst.[15]

While one enemy counterattack was being repulsed, however, other North Korean soldiers climbed Hills 80 and 85 unopposed. The Marines initiated their counterattack against these hills by wheeling rows of towed 4.5-inch multiple-tube rocket launchers into position and sending volleys of rockets streaming directly into the enemy positions. Unfortunately, the full effect of this rocket fusillade was dampened by the unavailability of missile fuses for the rockets, and the failure of substitute fuses. The 1st Battalion of the 1st Marines tackled both enemy-occupied hills, and advanced through clusters of huts in heavy fighting to clear the slopes.

The final assault up Hill 85 involved close hand-to-hand fighting on the summit. Lt. Henry A. Commiskey climbed the hill ahead of his men and leaped into one machine gun nest armed only with his automatic pistol. He fired into the stunned crew and killed every soldier except one, whom he wrestled in hand-to-hand combat until he was able to kill him with a weapon taken from a fellow Marine just arriving over the crest.

About 10 A.M., while the 1st Battalion attack was proceeding, General Almond drove MacArthur to Colonel Puller's command post. They were briefed that a regiment of the *9th NKPA Division* had reinforced the *18th NKPA Division* defending Yongdungp'o. These formations were preparing a strong defensive network in the town's industrial area to shield frontal approaches into Seoul.

MacArthur authorized the Marines to use any amount of shellfire or bombing to soften the enemy's Yongdungp'o defenses. Looking at his watch, MacArthur then turned to Almond and suggested they catch a glimpse of the 5th Marines crossing the Han River farther north. MacArthur stepped into the jeep as Almond sat behind the wheel, and Gen. Edwin Wright, MacArthur's operations chief, rode in the back.

According to Wright, Almond drove like a madman as he careened down the meandering Korean back roads to cut across the countryside and reach the river site. They narrowly avoided being flipped and missed at least one truck by inches. MacArthur seemed oblivious to Almond's daredevil driving, but Wright was frightened as Almond lurched the jeep around sharp bends and sped down bumpy road paths at full throttle. The return trip to Inch'on was equally harrowing. At the end of the ride, Wright stepped out and asked Almond in all seriousness if he had a driver's license.[16]

Almond's jeep-driving zest became famous throughout the corps area as he sped from sector to sector, often assuming a personal role as enforcer of the roads. It was not unusual to find him chasing after speeding military trucks with the gusto of a police cruiser, reprimanding the drivers for reckless behavior after he pursued them to a stop.

One of Almond's favorite maxims was, "no tanks to the rear," explaining, "The place of a tank is at the front destroying the enemy. If it goes back, even though for gasoline, we lose two things: firepower and the morale of the foot soldier. The foot soldier moving up can well ask himself, 'What the hell?' if a tank passes him going to the rear." Almond stopped any tank he spotted on a rear road going in a direction he disliked, chided the crew, and ordered it turned around. If the tank was low on gas, he sent his own jeep after gasoline for it.[17]

While General Almond was racing over roads taken in the early advance, Colonel Beauchamp's 32d Infantry was moving painfully through mine-sown farming land close to the main north-south Seoul-Suwon highway. In this area, the North Koreans had recovered from the shock of invasion and established extensive mine fields to slow down the invaders. Several tanks were blown up by mines and Beauchamp was nearly killed himself just after leaving his command jeep. The detonation tossed the vehicle high into the air, killing his driver and wounding the radio operator. Combat engineers, armed with minesweepers and bayonets, pulled hundreds of mines from the ground. The day closed as Beauchamp's infantrymen fought up Copper Mine Hill, the last high ground in front of the highway leading south to eventual link-up with Eighth Army.

On September 21, the corps advance toward Seoul made remarkable gains, and events appeared to be hastening in accordance with Almond's schedule for taking the capital. On the northern corps flank, Colonel Murray's 5th Marines repulsed counterattacks and cleared more hills as they advanced down the railroad embankment along the Han River. By nightfall, the regiment had one battalion on the outskirts of Seoul itself, a scant three miles from the main downtown train station.

A thick pall of smoke rose from bombed-out Yongdungp'o and its factories as Colonel Puller's 1st Marines assaulted the city. North Korean gunners checked the advance as it reached the city's outer ruins. Enemy weapons hidden along the earthen dikes hammered the lead Marine platoons traversing the open rice paddies. North Korean mortar rounds exploded through the open fields as the Marines tried to crawl forward to recover wounded men or silence exposed machine gun nests.

Although the regiment was stopped cold in front of its objective, one company commanded by Capt. Robert Barrow (Company A, 1st Marines) slipped through a rice field with man-high grass and crossed a brackish part of Kal-ch'on Creek without being detected. Realizing that they were behind the North Korean lines, Barrow boldly led his men through the vacated center of Yongdungp'o. The Marines established blocking positions on the other side of town at a major intersection where one road was elevated along a thirty-foot-high dike. They dug into this excellent defensive barrier and used rocket launchers, grenades, rifles, and machine guns to withstand repeated attacks by tanks and infantry throughout the night.[18]

That same night, Colonel Beauchamp's 32d Infantry soldiers secured a crossing on the Seoul-Suwon highway. General Barr ordered his divisional reconnaissance company, along with a handful of tanks, to go straight down the road and seize the large airfield south of Suwon. Maj. Irwin A. Edwards, the division assistant G2 officer, commanded the mechanized mission and was joined at the last minute by Lt. Col. Henry Hampton, the division operations chief.

They raced down the road toward the walled city of Suwon. The city's colossal stone East Gate had been struck by naval gunfire that collapsed the wooden temple structure in front of the main entrance. This obstacle forced Edwards to swing his group through the town from another direction. Their shooting spree surprised and killed several North Koreans. The recon unit passed through Suwon but missed the airport in the darkness, and proceeded farther south before setting up a roadblock.

General Barr lost communications with Edwards's recon force and became worried. At 9:25 P.M., Barr formed a larger mechanized column under 73d Tank Battalion commander Lt. Col. Calvin S. Hannum to locate them. This unit sped south over the moonlit highway, reestablished radio contact with Edwards and Hampton, and stated they would be arriving shortly. Hannum's unit then encountered the same blocked gateway and tried to wheel through Suwon at another gap in the wall. This resulted in a confused nighttime melee with the thoroughly alarmed North Korean garrison. Several tank duels were fought at close range. Hannum's tankers decided not to proceed farther because of the danger of more fatal tank ambuscades.

Four T34 tanks of the North Korean *105th Tank Division* retreated from this clash. Upon hearing approaching tank engine noise, Colonel Hampton and Edwards went to greet what they thought was Hannum's mechanized relief unit. As the tanks drew closer, Hampton flicked his jeep lights and waved his arms. He was promptly machine gunned and the rest of the men scattered as the T34s rammed the jeeps, killed more soldiers, and disappeared in the night.[19]

At daylight, Hannum's tanks ventured south of Suwon and linked up with Edwards and his recon unit. Suwon was captured and another large airfield was placed under American control, but the death of Colonel Hampton, one of the finest officers in X Corps, was a serious blow to the 7th Infantry Division. General Almond was very upset over the tragic incident which reminded him of Stonewall Jackson's death in the Civil War.

Unfortunately, several more tragic mishaps resulted from General Almond's rush to link up his southern front with Eighth Army. Elements of the 7th Infantry Division utilized prearranged bright orange or cerise air identification panels to prevent strafing by Allied planes, but the rapid southward advance was sometimes too close to retreating enemy targets and subjected to mistaken air attack.

One of the most costly adverse incidents occurred at daybreak on September 24 when two Navy jet fighters hit a troop convoy racing south along the main highway from Suwon. The convoy's escorting M26 tanks displayed the approved air identification panels. The jets circled the speeding column once before strafing it on the second pass. The aircraft cannon exploded tank ammunition stacked behind the turrets, set trucks on fire, caused jeeps to overturn, and killed or wounded twelve soldiers. The jets refrained from making a third pass when Lt. Marion

E. Bailey, the armor platoon leader, ripped off one of the large signal panels and stood up waving it like a large flag.

Another incident happened on the afternoon of September 26 after a 2½-ton cargo truck was disabled by three flat tires while part of a 31st Infantry troop convoy near Sang-chon. The soldiers were transferred to other vehicles and the driver, Pfc. George F. Herdon, started to fix the tires. The truck was surrounded by a throng of curious civilians. Three Corsairs spotted the large concentration of indigenous persons and dived in from three thousand feet, raking the stranded truck and crowd with 20mm cannon fire.

Lt. Col. Thomas A. Taylor, the commander of the 49th Field Artillery Battalion, was aloft in his L-4 observation plane and observed the strike in the distance. By the time his aircraft reached the scene the truck was burning and Herdon was seriously wounded. Taylor recalled, "In a radius of fifty yards around the truck were located eight to ten dead or dying civilians in white clothing. Several women were standing over the dead and waving their arms and some were trying to move blood-spattered victims off the road. South Korean flags were waving from neighboring houses."[20]

In an attempt to control his scattered forces Almond toured the main front indefatigably, sometimes leaving his headquarters as early as 4 A.M. to drive his own jeep to some battalion jumping-off point. He became a familiar sight in his plain green field jacket and fatigue cap, with field trousers tucked into combat boots. His only insignia were two large white stars sewn on the jacket shoulder loops, and the distinctive gold-buckled general officer's leather belt worn around the jacket with a side .38-caliber revolver. Wherever he went, Almond carried an old leather map case and a little black book to record his observations. The first two of his *Nine Rules* neatly typed in his black book were, "(1) constantly keep in mind the objective of the unit you command" and "(2) insist on reasonable but positive methods to insure a sound discipline."

Almond's tendency to show up unexpectedly at forward locations and interrogate local commanders and soldiers about the ongoing situation caused considerable displeasure. A Marine battalion weapons officer, Maj. Edwin H. Simmons, remembered Almond showing up unannounced at his location with his black book to inquire angrily about placement of supporting fire, only to be distracted by the sight of a marine with a bloodied shoulder staggering down a hill from the front line. Almond reached into his pocket and summarily pinned the marine with a Bronze Star. Simmons was appalled at Almond's random disbursement of decorations. While the marine could have been a wounded hero returning to an aid station, Almond made no attempt to determine whether the man had simply injured himself in a fall or was supposed to be still manning his position.[21]

Although Almond abused the military awards system to a degree, his on-the-spot awards represented the forerunner of the "impact award" system later adopted in Vietnam to recognize battlefield achievement. Through his daily visits Almond became familiar with every corps officer through the battalion level, as well as scores of men in the ranks. One confided, "The soldiers here may not like him, but they sure as hell admire him. That's one general who sticks his neck out just like we have to."[22]

General Smith was miffed by Almond's rude failure to follow common precepts of military courtesy in conducting these visits. Throughout the Korean campaign, Almond constantly bypassed Smith and frequently interfered with Marine subordinate commanders down to the company level. Almond gained this attribute from his World War I machine gun command service, where it was imperative to coordinate frontline requirements with personal supervision over scattered weapon positions. Otherwise, the guns would lag behind battlefield requirements or worse, fire into one's own men. Even as a corps commander, Almond remained obsessed with total, direct control over every frontline aspect.

Almond never saw any problem with this tendency and felt fully justified in visiting any Marine units whenever he pleased. "My action was that of a [corps] commander who wants to succeed by coordinating his troops as much as possible. I always announced in advance, in both World War II and Korea, my intention to visit such-and-such units and I usually expected the commanding officer to be present. What I found out, especially in the case of General Smith, was that I could go to the front line and find out for myself the existing conditions more rapidly than I could get them through division headquarters. Any commander who is concerned about the current situation in any of his major units should go to those units and find out conditions as they exist, as rapidly as possible. If they come through channels, that's fine and if they don't, he can seek it for himself. And by his rapid and frequent visits to the front line fighting units—without disturbing the intermediate commanders concerned—the more his troops learn of the [senior] commander's own feelings about the danger and the objectives."[23]

During September 21, prospects appeared favorable for a rapid seizure of Seoul and General MacArthur departed Kimpo air base to take care of urgent business in Tokyo. He told Almond that he would return, as soon as Seoul was in American hands, to reinstate President Rhee properly in the chambers of the country's capitol building. MacArthur reminded Almond that the capital must be captured quickly for purposes of the ceremony. The event was designed and timed to achieve international significance. To Almond, Seoul was a symbol to Korea equivalent to the Rome of his own World War II Italian experience, and the first maxim in his black book urged focus on the target.

During the afternoon, Col. Homer L. Litzenberg's 7th Marines arrived at Inch'on harbor and began unloading. Although the 7th Marines were used initially for normal patrolling, the 1st Marine Division had its full fighting complement. The beachhead was well established and Admiral Struble transferred operational command to General Almond. At this time, Operation CHROMITE ceased to be an amphibious task. X Corps now exercised total jurisdiction over the campaign.

Notes

1. Eighth Army PSD Interview DTG 191855 (Lt. Col. Kenneth E. Lay files).
2. Montross and Canzona, Vol. II, pp. 149–151.
3. Goulden, p. 222.
4. Montross and Canzona, Vol. II, p. 176.
5. X Corps War Diary Summary, *Operation Chromite*, p. 11–12.
6. X Corps G3 *Periodic Operations Report # 13*, dated 1 October 1950, Section II-4.
7. Headquarters Third Logistical Command Port of Inchon, *Historical Report: Port of Inchon*, dtd 1 November 1950.
8. X Corps War Diary Summary, *Operation Chromite*, p. 12.
9. John G. Westover, *Combat Support in Korea*, Department of the Army, 1955, p. 227.
10. 7th Infantry Division Annual Summaries, 1949 and 1950.
11. 7th Infantry Division, *Bayonet: A History of the 7th Infantry Division*, 1951, p. 22.
12. X Corps CXCG-H 314.7 Special Reports, *War Diary Summary*, p. 13.
13. Montross and Canzona, Vol. II, p. 210.
14. Montross and Canzona, Vol. II, p. 188–194.
15. Sharp and Dunnigan, *The Congressional Medal of Honor*, 1984, p. 219.
16. Blair, p. 278.
17. "Command," *Time*, 23 October 1950, p. 28.
18. X Corps War Diary Summary, *Operation Chromite*, p. 15.
19. Appleman, pp. 520–522.
20. X Corps Inspector General Division, *Report of Investigation Concerning Alleged Strafing of Troops by Friendly Planes*, dtd 29 Sep 50, Inclosure B-2.
21. Conversation with Brig. Gen. E. H. Simmons, 15 November 1988.
22. "Command," *Time*, 23 October 1950.
23. USAMHI Interview, pp. IV-51 and 52.

CHAPTER 5

THE BATTLE FOR SEOUL

1. Preliminary Struggle

On September 22, X Corps began the battle for Seoul. Major General Almond, the corps commander, wanted to capture Seoul quickly and the relatively narrow direction of his attack aimed the corps at the city like an arrow.

The northernmost corps unit was Colonel Murray's 5th Marines, which was already across the Han River and just west of downtown Seoul. The center of the corps line was held by Colonel Puller's 1st Marines, which occupied Yongdungp'o on the morning of September 22 after outmaneuvering the North Korean defenses in the industrial complex. The Marine regiment, however, was prevented by destroyed bridges from crossing the Han directly into Seoul.

Army troops formed the southern portion of the corps front. Colonel Beauchamp's 32d Infantry was positioned east of the Seoul-Suwon highway and safeguarding the right flank of the Marines. The regiment occupied an expanse of pine-covered ridges and rough farmland crossed by trails and interspersed with thatched mud huts and small streams. General Almond was preparing to reinforce this unit with Colonel Paik's separate

17th ROK Regiment. Colonel Ovenshine's 31st Infantry was anchored at Suwon and moving south along the Seoul-Suwon highway to link up with the advancing Eighth Army.

The North Korean defenders of Seoul numbered about twenty thousand soldiers, positioned primarily around the western periphery of the city in front of the 5th Marines. The North Korean commander of this sector was Maj. Gen. Wol Ki Chan, who commanded the determined troops of the *25th NKPA Brigade* and *78th NKPA Independent Regiment*. General Chan took advantage of the excellent and familiar defensive opportunities offered by the old Japanese (and later Korean) training ground between Seoul and the advancing 5th Marines. This region was filled with gullies and hills extending from the Han River banks to a ridge dominating the Seoul-Kaesong highway. The rugged countryside was dotted with an assortment of concrete pillboxes and artificial obstructions designed for infantry practice, giving General Chan's troops a ready-made miniature Siegfried Line. This became Seoul's western rampart.[1]

Seoul was protected by steep hills which surrounded the city and projected into densely populated areas. The most formidable natural barrier to any direct attack on Seoul, however, was the tidal Han River. This river flowed out of the interior Korean mountains and curved around the sprawling metropolis in a wide loop on its course to the Yellow Sea. General Smith's 1st Marine Division was split by this river. The 5th Marines faced the main line of communist resistance to the north, but were physically separated from the 1st Marines across the river to the south.

The defensibility of Seoul was further enhanced by the central business district in the vicinity of Ma-Po and Kwang Who Moon boulevards. The district contained many reinforced concrete, multistoried buildings which could be turned into individual fortresses. These included the Yongsan railroad station, the embassy area, Duksoo Palace, city hall, Sodaemun prison, the middle school, and Government House. These structures had defensive utility even if bombed or shelled, because weapons could be situated within the remnants or rubble. The full weight of Allied firepower could not be brought against many buildings anyway, because MacArthur wanted to minimize destruction of the capital.[2]

As the struggle for Seoul commenced on September 22, Colonel Quinn's intelligence analysts conceded that the North Koreans could put up a stubborn fight for the city, even though the eventual outcome

Seoul Campaign

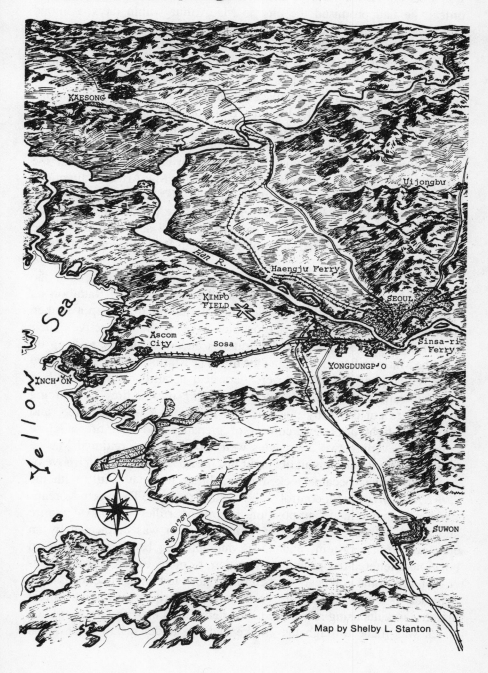

Map by Shelby L. Stanton

was a certain Allied victory. General Almond did not want a protracted ordeal; he had promised the city to MacArthur within days. Almond pressed the Marines to increase their attack momentum because of this urgency, but Smith considered his dictates burdensome and presumptuous.

According to the corps scheme of advance, Seoul was in the Marine divisional zone and its liberation fell within the Marine ambit. Smith wanted full authority to maneuver the Marines as he saw fit within his zone. The task of the 7th Infantry Division was in a screening and reinforcing capacity to the Marines, but Smith felt the division was substandard and he did not trust its staying power. Therefore, he wanted the capture of Seoul to remain a purely Marine operation, with the exception of the South Koreans forced on him. At MacArthur's direction, the separate Republic of Korea units attached to X Corps, the 1st ROK Marine Regiment and 17th ROK Regiment, were to have a hand in the capture of Seoul to appease the nation's political sensitivities. Of the latter units, Smith regarded only the 3d and 5th ROK Marine Battalions with any esteem.

General Smith ordered Colonel Murray's 5th Marines to clear the enemy from positions in front of Seoul. The attack by 2d Battalion on Hill 56 set the tone of the struggle when its men marched up a sunken road and crossed a series of rice paddies to reach their objective. Their supporting tanks became mired in ditches and were unable to keep up with the Marine riflemen climbing the hill. The Marines became embroiled in heavy combat with *NKPA* defenders near a railroad tunnel, while a communications mix-up prevented supporting mortar fire. Reinforcing troops were cut down by machine gun fire from a wooded ridge, and the tunnel fight became a contest of grenades and rifle fire at close range. By evening two companies were isolated, but continual Marine artillery shelling throughout the night discouraged enemy countermoves.[3]

The Marines became locked into a bitter four-day battle with the *25th NKPA Brigade* for control of the western rampart. The North Koreans steadfastly maintained their positions in spite of artillery and naval gunfire and aerial bombing. The enemy bunker system was connected by an elaborate trench system, and caves dug into the backside of forward positions sheltered troops and ammunition, as many concrete-walled caverns and machine gun nests seemed impervious to bombardment damage. In order to smash the enemy bastions, the Marines resorted to direct infantry assaults using rifles, grenades, demolition kits, and knives. Each attack was made through the smoke and fog under a hail of shrapnel and bullets. The North Koreans counterattacked to regain many fallen positions, and key areas sometimes exchanged hands several times.

2. Maneuvering into the Maelstrom

On September 23, as the Marines fought against the western rampart with unabated violence, General Almond moved his X Corps command post to the administrative area of the factory-warehouse complex in Ascom City, midway between Inch'on and Seoul. The 4th Signal Battalion, which operated the corps radio net and handled message traffic to the *Mount McKinley,* upgraded its arrangements. The battalion received fresh signal gear airlifted to Kimpo airfield and hauled in trucks to Ascom City. The battalion established communications and cryptographic centers, initiated telephone and wire operations, and established a radioteletype (RTT) link between X Corps and MacArthur's GHQ command center in Tokyo.[4]

General Almond was now in constant communication with Far East Command, and impatient to seize control of the government buildings in Seoul for MacArthur's ceremony. He was furious that the Marine drive had stalled in front of the city. Fearful that MacArthur's preordained timetable for the capital's liberation was evaporating, Almond hastened to Smith's command post and expressed his displeasure.

General Almond's motivation at this critical dividing point in the battle was simple. He believed that the Marines, and General Smith in particular, did not understand the higher strategic implications of the corps mission. In conformity with MacArthur's desires, Almond wanted X Corps to enforce United Nations policy by reinstating South Korean President Rhee in a politically decisive manner. For his part, Smith viewed MacArthur's political notions as rather whimsical, and detested Almond's demands for immediate action on this basis. Smith wanted to concentrate on the military objective—destroying the North Korean army—which he believed Almond was neglecting.

General Smith knew that the strength of Colonel Murray's 5th Marines was being diminished rapidly in its attempts to batter through the enemy's defensive wall. Smith wanted to bring the rest of his division together for greater striking ability. This meant bringing the 7th and 1st Marines across the Han River to join the 5th Marines. He deemed it essential to combine the 1st Marine Division and use its concentrated power to punch past the enemy defenses. In military terms, he wanted to mass forces and break through the enemy's main line of resistance.

Almond was incensed at Smith's plan to batter away at the same spot with more troops. He declared that these Marine frontal assault tactics resulted in horrendous casualties with small gain in territory. Almond charged that the Marine fixation for charging straightaway into the fray ignored the wider range of options. Almond suggested that Smith utilize his 7th Marines to maneuver around and attack the south flank of Seoul, dislodging the enemy from that direction. His envelopment plan would bring fluidity and flexibility to the battlefield.

Smith took the position that this maneuver would scatter his division on too broad a front. He disbelieved Almond's professed reasons, and recalled Operation CHROMITE's avowed purpose to isolate the North Korean army and destroy its supply lines. To Smith, meaningful envelopment meant cutting off North Korean escape routes north and east of the capital instead of maneuvering into the city from the south (which would fail to block enemy withdrawal). The southern approach also meant a river assault across the Han's swift current where it looped around Seoul under the shadow of South Mountain. He saw no purpose in splintering his regiments in such a dangerous attack for the sake of a rushed land-grab.

Almond was appalled at the tantamount insubordination of Smith's argumentive refusals. Given Almond's propensity to relieve subordinates who gave him dissatisfaction, it was obvious that only Smith's globe-and-anchor saved him from prompt sacking. Almond could not afford the wrath of the Joint Chiefs of Staff if he fired a Marine commander. Instead, he repeated his strong disapproval of frontal attacks against the city's western defenses, stressed that time was essential, and further delays would not be condoned. As Almond stated, "I think that General Smith thought it would be a great accomplishment for the Marine division, single-handed, to capture Seoul but he wasn't in the speed of mind I was."[5]

The animosity and distrust between both men was so pervasive that an amicable conclusion was impossible. General Almond was the corps commander, however, and gave Smith an ultimatum with only two options: (1) the Marine division could maneuver a regiment around the Han River south of Seoul and begin enveloping the city from that side, or (2) the Marine division could continue its frontal assault. He stated that if Smith selected the second option, and there was no progress within twenty-four hours, the Marine section would be narrowed to permit the 7th Infantry Division to attack into the city from the south.

General Almond needed Marine amphibious support if the 7th Infantry Division was used and related later, "In connection with this operation, having to cross the Han River which was some 200 to 250 yards wide and over head-deep (making it impossible for troops to cross without the construction of bridges), I decided to use amtracs from the Marines. In the initial landing, the amtrac is very useful because it really is a floating semi-tank, armed and amphibious. General Smith objected to this very strenuously by stating that 'those amtracs are Marine property!.' My reply to that was, 'They are the property of the United States government and I propose to use them.' Whereupon General Smith said, 'The 7th Division doesn't know how to use amtracs.' One of General Smith's staff officers—in fact the commander of the amtrac battalion—spoke up and said, 'All that General Barr would have to do would be to divide his men into groups of sixteen and have them situated on the part of the river that he wants to cross. These men can board the amtracs and we can transfer them over and they could reassemble in any formation that they desire on the other side.' This was the climax and made it possible for us to utilize amtracs as I had directed."[6]

During the night of September 23–24, Smith began consolidating the 1st Marine Division for the first time since leaving the United States. Colonel Litzenberg's 7th Marines moved north of the Han River as Colonel Puller's 1st Marines crossed the river and moved into positions near Colonel Murray's 5th Marines along the western rampart. After days of close combat, the 5th Marines were drastically below strength. During the fighting on September 24, some companies were fighting with three dozen personnel and one platoon mustered only seven non-wounded men.[7]

At 9:30 A.M., with the Marines still stalled in front of Seoul, Almond met with General Barr and selected members of the 7th Infantry Division staff. He told them to start preparations for a projected thrust at Seoul in the vicinity of South Mountain. He issued instructions to begin moving Colonel Beauchamp's 32d Infantry toward the Han River at the Sin-sa-ri ferry crossing, which was three miles east of the wrecked railroad and highway bridges. The infantrymen would cross the river, seize South Mountain, and drive east to secure hills dominating the highway and rail line entering the city in that direction.

Almond waited until the afternoon to permit Smith's full twenty-four-hours' notice to elapse. He called for a corps meeting in Yongdungp'o Circle at 2 P.M. sharp. Almond, Smith, Barr, Col. Harry I. Hodes (7th Infantry Division assistant commander), Colonel Forney (the Marine BLUEHEARTS planner, who now served as X Corps deputy chief of staff), Colonel Chiles (X Corps operations officer), and Colonel Beauchamp were present. Almond curtly issued his orders. The engines of the jeeps parked around the downtown plaza were still hot when Almond's subordinates climbed back in their vehicles to execute his new instructions.

Almond recalled, "In the presence of all I made the decision and gave the order. I took the map and redirected the front of the 1st Marine Division, moving the right boundary left so it would give the 32d [Infantry] Regiment the opportunity to move into the major tactical obstruction that was being offered to the Marine's [zone] advance [into Seoul], namely South Mountain. I issued an order there and directed General Barr to proceed with me and his regimental commanders to the crossing point, which had already been selected in that area and reconnoitered by General Barr."[8]

While the Army prepared to cross the Han River south of Seoul, the battle for the western rampart reached its point of greatest intensity. Hills 66 and 105, which dominated the center of the *25th NKPA Brigade's* line astride the railroad tracks leading into the city, served as pivotal strong-points in the chain of enemy fortifications. To take this defensive complex, the 5th Marines were reinforced with regimental clerks, mechanics, drivers, and every other Marine available, including wounded volunteers. Corsair aircraft and artillery pounded the heights for hours. The Marines charged up the slopes and into the sandbagged enemy trenches. The ditches were cleared in close-quarter combat.

Company D of the 5th Marines started the battle at Hill 66 with 206 men, but 176 were killed or wounded during the sustained fighting. A squad led by Sgt. Robert Smith suffered typically heavy casualties in one charge when nine members were killed, including the corpsman, and only three unwounded men returned. Two key Marine machine guns, manned successively by several replacement crews, were instrumental in defeating North Korean counterattacks to regain possession of the contested ground. Although heavy fighting continued for another day in the western ramparts, the capture of Hills 66 and 105 broke the stalemate in front of Seoul.

The Marine success along the western rampart came too late to change Almond's plans for his coveted Army river assault into southern

Seoul. At 4 A.M. on the morning of September 25, General Almond and members of his corps staff departed Ascom City and drove through the predawn darkness to watch the 7th Infantry Division river assault. Almond established a grandstand observation post near the river to watch the proceedings, much like his special post overlooking the hills northeast of Forte dei Marmi for his divisional attack of February 1945. Almond was anxious to show off his master plan in action, and invited Admiral Struble to leave the cruiser *Rochester,* anchored offshore, and watch the event with him (just as Fifth Army commander General Truscott had done in Italy). Almond was delighted with Struble's presence. "This to me was a great accomplishment to get an admiral sixteen miles inland at four o'clock in the morning."[9]

General Barr and Colonel Beauchamp made last-minute inspections of the assault infantrymen and then joined Almond's party at the observation post. He arrived at 4:30 A.M. The artillery started barraging the steep banks on the far side at 6 A.M. Exactly one half hour later the 2d Battalion, 32d Infantry, mounted amtracs and headed across the fog-shrouded river. They landed on the far side without casualties, scaled the sixty-foot-high bluffs, and captured South Mountain from the North Koreans. The attack was successful because the enemy had only lightly defended the area.

The entire regiment, along with its accompanying 17th ROK Regiment, dug in against possible counterattacks and strengthened overnight defensive positions. The 73d Engineer Combat Battalion constructed and operated a fifty-ton ferry across the Han River to keep the bridgehead supplied. Army and South Korean soldiers were across the river in roughly even numbers, because of the large number of Koreans within Army regimental ranks.

3. Fight for the City

The evening of September 25 would be marred by an incident that caused the Almond-Smith rift to widen even more. At 8:40 P.M., well after nightfall, X Corps flashed a message by teletype into Smith's Marine command post ordering his division to attack at once because "X Corps TACAir (Tactical Air) commander reports enemy fleeing city of Seoul on road north. . . . He is conducting heavy air attack and will continue same. You will push attack *now* to the limit of your objective [Seoul city] in order to insure maximum destruction of enemy forces."[10]

Lt. Col. Alpha L. Bowser, the operations chief of the 1st Marine Division, was incredulous when he received the X Corps order. Despite the message's assertion that the enemy was in full retreat, the North Koreans showed no signs of giving up their strong urban defenses in front of the Marine battle line. Colonel Bowser studied the message and found it contained several irreconcilable errors in its claim to enemy retreat, including erroneous grid coordinates. He called X Corps to check the order's veracity, but Colonel Chiles told him to execute the order as stated. Colonel Bowser then gave the message to Smith. Smith telephoned General Ruffner, the X Corps chief of staff, and objected that the enemy was not retreating. Ruffner replied that the orders were personally dictated by Almond and were to be carried out immediately.

At 10 P.M., Smith contacted Colonels Puller and Murray and explained the situation by field phone. Smith told them to advance their regiments down the main avenues for control purposes in the darkness, following forward patrols that would determine actual enemy dispositions. The nocturnal Marine patrols were counterattacked almost at once along the entire front. The attacks on the Marine sector lasted until 4:45 A.M.

One enemy force of fourteen armored vehicles and seven hundred infantrymen struck the 1st Marines at their main boulevard roadblock, and disaster was only averted by an intensive final artillery barrage, followed by close-in automatic weapons and rocket launcher fire. The lead enemy T34 struck a mine and Marine infantrymen destroyed several others. The North Koreans also counterattacked South Mountain in the early morning darkness of September 26, inflicting heavy casualties on the defenders and overrunning one Army company, Company F of the 32d Infantry.[11]

The Marine and Army troops were outraged by the failure of X Corps to properly analyze the enemy situation. Instead of retreating, the North Koreans spent the night attacking. Almond defended his presumption about enemy withdrawals by pointing out that aircraft detected large numbers of men exiting the capital in a northward direction around Uijongbu. Therefore, according to Almond, the North Koreans had executed a series of local counterattacks in an effort to mask their withdrawal.

The Marines pointed to several facts that contradicted this Army explanation. Not only were message coordinates in error (which Chiles admitted in his conversation with Bowser), but references to the aerial spotting indicated areas of retreat sixteen miles north of Seoul. In Marine opinion, X Corps had no basis for its immediate order to attack. Almond's overzealous ambition to jump into a major nighttime advance, coupled with his failure to properly anticipate enemy reaction, endangered the Marine division. Smith became convinced of Almond's lack of judgment and distrust of X Corps leadership deepened.

Marine disgruntlement with Almond was heightened by his premature pronouncement that Seoul was liberated. His announcement was made just before midnight on September 25, during the height of the North Korean counterattacks and at the onset of some of the hardest fighting within the city itself. Almond seized upon the aerial reports of mass North Korean desertion and the earlier capture of South Mountain to justify his determination. A UN communique was issued by MacArthur on the following afternoon:

General Headquarters
United Nations Command
Public Information Office

X Corps Communique No. 5   1145, 26 September 1950

Three months to the day after the North Koreans launched their surprise attack south of the 38th Parallel the combat troops of the X Corps recaptured the capital city of Seoul. In a short period of 10 days U.S. Marine and infantry units augmented by South Korean troops landed on the beaches of Inchon and rapidly thrust their way inland to this important communications center and severed the vital junction on the supply line of the enemy.

The liberation of Seoul was accomplished by a coordinated attack of X Corps troops. The attack started at 0630 hours with an amphibious crossing of the Han river south of Seoul by elements of the U.S. 7th Infantry Division coordinated with an attack by the 1st Marine Division to the west and north from positions along the outskirts of the city north of the Han river.

Heavy enemy resistance consisting mainly of intense small arms fire from well prepared positions along the streets and in the buildings slowed the advance of Marine units but steady progress was made during the day and the high ground west and north of the city was secured.

The 7th Division crossed the Han river in force against moderate resistance and drove forward to capture the 800-foot hill mass called South Mountain which overlooks the entire city and commands the east exits.

By 1400 hours 25 September the military defenses of Seoul were broken and the South Korean troops of the Capitol City Regiment began mopping up strong groups of defeated defenders. Reports at the end of this period indicate that the enemy is fleeing the city to the northeast.

The coordination of air, tank, artillery and infantry fire power made possible the seizure of the enemy's defenses in Seoul with minimum casualties.

The soldiers and Marines at Seoul knew the hurried announcement was a political fabrication but resented its impact on their efforts. After September 25, no word of the hard fighting still accompanying the battle for Seoul was released to the public, and X Corps censored all news reports that hinted the battle was not over.[12]

The bitter street fighting for Seoul was a house-by-house struggle that pitted Marine and Army tank-infantry teams against heavily defended barricades and buildings for several days. Progress was measured in blocks throughout the downtown and government areas. *NKPA* suicide tank-destruction members charged periodically from behind buildings to lob satchel charges against armored vehicles. A Marine flame-throwing tank following two Pershings was destroyed in this fashion by an enemy demolitions man who conducted a successful solitary charge.[13]

The North Koreans tore up the streets and erected sandbag-reinforced barriers of debris, barrels, and vehicles. Antitank mines were sprinkled around their positions. Stone walls and buildings were turned into small forts which gave protecting fire for the barricade defenders. Enemy mortars and machine guns were placed behind and on top of all structures. The bulk of Seoul's civilian population was rounded up and forced to build these defenses and endure the battle, while the populace was exposed to direct shellfire and bombings. Thousands of people were executed by the fanatical communist defenders. In many cases, the survivors were subjected to Allied retaliation as well.[14]

During September 26, Colonel Beauchamp's 32d Infantry and its attached South Korean regiment cleared the enemy around South Mountain and the hills to the east. The advance was initially uneventful for Company C of the 32d Infantry, which moved toward the urban district for more than an hour without encountering resistance. The company commander decided to place Lt. James O. Mortrude's platoon in the vanguard of his advance as a lone reconnoitering force near the Seoul city racetrack. Mortrude's men moved 250 yards through a low river valley before they were suddenly engulfed by a hailstorm of devastating enemy fire from the high road berm across the river. Six soldiers were killed instantly and many others were wounded. The shattered platoon's attempts to organize a hasty defensive perimeter were defeated by accurate enemy machine guns firing across the open ground. The acting platoon sergeant, Corp. Robert J. Malloy, made repeated dashes across this fire-swept zone to carry out and treat wounded comrades before he was killed by an automatic weapons burst.

Lieutenant Mortrude realized that their exposed position was untenable, but any unsupported route of withdrawal might wipe out his few remaining men. He spotted a trio of three tanks clanking forward to their assistance, and dashed twenty-five yards through withering enemy fire to reach them before more casualties were inflicted on his platoon. Grabbing the external interphone system phone on the rear box of the "buttoned up" lead tank, he yelled directions to commence firing immediately into the enemy-held roadway. The tanks smothered the road berm in geysers of blackened earth as the uninjured and walking wounded retreated to safety. Mortrude then ran twice to his platoon's former position to recover disabled soldiers and carry them back. The valiant acts of both Mortrude and Malloy were later recognized by awards of the Distinguished Service Cross.[15]

Later, Company E of the 32d Infantry linked up with the 1st Marine Division at the bottom of South Mountain's western slope, and X Corps was finally tied into a continuous front around the capital's lower rim. On the corps' southern flank, the 7th Infantry Division attacked south of Suwon but Colonel Ovenshine's 31st Infantry was making slow progress against the well-organized enemy defenses in that sector. General Barr pressured Ovenshine to conduct a coordinated regimental attack to clear out the North Koreans but by the time his orders reached the 31st, Ovenshine had already split the regiment and reached Osan-ni with a flanking column moving southeast. At 11:20 P.M., elements of the regiment met the leading tanks of the 1st Cavalry Division five miles south of Suwon. The juncture united Almond's X Corps with General Walker's Eighth Army and solidified the United Nations front in southwestern Korea.[16]

As the battle for Seoul raged on the ground, air power slashed enemy armored reinforcements trying to reach the capital district. When North Korean Col. Mon Jo Kim's *44th NKPA Independent Tank Regiment*, consisting of 594 men and seventeen tanks (mostly thirty-two-ton T34s), left Wonsan on September 17 to reinforce Seoul, it made a laborious cross-country journey, moving at night and hiding in tunnels during the day. After a five-day march, it arrived on the night of September

22, and aircraft were alerted to destroy it the following day. On September 23, the regiment was strafed and bombed with the result that all regimental heavy and light tanks were destroyed and the majority of its personnel were killed before the unit could even get into action.[17]

This aerial support was extremely important and General Almond basked in his control over the "X Corps tactical air force," consisting primarily of the 1st Marine Air Wing—an asset usually reserved for army-level commands. The Marine aviators provided overhead combat air patrol, aerial reconnaissance, and tactical air support exclusively for corps missions. Almond expressed general dissatisfaction with any air support not under his personal control and blamed the Navy for most adverse incidents, claiming that naval aircraft repeatedly violated his "carefully specified" bomb-lines.

The pitched battle for the capital continued. The North Koreans defended their barricades even after their positions became untenable, determined to make the conquest of Seoul as costly as possible. Enemy resistance was particularly fierce along the main boulevards, in the Duksoo Palace, city hall, capitol, and the East Gate.

Army Lt. Robert L. Strickland of the 71st Signal Service Battalion accompanied the 1st Marine Division during this fighting: "I'm afraid that silent film can't do it justice. The tanks started moving through an opening in the sandbag barrier. There was one Marine lying near the opening with his rifle pointed down the road. As the tanks moved through, all hell broke loose from the enemy antitank guns and rifles. The Marine by the opening jumped almost straight up and ran like a bat out of Hades. The spot he had been lying in had just got plastered, but I don't think he was hit. After that I shot [with a camera] some scenes over the sandbag barrier at the burning building in the background. It was exploding periodically. I caught one section of the building falling with a terrific roar amid clouds of dust and smoke. . . . The air was whipping with everything from flying stones to big antitank shells. When the sound boys get to this part they can dub in all the battle noises they can get and they still won't be realistic enough.

"I shot my next stuff [film] at a road junction where some Marines were running across the open toward a small, triangular building. There was a tank and a lot of buildings burning in the background. I finished shooting [my camera] and ran across after them, stopping at the corner of the building to shoot again. About four men passed me from behind as I stood shooting up the street. All of them ran right into a mortar shell and got hit, one of them seriously. He got the one that was intended for me.

"Right after this we got so much fire of all kinds that I lost count. There was more mortar shells, more antitank stuff, and more small-arms fire and then it started all over again. In a few minutes the little area back of the burning building that gave us cover was crowded with wounded men. They lay there in pain among burning debris and hot embers, hugging the ground to keep from getting hit again. . . . The tanks started firing their 90s. . . . right over our heads. The blast was so terrible that I still can't hear well today.

"There was only one medic—a Navy corpsman—so I put my camera aside and gave him a hand. I missed a lot of good pictures but there is no need to say the pictures were not that important. I have seen a lot of men get hit both in this war and in World War II, but I think I have never seen so many men get hit so fast in such a small area."[18]

The Marines fought day and night as they advanced grimly from building to building and stormed the barricades, silenced machine gun nests, destroyed antitank guns, and eliminated snipers hiding in trees and towers. The Marines methodically cleared each barricade, reconsolidated, evacuated wounded to frontline aid stations, and prepared to tackle the next obstacle. The Marines called the bitter, full-scale city battle resentfully, "Almond's mopping up." The fighting continued until the final enemy defenders were killed in the last flaming strong-points of the shattered city.[19]

During the main battle for Seoul, Colonel Ovenshine's 31st "Foreign Legion" Infantry maintained blocking positions thirty miles south of the city between Suwon and Osan that prevented enemy reinforcements from reaching the beleaguered citadel. On September 26, elements of the *105th NKPA Tank Division* struck Ovenshine's infantrymen and triggered a violent three-day battle for possession of the highway. A counterattack by Lt. Col. Robert R. Summer's 2d Battalion enveloped Osan and hit the North Korean armored force in concert with a mechanized-tank strike down the main road. Although Summers was seriously wounded in the battle, Colonel Ovenshine's maneuver destroyed the bulk of the enemy tanks and antitank guns (fourteen and six, respectively) and killed over four hundred enemy infantrymen. Although Almond felt Ovenshine was too old for the job and lacked offensive spirit, the crusty regimental commander had completely cleared the vital high-way between Osan and Suwon in sharp fighting with a minimum of casual-ties.[20]

4. MacArthur's Triumph

Throughout the battle of Seoul, Colonel Rowny's X Corps engineers were striving to construct a bridge over the Han River. General MacArthur had mandated the bridge as his prime engineering concern of Operation CHROMITE during its planning stages in Japan. Colonel Rowny had loaded the invasion fleet with bridging and engineer equipment, but the typhoon had swept much of this materiel overboard during the trip to Korea. The need to replace this bridging was so acute that transport of replacement items by other ships was dismissed out of hand. Immediately upon the seizure of Kimpo airfield, General Almond had switched logisti-cal priorities from air-delivered ammunition to emergency restoration of the missing bridge portions.

An undue stoppage of ammunition supplies might have jeopardized the entire success of the campaign. Logisticians argued that the bridge was not as critical as ammunition. The 1st Marine Division could use amtracs and the field-expedient pontoon rafts of its engineer battalion for tactical river-crossing purposes. The real purpose of a bridge leading into Seoul was to provide a convenience for General MacArthur's reinstall-ment ceremony of South Korean President Rhee. MacArthur did not want his party of dignitaries to use helicopters because this relatively new travel mode emphasized Seoul's isolation and "frontline" status. A bridge symbolized a secure capital linked firmly to the rest of the country.

At Almond's direction, General Ruffner personally supervised the airlift of bridge components into Kimpo airfield. The fortuitous discovery of the American ammunition at Ascom City enabled this substitution to gain approval from Far East Command. The 73d Engineer Combat Battal-ion landed at Inch'on on September 20, and two days later the first sections of a fully decked M4 aluminum army floating bridge were airlifted from Japan to Kimpo airfield. The battalion started moving this new equipment to the Han River.

The 19th Engineer Combat Group established headquarters at Yong-dungp'o to supervise bridge construction efforts on September 21. The

4th Signal Battalion established courier and radio relay communications between Ascom City, Kimpo, Yongdungp'o, and the Han River construction site. The 185th Engineer Combat Battalion landed at Inch'on on September 26, but lacked its equipment because of X Corps shipping problems in the Charlie echelon. The battalion was sent to Kimpo airfield to unload more M4 bridge materiel.

By this date, the low, flat sandy stretch of river land at the Han bridge site was congested with a variety of engineer units. Elements of the newly arrived 62d Engineer Construction Battalion prepared the M4 bridge site across the Han River. Their dozer tractors fitted with steel A-frames and pulleys shaped mountains of sand into approach ramps. Mobile cranes unloaded pontoons and placed them in the water as men of the 73d Engineer Combat Battalion pieced the M4 sections together. Marines of the 1st Engineer Battalion dismantled some of their rafts and floated the pontoons down to the army area to expedite completion. Frenzied Korean laborers surfaced the bridge roadway ramps with sandbag layers crushed flat by vehicular traffic. Racing against the clock, the X Corps engineers completed the M4 floating bridge across the Han River at midnight, September 28.[21]

At 10 A.M. on September 29, General MacArthur arrived at Kimpo airfield, where General Almond met him and South Korean President Rhee, as well as other important officials. The motorcade of sedans and jeeps rolled across the Han River bridge at 11 A.M., and proceeded through the hastily bulldozed, smoking ruins of Seoul. The 3d Battalion, 1st Marines secured the road from the bridge through the downtown area. Crowds of civilians waving small South Korean flags cheered MacArthur's entourage.

MacArthur and his guests stopped at the Government House and proceeded into the National Assembly Hall for the ceremony. The 3d Battalion of the 5th Marines guarded the bullet-riddled, shell-torn building but Almond kept them out of sight. He posted Army military policemen of his X Corps MP platoon—spruced up in polished helmets and white gloves—around all the doorways, halls, balconies, and marble staircases. Almond's efforts to keep the ceremony in a setting of peaceful tranquility were hampered by the sounds of distant artillery, fire-damaged glass falling from the high-domed chamber ceiling, and smoke wafting through the building from still-burning rooms.

With the exception of Marine division commander General Smith and his subordinates, who wore battle fatigues, MacArthur and most of his military guests were dressed in khaki or British naval white uniforms. Not to be outdone by the Marines, Almond showed up in his usual ordinary fatigue uniform and cap, with a .38-caliber revolver at his side. This attire set him apart from the khaki-dominant assemblage, but he also looked out of place for combat purposes. His field trousers were sharply creased and his starched field jacket was opened at the collar to reveal a black silken ascot.

General MacArthur addressed the gathered dignitaries in the hall from his flag-draped podium at noon. He turned to President Rhee, "In behalf of the United Nations Command I am happy to restore to you, Mr. President, the seat of your government that from it you may better fulfill your constitutional responsibilities." MacArthur then sanctified the proceedings by following a tradition copied from Stonewall Jackson's victory services that Almond heartily approved, the reciting of the Lord's Prayer.[22]

Immediately following the main ceremony, MacArthur presented Almond with the Distinguished Service Cross (DSC) for his "fearless example" in coordinating corps efforts and visiting the front lines. The citation was highly exaggerated, but in line with the glowing descriptions he received for two personal Air Medals, given for events of the same period.[23]

The DSC was the nation's second highest medal for valor, outranked only by the Medal of Honor, and signified great bravery on the battlefield. Many military personnel questioned not only the inflationary tone of the award, but the entire propriety of bestowing such an honor to Almond under circumstances connected with leadership instead of valorous front-line activities. His actions never compared, for instance, to the deeds of Corporal Malloy who was killed carrying out wounded soldiers and earned the same award posthumously. Almond accepted the medal and shrugged off criticism with the brisk statement, "I'm very grateful for his [MacArthur's] recognition."[24]

While MacArthur was bestowing honors on his favorite general, the newly arrived 17th Infantry landed to complete General Barr's 7th Infantry Division and was committed immediately to the battlefront southeast of the city. By the end of September, the 7th Marines were in hot pursuit of North Korean troops fleeing northward to Uijongbu beyond the capital. The X Corps campaign to seize Inch'on and Seoul and link up with the Eighth Army was completed.

5. Summary

The Inch'on-Seoul operation represented the first test of Maj. Gen. Edward M. Almond's corps leadership and was instrumental in deciding the future course of the Korean war. X Corps achieved victory in a well-executed end-run amphibian gambit that sealed victory fifty-three days after the operation was conceived. The military might of the Air Force-Army-Marine-Navy combination overwhelmed the enemy defenses. Daring feats added to the campaign brilliance, such as the alert Marine company that gave the corps its key to Yongdungp'o, and the Army flying column of tanks and jeep-riding infantrymen that brazenly seized Suwon airfield.

Nevertheless, X Corps was divided by the unhappy relationship and resulting disturbances between the Army and Marine commanders, a feud that diminished the mutual faith between each level of command and weakened its combined power. Both services must take blame for this outcome although, as corps commander, General Almond was ultimately responsible. Almond's acrid and dictatorial manner clashed with Marine pride and independence. Instead of displaying a good faith effort to resolve their difficulties, both Edward Mallory Almond and Oliver Prince Smith were content to find—and even relish—offense in any discovered wrong or perceived injustice. Almond's feud with Smith, like his underestimation of Oriental military prowess, had unfortunate future consequences.

Lt. Col. Frank T. Mildren described the Almond-Smith breach when he joined X Corps as the assistant chief of staff for operations in early October: "General Almond and the 1st Marine Division commanding general didn't get along at all. [General Smith] wouldn't take any orders from General Almond unless they were in writing. I could go up there with orders from General Almond for the 1st Marine Division, and the division commander wouldn't accept them. That's how rough things were."[25]

The Almond-Smith feud permeated Almond's tenure of corps command during 1950. To Almond, the Marines possessed fighting courage but lacked appreciation for higher authority. In his opinion, the Marine strategy was confined by training and mental objectivity to rigid and unimaginative tactics. Almond, always eager to classify masses—whether races or military services—into rigid stereotypes, believed the Marines possessed no real grasp of ''off-beach'' maneuver and disdained their operational methods. MacArthur, of course, must share the blame for placing a commander with such views in charge of a corps composed of so many Marine elements.

Almond's corps leadership must be divorced from his altercation with Smith in order to view it objectively. The historical fact remains that General Almond's X Corps achieved its military and political objectives with overwhelming success in the Inch'on-Seoul campaign. The port of Inch'on and capital of Seoul were seized in a daring amphibious gamble that, despite its critics, remains a hallmark of brilliant and incisive generalship. In contrast to the 1944 disaster at Anzio, where Maj. Gen. Lucian K. Truscott Jr.'s VI Corps dallied on the beaches thirty miles from the Italian capital of Rome until the Germans responded in force, Almond's X Corps raced inland twenty miles to capture the South Korean capital of Seoul before the North Koreans could react.

In one swift thrust, X Corps landed behind enemy lines despite considerable tidal, weather, and terrain obstacles, defeated all opposition, and severed the main enemy supply line southward. The *NKPA* was forced to abandon its conquest of South Korea, and the Eighth Army was released to chase the disorganized North Korean remnants to the border. X Corps achieved its goal of enabling the United Nations to repulse the North Korean invaders in minimal time, with relatively light casualties.

The question is, how much of this success can be attributed properly to Almond? The conduct of the operation was influenced by the personality of Ned Almond but was unmistakably forged and directed by MacArthurian authority. The actual planning was the product of several key BLUE-HEARTS and CHROMITE staff members, although Almond deserves credit for coordinating this program and serving as a loyal proponent. The actual invasion of Inch'on, being primarily a Navy responsibility under Admiral Struble, cannot be credited solely to Almond's direction of X Corps. There is even some basis for charging that Almond and his staff contributed to logistical flow problems because of their unfamiliarity with seaborne loading and transit procedures.

After September 20, when Almond was fully in charge of X Corps, the corps drive on Seoul was conducted in faithful compliance with MacArthur's dictates. Almond merely applied undeviating force in reaching preset corps objectives. He acted more as an aggressive chief of staff (which he technically was) during a nine-day absence of the senior commander. At the same time, his generalship was evident throughout the entire Inch'on-Seoul campaign period. He exhibited sound conventional military leadership by massing the weight of his corps against his primary objective. The only exception was one regiment sent south to link up with the Eighth Army below Suwon, a specific task justified by the importance of the mission.

During the entire campaign, X Corps fought as an integrated force of six regiments (out of five U.S. and two South Korean regiments available during most of the fighting) in a narrow geographical area aimed straight at Seoul. General Smith was not allowed to consolidate his Marine division as he desired, but the envelopment attack suggested by Almond on September 23 did not constitute a drastic separation of the formation. The crossing site was within two miles of current Marine lines and aimed at the same urban objective. The corps was not fragmented because the bulk of its maneuver force operated within conventional military supporting range and along relatively narrow frontages compared to other stages of the war.

Flank support was adequate and could have been bolstered by reserves if threatened seriously by enemy action. At least one regiment, usually the one in the process of disembarking, was always present as a reserve. The 7th Infantry Division was in reserve until the 32d Infantry was brought ashore on September 18; the 31st Infantry was in reserve until disembarked on September 20; the 7th Marine Regiment was in reserve from 21 September; beginning on September 24 the entire elite 187th Airborne Regimental Combat Team served as corps reserve. Considering that Admiral Struble conducted the amphibious stage until September 20, Almond certainly utilized sufficient flank and reserve forces while X Corps was under his control.

General Almond was a mobility-oriented commander. From childhood, he based his understanding of military strategy on the fast and bold Confederate raiders of the Shenandoah Valley. Almond's actual military experience confirmed these beliefs. In World War I, as a machine gun battalion leader, he had rapidly displaced machine guns forward to bring their fires into close supporting ranges at all times. Although Smith believed Almond hurried the Marines beyond prudent military preparations, the speed and shock of the X Corps advance carried the field at both Inch'on and Seoul.

In the final analysis, however, Almond's true leadership talents could not be ascertained by this brief campaign. The majority of the X Corps advance was under Admiral Struble's or General MacArthur's direct control, and Almond's corps was never opposed by an enemy force capable of inflicting serious damage. The real test of X Corps, as well as General Almond's true capability, awaited his next Korean campaign.

Notes

1. X Corps, *War Diary Summary*, Book II G2 Summary, 15 August–30 September 1950.
2. X Corps CXCG-H 314.7 Special Report, *War Diary Summary*, p. 23.
3. Montross and Canzona, Vol. II, pp. 240–241.
4. X Corps *Operation Chromite*, Signal Office Summary Report.
5. USAMHI Interview, p. IV-52.
6. USAMHI Interview, p. IV-54. X Corps possessed an Army amphibian tractor unit (which helped invade Inch'on): Company A, 56th Amphibious Tank and Tractor Company, which was part of the 2d Engineer Special Brigade. This Army element contained 50 amtracs. The Marine 1st Amphibious Tractor Battalion possessed approximately 170 amtracs of various types. To properly support the Han River crossings, General Almond used the Marine amphibious tractor battalion, less one company, and both amtrac platoons of the Army amphibious tank and tractor company.
7. 5th Marines *Special Action Report*, 1–30 September 1950.
8. USAMHI Interview, p. IV-54.
9. USAMHI Interview, p. IV-55.
10. Appleman, p. 532.
11. Appleman, p. 530.
12. Goulden, p. 228.
13. Montross and Canzona, Vol. II, p. 273.
14. Leckie, p. 152.
15. Far East Command General Orders No. 16, dtd 27 January 1951, and No. 17, dtd 29 January 1951.
16. X Corps War Diary Summary, *Operation Chromite*, p. 22.
17. X Corps Periodic Intelligence Report # 14, contained in X Corps War Diary, dtd 2 October 1950.
18. Westover, pp. 104–106.
19. Knox, p. 299.
20. Blair, p. 291.
21. 19th Engineer Combat Group, September Report of Operations.
22. Manchester, pp. 582–583.
23. GHQ Far East Command General Orders # 43, 22 October 1950.

Major General Edward M. Almond. 04666, United States Army, continually distinguished himself by extraordinary heroism in Korea as Commanding General, X Corps, during the period 15 September to 25 September 1950. During the seizure of Inchon, General Almond personally visited front line units, coordinated tactical efforts, and by his own fearless example aided them in seizing assigned objectives. Following the fall of Inchon, General Almond personally led his troops in their rapid drive through enemy-held territory to seize Seoul, and to speed the disintegration of the enemy forces. During the assault of the Han River, he moved to a forward position well beyond the line of friendly forces, to observe and control the river crossing. Despite heavy enemy mortar fire directed at him, General Almond remained to supervise the air and artillery support which was protecting the first units of the 7th Infantry Division crossing the river. Disregarding enemy mine fields and sniper fire, he proceeded to the crossing site to direct fire of amphibious tanks neutralizing enemy opposition which was impeding our crossing. By his inspirational leadership, his complete indifference to danger, and personal control of the battlefield, General Almond quickly concluded tactical operations which destroyed the enemy forces in the X Corps zone of action, and saved countless lives in the forces under his command. General Almond's extraordinary performance of duty is in keeping with the most esteemed military traditions and reflects great credit on himself and the military service.

24. USAMHI Interview, p. IV-55.
25. U.S. Army Military History Institute Proj. 80–3, Senior Officers Oral History Program Interview with Gen. Frank T. Mildren by Col. James T. Scott, 1980, p. 123.

CHAPTER 6

A NEW MISSION

1. Shifting Directions

Battlefield events in the latter half of September 1950 appeared to verify General MacArthur's prediction of a resolution to the Korean conflict before Christmas. Maj. Gen. Edward M. Almond's X Corps surprise amphibious assault at Inch'on, executed with total success on September 15, was followed by a swift advance toward Seoul. Within days, Lieutenant General Walker's Eighth Army smashed out of the Pusan pocket, crossed the Naktong River, and achieved a breakthrough in lower Korea. By midnight on September 26, the Eighth Army linked up with X Corps in the vicinity of Osan.

While X Corps was fighting through the street barricades of Seoul and Eighth Army was still pushing northwest to meet it, the U.S. Joint Chiefs of Staff and MacArthur were engaged in high-level discussions over future military direction in Korea. The North Korean Army, trounced on two fronts by successful Allied counteroffensives, showed signs of increasing disorganization and retreated toward the 38th Parallel—the international boundary partitioning the two Korean states.

The deterioration of enemy resistance in southern Korea offered tempting opportunities for classic wartime exploitation. The Allied forces were in excellent position to pursue the battered North Korean Army to its destruction. In MacArthur's view, such a crushing move, if executed promptly while the opportunity existed, promised complete victory. Communist North Korea would be rendered incapable of menacing world peace again, and the futility of unprovoked aggression against any nation under United Nations protection would be amply demonstrated.

The problem with this MacArthurian scheme was that, in order to deliver the final blow to the retreating North Korean Army, U.N. forces would have to move north of the 38th Parallel and occupy all North Korea. Many member nations of the world organization expressed opposition to pushing the war beyond South Korea's prewar border. The task of defeating enemy aggression was technically accomplished once the invaders were expelled and the Republic of Korea's territorial integrity was reestablished. MacArthur insisted that military exigencies justified "hot pursuit" of the North Korean Army if the enemy refused to surrender.

These legal distinctions were overshadowed by Chinese threats of intervention if North Korean soil was attacked. Fearful of an expanded war, some of President Truman's advisors and other prominent officials within the United States also opposed moving north of the demarcation line. MacArthur repeated his call for bold, decisive action to insure a quick and thorough victory. He asserted that China would not risk all-out war on North Korea's behalf. In Almond's words, "We might say that the grand strategy of the operation in Korea changed when General MacArthur decided that the North Korean Army had already been defeated and he doubted that the Chinese Army, the Reds, would intervene and come to the rescue of the North Korean government."[1]

On September 27, the Joint Chiefs of Staff granted General MacArthur authority to cross the 38th Parallel, destroy the North Korean armed forces, and reunite all of Korea—subject to approval of the U.S. government. The directive contained a proviso that there be no major Chinese or Soviet forces between the 38th Parallel and the Manchurian border. The latter limitation was inserted because the Pentagon high command was concerned about openly provoking these hostile powers. The U.N. force could be easily trapped and destroyed on the peninsula if China and the Soviet Union unleashed massive armies into the war.

MacArthur replied that he needed open permission to operate freely throughout Korea without the limitation of prior U.S. governmental clearance. President Truman, acutely aware of MacArthur's unassailable popularity and apparent infallibility following the daring Inch'on attack and liberation of Seoul, approved his request. The Allied ground situation appeared ideal for the next stage of operations. The Eighth Army's linkage with X Corps presented the chance for a final offensive along a united front. Unfortunately, MacArthur had already determined that the war's rapid conclusion depended on further offensives requiring separate Allied establishments.[2]

General Walker wanted to combine all U.N. forces in Korea under his direct control as quickly as possible after Eighth Army achieved its breakout from the Pusan perimeter. The lack of X Corps cooperation, in Walker's judgment, stifled his ability to capitalize on several unfolding tactical opportunities during the advance through southern Korea. On September 23, for instance, Walker notified MacArthur that his South Korean divisions were driving toward the important road junctions of Andong and Ch'ungju. "Control of these [cities] in conjunction with the seizure of Suwon by X Corps would cut off all major routes of escape for enemy forces remaining in southwest Korea."[3]

X Corps failed to respond to suggestions for a Suwon encirclement and shunned communications with Eighth Army. During this period, Walker's knowledge of the X Corps mission was limited to the sparse information contained in United Nations Command Order Number 1, which instructed the corps to land at Inch'on and make juncture with the Eighth Army. He still hoped that the corps would be incorporated into his organization upon link-up, consolidating all Allied forces in Korea under one command. Almond would be freed to resume his coveted chief-of-staff duties under General MacArthur in Japan. The original plan governing Operation CHROMITE's successful conclusion anticipated this arrangement when it was first adopted, and it was the course of action still favored by Generals Hickey and Wright of MacArthur's senior staff.

"The Big X" Corps was a veritable army of 70,457 soldiers and support troops with tremendous combat power.[4] Eighth Army planners looked forward to using this large, well-equipped, and relatively fresh formation as the spearhead of its continuing northward advance. General Walker's own contingents were worn down by both the recent breakthrough and the long battle for the Pusan perimeter. The Eighth Army mechanized column that reached X Corps was reduced to a single mixed multi-battalion vanguard of the 1st Cavalry Division ("Task Force Lynch"), exhausted by the rapidity of its running battle to clear peninsular highways and reach the Inch'on-Seoul salient. The rest of the Eighth Army was widely scattered, with many elements engaged in sharp fighting to reduce points of resistance and corral bypassed enemy troops along the various routes of march.

On September 26, just prior to the actual meeting between Eighth Army and X Corps elements, Walker was still operating in the dark regarding Almond's future command relationship. He had received no coordinating information. Walker sent a carefully worded message asking MacArthur for clarification: "To facilitate advance planning for the approaching junction with X Corps, rqst [request] this hq [headquarters] be kept informed of plans and progress [by] this corps to greatest extent practicable. To date X Corps operations plans have not been received."[5]

There was no reply until the following day. MacArthur informed Walker that X Corps would remain in GHQ Reserve under Far East Command, in occupation of the Inch'on-Seoul area, ready to undertake a GHQ-directed operation. Both X Corps and the Eighth Army would be present in the capital area, but there was no subordination whatsoever. Almond's force remained a separate entity accountable to MacArthur alone.[6]

The adverse impact of this decision was felt immediately. For instance, when the 1st Cavalry Division made contact with X Corps, it was operating at a great distance from its original supply point. In addition, Army stocks had been depleted by incessant fighting during the breakout. Eighth Army logisticians knew that X Corps could expeditiously support the division, but the cavalry was forced to rely on its own extended supply line instead. Corps supply officers relied on MacArthur's message of September 17, which stated that forward units of the Eighth Army would not be supplied by X Corps, except for emergency issues. This event proved to be just a foretaste of the logistical nightmare occasioned by continued corps independence.

The X Corps refused to respond to any Army operational request. Shortly after reaching the Seoul area, Eighth Army became aware that retreating North Korean units were streaming through the central mountains between Wonju and Ch'unch'on. A regimental-size force was urgently needed to block this critical gap in order to cut off approximately six thousand North Koreans still in the area. Almond refused to dispatch any of his troops on the premise that his lines could not be extended further, because his troops were commencing preparations for a new amphibious operation (these preparations were actually several days away). Eighth Army was forced to send the ROK 6th Division to capture Ch'unch'on on October 1. The city was secured on the following day, but thousands of enemy soldiers had already escaped.[7]

General Walker deeply resented Almond's refusal to employ X Corps units in assisting Eighth Army entrapment efforts against the fleeing North Korean forces east of Seoul. Almond was well aware of the danger posed by enemy partisans and bypassed troops, both from his Civil War studies and Italian front experience. On the evening of October 1, Almond was briefed that enemy activity had practically ceased in the capital area, but he was cognizant of the vulnerability of sudden attack from the largely unpatrolled region beyond the city's environs.

Almond formed his own personal guard, the 8222d Army Unit, Defense Platoon (Reinforced), which was the Korean War equivalent of General Lee's Virginia escort unit. Almond beefed up this new contingent with assets from military police units at the corps disposal, which were also being used as honor guards, bodyguards, and parade troops for his miniature army. This forced other units to take over normal MP functions. For example, the prisoner-of-war stockade at Inch'on was operated by the 69th Chemical Smoke Generator Company.

Other questionable tactical and logistical decisions were manifested by X Corps' utilization of Col. Frank S. Bowen Jr.'s 187th Airborne Regimental Combat Team, the "Rakkasans." This reinforced paratrooper outfit (technically part of the 11th Airborne Division from Fort Campbell, Kentucky) existed as the parachutist reserve of Far East Command. In accordance with Operation CHROMITE contingencies, it was available to assist X Corps. Almond was keenly aware of the generous cargo tonnage dedicated to its employment.

In an apparent effort to grab this tonnage for general corps purposes, Almond cancelled its projected parachute insertion and directed the "Rakkasans" to air land directly at Kimpo airfield from Ashiya, Japan, commencing September 24. He assumed that resulting cargo allocations to X Corps would be increased automatically to 850 tons daily. The supply situation was extremely tight and demanded equitable allocation. The Far East Command ruled, "Cargo tonnage lift made available through cancellation of airdrop of 187th Abn RCT will be distributed in accordance with overall theatre needs."[8]

Once the supply bonus disappeared, Almond expressed private resentment against Bowen's command. He was disturbed by stories of the unit's hard partying while departing Camp Stoneman in California just weeks earlier. Almond, who safeguarded classified information with obsessive fanaticism, was horrified by the unit's disregard of security precautions as reported by members of the 187th such as Maj. Francis L. Sampson: "Although all enlisted men of the regiment were forbidden to leave the post for security reasons, [Colonel] Bowen in an intoxicated condition brought a woman, whose name he (Bowen) could not remember, on the post and in her presence discussed the troop movement to Japan freely to the staff and weapons to be picked up before we left."[9]

The military necessity to keep the 187th Airborne Regimental Combat Team intact for future parachute missions, preferably in an isolated status near an air base, harmonized with General Almond's distrust of the "Rakkasans" around populated areas such as Seoul and Inch'on. The 187th, while under X Corps control, was relegated to clearing Kimpo peninsula, an area of relatively uninhabited wasteland between the Han River and the Yellow Sea. The paratroopers were otherwise used only as temporary, single-company reserves for frontline emergencies. The regiment, assisted by heavy cruiser gunfire from the *Toledo* (CA-133), completed mopping up Kimpo peninsula on October 1.

By September 27, X Corps' incessant demands for logistical priority and favored commodity support exasperated the Far East Command supply office. It issued a sharp rebuke to use normal requisitioning channels: "Since the beginning of the current X Corps operation, staff officers from X Corps have made requests for various types of supplies through the GHQ G4 [Supply] staff section. Every effort has been made to comply with the requests, but in two recent cases difficulty has arisen leading to the delay in receipt by X Corps of needed supplies. It is desired that staff officers [in] your hq [headquarters] be instructed to make their requests for supplies through appropriate channels to Japan Logistical Command in order that supply action on urgently needed supplies can be made more expeditiously."[10]

X Corps also suffered from increasingly serious command friction between its top leaders. The relationship between Generals Almond and Smith had gone completely sour. The extent of this disharmony was typified by a phone call from Lieutenant Colonel Williamson, X Corps assistant operations officer, to Major Hartness of the 1st Marine Division operations office on October 1. At the time, the division was skirmishing against roadblocks and clearing mine fields north of Seoul as it advanced against strongly defended Uijongbu. Williamson asked Major Hartness to transmit last night's activities, "to help us during the five o'clock briefing [for General Almond]. I want someone to give us a call and tell us what is going on! Due east of your north flank where the Han and Pukhan Rivers come together, it is reported that there are many ferrys in operation. We are having that investigated by air. It may be friendly troops.''[11]

These disturbing signs of corps mismanagement, as well as the pressing need for solidified Eighth Army control over all combat resources in Korea, went unheeded by MacArthur.

2. The Future of X Corps

During the last week of September 1950, MacArthur hurriedly formulated a new, independent amphibious mission for X Corps. The Far East Command Joint Strategic Plans and Operations Group was ordered to activate existing contingency plans for an amphibious landing against the former North Korean naval base of Wonsan on the eastern coast. MacArthur approved this plan on September 29, following his receipt of presidential authority to extend operational jurisdiction into North Korea.

When MacArthur received permission to cross the 38th Parallel, his next objective became the North Korean capital of P'yongyang. It was an important military and communications hub as well as an obvious political target. The best axis of attack toward the city led directly from Seoul along the west coast, but the enemy could be expected to defend this approach with almost suicidal tenacity. A multi-directional approach to P'yongyang would force the enemy to defend a wider area, flank his positions, and would isolate the capital from reinforcement.

The most satisfactory backdoor approach to P'yongyang was the east-west route leading from Wonsan on the opposite coast. This direction presented an ideal corps-sized zone of advance to be used in conjunction with the main Eighth Army thrust. It crossed the Korean peninsula at its narrowest point north of Seoul, minimized cross-country terrain obstacles, and offered the possibility of an advantageous rear attack. Once secured, the lateral Wonsan-P'yongyang corridor would form a barrier trapping North Korean elements to the south. Upper Korea was divided into two distinct geographic regions by the spine of the towering Taebaek mountain range, and basing X Corps at Wonsan also assured Almond an excellent field of operations toward the vital Hamhung-Hungnam industrial complex and other points in northeastern Korea.

MacArthur believed that a quick amphibious strike at Wonsan would ultimately achieve the best chance to unsettle any prepared North Korean defenses around P'yongyang. The U.N. forces would be temporarily split while the Eighth Army attacked north from Seoul in the west and X Corps attacked west from Wonsan in the east. When General MacArthur announced these separate roles, Walker and his staff (as well as members of the Joint Chiefs of Staff) were outraged that disconnected Allied command arrangements would continue to dominate the Korean battle-field. Their sentiments were summarized by a Von Schlieffen quote used by historian Roy Appleman to introduce the Army's official chapter on MacArthur's plan for complete victory, "It is better to abandon a whole province than to divide an army."[12]

The danger of splitting an army in the midst of wartime operations was a military hazard considered justifiable only under the most extreme circumstances. The lack of combined assets not only impaired overall effectiveness, but also exposed each separate wing of the army to locally superior enemy response and possible piecemeal defeat.

MacArthur stated that terrain and logistical hardships warranted sepa-rate combat establishments. He claimed that the dual assault could be efficiently coordinated from Japan—the actual base for all Korean opera-tions, even though it was seven hundred miles distant—without diminish-ing the combat power of either drive. MacArthur dismissed the risk of Chinese intervention, and was confident that the disintegrating North Korean Army posed no significant threat of counterattack to any prong of the advance.

General Almond claimed he operated in strict conformity with the anticipated course of action outlined by Operation CHROMITE, and that he was equally surprised by the new direction given the corps. Almond recounted that near the end of September he expected to return to Tokyo, Japan, and leave the X Corps behind to be absorbed by the Eighth Army. He stated, "The new plan, which was announced to us on the 1st of October, would involve operations into northeast Korea. This required that the X Corps be re-embarked on its transport and sail around from Inch'on by way of Pusan to the Wonsan harbor and land on Korea's east coast by the 20th of October, and directed to occupy northeast Korea. We learned this, as I said, on the 1st of October which was two days after the ceremonies [for President Rhee] that I explained on the 29th of September in Seoul."[13]

When MacArthur announced his intentions, Almond reacted with the zeal of a fervent disciple. He loyally adopted all of MacArthur's reasons with the unquestioning enthusiasm that his commander expected. The twin considerations of terrain and logistics were cited by both men as ultimately determining the destiny of X Corps in the first winter of the Korean war.

In MacArthur's judgment, it was necessary to secure Wonsan by seaborne attack because any overland drive would have to traverse formidable Korean mountains to reach the far coast. South Korean forces were moving up along the east coast but their ability to reach Wonsan was questioned. MacArthur ignored suggestions emanating from Col. John A. Dabney (the Eighth Army operations officer) that X Corps— already poised on the outskirts of Seoul—could push directly north across the peninsula to take Wonsan, a strategy that provided Eighth Army a unified front with good flank security. Dabney also predicted that the ROK drive would capture Wonsan before the projected amphibious movement could be completed.[14]

Almond thought that any overland route to Wonsan would subject his corps to a protracted struggle through the deep valleys and easily defended mountain passes of Korea's rugged interior. These disadvantages were sharply focused by his visit to the front on October 2. Even as X Corps was preparing to release responsibility for its zone to Eighth Army, the 1st Marine Division was engaged in hard fighting for the high ground three thousand meters south of Uijongbu, just north of Seoul. Almond decided to personally view the battlefield after he heard that the Marine advance was stalled by extensive mine fields planted alongside the road, which were covered in turn by heavy North Korean machine gun fire.

At 10:00 A.M., Almond directed his "mobile command post"—a motorized combination of gun-jeeps, staff cars, trucks, and headquarters vans—to move up the contested Uijongbu road. Only four miles north of Seoul, Almond's caravan was halted by an excited Marine who said several hundred enemy troops were "bearing down on the area." The machine gun vehicles were moved forward, and Capt. Lloyd E. Jones, Jr., one of Almond's aides-de-camp (whose jeep was outfitted with a pedestal-mounted Browning .30-caliber machine gun) was sent ahead to reconnoiter. Jones returned twenty minutes later to report that four North Koreans had been flushed from a small ridge by a Marine patrol a thousand yards down the road. Almond was upset that the entire Marine advance might be held up by equally minute encounters.

An hour later, the mechanized caravan arrived at the command site of the 7th Marines. General Almond, displaying his usual proclivity of personally supervising small unit activities, conferred with Colonel Litzenberg about regimental dispositions. The 7th Marines were battling against Hill 550 with two battalions, the 3d Battalion advancing on the left side of the main road and the 1st Battalion moving under fire on the right side (the 2d Battalion was in reserve). Almond decided to have a closer look and ordered his caravan to proceed a thousand meters farther up the road to the actual front.

Almond stopped his motorcade on the main road next to the command post of the 3d Battalion. The large, enemy-held hill mass was clearly visible. It was thinly wooded and deeply eroded by many ravines. White blossoms of smoke, intermixed with heaving geysers of blackened earth, erupted from the hillside as tank cannon and artillery shells pounded the slopes with white phosphorous and high explosives. Almond demanded to talk with the battalion commander, Major Roach, but was informed that he was leading his troops on the line. Almond looked in the distance where Marine riflemen could be seen maneuvering toward the hill through the rice fields.

An enemy mortar barrage suddenly exploded through the advancing Marine ranks. Almond glanced furiously at his watch. It was exactly noon and the attack was halted. Almond insisted that the tanks should go forward to assist the infantry, but a Marine artillery observer explained that North Korean 45mm antitank weapons were within range. At that moment (12:00 noon), one of these guns fired five rounds of armor-piercing ammunition at the large cluster of vehicles parked near the battalion command post. The X Corps war diary relates: "This cleared the road of personnel. Most rounds were over but one ricocheted off a ditch near the CG's [Commanding General] jeep. 1205: CG talked with Major Roach on SCR 300 [radio] and was briefed on the situation forward. Due to the lack of observation vantage points forward it was decided not to join the Bn [battalion] commander. 1210: Left CP, 3d Bn, 7th Marines.''[15]

Almond beat a hasty retreat, but his experience near the front convinced him of enemy capability to defend Korea's heights. The fact that the 7th Marines fought through Hill 550 to Uijongbu on the following day made no difference. He was now convinced that an amphibious assault would prevent a protracted overland drive through the mountains toward Wonsan, where North Korean defenders—armed with the same type mortars and antitank guns that caused his close call—could reduce the corps advance to an interminable crawl.

3. Guerrilla Warfare

X Corps planners prepared for the next phase of Korean operations with a keen awareness of the terrain factors involved. Corps Operation Order No. 4, issued on October 4, outlined the amphibious assault and later march across the peninsula on P'yongyang. Wonsan was situated in a pocket of clear terrain, but "inland from this coastal lowland is the northern Taebaek Range, with its steep slopes, narrow tortuous valleys, and peaks varying from 1,500 to 5,000 feet."[16]

The weather hazards were curiously understated. Korea's northern winter was accompanied by an onslaught of Siberian winds and freezing temperatures plunging far below zero. Whatever mobility advantages accrued from frozen ground and rivers was cancelled by the cliffs and goat paths the corps would be forced to traverse. The shock effect of northern Korea's arctic-type climate on the unshielded soldier was severe, because winterized clothing only offered marginal protection. Without warming tents and other heating measures, the corps was doomed to suffer crippling cold weather and frostbite losses. Yet the same corps operations order declared, "The period October through March is most favorable for ground operations from the standpoint of weather."[17]

The logistical reasons for a two-front campaign against North Korea hinged on the inadequacy of existing supply arrangements for both Eighth Army and X Corps. The port of Pusan was the major logistical base in Korea, but the roads and rail lines leading north of Pusan had been heavily damaged, either through bombing or enemy demolitions. Most bridges were either destroyed or seriously weakened, and railroads were unusable in many areas. It was estimated that months of repair work were needed to reconstitute South Korea's transportation network. In the meantime, its capacity was severely limited and MacArthur argued that supplying X Corps through seaside facilities would ease the strain.

All supplies for the U.N. forces were shipped from Japan and reached Korean ports for further distribution inland. The newly opened port of Inch'on had only a limited capacity to sustain a major offensive. Another port opened at Wonsan rendered a logistical alternative to resupplying X Corps, without increasing the burden at existing ports or overtaxing the poor road and rail system. Wonsan even promised great utility in its own right because of its direct east-west railroad connection to P'yong-yang.

Unfortunately, sending X Corps around Korea to make a landing at Wonsan also forced a pause in the Allied offensive beyond Seoul.

Although X Corps was already positioned in the capital area for immediate resumption of this attack, it was withdrawn from the front for embarkation. Eighth Army units exchanged positions with the corps in a time-consuming "relief in zone." The process of transferring jurisdictional and tactical responsibility delayed the Army's initiation of further pursuit operations for several weeks. Valuable time was lost while units coordinated arrangements, resurveyed their areas, conducted mutual inventory, and finally traded positions.

One of the logistical conveniences projected by the Wonsan option was the opportunity to reload the X Corps assault force into ships still at Inch'on, instead of having the same vessels return with empty ballasts to Japan. These shipping arrangements were first discussed at 12:30 P.M. on October 1, when Admiral Struble arrived at Kimpo airport on his way to Tokyo and discussed the pending operation with Almond. Struble was named to command Joint Task Force 7, which had the mission of transporting X Corps around Korea and landing it at Wonsan. A partial list of shipping was obtained, and an embarkation group was established the next day.

Difficulties arose immediately. Inch'on lacked the facilities to simultaneously embark X Corps elements and resupply Eighth Army. There were not enough cranes, warehouses, berthing spaces, barges, or landing craft. Adverse tidal conditions complicated all arrangements. Normal cargo unloading had to be abandoned in order to permit X Corps to meet its proposed landing date at Wonsan. From October 1 to 17, all discharging activities at Inch'on were drastically curtailed because of the need to load Marine troops and equipment. The rate of deliveries placed ashore was reduced to a negligible trickle, and many were actually diverted to embarking units.

General Walker desperately needed supplies in order to continue his northward offensive, but he was enjoined to give priority at both Inch'on and Pusan to out-loading X Corps units. The Eighth Army was forced to rely on a lengthy and dilapidated single-track railroad from Pusan. Eighth Army stock levels dropped at times to one day's sustenance of the main U.N. front. The logistical shortcomings impeded pursuit of the enemy and the main advance on P'yongyang.

The mutual resentment between the corps and Army supply agencies intensified. Colonel Smith of X Corps had stockpiled large quantities of supplies north of the Han River in anticipation of continued corps movement to the north. Upon notification of the Wonsan operation,

Smith began withdrawing these stores to accompany corps units embarking at Inch'on. The removal of pre-positioned supplies angered Eighth Army officials.

Army supply officers claimed that corps coffers had been overfilled in preparation for CHROMITE. Thus, any excess quantities—especially those already emplaced—should be available for Army needs. Smith replied that his staff had secured the bountiful supplies through "aggressive initiative," and they still belonged to the corps. He pointed out that substantial amounts of residual stocks (which the corps could not take with it) were "inherited" by Eighth Army, in addition to previous emergency issues. Army logisticians noted, however, that X Corps refused to leave any supplies behind unless they were exchanged for Eighth Army supplies being shipped from Japan.

These severe logistical problems were magnified by transportation complications. The available sealift and port capacity at Inch'on could only accommodate the 1st Marine Division and a few extra corps units needed for the assault landing. The rest of the corps had to travel south overland to Pusan for embarkation. The motor and rail move clogged the roads and interfered with the northbound movement of Eighth Army service units and cargo, eventually forcing the Army to bring critically needed ammunition forward by air. As the 7th Infantry Division of X Corps moved south, the Eighth Army displaced its 2d Infantry Division to the north. The cross-movement of these two divisions exacerbated transport hardships.

The cross-country trek involved the 7th Infantry Division and Embarkation Group Charlie, which included the corps medical, engineer, ordnance, transportation, quartermaster, chemical, and signal units. Road reconnaissance and general planning was initiated from the first of October, but hampered by constantly changing instructions. On October 3, the division assembled by regimental combat teams into three movement increments. The 31st and 32d Infantry were relieved on the front by the 1st Cavalry Division and assembled near Suwon.

At 9:20 A.M. on October 4, the L-5 *Blue Goose* landed General Almond at Suwon airstrip, and he spent the morning putting Colonel Ovenshine's 31st Infantry through a rigorous series of battalion combat exercises. Almond was sulky and cantankerous toward Ovenshine, whom he considered too old for the job. Incensed with Ovenshine's handling of the regiment a week earlier (which merited no real complaint), Almond expressed displeasure with the "many tactical and operational errors

X Corps Movement

N

Map by Shelby L. Stanton

Ch'angjin (Chosin) Reservoir

P'ungsan

Pujon Reservoir

Pukch'ong

Iwon

Hamhung

Hungnam

Yonghung

P'YONGYANG

Yangdok

Wonsan

Kojo

Kaesong

Ch'unch'on

SEOUL

Inch'on

Suwon

Wonju

Ichon

Ch'ungju

Mun'gyong

Choch'iwon

Andong

Yongdong

Kunsan

Kumch'on

Yonil
Air
Base

TAEGU

Chinju

PUSAN

GUADALCANAL
1

S⁴S © 1989

committed by units and individuals'' observed during the demonstration.[18]

Almond ordered each battalion of the 7th Infantry Division to conduct a similar exercise before departure. While battlefield rehearsal was normally sound doctrine, the division was simply too rushed by its compressed timetable. The directive actually imperiled preparations for the motor march. Staff officers and key NCOs at every level were in the midst of scheduling a major displacement. They were concerned about vehicle serials, march orders, convoy scheduling, and a host of attendant problems. There was insufficient supervision or time to properly control practice sessions using live ammunition.

The first fatal mishap occurred on the following morning, as the 17th Infantry was going through its ''crash'' training. Col. Herbert B. Powell had commanded the 17th for over a year—since September 22, 1949—but his ''Buffaloes'' had been the last corps regiment ashore and combat experience was slight. The regimental mortars fired into a cluster of troops, killing five outright and maiming fifty-five others. A life-saving chain of all available aircraft flew in doctors and plasma, and rushed the critically injured to hospitals. General Almond relieved a regimental commander by the time the day was over, but it wasn't Colonel Powell. Almond sacked Ovenshine, based on administrative shortcomings perceived during the previous day.

In the meantime, the first division convoy had started south at 4 A.M. that same morning, October 5. The meandering, 350-mile route of march extended from Suwon west to Ichon and south through Ch'ungju past Kumch'on, then southwest into Taegu and finally Pusan. The corps lacked sufficient motorization for the task, necessitating a hastily arranged truck shuttle by the 52d Transportation Battalion (which had landed at Inch'on for port clearance duty). The thirty-six-hour trip subjected the drivers to rough roads, numerous detours, sporadic fire from roving bands of bypassed enemy troops, and mechanical breakdowns. They were told to keep moving at all costs, however, because accessibility to stranded vehicles was hindered by the remote Korean wilderness.

Radio contact was lost just after the convoy disappeared into the predawn darkness. Aircraft were diverted for medical purposes after the mortar accident, and this prohibited flights to monitor the column's progress. At 2 P.M., Lieutenant Colonel Williamson at corps telephoned the division operations officer, Lt. Col. John W. Paddock: ''I can't tell you exactly where the columns are, but they cleared the IDP [Initial Departure Point] this morning on time and we haven't heard anything from them since they left this morning. They are supposed to check in every hour on the hour. We haven't got signal communication with them, although they have a [radio] set with each unit and one following them and are supposed to check in!''[19]

By the time Major Myers secured a spare plane and established aerial contact over two hours later, the leading vehicles were ninety-two miles south of Inch'on and the column stretched fifty-two miles to its tail at Ch'ungju. Despite the best efforts of convoy regulating parties, almost everything went wrong. The trucks and jeeps were marked by faded pink panels rather than orange and white as directed, and the division radio control truck was out of communication until 6:35 in the evening. Other segments of the column stopped for the night in towns scattered along the highway.

Early on October 6, as some convoys neared operating rail lines, they were directed to transfer troops from trucks onto railroad cars. This measure was intended to expedite vehicular turn-around time and speed final transit. Unfortunately, an ammunition train exploded in a tunnel near Andong. Engineers worked feverishly to clear the wreck, but rail movement was blocked until late afternoon. That same morning, the motor column of the 2d Battalion, 32d Infantry, was ambushed at a sharp bend in the road ten miles south of Ch'ungju. The enemy showered the lead vehicles with grenades and opened up with automatic weapons. The first vehicle burst into flames, another jeep careened off the cliff, and the convoy was stopped with eleven casualties. Snipers held up the motorcade for two hours.[20]

While the 7th Infantry Division struggled south through central Korea, Almond paid homage in a salutary farewell to the Seoul battlefield. The poignant ceremony was held at a hillside U.N. cemetery, where Marines had once clashed advancing on Seoul, which contained the graves of 540 American and 59 Korean soldiers.

The twenty-five-minute ceremony was the final tribute to the fallen soldiers of Operation CHROMITE. A thousand troops, representing each unit of the corps, attended in full combat gear. Four floral wreaths were specially flown in from Japan and laid carefully among the wooden white markers and barren cemetery graves. Almond himself delivered the memorial rites: "No spirit is so magnificent as that of laying oneself on the altar of sacrifice to preserve one's country and the democratic ideals for which it stands." He closed by quoting an inscription that he had noted while attending Arlington services for his own soldier-son:

"Not for fame or regard / Not for place or for rank / Not lured by ambition / Or goaded by necessity / But in simple dedication to duty / As they understood it / These men suffered all, sacrificed all / dared all, and died."[21]

4. By Land and by Sea

At noon on October 7, 1950, X Corps was officially relieved of its responsibility for the Seoul-Inch'on area. The 187th Airborne Regimental Combat Team and the Seoul Area Command reverted to Eighth Army control. The Marine Corps Air Wing at Kimpo was now operating under the control of Fifth Air Force. The usual logistical foul-ups were complicating embarkation (the daily corps summary noted, for example, "Shipment of 100,000 C-rations arrived [by plane] at Kimpo airfield and efforts are being taken for *reloading* these rations on ships at Inch'on"),[22] but the 1st Marine Division was finally assembled in the port area and ready for shipment to new objectives.

Almond departed his headquarters at 11:20 A.M. and flew to Taegu. He watched stragglers of the 32d Infantry being transferred onto trains bound for Pusan. Almond wrote General Barr a formal letter criticizing division performance. He charged that the training exercises showed "general weakness is evident in the application and control of supporting fires" and the existence of "command and staff weaknesses." He faulted crew-served weapons proficiency, tank-infantry teamwork, communications, and command structure.[23]

The letter thoroughly alarmed Barr, as it arrived just after Ovenshine's sudden relief. It was now obvious that Almond would be corps commander indefinitely, and as long as he enjoyed MacArthur's favor no Army officer could afford his retribution. Barr was not in the Marine Corps, where he might be shielded from career ruination at Almond's whim. Barr felt the intensified pressure and ordered his subordinates to react with immediate obedience to every Almond suggestion.

On October 8, Almond ordered the 2d Logistical Command at Pusan to embark the 7th Infantry Division and Embarkation Group Charlie with the utmost speed. The next day, the X Corps advance party arrived in Pusan. A conference was held to determine out-loading requirements, but the corps was unable to present estimates. Units arriving at Pusan had left Suwon without time to even hold shake-down inspections. Furthermore, several cargo ships, which were still unloaded at Inch'on, were being redirected to Wonsan, but their cargo manifests were either missing or unreliable. Almond's staff insisted that the corps be resupplied practically from scratch. The support officers at Pusan did not relish duplicating materiel, but were given little choice. The tremendous burden depleted depot stocks, ammunition reserves, operational rations, petroleum, oil, and lubricants.

One of the most critical items was winter clothing, which X Corps was relying on to mitigate the harshest effects of the upcoming Korean winter campaign. Instead of coordinating with the Eighth Army quartermaster corps, Col. Aubrey Smith ordered this support direct from the Pusan depot commander. An administrative wrangle ensued because the depot was under Eighth Army control. X Corps insistence on the highest priority (cleared by Far East Command) forced other quartermaster issues to be halted while winter items were furnished to troops embarking at Inch'on and Pusan. Filling this requirement also delayed sailing time in several instances and caused shortages in winter stocks for other Army divisions.

During October 8, Almond toured Seoul and visited Ambassador Muccio in the embassy. The corps chief of staff, General Ruffner, completed shipboard arrangements for the general's entourage aboard the command ship *Mount McKinley*. That evening Almond entertained Admiral Doyle with a stately dinner. In the meantime, the weary truck drivers of the 15th Antiaircraft Artillery (AAA) Battalion returned to Suwon to pick up more equipment. They reported being ambushed by enemy troops, armed with automatic weapons and grenades, along unpatrolled sections of the highway during both legs of their journey to Taegu and back.

On October 9, the 1st Marine Division began the embarkation process at Inch'on. The same fearsome terrain features (thirty-one-foot tides and extensive mud flats) that had threatened CHROMITE attack planners now presented severe obstacles to easy departure. Only seven landing points existed for LSTs or landing craft, and they were only usable at high tide. There was an absence of staging areas. The facilities at the tidal basin were completely swamped loading bulk cargo onto barges for transfer to ships offshore.

Vehicles at Inch'on initially had to wait until peak tide periods to cross one wooden pier overlaid with airfield matting and enter waiting LCMs. To offset this limitation, vehicles were crammed onto the top decks of LSTs, ferried into the harbor, and then lifted by crane onto attack cargo and transport ships. Ships' cranes were also continually at work transferring cargo to other vessels waiting in the main harbor, because of mistakes in loading routine and assault-package supplies.

On October 9, the 7th Infantry Division was also struggling southward at a faster pace in accordance with Almond's accelerated schedule. One headquarters convoy attempted to "run the gauntlet" of mountain roads in central Korea during the night. At 2 A.M., it ran into an enemy roadblock in a defile three miles north of Mun'gyong. The North Korean raiding party barraged the stranded column with machine gun and mortar fire for twelve hours. The convoy lacked both communications and enough defensive ammunition.

The signal detachment escorting the convoy had a jeep-mounted SCR-193 radio, which should have been capable of transmitting through the mountain wilderness for assistance. When an attempt was made to put the set on the air, however, the antenna would not load properly. Throughout the cold hours of darkness, lit only by exploding shrapnel and tracer fire, soldiers tried frantically to get the transmitter into operation. They were unsuccessful. The faint dawn light revealed that the antenna terminal on the set was broken. A later investigation by the division signal officer, Lt. Col. Clifford E. Roberts, revealed carelessness as the main culprit: the radio was an unchecked spare set and the faulty antenna condition was previously known but never fixed.

The 17th Infantry's 1st Battalion, reinforced by mobile guns of Battery C, 15th AAA Battalion, finally reached the column during mid-afternoon. Numerous trucks were destroyed or damaged, six Americans were killed, and dozens more wounded. Lieutenant Colonel Chiles, the X Corps G3, was infuriated and fired a message to Barr, "Our CG desires that each march unit be provided adequate protection of weapons and ammo to prevent interferences by enemy action. The reason for this request is that we have received reports that some of your march units had no ammo at all when they got jumped and as a result could not even fire back."[24]

On the evening of October 10, another division convoy was struck outside the village of Chigoing-ni, just seventeen miles south of the previous ambuscade. Nine soldiers were killed and scores wounded in the encounter. Ammunition trucks, loaded with ordnance for the 48th and 49th Field Artillery Battalions, caught fire and began exploding. The radio-equipped vehicles were too close to the dangerous blaze to permit communications. The fire storm engulfed the line of vehicles as well as the dwellings on both sides of the road, stopping all traffic for hours. Engineer bulldozers arrived but could not clear the road until the fire died down. The ammunition kept exploding past midnight. A bypass was found, but only jeeps could get through.[25]

By October 11, the divisional movement was coming to an end. Only a few elements remained to be moved, but many vehicles were out of commission either because of enemy action or maintenance problems. The division vehicles at Pusan were worn and some needed extensive overhaul. So many troops still were marooned at Ichon (the first checkpoint past Suwon), however, that over a hundred trucks were needed to move them out of the town.

Throughout the day, final truck convoys took the last isolated groups of soldiers south or back to planes at Kimpo airfield. In seven days, 1,459 tons of supplies and equipment and 13,422 soldiers were sent by truck a total distance of 281,600 driven miles by the 52d Transportation Battalion and the organizational vehicles of the 7th Infantry Division.[26]

On that same day, Almond closed his headquarters at Ascom City and watched the Shermans and Pershings of the 73d Tank Battalion being back-loaded into LSTs. He visited the Marines at the Inch'on waterfront and made inspection rounds of their staging camp. He questioned hundreds of individuals, "What's your name? Where's your home? How long have you been in the service?" and scolded a Marine who didn't remember his rifle number. He expressed the notion that a rifle was a soldier's best friend; if a soldier knew the rifle number like a friend's name he would never cast it aside.[27]

At 5 P.M., he boarded the *Mount McKinley,* which became the new X Corps command post for the next phase of operations. During that same hour the final 520 men of the 7th Infantry Division were airlifted from Kimpo and flown into Pusan. Almond sat down to a splendid shipboard dinner with Admiral Doyle and selected corps staff officers at 6:30 P.M.

Other news on October 11 far exceeded the importance of reports that X Corps had a division in Pusan or that both corps and Marine division command posts were anchored off Inch'on ready to sail. Since the end of September, the South Korean Army had been advancing relentlessly day and night, in vehicles if available but mostly by foot (even though many troops were barefoot) and without radio contact with higher headquarters. The forward ROK regiments traversed mine fields and bypassed or brushed aside enemy delaying forces. By October 11, the ROK 3d and Capital Divisions had battled their way through Wonsan on the east coast, and the Eighth Army was sealing off the Kumch'on pocket in the west. The latter engagement broke the main line of North Korean resistance in front of P'yongyang.

The need for an amphibious assault on Wonsan port or a backdoor approach to the enemy capital of P'yongyang—which had been the entire basis for X Corps' convoluted command and operational arrangements—had been preempted by South Korean divisions marching straight up the coast.

Notes

1. USAMHI Interview, p. IV-59.
2. Schnabel, pp. 181–183.
3. Message, CG EUSAK to CINCFE, in War Diary, EUSAK, dtd 23 September 1950, as paraphrased in Eighth Army Monograph, *Special Problems in the Korean Conflict*, dtd 5 February 1952, p. 32.
4. The X Corps actual strength was as follows: Corps Hq and misc. combat units—8,944 (8,344 Army + 600 Koreans); Corps service units—2,068 (2,039 Army + 29 Koreans); 1st Marine Div—21,996 (21,395 Marines + 601 Army); 7th Inf Div—23,581 (15,883 Army + 7,698 Koreans); ROK Marine Rgt—3,323; 17th ROK Inf Rgt—2,845; 187th Abn RCT—3,165; Corps controlled units in Seoul/Inch'on area—4,535 (4,452 Army and 83 Koreans). Source: *X Corps G3 Operational Report*, dtd 1 October 1950; and *Far East Command Situation Report*, dtd 30 September 1950.
5. Incoming Message, GHQ, from CG EUSAK to CINCFE, 26 September 1950.
6. Schnabel, p. 190.
7. Appleman, p. 611.
8. Outgoing Message, GHQ, from CINCFE to CG X Corps, dtd 27 September 1950.
9. Maj. Sampson Ltr of Complaint to LTG Ridgway, dtd 10 April 1951, copy in X Corps files.
10. GHQ Message to CG X Corps, Ref: Supply, dtd 27 September 1950.
11. X Corps G3 *Daily Journal*, 1 October 1950, Entry J-43.
12. Appleman, p. 607.
13. USAMHI Interview, p. IV-59.
14. Appleman, p. 611.
15. X Corps War Diary, 2 October 1950.
16. X Corps Operations Order No. 4, Appendix 1 to Annex 2, Estimate of the Enemy Situation, dtd 4 October 1950, Para 2c: *Terrain*.
17. Ibid., Para 2b: *Weather*.
18. X Corps War Diary, dtd 4 October 1950, Commanding General's Diary.
19. X Corps G-3 Periodic Report No. 17, Message Diary, dtd 5 October 1950, Item J-44.
20. X Corps G-3 Journal, 6 October 1950, Entry J-35.
21. X Corps Public Information Office Press Release 13, dtd 7 October 1950.
22. X Corps War Diary, 7 October 1950, p. 1, Summary of Activities.
23. MG Edward M. Almond, CG X Corps, Ltr to MG David G. Barr, CG 7th Inf Div, dtd 7 October 1950.
24. X Corps G-3 Daily Summary, dtd 9 October 1950, Entry J-13.
25. X Corps G-3 Summary, 10 October 1950, Items J-40, J-53.
26. X Corps War Diary, 1–31 October 1950, p. 22.
27. "Command," *Time*, dtd 23 October 1950, p. 27.

X Corps Casualties in the Inch'on-Seoul Campaign
15 September–7 October 1950

Unit	Killed	Wounded	Missing	Non-Battle
X Corps headquarters	0	0	0	5
2nd Engineer Special Brigade	0	2	0	12
Corps miscellaneous units	1	3	2	9
1st Marine Division				
a. Marine	427	1,961	5	1,122
b. Army attached	0	1	0	0
c. ROK Marine Regiment	29	96	0	0
7th Infantry Division				
a. Army	86	358	10	226
b. South Koreans attached	43	102	32	42
Total	586	2,523	49	1,416

Source: Personnel Daily Summary of X Corps No. 23, dtd 7 October 1950 (date X Corps was relieved of responsibility for Inch'on and Seoul areas preparatory to Wonsan-Iwon landings), posted at 1800 hours, as adjusted.

X Corps Casualties in the Wonsan—Hungnam Campaign
8 October–10 December 1950

Unit	Killed*	Wounded	Non-Battle
X Corps headquarters	29	36	137
2d Engineer Special Brigade	8	7	41
Corps miscellaneous units	19	26	147
1st Marine Division			
a. Marine	885	3,428	3,256
b. British Royal Marines	47	31	1
3d Infantry Division			
a. Army	227	266	502
b. South Koreans attached	132	102	94
7th Infantry Division			
a. Army	2,657	354	111
b. South Koreans attached	1,663	47	168
ROK I Corps			
a. ROK Capital Division	919	1,043	450
b. ROK 3d Division	253	476	349
Total	6,839	5,816	5,256

* Includes Missing in Action, the majority of whom were never recovered

Source: Personnel Daily Summary of X Corps, draft, dtd 10 Dec 50 (date X Corps filed last summary prior to evacuation at Hungnam). Although these statistics were adjusted by available records at The Adjutant General's Office and the Marine Corps Historical Center, discrepancies in various categories exist and the above tabulation must be considered as an estimate. The small number of casualties incurred from 10 December until the final evacuation from Hungnam on 24 December are not recorded because of insufficiency of records.

Maj. Gen. Edward M. Almond. June 29, 1950.

X Corps commander Major General Almond, carrying his map case, talks with paratroopers of the 187th Airborne Regimental Combat Team. Outside Seoul on October 1, 1950.

The 1st Marine Division commander, Maj. Gen. Oliver P. Smith, confers with Fleet Marine Force commander Lt. Gen. Lemuel C. Shepherd, Jr. during the invasion of Inch'on, September 15, 1950.

Major General Almond discusses the Wonsan landings with Vice Adm. Arthur D. Struble, Seventh Fleet commander, just prior to commencing X Corps's northeast Korean campaign on October 20, 1950.

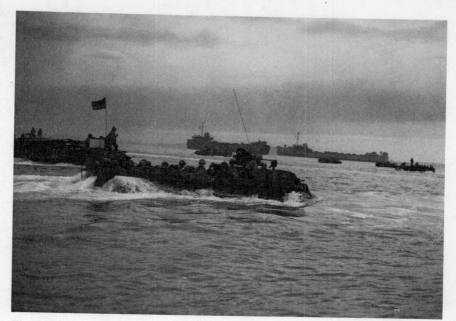

The 5th Marines ride amtracs toward Wolmi-do Island. September 15, 1950.

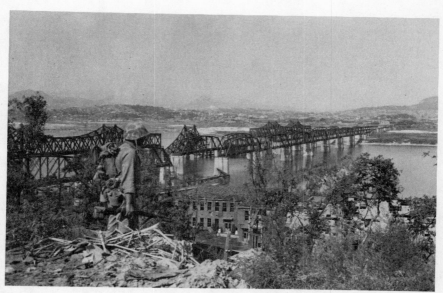

Marine views destroyed railroad bridges over the Han River. September 23, 1950.

Marine amphibious tractor refuels a Marine M26 Pershing tank during the advance on Seoul, September 17, 1950.

Marines advance past three North Korean T34 tanks destroyed near Inch'on on September 16, 1950.

3d ROK Division crosses into North Korea on a drive that would capture Wonsan and enable X Corps to avoid an east coast combat landing.

Puerto Rican troops of the 65th Infantry, shown with North Korean prisoners near Yonghung on November 15, 1950.

X Corps winter clothing included fur-lined parkas for the Marines (second from left) and overcoats and ski parkas for Army troops. December 3, 1950.

PLA prisoners taken by X Corps at Hamhung on October 30, 1950.

The Blue Goose *warms her engine while X Corps commander Edward Almond discusses the route of flight with pilot Capt. Charles Keleman.*

The 7th Infantry Division advances into Hyesanjin as X Corps reaches the Yalu River and Manchurian border, during the morning of November 21, 1950.

Air Force crewmen of a C47 transport prepare to parachute ammunition to the isolated soldiers of Task Force Faith on November 29, 1950.

Marine trucks are loaded on transports during X Corps's evacuation of Hungnam. December 14, 1950.

CHAPTER 7

THE SECOND INVASION

1. Deployment East

The seizure of Wonsan by South Korean forces gave sudden impetus to Almond's orders to stake a X Corps claim to northeastern Korea. Walker's Eighth Army was driving steadily closer to P'yongyang and MacArthur was concerned that the *NKPA* might turn their capital into a well-defended "communist hero city" for a final showdown. In the event Walker's forces became stymied in front of P'yongyang, MacArthur wanted X Corps in eastern Korea for an attack westward across the peninsula. A combat amphibious assault against the eastern shore was no longer needed after the South Koreans captured Wonsan, but beach landings remained the fastest means of establishing the corps in its objective area.

The X Corps was still in the midst of embarkation at two different ports separated by two hundred air miles. Almond chafed at the tedious loading schedules and employed liberal dosages of whip-cracking command emphasis to hasten their progress. On the morning of October 12, he left the *Mount McKinley* and flew south to Pusan in an L-17 Ryan Navion to inspect General Barr's 7th Infantry Division. Another

L-17 aircraft followed with his deputy chief of staff Lieutenant Colonel McCaffrey and Lt. Alexander Haig. Almond was accompanied by journalist Elmer Lower of *Time-Life* in his own plane.

Almond visited the 31st Infantry consolidation area first, where the new regimental commander, Col. Allan D. MacLean, was wasting no time while equipment was being processed and loaded. His battalions were engaged in accelerated combat training. The soldiers were stripped to the waist as they struggled through combat exercises that stretched the unit across rice paddies and up hillsides under the blazing Korean sun. MacLean's display of hard-driving aggressiveness caused Almond to note in his daily log, "Colonel McLain [*sic*] showed a high degree of leadership and the activities of this regiment were excellent."[1]

After lunch, Almond visited Col. Charles E. Beauchamp's 32d Infantry, where individual fighting loads were being reduced for the upcoming operation. The troops had landed at Inch'on with too much equipment and the Marines derided the regiment for abandoning gear on the battlefield. Beauchamp was now faced with the increased necessities of winter campaigning. Each soldier was clothed with a helmet and liner, cotton field cap, wool muffler and high-neck sweater, pile field jacket, wool and cotton field trousers, a pair of shoepacs and combat boots, and two sets of winter underwear, shoepac felt inserts, and ski socks. Almond inspected the unit and was infuriated that the men carried only two pairs of socks. He ordered that every man in the division carry six pairs, despite the protests of knowledgeable sergeants who realized the men would throw away extra pairs on the march.

Almond left Pusan after his whirlwind tour satisfied that Barr was responding to his directives for more speed in embarkation with reasonable alacrity. The division at Pusan, however, took weeks to complete outloading. The overland movement had taken a heavy toll on division vehicles and motorized equipment, and much time was consumed on repair and maintenance chores. The artillery battalions were forced to retread every tractor in the mechanized march from Suwon.

As the division languished at Pusan, the fear of potential supply shortfalls caused a creeping psychosis in units to acquire everything possible. Units began hoarding and demanding extra supplies. Upon arrival at Inch'on the division headquarters could move in twenty-five trucks, but at Pusan it took fifty. Regimental supply officers made deals with sympathetic Pusan logistic personnel, and carried their acquisitions in trucks overburdened with Korean desks, chairs, extra shoes, mess gear, stove parts, and other sundry items. One frustrated division supply officer lamented, "We had pressure to draw every piece of impedimenta that the Army designed."[2]

Many seasonal items such as squad tents, stoves, and mountain sleeping bags were necessary, but other common gear like shelter halves, tentage pins, and intrenching tools were later found useless in the frozen ground. When the division reached northeastern Korea, it possessed so much contraband equipage that it sought to fill train-loads of boxcars on sidings (permission was refused). Often the regiments forgot what they had already packed. One quartermaster later pleaded for rations, apparently forgetting that hundreds of cases had been smuggled into individual duffel bags, left unopened.

On Friday the 13th at Inch'on, the X Corps command group boarded the amphibious force flagship *Mount McKinley,* and the rest of the staff went on the assault transport *Gen. W. A. Mann* (AP-112). Although the corps was formally headquartered on these vessels, Almond decided to airlift a "small reconnaissance staff group" to establish an advance command post under Lieutenant Colonel McCaffrey at Wonsan airport. He secured permission from MacArthur and travelled to Wonsan with McCaffrey on Saturday morning to select the site and direct the aerial transfer.

Maj. Gen. Field Harris, the Marine aircraft wing commander, was at Wonsan airfield coordinating with Col. Boeker C. Batterton about the arrival of Marine Aircraft Group 12. The advancing South Koreans needed combat air support as quickly as possible. Almond interrupted their discussion and ordered Batterton's group delayed until his own "emergency" airlift was finished. Twelve C-119 aircraft shuttled the men and supplies of the corps forward command post into Wonsan. The 200 Marine and 175 Air Force personnel at the airfield undertook the added responsibility of protecting and supporting the secondary corps headquarters.

At 12:30 P.M., Almond drove a jeep to the field headquarters of Brig. Gen. Kim Paik Il's ROK I Corps, which was advancing rapidly toward the industrial center of Hamhung and its Hungnam port. Reports that the North Koreans were fleeing in utter disorder intensified Almond's concerns that his own corps might be unable to reach the battlefront before enemy resistance collapsed completely. Almond was also piqued that his nemesis, Lieutenant General Walker, had flown into Wonsan with Fifth Air Force commander Maj. Gen. Earl E. Partridge on the day of its capture, October 11, to coordinate forward support for the ROK I Corps.

Almond possessed no authority over ROK I Corps, but its zone of action was clearly within the anticipated province of separate X Corps operations. He expected to solidify command over all U.N. troops throughout the region within a week, and his meeting with General Kim's KMAG advisor, Colonel Rogers, was characteristically blunt. Rogers was informed tersely that Kim's corps should begin maneuvering in accordance with X Corps directives. "General Almond emphasized that he had no control over ROK I Corps at present and did not mean to influence them but, at the same time, he felt that they should be aware of what their mission would be on October 20," the day Almond was scheduled to take charge of all Allied forces in northeastern Korea.[3]

Lieutenant Colonel McCaffrey's X Corps advance command post installed radios and telephone circuits to provide a direct conduit for Almond's instructions and liaison with ROK I Corps and other units in the region. The forward headquarters was also ordered to prepare the Wonsan area for corps arrival. The discovery of dense mine fields covering Wonsan's seaward approaches jeopardized any landing. The Navy, which encountered increasing amounts of underwater mines throughout October, had not anticipated such dangerous concentrations off Wonsan. Helicopter overflights, however, confirmed that Wonsan waters were sewn thoroughly with enemy mines.

Lt. Col. Robert R. Glass of the advance command G2 intelligence section worked closely with South Korean agents to resolve the mine-laying mystery. They ascertained that Russian technicians assembled the mines and supervised their placement as Korean workers rolled the weapons off towed barges. Most of the four thousand mines had been sown before South Korean troops arrived in the area. Even so, the array contained three thousand contact inertia, contact chemical, pressure, and electronic mines—one of the deadliest mine fields encountered in naval warfare.

Admiral Struble assembled a twenty-one-vessel minesweeper flotilla by including eight minesweepers of the supposedly inactive Imperial Japanese Navy. The use of Japanese craft was a highly sensitive political gamble made by General MacArthur and Admiral Joy. The Japanese contract crews were given false promises about extravagant pay and employment conditions not to extend north of the 38th Parallel. They were also told that they would only perform safer secondary sweeps instead of first sweeps. The crews were later unable to complain to the Japanese Maritime Safety Agency because their radios were silenced in accordance with combat operational directives.

The tedious minesweeping process had to be completed before any seafaring troops or cargo could be unloaded at Wonsan. After two days of painstaking clearance, the minesweepers still faced ten miles of mine-clogged water in front of Wonsan's inner harbor. On October 12, in an effort to accelerate the process, carrier-based fighters tried to blast a passageway through the field between Reito and Koto islands with a hundred 1,000-pound bombs. Navy combat swimmers followed the raid by landing on Reito Island and conducting submerged reconnaissance.[4] The first minesweepers entering the channel after the aerial preparation, however, were sunk. Enemy shore batteries slowed minesweeping efforts for five more days until South Korean troops completed their mop-up of Wonsan's craggy peninsula and numerous islands.

On October 17, the amphibious task force sailed from Inch'on, led by the flagship *Mount McKinley* and followed by dozens of transports loaded with the men, artillery, and vehicles of the reinforced 1st Marine Division. The convoy sailed 850 miles around Korea and into the Sea of Japan, but was unable to disembark until the Navy completed its delicate sweeping mission. Almond raged in frustration at the snail's pace of the operation and urged more haste in clearing the mines. He impatiently criticized the perceived lack of naval skill (the sinking and disabling of minesweeping vessels continued), and the flotilla's high complement of "incompetent" Japanese boat crews.

A Japanese minesweeper conducting a first sweep struck a Russian-type mine and sank with heavy losses on October 19. The State Department expressed alarm over possible international repercussions and urgently cabled MacArthur to cloak the incident in the highest secrecy. MacArthur agreed, but assured the State Department that Japanese participation was not a militant act. He used the bizarre rationale that the North Korean free-floating mines were being cleared for "humanitarian purposes involved in neutralizing infractions of the accepted rules of warfare."[5]

2. Governorship

On October 15, just before the Marines departed Inch'on aboard Admiral Doyle's naval armada, MacArthur conferred with President Truman at

Wake Island. He reiterated his optimism that a quick victory would follow Eighth Army's plunge into North Korea. He categorized *NKPA* defensive tactics as an obstinate face-saving gesture (''Orientals prefer to die rather than lose face''), and predicted the collapse of organized opposition by Thanksgiving. MacArthur assured Truman that there was ''very little'' likelihood of Chinese intervention because the war was now lost to the communists and China had lost its chance to intervene effectively.[6]

On the following day, MacArthur returned to Japan and granted Almond his own wartime territorial fief. ''In order to exploit to the maximum all forces under CINCUNC [Commander-in-Chief, United Nations Command] and to implement the full concept of operations . . . X Corps, operating as an independent Corps of GHQ [General Headquarters] Reserve, will, effective at 1200 hours, 20 October 1950, and until further orders, assume operational control of all UN and ROK ground forces operating north of 39 degrees and 10 minutes north.'' The transmission confirmed the total freedom of Almond's X Corps from Walker's Eighth Army jurisdiction, formalizing the division of MacArthur's ground command.[7]

The Far East Command issued a U.N. alternate order creating parallel but separate zones of advance for the Eighth Army and X Corps toward Manchuria. The central interior Taebaek Range was stamped on maps as the boundary between the two forces. Thus, all of northeastern Korea— a West Virginia-sized chunk of 19,012 square miles—was given to X Corps as its own field of battle, ''in order to facilitate control and logistical support.'' Almond's exceptional latitude meant that his corps would operate as a separate army. The order became effective upon P'yongyang's capture October 19, and MacArthur's new directive automatically governed X Corps' fateful venture into North Korea.

On the previous day, the ROK I Corps secured both Hamhung and Hungnam against light resistance. Almond's X Corps was still trapped outside Wonsan's mined waters as the Navy hammered out passages to the shore, split between Marine-laden vessels rolling through turbid ocean waves and lines of soldiers clambering up Pusan's congested loading ramps. On the Korean battlefront itself, enemy defenses toppled as Eighth Army mechanized columns spearheaded toward P'yongyang. To an impatient mobility-oriented commander like Almond, the frustration of having his powerful command adrift at sea or locked in port during such a time was overwhelming.

The flagship *Mount McKinley* dropped anchor in outer Wonsan harbor on October 19 after a single berth was specially cleared by naval minesweepers. General MacArthur and Admiral Joy decided it was still too dangerous to risk troop transports close to the beach. Both leaders wanted to avoid the kind of risk that sank the World War II liner *President Coolidge* in Espiritu Santo harbor with the loss of a regiment's worth of equipment. There was no need to take chances in debarking the 1st Marine Division because ROK I Corps was making headway without need for Marine reinforcement. Both Navy and Marine officers sighed relief that the original plans to storm Wonsan beach (which had discounted underwater mine hazards) were negated by the South Korean advance; otherwise, the division might have faced disaster.

On October 20, in accordance with MacArthur's instructions, Almond became the principal commander of Allied forces in northeast Korea. The day presented a bleak background for such a momentous occasion. Misting rain and heavy seas prevented small boat travel and closed Wonsan to normal air traffic. Some remembered the murky atmosphere as an ominous portent of future misfortune. Almond instructed General Ruffner to transfer corps personnel ashore from the *Mount McKinley* when the choppy seas subsided. Almond transferred to the battleship *Missouri* for final conferences with Admirals Doyle and Struble, and then boarded a helicopter to assume his new duties ashore.

At precisely 12:00 noon, Almond officially took command of the Allied conquest of northeast Korea. His authority extended from the ROK I Corps scattered along the Korean roadways to the 1st Marine Division offshore, the 7th Infantry Division aboard ships at Pusan, and the 3d Infantry Division in Japan, being readied as corps reinforcement. Almond awaited the assembly of these formations on north Korean soil with restless anticipation, eager to begin MacArthur's final Korean offensive.

Shipping problems and landing postponements were annoyances to Almond, but he believed victory was close at hand. His confidence was shared by the Department of the Army, which was so encouraged by MacArthur's glowing reports that it was already planning the conflict's termination. The Eighth Army was tentatively scheduled for return to Japan by Christmas, with its 2d Infantry Division in Europe by January. MacArthur intended to keep X Corps in Korea with the 3d Infantry Division and supporting units. The corps would provide security for the U.N. Commission for the Rehabilitation and Unification of Korea, and many hoped that national elections before the New Year would preclude any need for prolonged military occupation.

Pentagon officials were so heartened by projections of reduced army requirements that immediate logistical retrenchment was initiated. The Far East Command was requested to cancel all unfilled requisitions from the United States and resubmit orders based on anticipated postwar force levels. The Army wanted to avoid turning around supplies at sea, and to curtail any shipments that might become excess and ruined while in sub-standard Japanese or Korean storage awaiting return to the United States.

On the same day that Almond assumed his new sovereignty at Wonsan the Far East Command issued Operations Plan 202, outlining military tasks after the abatement of combat. The plan envisioned no Chinese or Soviet interference and a rapid elimination of enemy forces, except for guerrilla bands in remote mountain regions. X Corps was specified as the Korean occupation force headquarters. It would exercise control over all United Nations, South Korean, and advisor military personnel remaining in the country following the United Nations victory.

MacArthur wanted to retain Almond at the helm of X Corps even after cessation of major hostilities. Almond was a trusted liege who would use this critical position in faithful adherence to MacArthur's postwar Korean policies, implementing his decisions with unquestioning exactitude. Before the Wake Island conference MacArthur had alerted Almond to these intentions. His corps command role would be greatly expanded as overseer of all military occupation duties within Korea.

Almond initiated preparation for this task as early as October 8, during his visit with Ambassador Muccio while still at Inch'on. His personal log for that date reveals: ''1130—Visited Mr. Muccio in Embassy Building and discussed future of South Korean Republic with respect to UN actions and pending national elections.''[8] Thus, when X Corps landed on Korea's eastern shore, Almond had much more on his mind than mere tactical deployments.

After landing at Wonsan, Almond devoted a large share of his initial time and energy to civil rehabilitation measures. He conducted a series of tours and conferences to organize local governments, emphasizing that ''every effort within reason must be made to convince the North Korean civilians of the sincerity of the United Nations effort to establish democratic practices in North Korea.''[9]

Almond was not naive about the realities of harsh Korean warfare conditions, where cruel and brutal civilian mistreatment was common-place, but he did utilize American Civil War antecedents to guide pacification efforts. Imprinted with the misery caused his Virginian ancestors by Union food thefts, he considered cash payments for Korean farmers the basis of a sound recovery policy for the entire nation.

He displayed obsessive interest in having farmers paid in cash for any requisitioned foodstuffs. On October 21, when Almond first met the esteemed ROK Capital Division commander, Brig. Gen. Song Yo Chan, his foremost business agenda involved the "civil situation in the Capital Division area concerning food, employment, and the general attitude of the civilians." Almond insisted that the tactical briefing would not commence until General Chan "stated that he understood this and that he would carry out General Almond's desires."[10]

Almond lectured General Chan at length about food procurement from civilians in liberated territory, and how it must be on an accountable payment basis. Chan was insulted by Almond's insinuation of thievery (Almond, remarking once on Korean stevedore thefts, stated all Koreans were thieves) and was puzzled over Almond's strong views on such a petty matter. After all, North Koreans robbed villages throughout the south and now these same traditional bounties belonged to his own advancing army. Korean civilians were murdered, tortured, and raped throughout the country, and reimbursement for food seemed a very low priority for restoring social order.

Three days later, General Almond held a conference with the city leaders of Wonsan. He made a welcoming speech through an interpreter, Mr. Ahn, and requested that the various representatives voice their concerns. He was besieged immediately with requests for lumber and oil to reconstruct the fishing industry, medical supplies, land reallocation, exchange of now-valueless "red money" for South Korean *won* currency, and solution of the problems of refugees and missing residents. The representatives were treated to cigarettes and candy for attending, but soon discovered the superficiality of Almond's visits. He repeated the same speech and promises in Hamhung on October 31.

By the end of the month, Almond's pacification policy revealed the same frenzied zeal for immediate results that typified his military endeavors. The program to prepare the people for unification was a rushed series of ceremonies and proclamations announcing U.N. elections. His city conferences were cosmetic forgeries because logistical limitations prevented the relief promised. The whirlwind organizational effort by his civil affairs teams established four city and twenty-four county government councils by December, but did little to restore public order. X Corps's installed civilian police were often outmatched by, and sometimes in league with, guerrilla bands marauding the countryside.

This new burst of Almond's activity raised the ire of Marine division commander General Smith, who thought the postwar planning encouraged a lax "end-of-war atmosphere" throughout the command. He chronicled his displeasure: "On 21 October, I received a dispatch stating that upon the conclusion of hostilities it was the intention to recommend to CINCFE that the 1st Marine Division, less one RCT, be returned to the United States. The RCT not returned to the United States would be billeted at Otsu, Japan. On 24 October, we learned that X Corps had received a document, for planning purposes only, to the effect that the present Corps commander would become the Commander of the Occupation Forces. One American division, probably the 3d Infantry Division, would remain in Korea as part of the Occupation Forces. Under this plan the Eighth Army would return to Japan. The receipt of information such as this cited above could not help but spread the impression that the war was about over. There was a noticeable let-down."[11]

3. The Landings

On October 21, the Marine assault convoy was still steaming in an almost comical, circuitous route awaiting orders to proceed ashore at Wonsan. The vessels alternately sailed north for twelve hours and then steamed south for twelve hours, a maneuver disdainfully nicknamed "Operation Yo-Yo." The Marines were uncomfortably crowded on cargo-filled ships where days of inactive monotony lowered morale and physical fitness, and dysenteric outbreaks eroded troop health.[12]

The most prominent X Corps problem was the absence of unloading facilities. The naval landing group with its Marine cargo circled in the Sea of Japan while the Navy slowly cleared lanes in Wonsan channel. In Wonsan itself, shore parties, engineers, and advance billeting construction troops were preparing for the main landing. The ROK 1101st Engineer Group was busy repairing bridges and roadways throughout the Wonsan area. The ROK I Corps continued its march up the coast but the colder weather was cutting through its soldiers' tattered summer clothing and torn footwear. The South Koreans lacked jackets, sweaters, socks, shoes, and winter underwear.

Essential fuel and ammunition for the South Korean troops was unloaded from Japanese- and South Korean-manned LSTs at the small port of Kojo, thirty-nine miles south of Wonsan. On October 21, Almond overflew Kojo in the *Blue Goose*. He was actively seeking ways to circumvent the mine barrier and get the Marines stalled offshore into action. He wanted a battalion to land at Kojo, on the grounds that it could secure the supply dump and release more ROK soldiers to rejoin General Kim's main advance. Admiral Doyle rebuffed the suggestion, pointing out that Kojo had not been swept for mines and Navy LST captains could not risk their vessels in the same reckless fashion as ROK crews.

After viewing Kojo, Almond directed his pilot to fly up the coast while he searched for a suitable landing place for the 7th Infantry Division. Reconnaissance of Hungnam harbor verified the port was also mined. Almond scanned the serrated hillocks and rugged mountains, looking for a lowland pocket with suitable beaches. Nearly 105 miles north of Wonsan, he circled low over Iwon and observed its beaches. In the distance, the leading elements of the ROK 1st Regiment were approaching Pukch'ong, a city near Iwon on a main north-south road leading to Manchuria. That afternoon he briefed General Ruffner and Lieutenant Colonel McCaffrey that Iwon was suitable as a division entry point.

On October 23, 1950, General Edward Mallory Almond became the cover celebrity for *Time* Magazine. Journalist Elmer Lower honored him with a lavish article that accompanied the cover selection entitled, "Sic 'em, Ned." The country's feature general, however, was still marooned at sea. During the next two days, he lashed out his frustration at Admirals Doyle and Struble in a series of heated conferences aboard the *Missouri*. He demanded quicker action. Perceiving Doyle as overly cautious and timid, he ruefully termed the Navy's tardy D-Day as "Doyle-Day."

Determined to accelerate the pace of Navy operations, Almond stated that the 7th Infantry Division would land a regiment in a beach assault at Iwon, while the rest of the Army formation would unload at Hungnam at the earliest opportunity. This action, he summarized, would allow Barr's division to advance north, straight to the Yalu River. He informed the admirals that the Army division would no longer be landed in the wake of the Marines at Wonsan, because he was moving his corps operational base farther north to Hungnam where superior logistical facilities existed.

Admiral Doyle was astounded at Almond's choices. Hungnam's seaward approaches were mined extensively, Doyle explained, and the Navy could not start sweeping until the inner harbor at Wonsan was cleared as first scheduled. He also reminded Almond that any landing at Iwon violated the express Joint Chiefs of Staff prohibition of September 27, that "no non-Korean ground forces will be used in the northeast province bordering the Soviet Union or in the area along the Manchurian border." Almond curtly informed them that MacArthur had lifted the restriction because North Korea refused to surrender.

A flurry of high-level cables confirmed that MacArthur had indeed chosen to ignore the Pentagon-imposed buffer zone along the Korean border with China. In an extraordinary order given October 24, MacArthur commanded Walker and Almond to drive forward to the border with all possible speed and using all forces under their command. Pentagon reaction was limited to a mild rebuke in the form of a query, leaving the Navy with little choice but to accede to Almond's "full speed ahead" demands. General Collins, however, later pointed to MacArthur's October 24 command as "an example of deliberate violation of orders by the U.N. commander."[13]

The 7th Infantry Division, anchored idly off Pusan with its headquarters aboard the command ship *Eldorado* (AGC-11) since October 16, received the welcome order to sail. These orders were tempered by last-minute orders directing Colonel Powell's 17th Infantry to land at Iwon instead. Regimental officers were informed that the area was unsecured and to anticipate hostile beaches. To prepare for a possible assault landing, the soldiers and stevedores at Pusan switched the regimental assault equipment from transports to LSTs. This last scramble was completed in record time and the division sailed a day after the Marines began landing in force at Wonsan.

On October 26, after a week-long hiatus off the coast, the 1st Marine Division and accompanying corps headquarters troops went ashore uneventfully near the Wonsan airport.[14] During the afternoon, about two thousand garrison soldiers and airmen were entertained by Bob Hope and his USO troupe in one of the airfield hangars. Following the show and cocktails with Bob Hope, Almond issued his marching orders.

A corps trident of three "flying columns" would conclude the Korean campaign. The trident's right prong was Major General Kim's ROK I Corps stabbing northward along the coast (some detached regiments were temporarily holding the left flank around the Changjin and Pujon reservoirs until the Marines reached that area). The central spear was Major General Barr's 7th Infantry Division that would land at Iwon and march through Pukch'ong and P'ungsan north to Korea's Manchurian border. The left prong was Major General Smith's division, slated to relieve the South Koreans at Hamhung and advance northward past the Changjin (Chosin) Reservoir* to the Manchurian border.

The temperatures were already falling with the advent of winter. The daytime high of October 27 plummeted from 58 degrees to freezing, producing the first snowfall of the season in the mountains and high passes. The streams around Unbung were frozen and a two-inch snow frosted the Obong-san ranges to the west. The corps still lacked sufficient cold weather clothing. Basic winter necessities such as glove shells and inserts, field caps, and heavy field trousers were issued to only half the Marines and army troops leaving Inch'on for the Wonsan operation.

4. Into Battle Again

On October 27, as fields of rice glazed with their first mantle of ice, the Marines established scattered positions around the Wonsan enclave. One of these was Kojo, where the Korean LST landing point was being dismantled (the opening of Wonsan cancelled further need for this small peripheral port). The 1st Marines sent its 1st Battalion into Kojo to safeguard the nearly empty Korean supply dump and relieve its previous guardians, a battalion of the ROK 22d Regiment.

Kojo was a small rail town tucked away in a sandy cove, hemmed in by rocky peninsula ledges plunging sharply into the sea. The railroad

---

* Chosin Reservoir was the Japanese name for Changjin Reservoir, just as Fusen Reservoir was the Japanese name for Pujon Reservoir. These Japanese names were used by X Corps in 1950 and derived from maps produced by the Japanese Imperial Land Survey of 1933–1943. The corps used erroneous Japanese occupation titles for these Korean geographical features despite a corrected 1950-series of 1:250,000-scale Korean maps produced by the Army Map Service (AMS) utilizing proper Korean place names. The latter maps were reproduced by the 62d Engineer Topographic Company in time for copies of the AMS-series Changjin Mapsheet to reach X Corps during the campaign. X Corps relied on older titles, however, which caused the action to be later identified as the Chosin Reservoir engagement. The Battle of Chosin Reservoir has gained historical acceptability, but the author uses the location title Changjin in this book as a matter of geographical propriety. As a final note on Korean place names, the book romanizes names in accordance with the McCune-Reischauer System used by the U.S. government in 1950.

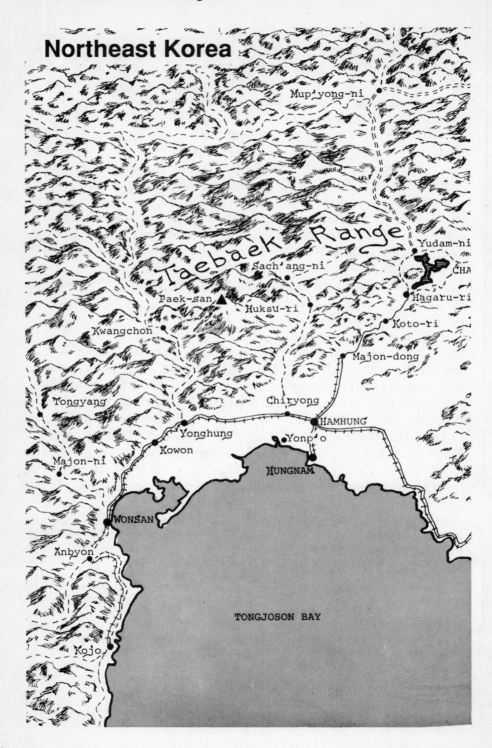

Northeast Korea

Mup'yong-ni

Taebaek Range

Yudam-ni

CHA

Sach'ang-ni

Paek-san ▲

Huksu-ri

Hagaru-ri

Kwangchon

Koto-ri

Majon-dong

Tongyang

Chiryong

HAMHUNG

Yonghung

Yonp'o

Kowon

Majon-ni

HUNGNAM

WONSAN

Anbyon

TONGJOSON BAY

Kojo

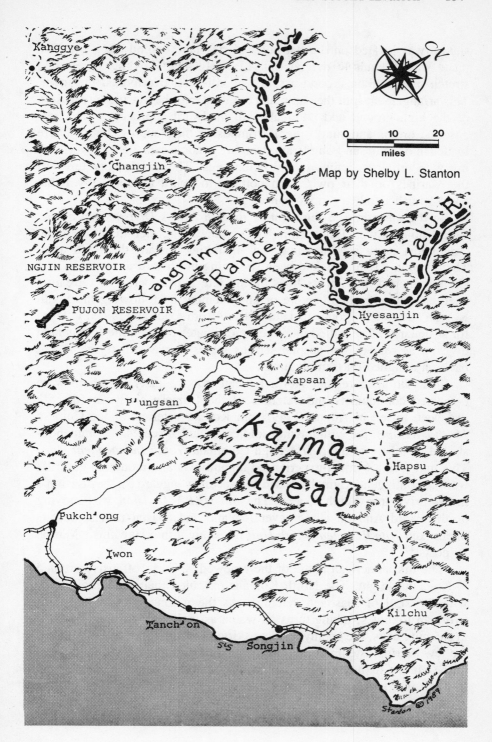

Kanggye

Changjin

NGJIN RESERVOIR

PUJON RESERVOIR

Yangnim   Range

Yalu R.

Hyesanjin

Kapsan

P'ungsan

Kaima
Plateau

Hapsu

Pukch'ong

Iwon

Tanch'on

Kilchu

S'S   Songjin

0   10   20
miles

Map by Shelby L. Stanton

Stanton © 1989

station was located on the flat bowl of rice land behind the town. The place was difficult to defend, but Lt. Col. Jack Hawkins decided to stretch his battalion around a series of hills that overlooked the town. This arrangement split the command but it offered the Marines possession of the high ground and dominated all landward approaches. The few gasoline drums and sundry items composing the "supply dump" were loaded into a Wonsan-bound train stringing gondola cars filled to overflowing with refugees, animals, and belongings. The train's departure left the Marines on their own, with nothing to guard except a town that had no further military significance.

In the meantime, a regiment of the *5th NKPA Division* led by Sr. Col. Cho Il Kwon (alias Kim Ku Yome, the former director of the communist party at Hamhung) was marching toward the Kojo area. The division's remnants had been streaming northward after the ROK I Corps punched through its lines during late September. The retreating enemy soldiers evaded capture or encirclement by following the South Korean advance in groups that shied away from roads and raided villages for sustenance. The Allied intelligence estimates counted the fragmented division as routed, but despite serious losses it was still trying to fall back on assigned reassembly areas.

In addition to regular North Korean troops, many of whom were dedicated communists and veterans of the Chinese civil war (the *5th* had been raised in August 1949 from Korean veterans of the Chinese *164th Division*), the withdrawing soldiers included scores of commando-skilled members of the *NKPA* High Command *766th Independent Unit*. This unit was a combat-experienced amphibious and mountain guerrilla warfare contingent originally raised as a special vanguard for the division's initial drive into South Korea. The *5th NKPA Division* was moving north toward Anbyon along several inland and coastal routes, and its intermixed *10th Regiment/766th Unit* ran straight into Hawkins's Marine outposts.[15]

The first American battle of the renewed X Corps offensive erupted at Kojo that night. The North Koreans executed their nocturnal attack with the skill of seasoned veterans. As the marines shivered in their two-man foxholes, taking turns on watch as their partners slept huddled in sleeping bags, the enemy soldiers skirted around or silently eliminated the few Marine listening posts. They crawled within hand-grenade range of the Marine foxholes in the darkness before being detected and shouted in English, "Don't shoot! We're friends!"

Suddenly the black sky was lit by red and green flares and the whistle of machine gun tracers pierced the night cold. The North Koreans stormed through the Marine lines of Company B, killing many marines in their sleeping bags and striking others down with rifle butts and bayonets. The Marine positions were toppled like a row of dominoes from both ends, and the enemy secured the hilltops in a welter of confused, close-in fighting.

The dazed Marines from the smashed company retreated in small groups or by individual effort. One decimated platoon managed to extricate itself after Sgt. Clayton Roberts manned a .30-cal. Browning machine gun and held off clusters of attackers, defending the weapon until he was killed. The battered company regrouped on the railroad south of the station and formed a compact perimeter. They spent the rest of night beating off prowling attacks with the assistance of supporting mortars that blanketed the darkness beyond.

The North Korean regiment, however, was just pushing through the area and swung inland after encountering the Marine defenses. The small airstrip was briefly captured and some forces entered the town, but combat became desultory after daybreak and ceased by 10 A.M. Company B accounted for many of its missing men and spent the morning withdrawing slowly through the leg-wrenching mud and water of the frosted rice paddies, carrying the wounded in sagging wet ponchos.

At 10:15 A.M., Almond was in conference with General Smith at Marine division headquarters. Their talk was interrupted when a message arrived from the Kojo defenders. The report stated that a determined enemy multi-directional attack from sunset to sunrise had overrun some positions and caused high casualties. The message had been transcribed in the heat of battle and overstated the danger (asking for a regiment "if the position is to be held"), asked permission to withdraw, and closed with a plea to "send all available helicopters for the wounded."[16]

Almond was infuriated at receiving first word of the Kojo engagement twelve hours after the action started, exclaiming "the delay in receiving the information is inexcusable!"[17] He was also peeved that the Marines considered pulling out and suspected they were either vacillating or panicked. Almond wanted no withdrawals under any circumstances. Almond's tantrum did not impress Smith, who believed that the situation was probably under control.

Almond scurried off to the command post of the 7th Marines to find the regimental commander and direct relief attempts, but Puller intercepted him on the road. He informed Almond that his Marines had the situation in hand, noting that the battalion had regained contact with the company cut off in the night fighting, that a destroyer had been bombarding Kojo with direct gunfire since daybreak and air strikes were being used against the town, and that a reinforcing battalion was moving into the area. The incessant air and naval pummeling reduced Kojo to burning shambles as the *5th NKPA Division* melted into the mountains.

General Almond toured positions around Wonsan and spent the evening moving his gear from the headquarters general-purpose tent into his personal van, which was brought ashore as priority cargo. The 2½-ton truck van and trailer included a refrigerator, alfresco shower, generator, heater, flush toilet, as well as fancy dining china and cutlery. The van's accommodations were sparse considering his three-star position, but enough to cause resentment. For instance, officers complained that fresh water was provided to Almond's heated shower tent, while troops in Wonsan went without sufficient drinking water until the engineers drilled wells.

On the same day that the Marines were mopping up Kojo and Almond was refurbishing his van, General Kim's ROK I Corps was advancing in conformity with orders to secure the X Corps flank until Marine arrival. The high mountains divided this South Korean advance into a series of disconnected reconnaissance ventures. Regiments and battalions became splintered as they followed the twisting roads into a broken wilderness of jagged mountain ranges. Vast barren river valleys and uncharted razorback peaks separated the minuscule pathways. As units stabbed farther inland, their military frontages were squeezed to the width of single oxcart lanes, and maps became useful only as fire starters in the stinging cold. The sharp, reverberating sounds of gunfire in the boulder-strewn canyons echoed their slender progress.

The 26th Regiment of the ROK 3d Division was moving slowly north of Sudong toward Hagaru-ri. The regiment had been activated just prior to the Allied September offensive by a KMAG captain, Frank W. Lukas, with the aid of two ROK interpreters and the Taegu police department. The Korean police garnered over one thousand "draftees" off the city streets in less than forty-eight hours and formed them into squads, platoons, companies, and battalions on the spot. Captain Lukas designated the "most intelligent-appearing recruits" as NCOs and platoon leaders. Those who helped find people were made into regiment and battalion officers. The new regiment marched outside Taegu, where each man was given a rifle and fired nine rounds. The soldiers, still clad in mixed civilian and army clothing or school uniforms, were in battle a few days later. The ROK 26th Regiment would receive no formal training until April of 1951.[18]

The hapless 26th smashed into the first Chinese defenders south of the Changjin reservoir. The South Koreans expected the encounter to be against a normal North Korean rear guard, which would retire after a certain amount of initial resistance. Instead the skirmish intensified until the South Koreans were forced to pull back. During the engagement, the South Koreans managed to take some prisoners and discovered they were fighting Chinese. They were members of the *370th Regiment, 124th Chinese People's Liberation Army (PLA) Division*, which had crossed secretly into Korea within the past week.

General Almond still believed MacArthur's assurances that no active Chinese participation was expected. Lieutenant Colonel Quinn, his intelligence chief, expressed disbelief that Chinese prisoners were actually captured. On October 29, his X Corps periodic intelligence report qualified the incident's importance:

> This information has not been confirmed and is not accepted at this time. However, should the presence of this unit later be verified, it would be the first definite evidence of large-scale intervention of Chinese forces as integral units in the Korean conflict. The significance of such a move would be to greatly augment the enemy's capability to defend or to *resume the offensive* [emphasis added]. . . . However, these individuals may have been sent as replacements and fillers rather than as members of CCF [Communist Chinese Force] units. It is possible that entire groups of reinforcements may have been employed as groups, thereby giving rise to the erroneous impression that CCF units may be engaged.[19]

Almond was more apprehensive about the impact of the Kojo attack on security in the southern portion of his extensive corps zone. He was infuriated with Fred Sparks of the *Chicago News,* who described a "Guerrilla Wall around Wonsan." Unfortunately, intelligence revealed that large groups of bypassed North Korean troops were being instructed to operate behind lines in their present areas instead of retreating north.

Almond decided to patrol his southern region with special task forces rather than displace units committed to the northern offensive. The X

Corps special operations battalion was sent to Manpo-ri with orders to intercept and destroy enemy troops moving around the western corps flank, held by the Marines. On October 30, Task Force Baker, commanded by Brig. Gen. Shin Hoyun-Jun and consisting of the 1st, 3d, and 5th Korean Marine Battalions, was organized at Wonsan. The unit was sent to Kosong with orders to control the coastline south to the 38th Parallel.

5. The Chinese Factor

The far more significant riddle of the Chinese front-line presence continued to plague the South Korean troops, who were engaged in costly combat for possession of the reservoir's large hydroelectric plants. Casualties were heavy, and the enemy fought with the vigor of fresh, confident troops instead of weakened, retreating survivors. Around Sudong, the ROK 26th Regiment clashed with Chinese troops who were supported by North Korean tanks and heavy mortars. On October 29, the regiment captured sixteen more Chinese prisoners before being counterattacked and driven back to Hadae-ri. General Kim of ROK I Corps telephoned Almond about the incident.

On the afternoon of October 30, Almond flew by L-17 aircraft to Hamhung to meet General Kim and view the prisoners. He was accompanied by Lieutenant Colonel Glass from the G2 office, deputy operations officer Lieutenant Colonel Mildren, and his aide, Captain Ladd. Almond conferred with Kim at the ROK I Corps headquarters, advising him that Marine units were moving to the Hamhung area immediately, and would proceed to the battlefront south of the reservoir to relieve the South Koreans on November 2.

General Almond then inspected the sixteen Chinese prisoners captured near Sudong. Most of the captives were from a heavy mortar company of the *370th PLA Regiment,* had not eaten for three days, and were somewhat disheveled—having been relieved of fur-lined caps and boots by their captors. Their bulky, shapeless padded cotton cloth uniforms were the standard basic unadorned issue of the Chinese People's Liberation Army. He interrogated each prisoner through an interpreter, out of hearing from the others, and marched them around to see if they could keep formation. Almond confided to his subordinates that these Orientals were "not intelligent" and ridiculed their appearance, calling them a bunch of Chinese laundrymen.[20]

Mildren remembered, "I'll never forget General Almond going up and looking at those Chinese we had captured. They were the most decrepit looking bunch you have ever run into. Some of them didn't even have shoes. They had big gunny sacks wrapped around their feet. General Almond tried to put them through some close order drill through an interpreter and they looked like a mob. And so, we couldn't believe the Chinese [regular army] was there. Still, Jimmy Polk, our [Army] G2, had been warning that there was going to be a [Chinese] build-up, but I'm convinced to this day that nobody in that [Far East Command] theater realized that the Chinese were there."[21]

Whatever Almond's initial impressions, Lieutenant Colonel Glass observed that the prisoners were well-fed and healthy, averaged twenty-eight to thirty years of age, were wearing Chinese winter quilted uniforms, and spoke in the Peking and North Manchurian dialects. They freely discussed their division activities. The *124th PLA Division,* stationed at Tianjin in China, had moved to Tonghua in southern Manchuria during July 1950, and had crossed the Yalu River in mid-October. Once in Korea, their division had marched southwest to the reservoir with their equipment on pack horses and mules. These captives, in Glass's opinion, were Chinese regulars and he briefed Almond accordingly. At 6 P.M., Almond dispatched a personal radio message direct to MacArthur, informing him that the corps had captured Chinese army troops.

Chinese forces were definitely on the front, although the extent of their presence was in dispute. Almond realized it was now imperative to get the rest of his corps into action. The 7th Infantry Division began landing over the Iwon beaches on October 29, but the seemingly routine, unopposed debarkation suddenly ran into difficulties as the seas roughened. Bulldozed sand ramps to the LSTs were washed away and the unloading of Colonel MacLean's regiment was cancelled by the worsening weather.

More ill winds were blowing in the political direction. On the afternoon of October 29, President Rhee was expected to make a triumphant arrival at Hamhung. Almond held extensive meetings with Major Sieminski that morning, lining up public information office coverage, and then flew out to Hamhung to inspect final arrangements for the liberation ceremony. After lunch, Almond was alerted that Rhee's trip was cancelled. The American Embassy was afraid such a visit might invoke China's wrath as well as taint sensitive U.N. plans to reunify Korea through disinterested elections.

By the end of October, X Corps redeployed over sixty thousand troops into northeastern Korea. Almond was still confident that his last thrust into the Korean interior could be accomplished quickly. Accelerated pursuit operations would keep the scattered North Korean army remnants in disarray and ease the job of completing their destruction. He felt the corps could achieve its goal before foreign intervention became a deciding factor.

Already the shifting winds of late fall were whipping tent flaps with cold strong winds. Allied troops huddled closer to their fire barrels throughout the corps zone. Although winter clothing and other logistical shortfalls remained, Almond believed that temporary wartime discomfort would be rewarded by mission conclusion in time to celebrate the New Year.

Perhaps the most prophetic October discovery, however, was made accidentally by a pair of rear-echelon clerks shifting through crated mountains of general cargo dumped on the sands of Wonsan beach. The Corps adjutant general, Lt. Col. Frank W. Roberts, had instructed the men to search through stacks of supplies and locate field desks, file cabinets, and other necessary shop gear. The two clerks conducted an exhausting three-day "hunt" before returning on October 30 with their only results: two cases full of Purple Heart medals.[22]

Notes

1. X Corps Commanding General's Diary Extracts, dtd 12 October 1950.
2. Dept. of the Army, *Combat Support in Korea,* pp. 175, 186.
3. X Corps Commanding General's Diary Extracts, dtd 14 October 1950.
4. X Corps G-3 Summary, 11 October 1950, Item J-61.
5. Schnabel, p. 210.
6. Schnabel, pp. 213, 214.
7. CINCFE Radio Cable 66549 to Eighth Army, dtd 16 October 1950.
8. X Corps Commanding General's Diary Extracts, dtd 8 October 1950.
9. X Corps Commanding General's Diary Extracts, dtd 21 October 1950.
10. Ibid., Item 1300 (a) and (b).
11. U.S. Marine Corps Historical Branch, Notes by Lt. Gen. Oliver P. Smith on the "Operations of the 1st Marine Division during the First Nine Months of the Korean War," p. 403.
12. Montross and Canzona, Vol. III, pp. 30, 31.
13. Schnabel, footnote on p. 218, citing the MacArthur Hearings.
14. Five LSTs carrying elements of the 1st Marine Division's engineers, shore party battalion, and combat service group landed at Wonsan on October 25. The main landing, however, was made October 26. Montross and Canzona, Vol. III, p. 39.
15. Far East Command Military Intelligence Section, *History of the North Korean Army,* dtd 31 July 1952, pp. 60, 61.
16. X Corps Chronological Narrative, dtd 28 October 1950, Item J-39.
17. X Corps Commanding General's Diary Extracts, dtd 28 October 1950.
18. Maj. Robert K. Sawyer, *Military Advisors in Korea: KMAG in Peace and War,* Department of the Army: 1962, p. 144.
19. X Corps G-2 Section Periodic Intelligence Report No. 33, dtd 29 October 1950, p. 3, Section V-2.
20. Quote from X Corps Commanding General's Diary, dtd 30 October 1950.
21. U.S. Army Military History Institute, Senior Officers Oral History Program Proj. 80-3, Interview of Gen. Frank T. Mildren by Col. James T. Scott, 1980, p. 117.
22. X Corps AG 314.7-G file letter, dtd 31 October 1950, contained in X Corps War Diary for 30 October 1950.

CHAPTER 8

MOUNTAIN WARFARE

1. Almond's Legions

At the beginning of November 1950, General Almond's X Corps in the east and General Walker's Eighth Army on the western front were poised for MacArthur's final strike of the Korean war. Both UN field commands, however, were separated from the distant Yalu River— MacArthur's objective for victory—by an immense swath of mountainous territory. X Corps alone was assigned a smaller-sized chunk of real estate with a four hundred-mile-wide front that approximated the length of the Franco-German border. Unless conquest was achieved early, the 84,785 troops of X Corps faced an uncertain winter campaign across this rugged Korean hinterland.[1]

There was little likelihood, in the viewpoint of most corps analysts, that North Korea could resist effectively much longer. Except for guerrilla nuisances and a final stand "somewhere" in the remote back country, the *NKPA* was judged to be finished. The real concern revolved around Chinese military intentions. MacArthur was confident of China's unpreparedness to confront the United Nations in open warfare, but he expected masses of Chinese troops to enter Korea under the guise of volunteer assistance.

According to MacArthur, the only way to strip away this artifice of Chinese intervention was to unify Korea quickly under American-backed UN protection. He wanted the southern bank of the Yalu River, a clearly defined international border, manned by infantry at critical crossing points. Other river crossing points could be sealed with aerial and naval weaponry, prohibiting further Chinese military "adventurism" to the south.

To solidify UN mastery over the Yalu, it was imperative to reach the Manchurian border on a broad front. MacArthur was convinced that rapid emplacement of Allied forces along Korea's northern border would terminate the Korean communist regime's claim to territorial legitimacy. This fait accompli would deprive China of any valid excuse to intervene in North Korea's behalf. Thus, the supreme commander believed that a quick push to the Manchurian border offered the best chance to end the war and safeguard against Chinese action.

Almond deployed his corps in strict compliance with MacArthur's instructions. To reach its designated Yalu River boundary, X Corps would have to traverse a jumbled tangle of high mountain ranges. The projected offensive presented difficulties that Almond had never experienced in his wartime Italian campaigning. In Italy, his division had hugged the coast in a supplemental drive that merely brushed the fringes of the Italian Apennine spine. Flank support in Italy had been assured by an Allied army advancing in unison; fire support was provided by scores of heavy artillery battalions and bomber squadrons; detailed charts benefitted from centuries of recorded surveys; and enemy dispositions and strengths were known.

In Korea, Almond's corps would have to stab across a huge mountain wasteland as a sole venture, largely away from the sea, devoid of heavy artillery or concentrated aerial support, and reliant on antiquated Japanese maps (which marked many areas as unexplored). The broken terrain prevented the corps from striking on a united front, because units following the road defiles were forced to split along divergent routes of advance. Knowledge of enemy dispositions was limited to a few prisoners and suspicions about *NKPA* opposition, while the extent and intentions of newly discovered Chinese forces were unknown. Intelligence analysis of Chinese motivations ranged from token late-war stiffening for their Korean ally to preparations for a third world war.

Against this backdrop of uncertainty, Almond adopted MacArthur's philosophy. He decided to tackle his assigned chunk of Korean mountain wilderness by speed of action and liberal use of multiple-unit spearheads. Almond envisioned moving X Corps northward in a broad fan-like advance against melting North Korean resistance. While regimental task forces would be separated beyond mutual supporting range, their exposed flanks could be safeguarded from overland counterattack by momentum, the nature of the difficult terrain, and enemy disorganization. Almond committed the bulk of his corps to the main attack in order to reach and maximize border security along the Yalu. Few units could be spared for anti-guerrilla duty, line-of-communication protection, or as precautionary corps reserves.

At the same time, three divisions of the world's largest military force, the Chinese People's Liberation Army, were already marching rapidly through North Korea on a collision course with X Corps. Although Allied intelligence remained mystified by Chinese intentions, an agent confirmed indications of lasting PLA entry into northeastern Korea during the first week of November. He reported all Korean road signs between Hoeryong and Chongjin had been taken down and replaced with signs containing Chinese characters.[2]

X Corps was also being bolstered by another division, the 3d Infantry Division under Maj. Gen. Robert H. Soule. This division had been stationed at Fort Benning, Georgia, at the outbreak of the Korean war, but manned at one-third cadre strength (5,179 men when authorized 18,894) as late as August 6. When the Joint Chiefs of Staff decided to send the division as emergency reinforcement to Japan, additional personnel were taken from almost every post in the United States. Its two regiments, the 7th and 15th Infantry, filled slowly because all installations had been previously combed for Korean-bound replacements.[3]

Even these drastic measures failed to boost regiments to wartime complements, and both regiments received the usual KATUSA (Korean Augmentation to U.S. Army) boost while in Japan undergoing final training for Korea. Empty places in the ranks were filled by 8,500 freshly dragooned South Korean recruits without knowledge of English, sanitation, or military skills. Division pilot Benjamin S. Silver recounted, "One day an American sergeant was teaching the disassembly of the machine gun. When he came to a particular part, he stopped and scratched his head because it itched, and then continued. When asked to take the same gun apart one of the Korean recruits did it precisely as the sergeant had shown him, to include stopping at the same step to scratch his head."[4] Ten-man squads often contained eight Koreans, and the hapless

3d Infantry Division was consigned to mediocrity under such circumstances.

The Puerto Rican 65th Infantry was added hastily on October 6 as the division's third regiment. The 65th Infantry had been constituted in March 1899 as the Puerto Rico Regiment of Volunteer Infantry, and had served as the main Puerto Rican component of the regular army since 1908.[5] When the understrength "Sixty-Feeth" was assembled hastily for combat in Korea, the move provoked harsh criticism and even outrage. Pfc. Rafael A. Zapata of Company K complained to the highest inspector general office in Puerto Rico, writing on behalf of a group of 172 fellow soldiers who had just enlisted in the Army at Fort Buchanan on May 18. "We signed papers stating; 'I agree to enlist for service at the Department of Panama Canal Zone Units.' How is it that we are been [sic] sent over to the Far East Command? Request that for the benefit of future enlistees in the territory of Puerto Rico, appropriate action be taken to correct this situation."[6]

The situation was correct: the U.S. Army was sending all available resources into the maelstrom. In fact, the 65th Infantry continued to fill its ranks as it passed through the Panama Canal. Acting on War Department orders, the commander skimmed troops from the 33d Infantry at Fort Kobbe, Canal Zone. The post commander obliged by ridding the fort of soldiers he considered less desirable, especially blacks. The need for infantry was so great in Korea that the 65th Regimental Combat Team was unloaded directly at Pusan and spent two months battling on the Eighth Army front before being released to join X Corps on the last day of October.

General Almond—who had boasted that, "I do not agree that integration improves military efficiency; I believe that it weakens it" because "there is no question in my mind of the inherent differences in races"— was obviously displeased when he received the mixed white-black-hispanic 65th Infantry (described officially by the Army as being composed of white Puerto Ricans, Virgin Island negroes, negroes from the United States, Americans of Japanese descent, and South Koreans). Almond was equally upset with Lt. Col. William W. Harris, the regimental commander who championed the unique character and battle-worthiness of his mixed unit. Almond stated, "These persons who promulgate and enforce such [integration] policies either have not the understanding of the problem, or they do not have the intestinal fortitude to do what they think if they do understand it."[7]

Almond inspected the 65th Infantry's debarkation at Wonsan on November 5 and curtly informed Harris that he "didn't have much confidence in these colored troops," leaving Harris to plead the "whiteness" of many of his soldiers and how others with "Latin pride" had already excelled in earlier Korean fighting.[8] This argument, of course, left little impression on Almond, whose prejudice was so ingrained that he classified integration-minded officers as dangers to the military establishment: "There is no question in my mind of the inherent differences in races. This is not racism—it is common sense and understanding. Those who ignore these differences merely interfere with the combat effectiveness of battle units."[9]

By this stage of the conflict, the mobilization and reserve call-ups sparked protests from many concerned citizens. Mrs. Oard wrote a letter of complaint that reached X Corps in December,

I'm writing in regard to my husband, Ed L. Oard, being in the Enlisted Reserve Corps. He was a reserve in the signal corps, with a critical MOS [Military Occupational Specialty] number 766 High speed radio operator. When they swore him in the 19th day of January 1946 he was told that if he was ever called back into active duty he would go back into the same branch, Signal Corps, with the same rating and he would not ever have to go overseas again. That was the main reason he stayed in the reserves. He was in combat (4 battle stars, 2 [invasion] arrowheads) almost two years in World War II and he didn't want to have to go through it again. They were lied to as usual because my husband was called back August 21 because of his MOS number. . . . He was put in Field Artillery instead of Signal Corps and was told there wasn't any 766 MOS anymore and no high speed radio operators. . . . Now, just what kind of a deal is it? My husband has also been alerted [for Korea].

These fellows go out and risk their lives and then fall for all this bunk they were told and look how they were treated. Maybe they do need experienced guys over there [Korea]; but fellows that were in combat before, just aren't able to take it again. There are so many that were in the service; but never overseas, that should go before veterans that were in combat before. I'd just like an explanation of such low methods. My husband should be in a signal outfit training troops on this side; like he was told.[10]

The letter was answered briskly by the assistant adjutant of X Corps, informing her that Oard was now a sergeant first class on the front line, and concluding with the hollow ring of a higher headquarter's suggested format,

> It is regrettable that the present critical international situation has necessitated the recalling to active service of so many men and women of our reserve forces. No doubt this has separated many families in our country and has caused increased hardship for them. It is through the patriotism of Sergeant Oard and others with prior military service, which has enabled us to form a reserve force to meet emergencies such as exist today.[11]

Many letters of complaint received by X Corps addressed the growing unpopularity of sending particular persons into this non-declared war, while others underscored the sometimes-harsh practices of the "old Army." One group of six soldiers fled the 32d Infantry "because conditions had become unbearable and there appeared no way of obtaining relief within their unit":

> Upon their arrival in Iwon, on or about 5 November 1950, they were segregated from the rest of the company and placed into a unit publicly announced as the Eight-Ball Squad. Originally eight men were so assigned. This squad performed all fatigue details for the company, including digging of latrines and sumps, kitchen police, cutting of firewood, etc. All other members of the company were forbidden to associate with them. At meal time this included their being required to wait until the rest of the company had been fed, then being marched to mess. Note: half of the group were detailed as KP's each day, those off KP that day were required to march.
>
> They requested permission to see their company commander, who interviewed them once, telling them, in effect, that they were 'eight-balls' and would stay in that squad until he saw fit to relieve them. His reply to their request to see the regimental commander or an inspector general was essentially the same. They were required to perform hard labor from approximately 0600 hours until well after dark, thus having no time to write letters. Petition to the First Sergeant for sufficient daylight time to write resulted in additional work. . . . On November 18, they informed Sergeant [name deleted] of their intent to leave the unit AWOL [absent without leave], but he made no effort to deter them.
>
> Three of the four soldiers [who returned from AWOL] admit having been in trouble before, but all state they have not been in trouble since arrival in Korea, further stating they had been awarded the Combat Medical Badge. All claim the only reason given to them for being punished was

loss of individual equipment which they allege was lost under combat conditions and during periods of action when the items were not under their control. All four of the soldiers stated they did not want to return to their unit because they feared corporal punishment at the hands of the First Sergeant.[12]

Despite the misunderstanding of several soldiers regarding their enlistment contracts, the concern of loved ones back home, and the unfortunate treatment dished out to selected soldiers in some units, the overall fighting spirit of X Corps was quite high. The air of impending victory encouraged by the high command included the knowledge that speedy resolution of the conflict would wipe the slate clean of most war-related problems.

2. The Advance Begins

On November 1, as the advance party of the 3d Infantry Division landed at Wonsan, X Corps was still largely confined to the lowlands and wooded foothills around Wonsan and Hamhung. This strip of coastline was hemmed in by the wall of the Taebaek Range in the west and the even higher Yangnim Range to the north. The elevations of both mountain barriers rose seven to eight thousand feet. Allied wheeled movement was blocked in many places. Where narrow corridors existed, advancing Allied columns were compressed along highland roads with scant maneuver option.

The southern corps operational area was dominated by the steep Taebaek range, while its western area of operations fell under the shadow of the snow-capped Yangnim mountains. The rocky domes of the barren, snow-scraped Kaima Plateau composed the eastern portion of the corps sector. The ROK I Corps advancing along the coastal route had already reached the critical crossroads of Kilchu, midway between Hungnam and the Russian border. The ROK Capital Division pushed inland as far north as P'ungsan in this mountain heartland east of 6,274-foot Puksubaek-san, one of Korea's highest mountains.

On the last day of October, Colonel Powell's 17th Infantry of the 7th Infantry Division moved by truck 120 miles north along a dirt road from its landing beaches at Iwon to P'ungsan. This route was designated as the division's main axis of attack toward the border. The American combat team of two infantry battalions, an artillery battalion, and an engineer company reached P'ungsan in the late afternoon. Powell's men prepared to relieve the ROK Capital Division's 1st Regiment at the town and advance to the border fifty miles further north. With daylight fading fast, however, Colonel Powell established a quick perimeter. American units were intermixed with South Korean units already present, and there was insufficient coordination.

Two leading howitzer batteries from the 49th Field Artillery Battalion were emplaced before dark, but during the night enemy probing attacks drove the South Korean troops from their positions and unmasked these emplacements. At 5:50 on the morning of November 1, before the 17th Infantry could jump off on its own offensive, a withering barrage of North Korean artillery and mortar fire swept across regiment elements situated west of the town.

About an hour later the barrage lifted and the *71st NKPA Regiment* stormed the American lines. Intense enemy machine gun fire engulfed the artillerymen of Capt. William T. Kidd's Battery B, as North Korean troops outflanked the infantry company protecting the 105mm howitzers and charged the battery through gaps left by the South Koreans. Enemy troops rushed the howitzers and engaged the crewmen in a melee of close-range combat that prevented them from firing their lowered tubes. Supporting units ringed the endangered battery with a curtain of final protective mortar and artillery fire that killed many *NKPA* shock troops, but the proximity of the fighting prevented any closer shelling without hitting friendly troops.

The artillerymen dueled with North Korean infantry for possession of their howitzers, using rifles and vehicle-mounted machine guns. The firing was almost continuous but a temporary lull developed when the North Koreans seemed to be running low on small arms ammunition. Sergeant Mitchell used this opportunity to dash forward with a handful of volunteers and get a howitzer into action. Mitchell's men braved enemy snipers and submachine gunners to fire twelve rounds of high explosive and white phosphorous directly into concentrations of nearby enemy troops. The North Koreans renewed their rate of fire and drove the cannoneers back to their foxholes.

For over an hour, the battery's survival was in doubt as more North Koreans hurled themselves at the battery's weakened lines. Captain Kidd, the artillery commander, directed the supporting fire of the other battery seven hundred yards away. He maintained the barrage of whirling steel and heaving earth around the trapped Americans. Scores of enemy troops were killed as they rushed forward and a cluster of huts suspected of concealing enemy crew-served weapons was destroyed. The fury of the sustained protective fire finally broke the back of the enemy assault, and Marine fighter-bombers chased the North Koreans into the granite badlands.[13]

As the smoke cleared over the shabby outskirts of P'ungsan, the L-5 Stinson *Blue Goose* arrived with General Almond on board. From the air, the Kaima Plateau's bleak landscape of jagged ridges and clay-stone river valleys stretched endlessly into the distance, appearing almost like the surface of a barren alien moon. After a hasty frontline inspection, the *Blue Goose* carried Almond back to Iwon and landed right on the beach where the division was continuing to come ashore.

At the same time, General Kim's ROK I Corps was speeding northeast along the coastal road past Songjin. The point motorized "flying column" was the hard-hitting mobile Cavalry Regiment of the Capital Division. These wheeled Koreans were supplied by LSTs. Their blitzkrieg-style advance covered ground so fast that they outdistanced the security troops and engineers needed for reliable service on the coast highway. The regiment, however, was forced to swing temporarily inland just north of Songjin, where the coast route branched away from the sea to cut across a jagged patch of mountains.

The major town on this interior stretch of highway was Kilchu and the *507th NKPA Brigade* occupied the choke-point with its defenses safely beyond the range of naval gunfire. On November 3, the South Korean column became embroiled in a major battle outside the town. The ROK Capital Division committed another regiment to outflank Kilchu when the 1st Regiment from P'ungsan arrived to join the attack. The reinforced South Korean maneuver succeeded in capturing the town within two days.

In the meantime, the spearhead 17th Infantry brushed past light resistance as it advanced slowly north in conjunction with strong patrols monitoring the P'ungsan vicinity. By November 7, the greater portion of the enemy forces had withdrawn north of the Ungi River and were preparing defensive positions on the high ground overlooking the river. The division was completely ashore by November 9, when Colonel Beauchamp's 32d Infantry landed behind Colonel MacLean's 31st Infantry, which had arrived November 4. While Beauchamp moved up the P'ungsan road, MacLean was moving his regiment into the wall of mountains between the advancing 17th Infantry and the Pujon Reservoir, just east of the Changjin Reservoir close to the Marine sector.

On November 1, Colonel Litzenberg's 7th Marines were trucked to the front north of Hamhung to relieve the ROK 26th Regiment near Majon-dong. The South Korean troops had smashed into Chinese defenses just beyond this town, where the flat rice-valley road ascended into rolling, tree-covered 2,500-foot foothills. During the night and early morning, radiation fogs formed in the mountain pockets. On November 2, as the fog dissipated, the Marines began their offensive to clear the main road leading to their first objective, Sudong.

Enemy observers watched the Marines advancing along the gravel-dirt road and fanning out to climb the wooded elevations on either side. Chinese machine guns, sandwiched between boulders and protected by rocky overhangs on the higher ground, clattered incessantly throughout the day. Air strikes and artillery were used against the commanding ridges as the tempo of fighting increased. Marine fire teams were exposed to accurate enemy fire as they clambered over rocks and struggled uphill to reach designated summits. Cries for corpsmen rang out as marines dropped in the meadow grass and conifer forested slopes.

By nightfall, Litzenberg's battle-weary troops halted on the lower flanks of two prominent mountains overlooking the road. Efforts to reach the summits of both Hills 678 and 727 were suspended until morning. The leading battalion, however, was just a road-bend short of reaching Sudong. The elongated regimental perimeter stretched over three thousand meters along the main road, but it was actually a series of disconnected company positions staked out in foxholes along the ridges and road bed.

Just after midnight, the *371st Regiment, 124th PLA Division* stormed both sides of this Marine line in a well-executed double envelopment. The nocturnal solitude was split by blaring bugles, the booming of detonating grenades, and the rattle of rifles and submachine guns. The crescendo of fire echoed and reverberated among the rocks into a deafening roar. Marine positions crumpled under the shock of the attack as grenade exchanges showered the slopes with flashing explosions. The Chinese surged downhill through undefended gaps and spilled out into the valley road. In the midst of this confusion, a T34 clanked down the same road unchallenged, fired some poorly aimed rounds, wiped out a 3.5-inch rocket team after taking a hit in exchange, and disappeared around a bend in the road.[14]

The situation at daybreak on November 3 appeared bleak. The Chinese were in control of the dominating peaks and part of the main route where they established a roadblock. The two leading battalions of the

7th Marines were isolated. Emergency ammunition resupply was parachuted to one beleaguered group. The Marines spent the day in hard combat that slowly reduced the Chinese grip on the main supply lane. Massed artillery fire and aerial bombing pummelled the high ground as Marine infantry recaptured lost positions. Working close to the raining shield of high explosive and white phosphorous shells, the Marine riflemen methodically eliminated the enemy defenders and eradicated the roadblock.

During the night of November 3–4, the *124th PLA Division* pulled back to new blocking positions. The Marine route of advance lay along one narrow road that wound through a deep gorge before climbing along the edge of cliffs some twelve miles to the top of the plateau leading to the Changjin Reservoir. This tortuous segment was known as Funchilin Pass.

The 7th Marines followed this withdrawal by dispatching its reconnaissance company in jeeps, some trailing cart-loads of 75mm recoilless rifles and 3.5-inch rocket launchers. Covered by Marine aircraft overhead, this jeep convoy barrelled up the main road and into Chinhung-ni at the base of the steep Funchilin Pass incline. The motorized recon marines surprised and killed several Chinese soldiers in the town and roared up the road opposite the cable-car station, which they took under fire.

Hidden alongside the road opposite the tramway station were four camouflaged North Korean tanks. The recon platoon leader and two of his men climbed on the turret of one tank they found nestled in piles of leaves and brush. Corp. Joseph E. McDermott smashed the glass out of the periscope and SSgt. Richard B. Twohey tossed in a grenade as the tank began moving forward. A second grenade was used in the same manner to finish its crew. The next tank was destroyed in a more conventional manner after it roared out of a thatched hut, by concentrated antitank fire followed by Corsair five-inch wing rockets. The crews of the remaining two tanks surrendered and the Marines claimed final destruction of the *344th NKPA Tank Regiment*.

The battle to clear Funchilin Pass revolved around the fight for the high ground overlooking the looping hairpin turn as the road scaled the most treacherous portion of the pass. The commanding heights of Hills 987 and 891 were turned into mountain bastions by the Chinese, whose timber bunkers and entrenchments were backed up by mortars in rocky enclaves. The main supply road was cut into Hill 891, and clearing this formidable terrain obstacle became the main focus of Marine action.

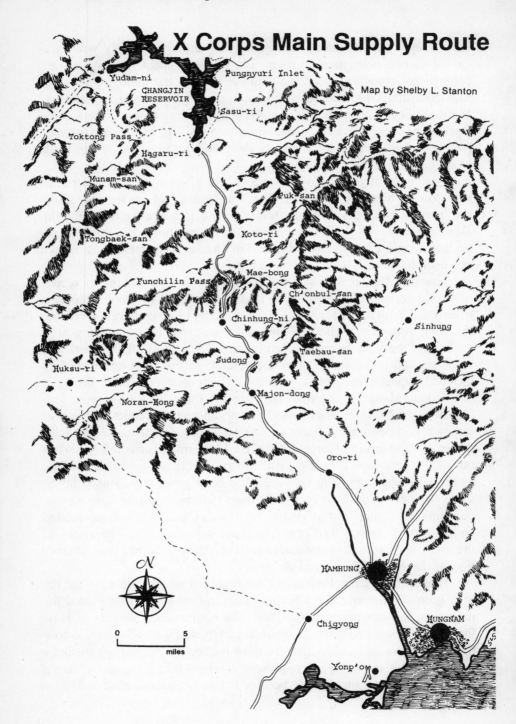

X Corps Main Supply Route

Yudam-ni

Pungnyuri Inlet

CHANGJIN
RESERVOIR

Map by Shelby L. Stanton

Sasu-ri

Toktong Pass

Hagaru-ri

Munam-san

Puk-san

Tongbaek-san

Koto-ri

Mae-bong

Funchilin Pass

Ch'onbul-san

Chinhung-ni

Sinhung

Taebau-san

Huksu-ri

Sudong

Noran-Hong

Majon-dong

Oro-ri

N

HAMHUNG

0   5
miles

Chigyong

HUNGNAM

Yonp'o

During November 4 and 5, the Marines slowly advanced as artillery and air power pounded the entrenched Chinese positions.

On the afternoon of November 6, Company H of the 7th Marines went forward up the steep rock walls, lugging machine guns and ammunition boxes up the slope as they climbed toward the summit under a shower of grenades and submachine gun bursts. A fierce Chinese counterattack drove the Marines back down the hill at heavy cost, but during the night the *124th PLA Division* retreated again. The Marines took Funchilin Pass on November 7, and General Almond visited the site of the Company H mountain assault on the following day. Hearing of the valiant deeds of Capt. Thomas E. Cooney, who had been wounded twice charging enemy trenches on Hill 891, the corps commander reached in his pocket for a medal. Discovering that he had run out of medals, he pinned a scrap of paper on Cooney's field jacket inscribed "Silver Star Medal for Gallantry in Action—Almond."[15]

3. The Wild Frontier

One major Marine difficulty remained the dispersion of its forces. While the 7th Marines were battering the *124th PLA Division,* other division elements were scattered on a multitude of screening assignments throughout the corps sector. Typical of these roles was the assignment of the 3d Battalion, 1st Marines, to the picturesque mountain village of Majon-ni on the icy Imjin River since late October. Majon-ni was the farthest corps outpost west of Wonsan. The interior road connecting it with coastal Wonsan twisted twenty-eight precipitous miles through a maze of towering mountains, known to the Marines as "ambush alley." Past Majon-ni the road forked into three directions and Marine companies patrolled these rocky pathways in an effort to police Korean travellers and detect retreating *NKPA* soldiers.

On November 2, the first Marine jeep patrol was bushwhacked in a deep ravine by local elements of the *15th NKPA Division*—rumored to be holed up in the nearby Imjin River highlands. On four separate occasions during the next ten days, convoys attempting to reach the battalion at Majon-ni were ambushed. The enemy cratered the narrow cliffside road or triggered landslides to make impassable roadblocks, covering these sites with automatic weapons on the heights. Trucks caught in the killing zone were either destroyed by enemy weapons fire, careened off the road into yawning chasms below, or were forced to turn back. Relying partially on parachuted supplies, the Marine garrison defied isolation and enemy probing attacks to maintain its position. Even radio communication was uncertain, because the Majon-ni defenders could only transmit over the intervening peaks during crystal-clear nighttime atmospheric conditions.

On November 5, the first regiment of General Soule's 3d Infantry Division, the 65th Infantry, began landing at Wonsan. The main mission of Soule's formation was to relieve the 1st Marine Division of its burdensome security duty south of Hamhung, to guard Wonsan and adjacent areas, and to cover the main roads throughout the X Corps southern zone.[16] The division's sector was only slightly smaller than the state of Connecticut, but immeasurably more rugged.

That night the North Koreans stormed the town of Yonghung along the coastal Wonsan-Hamhung trunk road, breached the perimeter of the 96th Field Artillery Battalion and wiped out six 155mm howitzers along with tons of ammunition and other materiel. The 96th was a black outfit that Almond had no confidence in, and he had left the unit devoid of infantry protection. The disaster deepened his contempt for black troops, but he finally ordered supporting infantry in their behalf.

Almond directed the 65th Infantry regimental command group and its 2d Battalion to secure the town on the following day. The motor march was painfully slow and the long procession of trucks took most of the day to cover the forty-mile distance. The trucks frequently halted while the nervous soldiers checked any clusters of Koreans by the road and sent forward investigative patrols into every village. The infantrymen finally reached their destination and linked up with the artillerymen on the north edge of town.

The trucks were reassembled for the return to Wonsan but were delayed by a long Marine tank convoy. It was already dark when the empty trucks started south out of town. In the morning darkness at 3:20 A.M. the 65th Infantry troops at Yonghung, together with members of the 96th Field Artillery Battalion, were attacked by five hundred to eight hundred North Korean troops. The five-hour engagement lasted until well after daylight. Several defending companies ran out of ammunition in the midst of the battle because insufficient amounts had been brought forward from Wonsan (apparently the hasty debarkation and immediate movement to a distant base had complicated things). The results were grim and scores of positions were overrun.

The North Koreans penetrated numerous points in the artillery perimeter and gained several observation and firing positions. Lt. Paul R. Schultz of the Battery C, 96th Field Artillery Battalion, and six other men occupied positions designed to prevent enemy flanking movement against the main command post. As the enemy tried to infiltrate closer through the darkness, he dashed through a hail of gunfire to a weapons carrier and turned on the headlights for illumination. The enemy immediately concentrated their fire on this truck, and Schultz returned to his post to heave grenades and direct rifle fire. Soon afterwards, a mortar detonation ignited a nearby vehicle which threatened to set fire to the ammunition trucks. Schultz extinguished the blaze despite the intense enemy fire directed at him, but was mortally wounded by mortar explosions. His bravery, later recognized by the Distinguished Service Cross, was one of the few heroic episodes in a battle marred by serious tactical blunders.[17]

In the meantime, the convoy was stopped just beyond Kowon, midway in its darkened journey, by an ambushed truck blazing as its cargo of gasoline drums burned and lit up the night sky. The fiery truck blocked the narrow roadway squeezed between rice fields, but Lieutenant Catania remembered a nearby westerly road that crossed a village bridge and looped back to intersect again with the main road. His sergeant conducted a quick jeep recon that confirmed the bridge's location. The convoy was diverted down this side road, but suspicions were aroused as they neared the village. Groups of Koreans defiant of curfew stood around the road waving them on, but the Koreans near the bridge scattered when they saw headlights.

The number of drivers was insufficient to defend the column when it was attacked at the bridge site. The Americans abandoned most of the trucks and retreated to the last ones. They unhitched the trailers under fire from a forward truck-mounted .50-caliber machine gun turned against them. The transportation crews headed back up the road in three trucks, leaving Catania behind. He turned around the fourth truck and sped away also. He soon reached the other three trucks where they were ambushed a thousand yards farther up the road. The trucks were either blown off the embankment or blocking it, and the thirty transportation troops were pinned under heavy fire. The cab and hood of Catania's own truck was riddled with enemy gunfire and he scrambled out to hide in a ditch.

Throughout the night the enemy drove U.S. trucks from the captured convoy up and down the road. They scoured the area looking for the drivers and capturing several. One soldier caught by the Koreans related that they had argued whether to kill him or not, but settled on taking his wallet and jewelry, hitting him over the head with his rifle, and then kicking him as they let him go. After a night of joy-riding, the Koreans burned all the vehicles. Catania, whose trousers were torn by bullets that miraculously missed his legs, walked cautiously back toward Wonsan—hailing a jeep only after he was sure it contained Americans.[18]

During the morning, the *Blue Goose,* with General Almond aboard, landed on a rice paddy near Yonghung where only a furrow had been knocked out to make a strip. Typically, it landed right in the thick of a fight. Guerrillas hidden in the haystacks still covered one end of the strip with rifle and machine gun fire. The soldiers had to smoke them out before the little two-seater *Blue Goose* could take off again, and Almond himself experienced a close call.[19]

The action at Yonghung reinforced a sudden turnabout in Almond's attitude regarding the pace of the campaign. Not only were hordes of Chinese menacing his corps, but in his opinion he was again saddled with inferior non-white troop units being sent to him from all over the globe. His change of heart might have also resulted partially from his own encounter at Yonghung. At any rate, the wary tone of messages received that same day from General MacArthur revealed the supreme commander's great concern over reports of the increasing Chinese buildup, and Almond reflected MacArthur's viewpoint unerringly.

During the day, Almond held three conferences in which he aired a more cautious approach to Korean domination. He discussed prospects of a winter campaign and his concepts for tightening the corps area of responsibility. His first meeting of November 7 was held with General Kim, commander of ROK I Corps and Colonel Rogers, his KMAG advisor. In his second meeting, held with General Barr, Almond explained reducing the corps perimeter with regard to the 7th Infantry Division. The final conference involved a meeting with Marine General Smith. When Almond mentioned pulling the corps in for the winter, Smith recommended holding only the enclave area of Hamhung, Hungnam, and Wonsan. Almond wanted an advance picket line as far north as Hagaru-ri, but he relented on this point and agreed that more contraction was needed.

During the next few days, however, no sightings of large Chinese forces were reported and no major contact developed. The Far East Command strategists relaxed their initial concern. Almond adopted a more aggressive posture in line with his original intentions to push on to the border. Plans were prepared again for a maximum corps offensive to reach the Yalu River.

One of the most daring X Corps ventures into the forbidding and trackless mountain interior was conducted by Colonel Harris's 65th Infantry in a forlorn effort to make physical contact with the Eighth Army to the west. An actual junction between the two field forces would tie in the United Nations front and ease concern over possible enemy flanking movements against either front. To date, the most meaningful operational juncture between Walker's and Almond's forces was the 120-mile flight of the *Blue Goose* from Wonsan to the North Korean capital of P'yongyang. The *Blue Goose* carried an important intelligence agent to the city just after it was captured. For a long time, its trip remained the longest light aircraft flight over enemy-held Korean territory.

On November 9, Lt. Col. Howard B. St. Clair's 1st Battalion of the 65th Infantry began trekking west of Yonghung in an effort to reach patrols from the Eighth Army. Radio signals from IX Corps were picked up during the day on the 1st Marine Division communications net. This was the first direct radio contact between X Corps and Eighth Army.[20] The 65th Infantry task force continued to probe westward, completely unopposed by the enemy.

Almond was very concerned about establishing a link-up at the X Corps–Eighth Army boundary and he personally flew over the battalion's route of march on November 10. Although the narrow cliff-hugging road twisted through narrow passes and wrapped around hillsides, Almond decided the battalion was not moving fast enough. He dismissed their pleas for prudence in such a hazardous solitary undertaking. When informed that St. Clair's men were unsure about some bridges, Almond raged the battalion "had not been energetic in its movement west from Yonghung."[21] He intended to check out whether there was any major breach in the road. After observing no bridges down, he landed and rushed into the 65th Infantry command post at Yonghung. He stormed furiously at Colonel Harris that he wanted the battalion's movement expedited. By that evening the lone column was thirty-one road-miles back into the frozen Obong-san ranges.

On that same morning, the 7th Marines entered Koto-ri at the northern elevated terminus of the Funchilin Pass, which emptied into an iced-over plateau. The freezing high mountain air swept across the frigid uplands at thirty-five miles per hour, a moderate gale on the Beaufort scale of wind force, and the temperature registered a numbing eight below zero. The 1st Marine Division set up warming tents as patrols scouted the immediate area. The men strained to see through the eye-stabbing cold blasts of sub-zero air. Their parka hoods were tightly drawn and fringed in ice. They reported sighting only small bands of enemy troops who vanished upon hearing rifle shots.

This information bolstered Almond's conviction that the Chinese might not be interested or prepared for further battle, justifying his drive to the border as the right choice. The Marines had trounced the *124th PLA Division,* and if the remaining two division-sized formations identified in northeast Korea were the extent of the Chinese volunteer effort, the danger might be past. At midnight on November 11, he issued X Corps Operation Order 6, ordering an immediate advance to the Yalu River.

The 65th Infantry's battalion set up an advanced patrol base at the mountain crossroads of Kwangchon, still eight miles short of the mapped boundary between X Corps and the Eighth Army. On November 12, a corps light plane flying over the patrol spotted what appeared to be South Korean troops moving west. A message was dropped arranging for a meeting. This was the closest claim that the two forces ever made to contact. There were too many landslides and too many cratered road-ways to support jeep rendezvous. Without supporting jeeps and their radios and machine guns, foot patrols would not venture farther.

On November 14, the 7th Marines followed up the light screening withdrawal of the *126th PLA Division* and reached Hagaru-ri on the southern tip of the Changjin Reservoir. The sky was relatively clear and a dusting of light snow covered the frozen ground, except where local drifting caused accumulations in the mountain valleys. The reinforcement of the corps' southern front with additional regiments of the 3d Infantry Division enabled the 1st Marine Division to pull its units into close operating distance. On November 14, Colonel Puller's regiment was relieved by the 15th Infantry and relocated to Chigyong, just south of Hamhung. By this date, the 5th Marines were moving to Koto-ri. The 1st Marine Division began to assemble slowly along one axis of advance for its own push into the Korean mountains.

One major problem hindering divisional consolidation was the lack of Marine motor transport. Even with the separate Marine 7th Transport Battalion, Smith's Marine division had only 1,219 vehicles compared to an Army division's standard allotment of 2,098 vehicles. As the Marine division logistician, Col. Francis A. McAlister, noted, "Marine divisions are not equipped basically for overland operation on large land masses." The X Corps operations planning chief, Lt. Col. Frank T. Mildren, recalled, "They [Marines] did not have all the equipment and vehicles [Army units possessed]. We had to supply them with vehicles to enable them to move like an infantry division. Every time we moved the 1st Marine Division it took every [non-divisional] vehicle we had in the corps."[22]

The corps command post had scarcely settled down at Wonsan when Almond decided that the future advance of X Corps necessitated its relocation to Hamhung, which offered superior communications and access to the major port of Hungnam. Hungnam was still being cleared for mines at this time. The entire 52d Transportation Truck Battalion was used to make the transfer, supplemented by rail transportation, and it was completed by early afternoon on the following day. Almond instructed the 8224th Engineer Construction Group to renovate three railroad cars into headquarters and private coaches for his mobile railroad command post. The plans were rushed to completion, but the conversions were never made because of adverse tactical developments just three weeks later.[23]

Notes

1. The X Corps actual strength was as follows: Corps headquarters, service, and attached units—6,399; corps combat units—1,479; 1st Marine Div—23,430 (23,334 Marines + 96 Army); 7th Inf Div—26,641 (18,837 Army + 7,804 Koreans); 2d Engineer Special Bde—1,393; Task Force Baker (ROK Marine Rgt)—2,206; ROK I Corps Headquarters—661; ROK Capital Div—11,261; ROK 3d Div—11,315. Source: X Corps *Personnel Daily Summary,* dtd 1 November 1950 (excluding tactical air support elements).
2. X Corps Periodic Intelligence Report No. 71, Para II-5 (f).
3. The division's regular third regiment, the 30th Infantry, was reduced to zero strength at Fort Benning by transfers to the 7th and 15th Infantry, and did not deploy to Korea.
4. Correspondence with Col. Benjamin S. Silver, 28 March 1987.
5. Department of the Army, *The Army Lineage Book: Vol. II, Infantry,* Washington, D.C., 1953, p. 253.
6. Ltr fm Pfc Zapata to IG, US Army Forces Antilles, Ft. Brooke, Puerto Rico, dtd 17 September 1950. Copy in X Corps IG records.
7. Morris J. MacGregor, Jr., *Integration of the Armed Forces, 1940–1965,* Defense Studies Series, Center of Military History, pp. 440–441.
8. Blair, p. 407.
9. MacGregor, p. 441.
10. Ltr fm Mrs. Ed Oard to Fifth Army Hq, relayed to X Corps IG for reply, 23 December 1950.
11. X Corps Asst Adj Gen Ltr dtd 29 March 1951, in X Corps IG file.
12. X Corps Ltr AG 333.3, dtd 20 November 1950, Subj: Mistreatment of Soldiers in Medical Company, 32d Infantry Regiment, in X Corps IG files.
13. 17th Infantry Regiment Ltr dtd 25 January 1951 with extract copy of statement by 1Lt. Wallace N. Fluckey.
14. Lynn Montross and Nicholas A. Canzona, *U.S. Marine Operations in Korea: 1950–1953,* Vol. III, *The Chosin Reservoir Campaign,* Washington, D.C., 1957, p. 105.
15. Montross and Canzona, Vol. III, p. 120.
16. Appleman, p. 740.
17. Far East Command General Orders No. 137, dtd 26 May 1951.
18. Westover, pp. 50–53.
19. Lt. Col. Kenneth E. Lay, "Korea's Blue Goose," X Corps files.
20. X Corps War Diary, November 1950, p. 38.
21. X Corps War Diary, November 1950, p. 14.
22. 1st Marine Division Special Action Report, *Wonsan-Hamhung-Chosin: 8 October–15 December 1950,* Annex Dog, dtd 28 February 1951, p. 10, and USAMHI Interview of Gen. Mildren, p. 124. The comparisons in Annex Dog were as follows:

	Marine Division*	Army Division
¼-ton truck	592	1,020
¾ and 1½-ton truck	63	336
2½ ton cargo truck	436	621
2½ ton truck, other	128	121

* reinforced with 7th Motor Transport Battalion.

23. 8224th Army Unit, Engineer Construction Group, *Command Report,* December 1950, Pt. III-Summary, p. 8.

CHAPTER 9

DRIVE TO THE YALU

1. A Plan to End the War

Original corps plans to drive west after landing and assist the Eighth Army in capturing P'yongyang were superseded when the North Korean capital fell in October. X Corps was now simply directed to reach the Yalu River and the Manchurian border as soon as possible. The attainment of this objective across the front would bring all of Korea under Allied jurisdiction. By the third week in November, as the 7th Infantry Division reached the Yalu River, this goal appeared on the verge of accomplishment.

On November 15, the division's 17th Infantry had stormed across the waist-deep freezing water of the Ungi River under enemy fire and secured the far bank in two days of heavy fighting. Colonel Powell's regiment battled past Kapsan on November 19 and entered Hyesanjin on the Yalu River unopposed during the morning of November 21. General Almond had arrived in the *Blue Goose* at the 17th Infantry command post the previous evening and now marched down the final hill on Korean soil.

He described the moment, ''The Yalu River was frozen over, the ground was covered with snow and at this point, the river was very little of an obstacle to the possibility of an enemy advance across the river from the north side in raiding operations. We had to watch for this but otherwise there was no serious concern. I accompanied General Barr, the division commander, General Hodes, the assistant division commander, and General Kieffer, the artilleryman, with the regimental commander, Colonel Powell. We all walked the lead company down the road to the river bank. This was the first element of the American forces to reach the Korean-Manchurian border, although earlier elements of the ROK 6th Division with the I American Corps on the west flank, the Eighth Army front, attempted to get to the river but did not succeed in remaining there.''[1]

Eighth Army plans to reach the border supposedly controlled the rate of X Corps advance. While the general UN advance appeared closely coordinated on MacArthur's wall map in Tokyo, northern Korea's rugged geography fragmented field commands into separate ventures linked only by radio transmission. The divisions stabbed north through the bleak mountains along the few winding roadways available.

The principal routes were the coastal highways on each side of the Korean peninsula. Between these were the more difficult routes, ancient trading paths snaking through the high mountains with the assistance of innumerable bridges and tunnels. In this fashion the broad inland advance was reduced to a series of dangerously narrow thrusts. Regimental frontages were squeezed to the width of a single ox-cart lane, and units were physically separated by an uncharted expanse of razorback peaks and frozen river valleys.

The tortuous overland road system imperilled logistical efforts to keep the forward soldiers fed, clothed, and resupplied with ammunition. Sustenance of the X Corps front lines required the transport of three thousand tons per day, six hundred tons for each division and even larger quantities to maintain the critical supply pathways to them. Only four engineer battalions existed beyond those at division level, and these were expected to upgrade and clear roadways of snow and enemy obstructions under winter conditions. Less than ten truck companies existed within the corps to haul troops and materiel, and these were subject to mechanical breakdown, enemy attack, and accidental destruction along roads slippery with ice or hidden by snow.

Weather dominated all activity. November through March constituted the Korean dry season, with light snowfalls predicted, but the winter was already bitterly cold. The northern sky was either streaked with high cirrus clouds propelled by arctic winds, or was blanketed by massive cloud banks that hid the upper mountains. Light winds or periods of calm shrouded the morning atmosphere with overcast and haze. Snow drifts piled up to dangerous heights in the mountain valleys. Temperatures plunged to minus thirty degrees in the interior, and were often accompanied by the severe chilling of wind gusts that snapped tent lines and knifed through the heaviest layers of clothing.

The military situation was far murkier than weather and supply considerations. Those difficulties could at least be measured. Far East Command was unable to gauge accurately the strength of the opposing enemy forces. The general headquarters (GHQ) intelligence summary for November 25 estimated that elements of nine North Korean divisions, totalling about 49,000 men, still lurked ahead of the 120,000-man Eighth Army, reinforced by perhaps 40,000 Chinese. While this estimate excluded the X Corps zone, it reflected a high-level consensus that the UN still enjoyed numerical superiority.

Expectations of total success were still quite high at Far East Command in Japan and at X Corps in Hamhung. The prevailing headquarters attitude was that the fleeing remnants of the *NKPA,* considered to be in shambles, could no longer seriously challenge the superior resources available to Almond's command. The Chinese formations identified in front of the Marines were still viewed as a delaying gambit to help broken Korean communist cadres escape for rebuilding. Almond felt certain that a de facto United Nations boundary established along the Yalu, with the assistance of troops like his 17th Infantry at Hyesanjin, would prevent stronger Chinese intervention.

In the meantime, MacArthur's intelligence sources identified the Kanggye area—deep in the north-central mountain fastness of Korea—as the assembly area for reconstitution of the North Korean People's Army as well as the possible main avenue of march for reinforcing Chinese contingents. MacArthur believed that a lateral advance by X Corps, slightly to the northwest beyond the Changjin Reservoir, could secure this key geographical sector.

The seizure of the road junction of Mup'yong-ni, halfway across northern Korea and just below Kanggye, promised to speed up Allied control of the region. If X Corps could reach and establish a choke point at this town and its mountain passes, the primary enemy interior supply network south from Kanggye would be cut. This in turn would effectively prevent the enemy from organizing a strong defensive redoubt facing Eighth Army columns moving up Route 7. Communist attempts to stabilize the military situation would be crippled, in MacArthur's opinion, and the war's rapid conclusion assured.

General MacArthur believed that this bold corps thrust against Mup'yong-ni was crucial and Brigadier General Wright, his operations chief, agreed. The great gulf dividing the UN forces would be closed by means of interlocking roads. Without resupply, enemy resistance was doomed to wither in the icy mountain wilderness between. A starving, ill-equipped army reduced to desperate guerrilla raiders and bands of brigands could be mopped up and eradicated at the leisure of Korean police under UN sponsorship.

Wright had sent a personal letter to General Almond on November 10, emphasizing the importance of rendering all possible assistance to the Eighth Army. Five days later, as the temperature dropped to four below zero and Colonel Litzenberg's 7th Marines occupied the scrubby town of Hagaru-ri on the southern edge of the Changjin Reservoir, Almond responded. He stated that X Corps could best assist the Eighth Army by continuing to attack north with all forces to reach the Yalu.

On the same day, however, MacArthur sent a radio message ordering a change in direction. He wanted the corps' main offensive shifted to attack west from the Changjin Reservoir through Mup'yong-ni to reach Manpojin on the Yalu River. On a map the objectives, while graphically distant, appeared attainable.

This new direction of march would engage the corps in a long and arduous march over unknown roads and barren mountains in the dead of winter, with extreme temperatures predicted to drop as low as forty degrees below zero. The Yangnim mountains were the highest and most inaccessible of Korea's fearsome northern ranges. The peaks reached heights over eight thousand feet and their steep rocky slopes were cut by icy gorges and waterfalls plummeting into the forested valleys far below. The harsh terrain conditions and ferocity of Korea's upcoming winter storm season did not dampen the optimism of the corps commander and his planners. Enemy opposition was only expected to be in the form of scattered delaying actions.

In actual fact, X Corps was woefully unprepared for such a mechanized winter maneuver. The tenuous single road leading from Hamhung through the heights of Funchilin Pass extended only fifty miles inland, as far as the Changjin reservoir, and even it was in deplorable condition.

An airstrip constructed at Koto-ri was already non-operational because of mud from melted snow. Combat engineers dumped cinders and coal into the quagmire for filling purposes.[2]

The primitive roadway and the rudimentary air facilities being established along its path hardly befitted a reinforced corps drive. Almond was confident that intensified efforts by the 73d and 185th Engineer Battalions, even with their limited assets on hand, could remedy these defects. He ordered the sole roadway twisting from Hamhung port to the high plateau at Hagaru-ri bulldozed, graded, and hammered into the major corps supply route. Unfortunately, the narrow gauge railroad and cableway up the Funchilin Pass incline required such extensive repairs that the system could not be put into operation.

Typical of the plight facing the forward combat engineers was one bridge damaged by an Air Force five hundred-pound bomb near the Changjin Reservoir. On November 23, a company of the Marine 1st Engineer Battalion overcame the problems of constructing the bridge foundations in a frozen stream. The entire stream was first dammed and rerouted, then the ice was melted and kept fluid by burning drums of carbide, and the Marine engineers built foundations to support the piers of a new bridge.[3]

Marine General Smith knew his Marines could tackle the most demanding tasks, but he balked at needless sacrifice. He was aghast at any plan to reach the Yalu without proper flank safeguards in the face of potential Chinese resistance. He wrote to General Cates, commandant of the Marine Corps, "We would simply get further out on a limb. . . . I believe a winter campaign in the mountains of North Korea is too much to ask of the American soldier or Marine, and I doubt the feasibility of supplying troops in this area during the winter or providing for the evacuation of sick and wounded."[4]

The X Corps plan to reach Mup'yong-ni was coded Operation Plan number 8. The first draft presented for Almond's consideration opted for an even wilder scheme than the straight Mup'yong-ni approach. Upon attaining positions in the Changjin Reservoir vicinity, the corps would continue north along the Changjin River another fifty miles and then turn due west to take Kanggye, *behind* Mup'yong-ni.

The concept counted on surprising enemy defenders who might misplace their delaying forces to confront the corps as if it were heading north all the way to the border. It also reflected Almond's desire to please the original objective dreamers at MacArthur's headquarters. While this course would give X Corps an advanced position astride all infiltration routes into central Korea, it was too logistically impractical even for Almond. He rejected it as being much too reckless in view of his currently precarious supply line. He envisioned the corps advancing in stages, contingent on reduction of possible enemy strong points and strengthening supply arrangements.

On November 21, Almond selected the second draft of Operation Plan number 8. The push toward Mup'yong-ni would be made directly west from Hagaru-ri, where the Marines were already located. Since Changjin Reservoir and Mup'yong-ni were so widely separated by rugged terrain impassable to wheeled traffic, one division was deemed insufficient to take both objectives. The 1st Marine Division was scheduled to attack Mup'yong-ni, but the plans were modified so that the 7th Infantry Division would capture the Changjin vicinity and advance to the Yalu River. Another potential enemy reinforcement corridor would have fallen under Allied control, the Marine right flank would be secured, and the division could later link into ROK I Corps lines for a continuous front.

In the meantime, the ROK I Corps continued its coastal march to the Yalu by way of Ch'ongjin, where six thousand North Korean troops were believed concentrated. The South Koreans advanced past Kilchu and continued through Myongchon and across the Orangchon River, where they met renewed enemy opposition. The ROK 18th Regiment was forced back across the river and the enemy started to turn the east flank of the ROK Capital Division. Enemy moves were countered by coordinated naval gunfire and air support, and Hapsu was seized on November 22.

Fragments of other *NKPA* forces, three thousand from the Naktong River front and perhaps another ten thousand regrouping southwest of Wonsan in a guerrilla warfare role, offered a mild threat to X Corps' western flank. The 3d Infantry Division, which completed landing on November 21, was to secure this area, destroy remaining resistance around Wonsan port, and redouble efforts to gain physical contact with the Eighth Army. The division would also plug the gaps along the Marine west flank.

The sum of all these preliminary moves would disperse X Corps over nearly a five hundred-mile front, but Almond believed this disadvantage was offset by the lack of enemy offensive capability. Intelligence officers had low regard for the fighting stamina of disorganized enemy troops and recommended pursuit to the fullest extent to prevent their chances of reorganization. The Chinese divisions identified in the Changjin Reservoir were becoming mysteries. Intelligence sources lost track of the *124th PLA Division* and the *126th PLA Division* which had "side-slipped to the southwest."[5] A newly identified Chinese formation, the *89th PLA Division* was reported around the reservoir. Instead of alarming Almond, this information confirmed his anxiety to reach targeted areas before the enemy could consolidate, form a defensive barrier, and cause a stalemate over the winter months.

On November 23, Lt. Col. John H. Chiles, the X Corps operations chief, took the third draft of Operation Plan number 8 to Tokyo for presentation to General MacArthur. On the following day Chiles briefed the supreme commander on the revised concept. MacArthur approved it with one change: he ordered the proposed boundary between X Corps and the Eighth Army shifted even farther west and south in the 1st Marine Division zone. The completion of this ambitious plan called for nothing less than total X Corps control of most of northern Korea along the Yalu and Tumen River borders of China and the Soviet Union.

2. Men in Battle

On November 24, the same day that Lieutenant Colonel Chiles was presenting the X Corps plan of final attack in General MacArthur's stately office in the Dai-ichi building, another lieutenant colonel was at a frozen medical command post near P'ungsan, Korea. Lt. Col. Oren C. Atchley, Medical Service Corps, was commander of the 7th Infantry Division's medical battalion. He received information that an ambulance evacuating five patients from the front was missing on the trip from Kapsan back to Pukch'ong, a route necessitating passage through enemy territory. Atchley was extremely worried about the safety of the wounded men and personally organized a search party.

He left with five enlisted medics in an ambulance and jeep. They followed vehicular tracks in the snow to Wonpung-ni, where Atchley reconnoitered the surrounding area in his jeep. He returned and spotted enemy troops closing in on the ambulance from the main road. Atchley quickly hand-signalled the ambulance to follow his jeep and the two vehicles moved out from the village along a side road that stopped abruptly at a dead end. The pursuing enemy made return impossible. The six medical personnel took all the weapons, ammunition, and food out of the jeep and ambulance and set out on foot for the perilous trip back to friendly lines.

During this attempt, about thirty hostile troops fired on the rescue party and engaged them in a brisk fire fight. During the action, Colonel Atchley's driver was mortally wounded and Atchley became separated from the other men. Realizing the desperate situation and fully aware of the odds against him, he took up a firing position to afford time time for the others to escape. Atchley was last seen "fearlessly maintaining his stand and urging the sergeant of the four men to withdraw," an act that was later recognized with the Distinguished Service Cross. The episode also underscored the vulnerability of corps lines of communication between units thinly spread across the Korea hinterland.[6]

Hundreds of miles away, Colonel Litzenberg's 7th Marines advanced through Toktong Pass. The Marines cleared road blocks, some of which were booby-trapped, and used air strikes to knock out the few machine guns that opposed their march. On November 25, the Marines entered the village of Yudam-ni on the southwest side of Changjin Reservoir. The road passed through the town and a branch forked off to the west. This was the road that led to Mup'yong-ni.

In the meantime, the ROK Capital Division continued its advance along the east coast in a column of regiments. Continuing to advance rapidly, the Capital Division passed around the west side of Nanam and by November 25 it reached the outskirts of Ch'ongjin a scant fifty miles from the Russian border. Both Yudam-ni and Ch'ongjin would mark the farthest limits of the X Corps advance into North Korea.

At 10 A.M. on the morning of November 26, Almond presented General Smith the final X Corps offensive plan. X Corps was to commence a general attack on the following day, November 27, to sever enemy lines of communication at Mup'yong-ni and destroy the enemy in a zone up to the Yalu River on the left and to the mouth of the Tumen River on the right.

Major General Smith's 1st Marine Division was ordered to attack and seize Mup'yong-ni and advance to the Yalu River. Major General Barr's 7th Infantry Division elements on the eastern side of the Changjin Reservoir were ordered to attack north and advance to the Yalu River. General Kim's ROK I Corps was ordered to advance from the Hapsu and Ch'ongjin areas to the northern boundary of Korea. Major General Soule's 3d Infantry Division was ordered to establish contact with the right flank of the Eighth Army, protect the western flank, and support the 1st Marine Division on corps orders. The die was cast.

The first Chinese divisions that confronted X Corps belonged to the East Liaodong *42d PLA Army* (*124th, 125th, 126th PLA Divisions*) which had crossed into Korea during mid-October. The army had not performed well against X Corps. The Marines had decimated its *124th PLA Division* in heavy fighting around Sudong and the *126th PLA Division* had conducted a lukewarm screening retreat to Hagaru-ri. The *125th PLA Division* farther west was barely engaged. During the latter part of November, this army moved west and eventually encircled the ROK 6th, 7th, and 8th Divisions in the Eighth Army zone. Unknown to Allied intelligence, in late November the *42d* sector in front of X Corps was taken over by three new Chinese armies. Instead of facing three depleted divisions, Almond's organization would be confronted with three fresh *PLA* armies. Among their sixteen divisions were some of the best troops China fielded during the Korean war.[7]

The elite *27th PLA Army* (*79th, 80th, 81st, 90th PLA Divisions*) deployed mainly east of the Changjin Reservoir. This army stemmed from the 9th Column of the East China People's Liberation Army of the civil war period, where it became distinguished in battles ranging from Jiaoxian to Laiwu. Considered one of the most combat-proficient communist units, the column demonstrated great mobility and effectiveness in storming fortified positions. In January 1949, when the column was redesignated the *27th PLA Army,* it took hand-picked replacements and became divorced from the provincial nature of most Chinese armies. The *27th* was also unusual because of its amphibious specialization, having trained in Hangzhou Bay until mid-1950. The army had been sent to Linjiang, Manchuria, in October and crossed the Yalu River as a crack "volunteer force" for Korea.[8]

The *20th PLA Army* (*58th, 59th, 60th, 89th PLA Divisions*) went into positions north and west of the Changjin Reservoir. This force was rooted in the old 1st Column of the East China People's Liberation Army and was redesignated the *20th* in the spring of 1949, as it moved against Shanghai. Although trained in amphibious operations, it was a regular territorial Chinese army with strong links to the northern and western districts of Shandong Province. Railed from that area to Ji'an, Manchuria, on November 10, the army was hurriedly dispatched into the Yudam-ni sector of Korea.[9]

The *26th PLA Army* (*76th, 77th, 78th,* and *88th PLA Divisions*), also from Shandong Province, was initially in reserve. This army originated as the 8th Column of the East China People's Liberation Army during the latter stages of the Sino-Japanese war, being redesignated as the *26th* in November 1948. The army had conducted occasional anti-guerrilla campaigns in Fujian and Zhejiang Provinces before resettling in Shandong Province. On November 5, the *26th PLA Army* crossed the Yalu River into Korea and was quickly moved south.[10]

The *PLA* was basically a peasant infantry force with limited firepower, wheeled mobility, communications, and logistic systems, but it had just defeated a far better equipped and more numerous army through skillful maneuver and toleration of extreme hardships. In the recent three-year Chinese civil war of 1946–1949, the communists had controlled the countryside and waged a war of attrition against the Nationalists concentrated in the cities and along main lines of communication.

The *PLA* had embarked on large-scale offensive operations during the summer of 1947 and destroyed the Nationalist army piecemeal using both guerrilla raids and conventional, open attacks. Nationalist resistance had virtually collapsed after Beijing (Peking) fell in January 1949. In March the *PLA* had crossed the Yangzi (Yangtze) River, capturing Nanjing and Shanghai in quick succession. That August the Nationalist government withdrew to Taiwan and the People's Republic of China was established October 1, 1949. Only one year had passed between this victorious event and MacArthur's drive into North Korea.[11]

The successful maneuvering strategy of the Chinese People's Liberation Army should have been obvious to General Almond. He served as MacArthur's chief of staff in Japan throughout this tumultuous period, and his two army division commanders David Barr and Robert Soule had actually witnessed the Chinese civil war. The Chinese style of warfare was predictable enough to conclude that they might concentrate in the interior Korean mountains—while opposing forces clung to towns or roadways—awaiting an opportunity to strike decisively against lines of communication.

There were many differences between the North Korean People's Army encountered up to this stage of the war, and the Chinese People's Liberation Army about to enter it. *NKPA* forces used equipment donated by the Soviet Union, but the *PLA* possessed ordnance from practically every major arms-manufacturing country in the world. *PLA* formations were outfitted largely with ex-Chinese Nationalist Army materiel—produced originally in the United States—but they also contained weapons garnered or copied from many other countries, including Japan, Germany, and Russia. This bewildering array of different weapon and munitions types caused logistical and replacement problems, but it also confused U.S. efforts to quantify the effectiveness of *PLA* formations.

Chinese People's Liberation Army divisions had theoretical strengths of 12,225 men, compared to the 11,000-man ideal standard of North Korean Army divisions or the actual 23,400-soldier Army and 26,600-marine divisions fielded by X Corps. The real *PLA* divisions, however, were somewhat smaller than their organizational tables and averaged about ten thousand personnel. There were rarely enough weapons to equip everyone, and normally one third of a unit's manpower comprised unarmed soldiers waiting to receive either captured stocks or equipment from fallen comrades.

The Chinese battle tactics usually exemplified patient combat skill and reliance on supporting arms rather than mob attacks by "suicidal hordes." For example, Chinese skirmish lines never took on the appearance of unbroken waves of hundreds of men, but rather consisted of forty-man groups that took full advantage of cover from boulders, ravines, or natural draws. American machine gunners were rarely presented clustered targets numbering more than five troops at a time. These groups often followed each other to build pressure against selected points of attack in strict adherence to preset plans. Where caught by enfilade or heavy defensive fire, however, successive decimation of these groups sometimes resulted in awful spectacles of slaughter.

The Chinese rarely overwhelmed positions in close assault, preferring to advance within grenade range and wear down the defenders with machine guns, grenades, and mortar fire. They placed primary reliance on grenadiers, liberally equipped with belt pouches of potato-masher grenades, who were supported by riflemen or submachine gunners fighting alongside. The Chinese favored showering targets with concussion grenades, although the low charge of these weapons caused much wounding but little lethality. Many Allied positions survived heavy dosages of grenades thrown at close range. The Chinese light machine guns caused most Allied casualties, followed by medium mortars. During actions against X Corps, however, the Chinese constantly ran low on ammunition, at which point their effectiveness either declined markedly or ceased.[12]

Chinese officers and enlisted men evidenced little concern over rank compared to the status-conscious North Koreans. Many *PLA* troops only thought of themselves as "soldier" or "officer" rather than various grades of private, sergeant, and junior and senior officer categories. Many officer uniforms were plain but some had 1/8-inch red piping on the collar edges and inverted V-trimming near the sleeve cuffs. Rank was still recognizable, however, because lieutenants were armed with submachine guns, captains and majors had Mauser-type pistols, and lieutenant colonels and higher possessed both pistols and personal bodyguards.[13]

The Chinese soldiers were garbed in quilted mustard-brown or navy-blue winter uniforms made of heavy cotton cloth with ribbed cotton padding to provide extra protection in cold weather. Unlike *NKPA* winter apparel there was no cross-stitching to secure the padding in place. For extra warmth, as many as three summer uniforms were worn underneath. Headgear consisted of cotton-padded caps with brown tops and pile lining on the ear and neck flaps and visors. Ordinary footwear consisted of canvas-padded, high-top cloth shoes with rubber soles ("sneakers"). They assisted infiltration tactics because of their quietness, but they were not good for climbing or protecting the feet from frostbite. The general absence of suitable winter clothing and blankets caused great suffering from freezing, trench-foot, and other cold-weather injuries.

The U.S. soldiers were also susceptible to the extreme cold, although they were much better clothed. Marine combat uniforms consisted of fur-lined parkas, field trousers, and gloves with wool inserts. Army uniforms consisted of either fur parkas or ski parkas with field trousers and gloves. Both services had cold-weather undergarments, pile caps, wool mufflers, and trigger-finger arctic mittens with inserts.

The shoe-pac footwear was a combination boot featuring an ankle-length rubber bottom and thick leather uppers. The shoe-pacs were designed primarily for cold weather static duty, such as guard posts, instead of sustained activity. They trapped foot perspiration which froze and formed ice inside the liner. Although frequent sock changes and less marching could reduce the foot moisture, these were not viable options under conditions of constant combat. As a result, Americans also suffered from frozen feet, frostbite, and cold-related impairments.

The cold weather took a toll on the operating effectiveness of M2 carbines and 4.2-inch mortars. These mortars had a high rate of ammunition failures and parts breakage. Many troops also experienced difficulty with the Browning Automatic Rifle (BAR), a decisive weapon against Chinese onslaughts. Many other weapons malfunctioned because their handlers were unable to properly clean and lubricate them. Oil preservatives thickened and caused machine guns to become sluggish. Some munition types, such as 3.5-inch rocket rounds, split apart under low temperatures.[14]

The cold caused severe vehicular problems, which were compounded by the snowy and iced-over terrain. The prolonged sub-zero weather caused tank starters to malfunction. Tank crews resorted to running Waukesha generators for a long time and then using jumper cables. Plans for periodic tank engine warmups were often abandoned because of the lack of fuel. Tank batteries suffered high failure rates, attributed to excessive cold-weather demands and an inferior grade of electrolyte that prevented full battery charges. Water in the gasoline, condensation, and vapor caused fuel pumps and fuel cut-off valves to freeze.

When armored crews opened their hatches—a periodic necessity because of smoke and fumes—their breath caused frost or a thin film of ice to glaze over the entire interior of their tanks. Periscopes frosted over on the outside. Tank machine guns had to be hand-loaded for the first few rounds until the weapon warmed enough to fire automatically. A big scare developed when anti-freeze supplies became exhausted, but diesel oil was found to be a satisfactory substitute.[15]

The Americans were well endowed with medical supplies, but these were also adversely affected by the extreme cold. Whole blood supplies froze and hemolyzed, zepherin chloride solutions froze, and plasma units froze. While thawing could make plasma units serviceable, any cold water introduced into the plasma would cause the solution to gelatinize and refuse to flow. Thus, in order to use plasma, water had to be warmed thoroughly before mixing and a hot water bottle needed to be fastened to the flask. Thus, troops in open winter field conditions could not use plasma, and many soldiers died as a result.[16]

3. Fighting on a Thread

As X Corps moved farther inland under darkening winter skies, its slender logistical lifeline was stretched farther into the contested defiles of the frozen Korean highlands. The corps' slim transportation system depended on one rail line and a few poor roads that twisted past rocky outcrops and guerrilla-infested villages to reach a few small ports, weather-dependent airfields, and unsheltered beaches. Wonsan sufficed as the only decent port facility until the middle of the month, when Hungnam was finally cleared of mines. Even then, the hazard of floating mines continued. On November 16, an Army tug and crane barge sank with a loss of thirty men (out of forty) after striking a mine off Wonsan.

The main supply route along the eastern coast was a single road a lane and a half wide that meandered in sight of the storm-tossed waters of Tongjoson Bay. Its gravel surface began disintegrating under truck usage in the freezing weather. A few precarious roads leading inland were chosen as resupply lines, but they threaded through deep divides and stone-walled passes that curtailed or prevented engineer upgrading. Other trails were impassable because of flimsy foot bridges, frequent washouts and landslides, or enemy action.[17]

These resupply difficulties were complicated by the scorched-earth policy of the retreating North Korean Army, which displayed a high degree of sophisticated demolition expertise. Railroads and piers were destroyed, roads and airstrips were mined, power plants and utility systems were idled, and factories were demolished. The corps chemical section surveyed the Hamhung-Hungnam area and reported that the entire industrial complex was leveled. The ammonia-synthesis and sulphuric-acid plants, dye works, machine manufacturing centers, and fertilizer, munitions, pharmaceutical, magnesium, and chemical factories were totally destroyed.[18]

The laborers of the ROK 301st Quartermaster Railway worked around the clock to repair the vital single-track railroad from Kojo through Wonsan to Hamhung. The seemingly impossible task was accomplished by gangs of workers pushing aside fallen boulders, filling in craters, and fixing the roadbed with shovels and picks. Major Meisell of the corps transportation section directed the Korean railway soldiers as they rehabilitated seven locomotives and thirty cars, fixed fifty sidings, and repaired the marshalling yards.[19]

The Kojo-Hamhung railway was put into operation, but there were numerous problems. The Korean steam engines needed large amounts of water but pumps were either broken or out of power. Generators were hauled into pumping stations and shops to give emergency electricity. Reliable communications, however, were never restored between terminals. Maintaining the main track was a major task, and there was never enough manpower, cranes, or power equipment to open the devastated spur lines. Most Korean rolling stock remained trapped behind the wreckage of way-stations and missing track for the duration of the campaign.

The single track forced careful scheduling of directional travel, and mishaps or blockages shut down the rail artery for hours and sometimes days. Any delays were costly, and the corps transportation section sent supervisors with each train to insure that cargo was unloaded expeditiously and the engines were turned around promptly.

Each train on the emergency run north was exposed to sudden guerrilla ambush, and large guard contingents were required for the hazardous trips. On November 6 a supply train was attacked at Kowon rail station. The next day another train was wrecked between Kowon and Yonghung when guerrillas destroyed a bridge. The enemy anti-rail campaign forced adoption of unusual line-clearing methods. A roadbed-repair ''work train'' was prepared using flat cars fitted with machine gun mounts behind sandbag revetments.[20]

Trucks were essential in sustaining the primary corps support effort. The first transportation unit reached Wonsan before the sea lanes to the port were cleared. Unable to reach the docks, the ship crews transferred the vehicles to LSTs ferrying equipment ashore. The heavy seas buffeted the hulls of the transports, unbalancing lines and straining gear as cargo booms hoisted trucks over the sides of transports onto LST decks, often causing serious damage to the vehicles. On November 2, the 377th Transportation Truck Company, pre-loaded with gear for the 37th Evacuation Hospital in Hamhung, initiated the seventy-five-mile ''Wonsan-Hamhung highway run,'' a staple of corps truck movement, after the Marines cleared several North Korean roadblocks.

The 7th Infantry Division landed at Iwon and its infantry regiments moved rapidly into the Korean back country. The main supply base at Iwon, however, was not transferred to Pukch'ong until division troops were nearing the northern border. The distance between the coast and division elements placed a severe strain on the truck convoys, which made continuous long hauls carrying rations, ammunition, and gasoline without maintenance or rest periods. The key highway pass in the division sector went over the difficult mountains between Pukch'ong and P'ungsan.

Truck convoys had to drive over a mountain eleven miles uphill and nine miles downhill on the other side. The roadway was too narrow for two-way traffic, which snarled as vehicles jockeyed for passing space going both ways. Military policemen with telephones and radios were finally posted on each side of the mountain to exercise movement control. The situation was only alleviated in late November after engineers cut a crude bypass and reserved the main pass for north-bound convoys. Returning vehicles carrying troops, prisoners, or empty fuel drums were detoured around the Komdok-san range and rejoined the highway farther south. By that time, temperatures were routinely ten below zero in the road's higher elevations.[21]

The division resorted to unorthodox measures to sustain its forward units. Aviation was used to the fullest extent possible. The division relied on emergency airlifts from Japan and utilized its own observation planes to patrol the roads and supplement critical deliveries. The quartermaster section also cranked up a ten-mile conveyor system fortuitously discovered near a rail line. The conveyor transported fifty-five-gallon petrol drums from the railhead at Honggun-ni over the very rough mountains to within twelve miles of P'ungsan. As division quartermaster Lt. Col. Kenneth O. Schellberg related, "We hauled gasoline all day and fought off guerrillas from our conveyor installations at night."[22]

All this effort caused Lieutenant Colonel Scherer of the division G4 section to bristle at continuing demands for lavish supply. Scherer related, "Occasionally, a regimental commander would test our ability to produce. One regimental commander, while advancing to the Yalu River against moderate resistance, insisted on fifty tons of 4.2-inch mortar ammunition. We figured he didn't need that much, but we piled it right in his front yard so he could see we could deliver it. Unfortunately, we could not evacuate it when we withdrew, and it had to be destroyed. The artillery battalions near the Yalu River requested two extra basic loads of fire to be stored in a division ammunition supply point, and they gave strong arguments for it. I had mental reservations about getting so much heavy ammunition so far forward when resistance was light. When the fighting around the Chosin [sic] Reservoir forced us to leave our exposed position on the Yalu River, this ammunition too had to be destroyed."[23]

Only two corps-level ordnance companies and one explosive disposal squad were on hand to furnish munitions and vehicular maintenance support across the far-flung Allied front. Emergency airlifts of automotive parts, especially front springs, kept the long-haul operation in business over Korea's rough roads, but hardly any vehicle winterization kits or new trucks were available. Special ammunition stocks for artillery and mortar illumination rounds—desperately required to curtail enemy night infiltration tactics—were woefully inadequate.[24]

Prompt medical evacuation of cold-weather injuries and battle casualties became increasingly imperative as winter set in, but shortages of blankets and lack of motor ambulances (there were only sixty in the whole corps area) hampered efficient transfer of wounded or frostbitten soldiers. All resources were pooled under the direct control of the corps surgeon, who managed to convert six Korean railroad cars into lifesaving hospital coaches manned by medical personnel. The crucial availability of whole blood was assured only by frequent aerial delivery from Japan—a tenuous connection easily severed by bad weather or unusable runways.

Grave registration was left to the divisions, and the 7th Infantry Division established its cemetery on November 4, a half mile from Puk-ch'ong where the dry rocky soil had good drainage and was not under cultivation. Maj. Jacob W. Kurtz, the division graves registration officer, located his ten-man section with the quartermaster company. A nearby obscure building was used for processing the bodies, but the operation was so quiet that few people noticed it. When a body arrived, the section encased it in a mattress cover and insured that an identifying medical tag was present. A dozen Korean laborers were hired to dig the graves and worked faithfully at a daily wage of two canteen cups of polished rice.

Four or five open graves were maintained at all times. A pyramidal tent at the cemetery protected the crews against the weather as they screened the bodies prior to burial. Major Kurtz recalled, "When a body arrived it was lowered into the open grave, face up. Then one of my men would reach into the mattress cover and place the burial bottle, containing a report of internment, under the left arm. The grave was closed and a temporary marker placed. Unless a chaplain happened to be present when the body was interred, there was no ceremony at that time. Sometime during the day of internment, however, a chaplain of the soldier's faith came to the grave for a short service. If the soldier's faith was unknown, chaplains of all faiths visited the site. In digging graves, our laborers turned up many stones. With these we built a cemetery wall. Three flags flew over the cemetery: the United Nations color at the front entrance, the United States color in the center of the cemetery, and the Republic of Korea color toward the rear."[25]

On December 1, the cemetery was closed as the 7th Infantry Division began its long trek back from the Yalu River to coastal Hungnam. Major Kurtz's section finished their official location sketches and internment register. Bitter cold winds howled past the barren cemetery rocks as the last U.S. troops disappeared beyond the small summit, never to return. That night the graves of fifty fallen Americans and twenty-four South Koreans were not saluted by snapping flags or praying chaplains, but covered silently by the eternal winter snow of northern Korea.

Notes

1. USAMHI Interview, p. V-1.
2. X Corps War Diary, *Monthly Summary, 1 November 1950–30 November 1950.*
3. 1st Marine Special Action Report, Annex Nan Nan, dtd 15 January 1951, pp. 9–10.
4. Montross and Canzona, Vol. III, p. 133.
5. X Corps G2 Estimate of the Enemy Situation, dtd 24 November 1950.
6. Far East Command General Orders No. 164, dtd 26 June 1951.
7. US Army Pacific *Order of Battle, Chinese Communist Army,* dtd 1 February 1958, p. 144.
8. Ibid., p. 131.
9. Ibid., pp. 120–121.
10. Ibid., pp. 129–130.
11. Defense Intelligence Agency, *Handbook of the Chinese People's Liberation Army,* November 1984, p. 2.
12. S.L.A. Marshall, *CCF in the Attack,* Part Two, dtd 1951, quoted in William B. Hopkins, *One Bugle, No Drums,* Algonquin Books of Chapel Hill, 1986.
13. Eighth Army Historical Service Detachment (Provisional), *Enemy Weapons and Equipment,* 3 August 1951.
14. 1st Marine Special Action Report, Annex Sugar, dtd 15 January 1951, p. 6.
15. 1st Marine Special Action Report, Annex Oboe Oboe, dtd 15 January 1951, pp. 42–43.
16. 1st Marine Special Action Report, Annex Dog to Annex Howe Howe, p. 3.
17. Dept. of the Army Assistant Chief of Staff G-2, *Korea Handbook,* September 1950.
18. X Corps Chemical Section, *Special Report,* included in X Corps October 1950 summary.
19. X Corps War Diary, 1–31 October 1950, p. 25.
20. X Corps, *Report of Transportation Section,* October 1950.
21. X Corps War Diary, November 1950, p. 36.
22. Report of 7th Inf Div Quartermaster, December 1950.
23. Westover, p. 185.
24. X Corps War Diary, November 1950, pp. 36, 37.
25. Maj. Jacob W. Kurtz, "Pukchon Cemetery," Westover, p. 182.

CHAPTER 10

WHITE DEATH

1. Battle at Yudam-ni

On November 27, the western side of the iced-over Changjin Reservoir was held by the 5th and 7th Marines. Both regiments were located in forward positions at Yudam-ni or its surrounding heights, and oriented to attack westward in compliance with General Almond's offensive. The 7th Marines also manned a few security points along the fifteen-mile stretch of mountain road connecting this advanced base with Hagaru-ri.

General Almond and Marine Lt. Col. George F. Waters, the corps liaison officer to the Marine division, traveled up the main supply road to Hagaru-ri and flew to Yudam-ni for a brief inspection of the front. Along the way Almond grumbled that the roads were jammed with vehicles and troops. He was dissatisfied with the few traffic control stations along the roadway and complained that drivers were not practicing convoy discipline. He demanded that the Marines take immediate steps to enforce traffic control, but these secondary considerations were soon overtaken by battlefield events.

For the big offensive, Colonel Murray's relatively fresh 5th Marines moved through the positions of Colonel Litzenberg's 7th Marines at Yudam-ni, as both regiments prepared to attack west along the main road leading to Mup'yong-ni. The night had been extremely windy with temperatures far below zero, and elements of the 5th and 7th Marines marched stiffly into attack positions. The assault began at a frosty 8:15 A.M. as Lt. Col. Harold S. Roise's 2d Battalion, 5th Marines, advanced to clear the roadway. The 3d Battalion of the 7th Marines rendered flank protection by advancing into the rugged slopes of two hills on either side of the road.

As the Marines started their attack, they were hit by heavy fire from Chinese bunkers hidden in the mountains. These bunkers consisted of logs wired together in double thickness, timbered ceilings, and rock and soil protection several feet deep. They seemed impervious to most artillery fire and air strikes, and could only be silenced by direct rocket hits. Throughout the day, fighter-bombers roared across the sky to deliver ordnance against the stone ridges. Howitzer barrages clouded the steep enemy-held mountains in smoke, but enemy machine guns and mortars hidden among the high rocks flared into action whenever the Marines tried to move forward. The Marine attack was stopped at 2:30 P.M., although some elements pinned by Chinese weapons received heavy fire until dusk.

The corps attack started with the expectation of brushing aside Chinese delaying forces, but by evening Marine commanders realized they were being checked by strongly entrenched defensive lines. The temperature was twenty below zero and was still dropping. At midnight, the jagged ice landscape and black mountain skyline glittered starkly under the full moon. The Marines were unaware that the Chinese were about to commence their own major offensive. The *79th* and *89th PLA Divisions* were moving into final positions aimed at crushing the Marines at Yudam-ni, while the *59th PLA Division* was making a wide sweep southward to seize Toktong Pass and cut the Marine supply road to Hagaru-ri. Their goal was nothing less than eliminating the entire Marine command.

The enemy attack against the Marine lines anchored outside Yudam-ni was initiated in the freezing darkness of November 27–28 by probing actions and intense mortar bombardments. The barrage was followed by Chinese probing parties who grenaded Marine outposts and disclosed targets for supporting machine guns. Suddenly, the chill air was pierced by hundreds of blaring bugles and shrill whistles all along the front. Thousands of *89th PLA Division* assault troops rushed across the moonlit snow and charged into the Marine hillside positions east of Yu-dam-ni.

The wave attacks continued as the onrushing ranks of Chinese were torn apart by Marine machine gunners, riflemen, and mortars, causing frightful carnage. Sections of the Marine front collapsed under this heavy pressure and Chinese infiltrators poured through gaps in the line. The Chinese who accomplished this breakthrough, however, were silhouetted by burning huts on the battleground and eliminated by Marine direct weapons fire. During the early morning, the Marine defenders made a fighting withdrawal from Hill 1403 overlooking the road junction at Yudam-ni.

At the same time, the *79th PLA Division* stormed across the high ground towards Yudam-ni from the north, with the objective of taking the ridge line between the town and the Changjin Reservoir. Marine companies posted on the three key hilltops of North Ridge were assaulted continuously in standard Chinese fashion, by groups of grenadiers and riflemen trying to wear down the defenders in conjunction with machine guns and mortar fire. The Chinese also surged through gaps in the line and occupied the high ground overlooking the road junction at the edge of town. In hours of bitter fighting through the icy cold darkness, the Marine lines were slowly driven back.

The key heights of Hill 1282 and 1240, overlooking Yudam-ni on its east (or rearward) side, were silhouetted by the flare-lit haze of battle as Chinese troops made repeated charges to secure the summits. The close-in fighting was often hand-to-hand, splitting Marine companies and destroying entire platoons. Throughout the night, the flashing howitzers of the 11th Marines, located on the frozen low ground, blasted the Chinese attackers along the semi-circular arc of contested ridges, but ammunition stocks were dwindling fast.

The Chinese finally took Hill 1282 in fierce combat. Several counterattacks by depleted Marine reserves failed to dislodge the victors. By dawn, the Chinese were also on top of Hill 1240, although a decimated Marine company managed to regain the lower slope. The combined attacks of the *89th* and *79th PLA Divisions* from the west and north never succeeded in smashing completely through the Marine perimeter, but they gained high ground which threatened the continued Marine ability to hold Yudam-ni.

While two Chinese divisions attacked the main Marine perimeter around Yudam-ni, the *59th PLA Division* moved south of the town to slice the fourteen-mile Marine logistical life-line to Hagaru-ri. Two companies of the 7th Marines, Company C under Capt. John F. Morris on Hill 1419 and Company F under Capt. William E. Barber in Toktong Pass, served as isolated sentinels along this roadway.

The battle for Hill 1419 commenced at 2:30 A.M., November 28, when Chinese infantrymen descended in force from the mountain crest and fought to eradicate Captain Morris's company situated on the slope. The seesaw battle lasted until dawn as Morris desperately reshuffled his scant headquarters reserves and 60mm mortars (his only source of supporting fire) into the hardest-pressed sectors. The radio was knocked out by enemy bullets and the Marines were nearly out of ammunition. Several Marines were killed by machine gun fire while trying to scale the rugged incline and drag wounded outpost members to safety. By the morning the Marines were still holding but pinned down by close grenade and automatic weapons fire.

The Chinese effort to gain possession of Toktong Pass began at the same time the Hill 1419 battle erupted. Captain Barber's Marine company, the "ridge-runners of Toktong Pass," was positioned to cover truck traffic in the three-mile gorge of this vital mountain pass. The Chinese assaulted the company from three sides, overwhelmed the forward squads on the summit, and quickly gained control of the peak. Hours of close combat and grenade exchanges followed as the enemy tried to drive a wedge between the company lines. Another Chinese attack was made uphill through the trees, forcing Barber to move his command post higher on the slope. Marine machine guns overlooking the roadway created a fire zone that the Chinese could not cross. At dawn, after seven hours of bitterly fought combat, the tempo of combat decreased but intermittent fire and grenadier assaults continued against the Marine defenders.

On November 28, two *PLA* divisions surrounded approximately eight thousand troops of the 5th and 7th Marines at Yudam-ni. Another division cut the main supply route at several points between the town and Hagaru-ri. Wheeled traffic was impossible, although two cut-off Marine companies stubbornly maintained positions along the road. Colonels Litzenberg and Murray switched their Marines to the defense and cancelled further attacks westward. Their first priority was security of Yudam-ni. In the early morning, the two Marine regiments began a series of counterattacks to push the Chinese off the commanding ridges behind the town. The northernmost hilltop along North Ridge was retaken, and Company C of the 5th Marines made a two-hour climb in the bone-chilling predawn air to reinforce the battered Marine survivors on the down-slope side of Hill 1282.

The Marines mustered their forces against Hill 1282 and conducted a frontal assault through a rain of grenades, forcing the Chinese off the military crest in close combat. Machine guns were emplaced and several Chinese counterattacks to regain this part of the hill were defeated. Fighting raged across Hill 1240 during the day, but the Chinese held on to the summit. The snowy peaks and rock slopes of North Ridge were covered with smashed equipment, wounded troops immobilized by the freezing conditions, and scores of bodies piled up around boulders and gullies.

Colonel Litzenberg's 7th Marines also attempted to reopen the main supply line south and rescue Companies C and F. After five hours of marching, climbing, and fighting, the relief column reached Company C and pulled back to Yudam-ni. Captain Barber of the Company F Toktong Pass ridge-runners gave assurances that he could hold if supplied by airdrops, and requested permission to stand fast when he was radioed to fight his way back after the relief attempt failed to reach his isolated men. The company called in continual air strikes and sent out patrols despite persistent sniper fire. Many of the wounded died because the plasma was frozen. Throughout the night of November 28–29, the thinning ranks of Marines countered another series of close assaults and probing attacks.

The duel at Toktong Pass continued the following day. Captain Barber was aware that enemy possession of this canyon would jeopardize withdrawal chances of the two Marine regiments at Yudam-ni. Many members of his shrinking force were now casualties, and Barber was severely wounded in the leg. The open ground was marked with colored parachutes from the previous day's air drops. These served to mark their positions for fighter-bomber support as well as cargo transport planes. The Air Force Combat Cargo Command sent C-119 Flying Boxcars to resupply the surrounded Marine unit, but much of the crucial mortar ammunition parachuted in the afternoon landed west. The Marines formed groups to retrieve the precious cargo, and these fought through concentrated enemy fire to bring back boxes of materiel littering the contested slopes.

A composite battalion of the 5th and 7th Marines was sent from Yudam-ni to reach Toktong Pass but the Chinese started massing in the broken hills and hidden draws on both sides of the road. During the afternoon, Colonel Litzenberg, the senior commander, was alerted to these ominous developments by aerial spotters, and he called off the relief attempt to prevent enemy entrapment of the composite battalion. In the meantime, the Marines carefully collapsed their extended perimeter around Yudam-ni to manageable proportions. At 7:30 in the evening, as the Marines braced for another bitter cold, sleepless night, General Smith directed Colonels Litzenberg and Murray to prepare plans for a breakout. Yudam-ni was destined to be the farthest point of the Marine advance in the northern offensive.

The freezing night of November 29–30 was spent huddling for warmth as illumination rounds cast shadows across the trees and snowy ground. Machine guns constantly opened fire to either keep the weapons operating or cut down Chinese infiltrators. The Marine ridge-runners of Toktong Pass spent the whole night miserably awake on guard listening to Chinese enticements to surrender for warmth in prisoner-of-war compounds.

On November 30, the Marines at Yudam-ni regrouped for the breakout attempt. Artillery and air strikes covered withdrawals from the final perimeter. The *Blue Goose* made a daring and successful sortie into the town to rescue some wounded. The light plane landed on the ice of the streambed as rifle bullets ricocheted over the frozen surface. The tip of her wing barely cleared the barrels of artillery howitzers firing near the end of the runway. Captain Keleman stated, "I was afraid our Goose was cooked that time."[1]

On December 1, the two regiments formed for the march. Most of the artillerymen became provisional infantry, and the soldiers of the composite battalion began wearing green parachute scarves and referring to themselves as the "Damnation Battalion."[2] In general, the Marine vehicular road march was protected by air strikes and columns of riflemen battling to clear the wooded hills on either side. The spearhead battalions were Lt. Col. Robert D. Taplett's 3d Battalion, 5th Marines, and Lt. Col. Raymond G. Davis's 1st Battalion, 7th Marines.

The Marine road column was led by M26 Pershing tank Number D-23 under the command of SSgt. Russell A. Munsell. This tank entered the Yudam-ni perimeter on November 27 on a trial run to test the ability of armored vehicles to traverse the icy mountain road. The crew was sent back to line up other tanks, but the Chinese cut the road. Staff Sergeant Munsell and another crewman were flown into Yudam-ni by helicopter, checked the tank over, and installed air-delivered fan belts and a new battery. At noon on December 1, Tank D-23 rumbled onto the road behind the point company, which would give fire missions to the tank.

During the night, Munsell's tank knocked out two enemy machine guns and an antitank crew. At dawn on December 2, Tank D-23 again led the Marine attack, destroying two Chinese roadblocks before its engine quit at 10 A.M. The crew changed batteries within a half-hour despite enemy rifle and sniper fire. Three hundred yards farther up the road, Munsell's tank encountered a third roadblock. The tank's 90mm gun was used to destroy the buildings and machine gun nests around this log-and-rubble obstruction, and the Marine infantry cleared the pathway by dark. By now the tank was running low on fuel and machine gun ammunition, and at 8 P.M. the crewmen walked back to get more petrol from other trucks. They returned with fifteen gallons of gas and bandoleers of ammunition donated by grateful Marines.

As Tank D-23 was moving down the primitive icy trail, the Marine riflemen covering the flanks of the motorized column trudged through waist-deep snow drifts. When opposition was encountered from entrenched enemy forces commanding the high ground overlooking the path of the advance, the Marines conducted repeated assaults up the steep, ice-covered slopes in the face of withering fire. Lieutenant Colonel Davis led his fatigued battalion over three successive ridges in the deep snow during continuous fighting that was sometimes hand-to-hand. Davis's battalion reached Barber's beleaguered rifle command late in the morning. The epic week-long stand by this lone company in bitter sub-zero weather had kept the Chinese from overrunning Toktong Pass, but only eighty-two of the original 220 men were able to walk away from their positions.

At 10 P.M. that night Munsell geared his tank into action against a fourth Chinese roadblock. During this fire fight the point company commander ordered the tank to back away from the enemy logjam, and while executing this maneuver Tank D-23 "bellied up." Most of the night was spent affixing cables and righting the armored monolith. In the meanwhile, the Marine riflemen repulsed several determined enemy attacks launched from the mountain crests against their positions.

The rearguard 3d Battalion of the 7th Marines was also hit hard. One valiant squad leader of Company J, Sgt. James E. Johnson, encouraged his men to hold their positions through an intensive enemy barrage. The bombardment was followed by an overwhelming attack by Chinese dressed in Marine parkas and field trousers, making identification difficult in the desperate battle. Wounded several times while he rendered covering fire, Johnson was last seen singlehandedly engaging the enemy troops in a grenade duel. He was declared missing in action on December 2 and after nothing further was heard, his status was changed on November 2, 1953, to deceased. His actions were recognized by the posthumous Medal of Honor.

At dawn on December 3 in Toktong Pass, the ground was covered with six inches of fresh snow. Lieutenant Colonel Davis deployed his battalion to secure the vital mountain pass and held these positions until the rest of the Marine column passed through. The Chinese roadblock was finally destroyed at 8 A.M., and the Marine advance continued with Munsell's tank in the lead. By this time, the entire tank crew was exhausted from lack of food and rest, as well as the constant smoke and fumes inside. The loader passed out and had to be replaced by a rifleman.

The Marine infantry on the flanks conducted a punishing overland march. To the men, it seemed like an interminable ordeal as they cleared Chinese from dug-in mountain positions and suffered high casualties and cold-weather injuries. As the overcast lifted, remaining Chinese-held positions along Toktong Pass were scorched by napalm and bombs. Air support was provided by carrier-based naval aircraft as well as B-26 light bombers of the Fifth Air Force.

The tank ran out of .30-cal machine gun ammunition while supporting a flanking attack by Marine infantry against a Chinese-held hill. The Marine column and its tank pushed through a fifth roadblock late in the morning. During a fierce mid-afternoon skirmish from the heavily defended sixth roadblock, the 90mm gun proved decisive. The attack on the seventh and final roadblock was coordinated with an air strike. Munsell's armored vehicle ran out of gas again in the evening, but the accompanying engineers poured in ten more gallons. Two hours before midnight on December 3, the leading elements of the 7th Marines followed Tank D-23 safely into the Hagaru-ri perimeter.[3]

Throughout the morning of December 4, the 5th and 7th Marines marched into Hagaru-ri. At 2 A.M., the prime movers towing eight 155mm howitzers ran out of diesel fuel. The tractors and their artillery pieces were moved off the road. A ninth tractor and medium howitzer skidded off the road and toppled down a ravine. Airstrikes were used to destroy any equipment left behind.

The last unit in line, the rearguard 3d Battalion of the 7th Marines, arrived at Hagaru-ri at 2 P.M. following a seventy-nine-hour running battle all the way from Yudam-ni. When the Marine drivers were asked how they managed to plug their bullet-riddled, leaking radiators during the long march, the men replied they had resorted to using Tootsie Roll bars.[4]

2. Regimental Destruction

On November 27, the eastern side of the iced-over Changjin Reservoir was held by a two-battalion task force of Colonel MacLean's 31st Infantry, supported by a weak battalion of light howitzers. The Army regiment was not organized in a compact defensive line, but was strung out ten miles in seven separate knots along the winding ribbon road paralleling the reservoir.

The forward element occupied a stark, snow-covered hill mass near the middle branch of the reservoir. This was the 1st Battalion of the 32d Infantry, led by Lt. Col. Don C. Faith, Jr. Farther south, tucked away in the hollow of an inlet where the roadway bridged Pungnyuri stream, was the 3d Battalion of the 31st Infantry under Lt. Col. William R. Reilly. His isolated perimeter also included the 57th Field Artillery Battalion's two firing batteries. The rest of the artillery, along with four 40mm antiaircraft self-propelled mounts and four quadruple machine gun half-tracks, was located even farther south. A tank company was situated well to the rear of these main groups and a solitary service company was encamped below Sasu-ri village. The summit of Pokko-chae separated this village from the Marine bastion of Hagaru-ri fourteen miles away.

The atmosphere was unsettling. Contrary to the pure-Marine units, every fourth man in MacLean's outfit was a South Korean KATUSA soldier unskilled in English or proper weapons handling. Now in the midst of a remote and barren wasteland, MacLean's troops were further handicapped by their inability to converse intelligibly with or depend on their own squad mates. The Koreans were unwilling soldiers, and any attempt to prod them into battle invariably caused casualties among their Army leaders.

In addition, the regimental jeep reconnaissance platoon had already "vanished" while scouting the dirt trail leading east along the Pungnyuri to the Pujon Reservoir. The regimental efforts to contact the missing men by radio were futile, because the lost platoon members were already dead or captured by the *80th PLA Division* which was moving closer to entrap MacLean's command.

The Chinese struck the vanguard of the mixed Army regiment in force just after midnight. They moved down the main road and infiltrated through the positions of the 1st Battalion on the left side, where many of the troops were caught sleeping. Achieving total surprise, the Chinese shot Americans in their foxholes, grenaded bunkers, and forced the mortar crews to abandon their weapons. Fighting became confused and savage, and at least one KATUSA soldier was decapitated when a Chinese pole-charge was rammed into his head.[5]

Shortly afterwards, other enemy attacks drove in the American lines on the right side of the road and succeeded in capturing the high ground. A Chinese attack down the main road using a T34 and SU76 self-propelled gun was halted, however, when Corp. James H. Godfrey destroyed both with his 75mm recoilless rifle. Faith's battalion partially restored its perimeter in brisk fighting that lasted until dawn, but suffered heavy casualties as ammunition ran low.

Farther south, another main Chinese assault force stormed the 3d Battalion and its associated artillery emplacements on the slopes overlooking the icy Pungnyuri inlet, where this stream entered the reservoir. The Chinese attackers in this area broke through the front lines and destroyed the battalion command post, killing almost everyone inside the hut. Lieutenant Colonel Reilly was wounded four times and knocked out by grenade blasts, and the Chinese left him for dead.

Surviving riflemen of the shattered line companies retreated and became intermixed with advancing Chinese grenadiers and burp gunners. The night fighting deteriorated into a vortex of close combat, where the babbling of Korean, Chinese, and English voices was drowned by screams of the wounded, a crescendo of gunfire, and enemy bugles and whistles. Trucks were set afire, the medical aid station was riddled with machine gun bullets (killing the regimental surgeon), and several howitzer and recoilless rifle positions were overrun. Lieutenant Colonel Embree was wounded and incapacitated. The Chinese withdrew from this smoldering battlefield at daybreak.

The Chinese also established a strong roadblock on Hill 1221, overlooking the main road leading from the Pungnyuri inlet to Sasu-ri village. Any wheeled journey would have to pass around this rugged height because the road veered away from the reservoir banks and looped around the hillside. The key summit provided an ideal site for passage obstruction, and the Chinese ambushed several medical vehicles from this vantage point in the early morning darkness. A final Chinese thrust was aimed at the separate artillery headquarters area where the tracked antiaircraft vehicles were located. One enemy column was decimated by the 40mm twin Bofors guns, but the cold froze up some of the quad machine guns and one 40mm mount was destroyed in exchange.[6]

At dawn on the cold, snowing morning of November 28, MacLean's command was under heavy enemy pressure and sliced in two. The regiment's battered infantry components were cut off completely from units below the roadblock. Sgt. James J. Feund, a mortar squad leader, remembered,

> It was after they [Chinese] started coming through on us they would start blowing these bugles and blowing whistles and everything else but that didn't bother the GIs. They would just fire all the more. During the first night we lost our sights, somehow they were busted. But the next day we fired better than 300 rounds. We didn't have anything . . . aiming stakes or no sights; just by moving the mortars from left to right. And we used pass-back communications. Just yelled from one man to the other. We had about five men strung out and used that [chain] for communications.[7]

General Almond flew by helicopter into Faith's 1st Battalion perimeter, where MacLean had also shifted his forward headquarters. It was apparent that no one understood the gravity of the situation. Almond lectured Faith that he should try to regain the lost high ground, and concluded by handing the battalion commander a Silver Star. He told Faith to select two other deserving recipients.

T. R. Fehrenbach described the incident in *This Kind of War*: "What Faith did next indicated something of his frame of mind. He snapped to a wounded young officer, Lieutenant Smalley, sitting on a five-gallon water can and waiting evacuation, 'Smalley, come over here and stand at attention!' Bewildered, Smalley obeyed. The next man to pass by was Sergeant Stanley, a mess steward. Faith called, 'Stanley, come here and stand at attention next to Lieutenant Smalley.' A dozen men, clerks, wounded and the like, were assembled to watch, while General Almond pinned Silver Stars on Faith's, and the other two men's parkas." After Almond departed this impromptu ceremony, Faith ripped off his medal and tossed it into the snow.[8]

During November 28, south of Hill 1221, the 7th Infantry Division assistant commander, Brig. Gen. Henry I. Hodes, directed Capt. Robert L. Drake's tank company to launch a counterattack against the reinforced Chinese roadblock. The pair of leading tanks were knocked out by enemy 3.5-inch rocket launcher teams and one was left blocking the road. Chinese soldiers swarmed over several other tanks and tried to lift hatches to toss in grenades, but they were killed by dusting fire from other supporting tanks. The rest of the tanks attempted to go around the icy sloping ground, but one crashed over a cliff and another bogged down with a thrown track. After watching the unsuccessful armored attack, General Hodes departed with another tank for the Marine base at Hagaru-ri. Captain Drake conducted another armored assault on Hill 1221 the following day, but lost two more tanks and on the afternoon of November 30 the tank company was called back into the Marine perimeter at Hagaru-ri.[9]

During the night of November 28–29, the *80th PLA Division* renewed its efforts to annihilate the 3d Battalion at the Pungnyuri inlet. Light snow was falling but some moonlight beamed through the overcast. Chinese attacks in the 3d Battalion's isolated sector made local penetrations, but most of the attackers were repulsed by concentrated 40mm and quad machine gun supporting fire from the tracked antiaircraft weapons.

In the forward zone of Faith's 1st Battalion, mortar fire broke up several Chinese attempts to rush down the road. The Chinese, however, used their commanding positions on the high ground, secured the night before, to make repeated charges on the battalion's right flank. At 2 A.M., Faith ordered the battalion to fall back toward the 3d Battalion. The sixty trucks in the perimeter were unloaded and filled with wounded. First Sgt. Richard S. Luna stated, "I saw all the casualties that had come down. There were a lot of dead. I saw them being drug in, frozen stiff already, and a lot of casualties also that had already been loaded on the trucks that had been pushed forward. Some had frostbite, frozen hands, frozen feet."[10]

At 4:30 A.M., November 29, the motorized column began moving south. The companies pulled out of their positions under fire, and this led to some instances of panic-stricken abandonment. The rear guard fought off several close assaults and then formed along the back of the column. The Chinese contented themselves with looting the rich stores of food and materiel left behind. The pursuit was close but not aggressive.

When the Chinese did not engage the tail of the column, the retreating men hoped to enter the other battalion perimeter at the Pungnyuri inlet without difficulty. When Faith's leading troops rounded the bend in the road and approached Pungnyuri stream, they were shocked to see the smoking battlefield and the log block across the bridge. Both the causeway and the bridge were under sniper and machine gun fire. The perimeter on the other side was smoldering from burning tents, vehicles, and positions destroyed in the previous night's fighting.

Faith realized that his men needed to get through as quickly as possible before the enemy charged their extended file. He sent infantry and recoilless rifle teams to secure the slopes of the hill overlooking the bridge. The troops conducted a strenuous climb over the snow and ice to the crest of the ridge line, and covered Faith's attempts to clear the bridge logjam. Although accounts of the action are hazy, the obstruction was probably cleared by a number of forward troops led by Faith and supported by some weapons fire from the other side. Apparently, many of the troops descended the ridge to assist, but the slippery trek downhill caused many injuries and lost weapons. The log obstruction was removed and the link-up accomplished.

During this episode, senior commander Colonel MacLean disappeared. The Army's official Korean War historian Roy Appleman conducted an extensive investigation into the circumstances of his disappearance. He concluded that MacLean was issuing battle orders and tried to cross the frozen inlet near the mouth of the stream where the Chinese were hidden around the bridge. He fell several times as he was hit by Chinese fire or slipped on the ice after being wounded. He was captured by Chinese who dragged him into some brush-covered islands. The mystery was resolved when an American prisoner released by the Chinese stated that MacLean died from his wounds four days later, during his journey to a Chinese prison camp, and was buried in a grave near the roadway.[11]

The remnants of the Army force at the Pungnyuri inlet assumed the designation of Task Force Faith. The task force was in bad tactical shape, with over five hundred wounded and low on critical ammunition. The troops were balled up in a tight perimeter on the lower slopes and flatland south of Pungnyuri stream, and dominating Chinese positions on the higher ground looked down their throats from all sides. The force was out of radio contact with other ground forces—either because of terrain interference with radio transmission or incompatibility of Marine and Army sets—and thus unaware of the strong Chinese roadblock at Hill 1221. The only way to reach the cut off unit was by helicopter and only three landings were made, twice to evacuate wounded (including Lieutenant Colonels Reilly and Embree), and once to whirl in General Barr for a hasty battle session with Faith.

The task force held its ground for two more frigid nights of harrowing combat in which temperatures dipped to thirty below and men froze sitting up in their foxholes. The only sliver of hope was the close air support that strafed and napalmed Chinese positions and dropped a few precious cargo bundles during the daylight hours. The Chinese tightened their vice inexorably around the isolated unit, and combat intensified through a snowstorm-laden overcast that threatened further aerial assistance. On the morning of December 1, Faith decided to attempt a breakout from the Pungnyuri inlet and reach safety in the Marine lines.

The wounded were placed in the trucks. There were so many casualties that one 2½-ton truck was triple tiered with rows of prostrate litter cases on jerry-rigged decks built up over the cargo bed. The crucial 40mm mounts were apparently counted on to deliver the infantry-killing firepower that might get the caravan the final eight miles to Hagaru-ri. Unfortunately, three of these had been either destroyed or immobilized in previous fighting, and the lone operable machine was out of 40mm rounds. Two of the quad machine gun half-tracks were also abandoned because of dead batteries, and the other two were very low on gas and ammunition.[12]

The column started moving between noon and 1 P.M., when a few Marine Corsairs from the aircraft carrier (CV-32) *Leyte* managed to fly through the clouds and lend close air support against the Chinese positions surrounding Faith's perimeter. One aircraft, however, dropped a napalm tank prematurely and enveloped the leading contingent of Faith's task force in a sheet of flame. The jellied wall of fire burned the leading troops to death and threw the breakout effort into chaos at the outset. First Sergeant Luna stated,

> I could see when the first napalm bomb was dropped and they got some of our men. You could see them running all around just ripping their clothes off, just keeping on running. I mean both the ROKs and the GIs. And it was only within a matter of 200 or 300 yards, just outside our perimeter. And it was a matter of another 200 or 300 yards that the enemy was. . . . I had to step right over the enemy [killed by the air strikes], over the enemy dead. We had to take the enemy dead off the roads so the trucks could get through. We made a break forward [down the main road] and there was just a mass of wounded being put on the trucks, one on top of the other. The trucks still kept on moving forward. We got what wounded we could out. I mean just kept loading them on and onto the trucks. It was impossible to get all of them on. I do not recall right now just how many were left behind.[13]

Lt. Cecil G. Smith of the 32d Infantry recalled the conditions of the retreat,

Because the (left) flank was on rather rough terrain and the men were getting shot, the men were inclined to move across the railroad track on to the road. All the officers and non-coms [sergeants] were continually pushing the men off to the left flank which was the ridge. The men did not care to get up on that part because there was quite a few Chinese. We continued on down the road until we hit the road block, at which place the road [bridge] was blown [at Paegamni creek].[14]

The destroyed bridge at Paegamni Creek was an unpleasant surprise (no one knows why this obstruction was not reported by air) that forced traffic into a low, marshy area that could only be traversed by tracked vehicles. The trucks bogged down after they broke through the ice and into the swamp grass. The self-propelled 40mm carriage went across the streambed and then its winch cable was hooked to each truck in turn to pull it across. Almost every truck had to be towed over the creek in this fashion, taking precious time and allowing the enemy to reorganize. The wounded were screaming as the trucks were rough-handled over the broken ground and enemy fire peppered the troops. It was dark before the entire convoy was able to negotiate this difficult bypass around the blown bridge.[15]

Task Force Faith reached the main enemy road block at Hill 1221 as nightfall eliminated all chance of air support. The 40mm gun carriage would not restart after its engine was turned off, and the Chinese riddled the stalled convoy with automatic weapons fire that cut into the trucks and the wounded on board. The roadblock was placed in a ravine with more automatic weapons on both sides of the hill. There was little choice but to storm the hill by direct frontal assault. Lieutenant Smith relates,

We tried to advance troops around the left flank of the roadblock and they were immediately driven back by the heavy fire. The men all started gathering up and they were getting hit very rapidly. So a few of the non-coms and officers decided that we would push them across the hill and overrun the Chinese positions on top of the hill. After we got on the hill we threw hand grenades at the machine gun position, but we did not knock it out. The point of approximately 40 men flanked the machine gun position and kept moving on the road and later they got in the valley. There was approximately fifteen men left on the hill with Lt.

Barnes and myself. After we had seen that the point had advanced there was no chance to withdraw from this position. We decided that we would move forward and try to catch the point. We got on the road and marched forward for approximately one mile without getting a shot fired at us. Just prior to reaching the ice [of the reservoir] approximately 25 Chinese came off the hill from our left and chased us on the ice. We could not return fire because at that time we were out of ammunition. After we had reached 500 yards out on the ice there was one wounded man who had fallen back on the ice. One fanatic Chinese came out on the ice and bayoneted him.[16]

The struggle to get around the main roadblock was also described by Capt. Robert J. Kitz, the commander of Company K, 31st Infantry,

The ice broke in a couple of places [near the first blown bridge at Paegamni Creek]. People fell in the water. Some got in and some didn't. I got in the water and was lucky to get out. The vehicles moving along the road were being shot at. . . . We got to the place where the big roadblock was. The terrain was ideal for a roadblock. These were a hairpin curve, a big nose [of high ground], and a long ridge we had to go around. I was under the impression that our friendly forces were right on the other side of that ridge. . . . So the vehicles got caught on the road on the side of this hill. We couldn't move because of the roadblock. The Gooks were on top shooting down and the Gooks were on the bottom shooting up. And we were caught in the middle. The vehicles were caught. The wounded were in the vehicles and a lot of lead was flying.[17]

The strongest of several Chinese blocking positions echeloned down the road consisted of logs stacked around the two destroyed tanks of Drake's command. One of them was upside down, resting on its turret.

The logs were removed in heavy fighting, but only a few trucks negotiated the hairpin curve around Hill 1221. Most of the wounded were either left in stalled vehicles, or lined along the road as inoperable vehicles were thrown off the side in an effort to get the convoy moving again. The column broke apart in the darkness and was destroyed piecemeal as it moved across a ford near the Marine-repaired concrete bridge south of Hill 1221. Lieutenant Colonel Faith himself was seriously wounded just above the heart by a grenade at the tank-log trap and was placed in the cab of the lead truck. According to Roy Appleman's investigation into his death, Faith was killed when this truck made a final dash toward Sasu-ri and was stopped by enemy fire only two miles from the Marine encampment at Hagaru-ri.[18]

Several splintered groups of Task Force Faith soldiers struck out for Hagaru-ri over the ice of the Changjin Reservoir, using the North Star as a point of reference. Not one vehicle, crew-served weapon, or piece of baggage was brought out. The only rifles, pistols, and ammunition ever saved were carried by soldiers straggling into Hagaru-ri over the next several days. The *80th PLA Division* virtually annihilated Colonel MacLean's 3,300-man command.

No one ever knew how many troops were killed by enemy fire, captured and died in captivity, froze to death along the roadway, or perished in individual efforts to escape across the reservoir. When the Marines pulled out of Hagaru-ri, only 385 able-bodied soldiers were left from MacLean's organization. They were merged with the other 490 Army soldiers stationed in the Marine perimeter and formed a composite Army battalion.

3. Nights of Fire

The Marine advanced command post of Hagaru-ri, at the southern tip of the Changjin Reservoir, was occupied by three thousand Marines. Division commander General Smith was also at Hagaru-ri, far in advance of corps headquarters, where he only had to endure transitory visits from Almond. Lt. Col. Thomas L. Ridge, the commander of the 3d Battalion, 1st Marines (the largest unit at the site), was in charge of the town defenses. He formed a perimeter composed of his Marine reinforced rifle battalion, cannoneers of the 11th Marines, corps signal troops, elements of Marine 1st Service Battalion, Army and Marine engineers, and various headquarters elements. The Chinese offensive also isolated Hagaru-ri. Ridge sent a tank-escorted patrol to probe the road southward across the plateau toward Koto-ri, but he ordered it back after being notified by aerial observers that three hundred Chinese were about to surround the patrol.

About an hour before midnight on November 28, as light snow began to fall, the Chinese conducted their first direct assault against the Hagaru-ri perimeter. The Marines occupied good defensive positions along most of the perimeter. Many foxholes had been dynamited out of the ground by using explosive charges in ration tins, and reinforced by dirt-filled sandbag parapets. These positions were protected by strands of concertina wire filled with booby traps. Other parts of the perimeter were not as well guarded, and hastily occupied just prior to the attack.

The Chinese fired red flares and blasted whistles as they charged into the wire barriers, dousing the Marine and Army positions with a barrage of white phosphorous mortar shells. The defensive machine guns and artillery responded and tracers and exploding shells lit the darkness. Groups of Chinese dodged through the shadows and some rolled down a hillside to rise up suddenly on the very edge of Marine positions. In the confusion of this hard-fought action, Chinese infiltrators who penetrated the defense lines near the airstrip started roaming the inner area. By midnight, the combat was general everywhere along and inside the perimeter, and the wooden medical clearing station was riddled by enemy machine gun fire.

One of the key defensive points at Hagaru-ri was East Hill, a steep rocky ridge that rose three hundred feet straight up on the northeast side of the perimeter across the Changjin River. East Hill was occupied in the evening by Army engineers of the 185th Engineer Battalion (reinforced by Company D, 10th Engineer Battalion) and Army signalers of the 4th Signal Battalion after an exhausting climb to the top. Darkness prevented proper organization of a coherent defensive line. There were plenty of crevices among the jagged rocks and the soldiers occupied these holes randomly. The defenders of East Hill had machine guns and a few rocket launchers, but no mortars or recoilless rifles with them.

The Chinese stormed East Hill in conjunction with their attack on the entire Hagaru-ri perimeter and quickly cut through the South Korean labor units placed on the mountain top. Despite the continuous Marine howitzer and heavy mortar fire placed on the blackened hill mass, the Chinese assault troops soon chopped the defensive line into separate pockets of resistance along the rocky moonscape.

Lt. Norman R. Rosen of the 10th Engineer Battalion was forced to shift part of his platoon to confront flanking enemy grenadiers after a contingent of South Korean construction workers fled down the slope early in the battle. This costly maneuver was executed in the midst of the fire fight, and a number of engineers were cut down as they tried to occupy new positions. His company had experienced so much turbulence in recent personnel assignments that some of its members were more acquainted with its KATUSA Koreans than the newly arrived Army replacements. Unfortunately, the KATUSA soldiers became completely demoralized early in the battle and cowered in their holes, refusing to even hand out ammunition—claiming to be out. Later the American engineers discovered that most of the South Koreans never fired a shot and their pouches were full of M1 rifle and carbine bullets.

Company D withdrew to a tight perimeter on the hill crest, but suffered heavily from concentrated enemy mortar barrages. Although some radios were on hand, the devices were short-range. One engineer lieutenant remembered having exceptionally good communications with the Marines through most of the night, only to discover the next morning that he had been talking to the Marine liaison officer attached to the engineers, who was located just a few holes over from his own location. The communications had ceased abruptly when this Marine officer was killed.

The Army engineers ran low on ammunition, but they repulsed charge after charge as the Chinese attacked incessantly with thirty- or forty-man groups led by whistle-chirping leaders. The Chinese never massed into large clusters, but swarmed from the boulders and across the ravines, forcing 3.5-inch rocket launcher teams to blast individual targets. In their haste to occupy the summit, the engineers never wiped the oil off their machine guns and the weapons sputtered or jammed in the subzero cold. The soldiers scooped up scores of Thompson submachine guns dropped by enemy dead in front of their rock ledge and used these to keep fighting.

The Chinese penetrated the lines at East Hill in several areas, primarily where South Korean troops were forced off the summit. The engineers of Company D held their isolated position despite heavy casualties until a composite Marine relief force reached them later in the day. Lieutenant Rosen recalled, ''The Marines tended to be critical of our company for its operations of the night, in spite of our holding the position. They estimated that we had been hit by an enemy battalion of 1,000 and we counted more than 400 bodies in front of our positions when daylight came. No account was taken of our inexperience, or that we were thrust into a combat role suddenly, without orientation or support. Months passed before the Marines gave us recognition for even having been in their perimeter.''[19]

During the predawn darkness of November 29, Marine Maj. Reginald R. Myers gathered a composite unit of Army and Marine service and headquarters elements totalling about two hundred fifty men to retake East Hill. The ad hoc force was severely handicapped by lack of trained riflemen and experienced leaders, but Myers valiantly led his men forward in persistent attempts to regain the maximum ground prior to daylight. During the day, Myers launched further counterattacks on East Hill. The troops moved up the steep and icy, fog-enshrouded mass of jumbled rock, but were challenged immediately by Chinese grenadiers and snipers posted among the rocks and deep ravines.

Myers's attackers moved forward despite slippery footing on the new-fallen snow and the treacherous jagged rock, but were exhausted from cold fatigue and the all-night battle. After fourteen hours of raging combat in subzero temperatures, Myers's force suffered 170 casualties. The force was defeated just short of the summit, but Myers directed close air strikes and Marine howitzer barrages which mauled the remaining enemy positions on East Hill. The following night passed quietly without incident along the main perimeter.

The snow-covered East Hill commanded the entire valley southeast of town as well as the line of march to be used in event of a breakout to the south. At 8 A.M. on November 30, Capt. Carl L. Sitter's Company G of the 1st Marines tried to retake this strategic objective. Sitter led his depleted Marine company up the steep, frozen hillside under blistering fire from well-entrenched enemy machine guns. As casualties thinned the Marine ranks, Sitter realigned his men and personally directed his forward platoons as they continued the drive to the top of the ridge. The Marine infantry were also thwarted by the nature of the jagged mountain, however, which prohibited them from closing against the enemy machine gunners concealed in rocky crevasses without taking unacceptable losses.

Major General Smith decided that relief expeditions could neither be mounted in the direction of his own Marines struggling to escape the Yudam-ni trap, or in the direction of Army troops cut off on the east side of Changjin Reservoir. The continued survival of the Hagaru-ri garrison was in doubt.

4. Relief from the Sky

When the Chinese moved into positions dominating the vital Allied supply lines, the forward Marine and Army units became dependent on air-delivered or parachuted supplies and equipment. The Far East Command took most of its C-47 and C-119 cargo planes off routine assignments during this emergency, and detailed them to Korean airdrop missions. The principal aerial-resupply base at Ashiya, Japan, was reinforced with extra workers and Japanese laborers and round-the-clock relief measures were instituted. The magnitude of this effort increased from the twenty-four short tons of ammunition, medical supplies, and rations dropped to X Corps on November 28, to over 256 tons airdropped from Japan alone on December 5. During this eight-day period, the overall weight of supplies and equipment requested by the 1st Marine Division alone totalled 1,237 short tons.[20]

The Air Force relied on two types of aircraft to deliver these life-sustaining combat cargos over the frozen Korean ranges. The venerable Douglas C-47 Skytrain of World War II fame served as a sturdy workhorse of these operations. Cargo ejection from C-47s was accomplished by "kickers" who pushed the cargo out the side door as the aircraft flew over the drop zone. The amount of supplies delivered to any given drop zone depended on the skill of the kickers. This method also required the C-47 to make four to six runs over a drop zone to deliver any appreciable amount of supplies. Resupply efforts were greatly assisted by the Yonp'o-based Marine 1st Air Delivery Platoon, a Fleet Marine Force unit specializing in C-47 use.

The newer C-119 Flying Boxcars could carry an airdrop payload of six tons, compared to the two and a half tons carried by a C-47. Some Japan-based C-119s were even sent to Yonp'o for more immediate response. Troops from the 2348th Quartermaster Airborne Air Supply and Packaging Company provided the technical expertise. On C-119 aircraft rigged for airdrops, the rear clamshell doors were removed and rows of skate rollers were installed on the cargo floor. The supply packages were bundled on four-foot square plywood pallets, tied down, and anchored into cables with their parachute static lines. As the aircraft approached the drop zone, the man riding in the cargo compartment untied the load and the pilot slowed aircraft speed to about 110 knots. Over the drop zone the pilot signalled release by ringing the emergency bell and the man pulled sharply on the shroud line. The load travelled free from the rollers and cleared through the open rear fuselage in three to six seconds as the pilots applied climbing power and raised the aircraft's nose.[21]

Unfortunately, C-119 aircraft often scattered their deliveries beyond intended drop zones. Many times the Flying Boxcars arrived over the drop zone and maneuvered into perfect dropping position but several seconds elapsed before the first chutes left the rear of the plane—causing the cargo to fall over a wide area (and sometimes into enemy hands). The problem was attributed to faulty C-119 release systems. Parachutes occasionally separated from their packages, a factor caused by pilots pulling up too steeply instead of leveling out.

Air dropping supplies was always a chancy business. Several planes lost their loads on take-off, or spilled them inadvertently between the airfield and drop zones. Some pilots missed the drop zones completely because of the high cross-wind, poor visibility, or loss of ground communications. The containers were either recovered by the enemy or drifted into fire-swept areas inaccessible to recovery parties. One pilot, who failed to heed the advice of a ground controller, dropped his cargo right over Hagaru-ri airfield and crippled three C-47 aircraft parked on the runway. High-speed aerial delivery containers, developed by the Marine Corps equipment board and designed to fit the external bomb racks of fighter-type aircraft, were not used because they were unavailable in Korea.[22]

High levels of failure were experienced with some critical types of cargo. About a third of all airdropped gasoline was lost because the five-gallon can handles (through which the webbing was tied) had a tendency to break when the parachutes popped open. These cans still proved superior to fifty-five-gallon drums, of which nearly half (40 percent) ruptured upon striking the ground. Less than half of all parachuted rifle and machine gun ammunition was recovered in usable condition. Poor packing of small-arms cartons overloaded parachutes and the speed of descent caused the cases to break open when striking the ground.

Standard artillery ammunition drops were the least successful of all, and only a fourth of the munitions requested ever got to the gun pits. Tank and artillery rounds were easily damaged by rough handling because comparatively light blows dented the cases or whacked the projectiles out of alignment far enough to render them unserviceable. Even in the best of drops, most containers sustained some breakage when they struck the frozen, concrete-hard ground. Parachute malfunctions caused the loss of some entire attached loads, and several Marine ground casualties were caused by this hazard. Fortunately, airdropped mortar ammunition had much higher rates of success, and reliance on these munitions became essential.[23]

The greatest air relief effort was devoted to flying out the ambulatory wounded who were trapped at Hagaru-ri because overland travel routes were cut by the Chinese. The condition of these patients demanded immediate medical attention, but a field capable of handling regular cargo planes was still being finished. In the meantime, the engineers blasted and bulldozed a makeshift airstrip out of a narrow streambed in a deep mountain valley. When it was finished, the crudely fashioned strip was so rough and short that landing even light planes beckoned suicide. 7th Infantry Division Aviation Section Maj. Lyle M. Wright recalled, "It would have been dangerous to land on it under perfect weather conditions, but due to the seriousness of the situation all pilots of the section volunteered to try."[24]

The mercy mission was titled "Operation Little Lift." Only the smallest corps aircraft could be used, and the light aviation sections of the 3d and 7th Infantry Divisions, as well as Marine and corps command assets, were diverted from their normal air recon, artillery spotting, and liaison missions to the task of casualty evacuation. The planes used were primarily L-4 Piper Cub Grasshoppers and L-5 Stinsons.

To reach this airstrip, pilots flew their unarmed two-seater aircraft from Hamhung sixty miles over the steeply rising mountains. Like most aircraft of this type, the small Grasshopper sixty-five-horsepower engines strained as they climbed higher, their power decreasing as altitude increased. The airmen used sheer muscle and grim determination to navigate through the gale-force winter winds and low-hanging storm clouds. During the twenty-minute flight to reach the field, it was not unusual for sudden snow squalls to completely envelop aircraft in a fog of zero visibility.

On the final landing approach, pilots were forced to guide their flimsy machines through cloud openings and run a gauntlet of close enemy fire from the mountain crests overlooking the tiny airstrip. The winds roaring through the treacherous canyon walls created a virtual wind tunnel, and the runway was often covered in treacherous snow. Pilot Capt. Thomas C. Jennings stated, "Descent to the Hagaru-ri airstrip was made over enemy-held terrain and machine gun and small-arms fire was directed at aircraft from ranges of less than five hundred yards. Icing conditions existed and descents were made between low-hanging clouds causing the aircraft to ice up and quit. Numerous dead stick landings were made."[25]

The planes brought in blankets and essential medical supplies. Weight limitations and plane design precluded the carrying of litter patients, but the pilots tore out the back seats of their L-5s and flew out two litter cases on each return trip. The mercy missions were flown from dawn to dusk, in weather that normally grounded all flights and under climatic conditions that prevented normal aircraft operation. Back at Hamhung, the mechanics worked through the night hours to patch up bullet-riddled frames, wind-damaged supports, and overworked engines for the next day's mission.

The *Blue Goose* joined the ranks of all X Corps aircraft in Operation Little Lift to fly the hundreds of wounded men to safety from the encircled Marine base at Changjin Reservoir. For six straight days the *Blue Goose* flew twenty-six times over the six thousand-foot "Chosin Range," hauling ammunition, stretchers, and medical supplies for the embattled troops and bringing out wounded men each trip. Miraculously, the *Blue Goose* came through this operation without a surface scratch, halting only long enough on landings to refuel and take on a new load.

Normal inspections were ignored as the plane chalked up fifty-five hours of straight flight time, flying seven hours a day during the evacuation. Even in the coldest days, when it was 26 below zero, her crew stuck an exhaust tube from a truck into the engine cowling and in fifteen minutes the aircraft prop was spinning. After Operation Little Lift, the *Blue Goose* still seemed in good external shape, apart from her faded blue color and a few frayed edges. But the Changjin ordeal had cost the aircraft in an unseen way, just as it had many units in X Corps. The plane lost some of its old power when she took off from the Ko-to-ri airstrip at four thousand feet with a two hundred-pound overload. The *Blue Goose* was finally worn out, and everyone knew she had to be replaced. "She may have heard about rotation," Keleman laughed,[26] but it was a hollow phrase everyone was using. The spirit may have been present, but the power of X Corps, represented by the valiant *Blue Goose*, was diminished.

5. The X Corps Predicament

On November 28, the second day of the Chinese offensive against X Corps, General Almond visited the 1st Marine Division command post at Hagaru-ri and helicoptered to Colonel MacLean's regimental combat team on the eastern shore of the Changjin Reservoir. That evening, Almond was reported missing.

The search for General Almond was begun at Hagaru-ri at once. The X Corps transportation officer called the Marine division command post and stated that Almond was supposed to meet Colonel Beauchamp but the corps commander could not be found. Numerous phone calls failed to locate the general. At 10:30 P.M., the corps called and requested active assistance in locating Almond. The Marine Provost Marshal responded by dispatching several patrols to aid in the search. Within twenty minutes, a X Corps staff member called again and reported that the general had been located. The weary rifle teams were called back inside the Hagaru-ri perimeter.[27]

The mystery of Almond's whereabouts related to General MacArthur's sudden top-secret council of war that necessitated the corps commander's departure from Yonp'o airfield for Japan at 5 P.M. General MacArthur notified Almond in his urgent summons that Walker would also be present, and Almond understood the session's importance at once, because both field commanders in Korea were being called back to Far East Command headquarters. Almond flew into Haneda airport on a C-54 Skymaster, accompanied by his most trusted wartime companion, Lieutenant Colonel McCaffrey, his prime intelligence chief, Colonel Glass, and his aide, Major Ladd.

Almond arrived at 9:30 and was told to proceed directly to General MacArthur's residence at the American embassy in Tokyo. MacArthur was waiting with a bevy of the top UN commanders of the Korean theater. Vice Adm. Charles Turner Joy (Naval Forces Far East), Lt. Gen. George E. Stratemeyer (Far East Air Force), Lt. Gen. Walton H. Walker (Eighth Army), Maj. Gen. Doyle O. Hickey (acting chief of staff for Far East Command), Maj. Gen. Charles A. Willoughby (FEC intelligence officer), Maj. Gen. Edwin K. Wright (FEC operations officer) and Maj. Gen. Courtney Whitney (MacArthur's military secretary) were also present.

The conference lasted from 9:50 P.M. until 1:30 A.M. on November 29, and involved a full discussion of the adverse situation occasioned by formidable Chinese intervention in Korea, as well as measures needed to counter the enemy onslaught. The Eighth Army had been hit by the full force of the Chinese offensive on a broad front since November 25. The army's reserves were consumed in the heavy fighting and its right flank was unprotected. Walker expressed his concern that the Chinese were trying to outflank and surround his army. He believed at that time, however, that he could still stabilize the front around the former North Korean capital of P'yongyang with help from X Corps. MacArthur authorized Walker to withdraw as necessary to negate the danger of encirclement.

The situation of X Corps was just as perilous because it was widely strung out through difficult terrain in a series of separated columns, and subject to piecemeal isolation and destruction. The Chinese offensive against the corps sector, however, was more localized (being directed at the central area) and thus the full extent of enemy involvement was not as readily apparent to Almond. Lack of communications prevented a full appreciation of the destruction being wrought against MacLean's regiment, and the level of combat along the Marine front was only entering its second night and still developing.

Under the circumstances, the conversation turned to how Almond's X Corps, being less seriously engaged, could assist the desperate situation confronting Walker's Eighth Army. Rather surprisingly, Almond expressed his view that X Corps could continue its attacks northwest from the Changjin Reservoir and help Eighth Army by cutting the enemy rear line of communication. It was apparent that Almond did not understand the reality of the Changjin disaster, even though he had just personally visited all units engaged on that front.[28]

Almond even agreed to use the 3d Infantry Division in a westward attack to connect his force with Eighth Army if Walker agreed to supply the division after it crossed to the west side of the Taebaek Mountains, the agreed line of demarcation between Eighth Army and X Corps. Almond went so far as to order the attack, but later cancelled it because, as he related to official Army historians, Walker failed to give assurances about logistical arrangements, the severity of the winter weather, and the possibility of strong Chinese forces in the gap between the two Allied commands.[29]

No decisions were made at the conference itself, but at noon MacArthur gave Almond new operating instructions as he prepared to return to Korea. He ordered Almond to terminate all offensive movement, withdraw, and concentrate in the area of Hamhung and Hungnam. He wanted X Corps safely consolidated, but still in position to "geographically threaten" the main line of supply for the Chinese forces striking either Walker's flank or pouring through the gap between his forces and into South Korea. Furthermore, MacArthur felt that any Chinese formations "diverted" to the X Corps front left them fewer divisions to use against Walker's Eighth Army.[30]

During the return flight to Korea, Almond began preparing a new corps order, concentrating X Corps for the protection of the Hamhung enclave and action against the enemy wherever possible. During the night of November 29, the staff developed X Corps Operation Order No. 8, which discontinued further corps advances and dictated withdrawal to insure overall corps cohesiveness.

At the end of November, as the subordinate corps units dutifully attempted to execute Order No. 8, the strength of the Chinese offensive was much clearer. Almond's corps was over-extended and fragmented in northern Korea's wind-swept mountain ranges and frozen remote highland plateaus. One Army regimental command was annihilated and the Marine division was virtually entrapped. Only Marine combatant skill could accomplish its extrication. Other corps forces were also threatened, and only quick action in reaching the main corps defensive perimeter could save them. X Corps was on the brink of disaster.

Notes

1. Lt. Col. Kenneth E. Lay, "Korea's Blue Goose," p. 5.
2. Montross and Canzona, Vol. III, p. 251.
3. 1st Marine Division Special Action Report, Annex Oboe Oboe, dtd 15 January 1951, pp. 20–32.
4. Montross and Canzona, Vol. III, p. 278.
5. Roy E. Appleman, *East of Chosin,* Texas A&M University Press, College Station, 1987, pp. 65–76.
6. Appleman, *Chosin,* p. 97.
7. Transcription of recorded statement by Sgt. James J. Freund, Mortar Squad, Co A, 1st Bn, 32d Inf, December 1950.
8. T. R. Fehrenbach, *This Kind of War,* MacMillan Company, New York, 1963, p. 361.
9. Tank Co, 31st Inf Regt Ltr, Subj: Operations Summary, dtd 12 December 1950.
10. Transcription of recorded statement by 1SGT Richard S. Luna, Co B, 1st Bn, 32d Inf, 3 December 1950.
11. Appleman, *Chosin,* pp. 146–147.
12. Appleman, *Chosin,* p. 200.
13. Statement of 1SG Richard S. Luna, p. 3.
14. Transcription of recorded statement made by 1Lt. Cecil G. Smith, Co A, 1st Bn, 32d Inf, 2 December 1950.
15. Appleman, *Chosin,* Chapter 16.
16. Transcript of Lieutenant Smith.
17. Transcription of recorded statement by Capt. Robert J. Kritz, Co K, 3d Bn, 31st Inf, dtd 3 December 1950.
18. Appleman, *Chosin,* pp. 275–277. Lt. Col. Don C. Faith was awarded the Medal of Honor posthumously.
19. "Combat Comes Suddenly," Dept. of the Army, *Combat Support in Korea,* Combat Forces Press, 1955, p. 210.
20. 1st Marine Division Special Report, Annex Dog, dtd 23 February 1951, Appendix 1, p. 3. This total was broken down in short tons requested as: 298.6 for Yudam-ni; 40.9 for Toktong Pass (Company F, 7th Marines); 372.7 for Hagaru-ri; and 524.9 for Koto-ri.
21. Capt. Charles C. Thebaud, *Problems in the Airdrop of Supplies and Personnel,* Far East Command, dtd 15 August 1952.
22. Annex Dog, Appendix 1, p. 6.
23. Ibid., Annex Dog, Appendix 1, pp. 4–5.
24. 7th Inf Div Light Avn Sec, *Recommendation for Unit Citation,* Certificate of Maj. Wright.
25. Ibid., Certificate of Captain Jennings.
26. X Corps files, Lt. Col. Lay, p. 9.

27. 1st Marine Division Special Action Report, Annex Easy Easy, dtd 15 January 1951, p. 19.
28. Appleman, *Chosin,* p. 170.
29. Schnabel, p. 279.
30. Schnabel, p. 280.

CHAPTER 11

X CORPS CRISES

1. The Nadir of Corps Fortune

On December 1, X Corps strength totalled 114,307 troops, minus those killed or missing and not yet tabulated into the daily morning reports.[1] The freezing morning was ushered in with heavy snowfall and low overcast skies. At the Hamhung "airstrip" outside the corps command post—a city street terminating at one end in a traffic circle complete with a battle-scarred Red Star-topped concrete monument—the stinging cold temperature at daybreak registered zero. It rose only ten or fifteen degrees during the course of the day, and the wind stiffened by afternoon to a matching ten to fifteen knots. The weather was much colder in the higher elevations.

The low visibility and snowed-over airstrips held Marine Air Wing sorties to eighty-eight during the day, and most of the air support was concentrated in the Changjin Reservoir sector where it was most needed for withdrawing Army and Marine troops on both sides of the frozen lake. By evening, however, the Navy Seventh Fleet sent the message, "Regret weather conditions preclude air operations by Task Force 77 to support 1st Marine Division." X Corps informed the Marine Division that land-based air support could be furnished, albeit to a limited extent, but that the crucial carrier aircraft strikes were cancelled by weather. The soldiers remarked ruefully, "the weather came straight from Siberia, just like everything else the Commies are using."[2]

Elements of the *58th PLA Division* attacked from midnight until dawn at the 1st Marine Division forward base of Hagaru-ri. The main attack came from the south and east, but a secondary attack was made from the west. The enemy directed his primary effort against the engineer and service battalion defensive areas, targeting the regimental command as the apparent objective. Heavy fighting lasted throughout the darkness of early morning as Chinese shock troops tried to get past rows of concertina wire, trip flares, and booby traps. Several enemy soldiers who swarmed through the entanglements were killed at bayonet point within the line of Marine foxholes.

The perimeter was silhouetted in brilliant light after enemy artillery shelling set fire to dozens of gasoline drums in the central supply dump. The enemy charged the American positions on the edge of East Hill during the night in a sudden, vicious counterattack that set the hill ablaze with mortar explosions and machine gun tracers. Many sections of the hill were never defended because of manpower shortages, and Marine artillery was relied upon to block these gaps with barrages.

Company G of the 1st Marines defended their positions in hand-to-hand combat as enemy soldiers made repeated charges and grenaded the command post. Captain Sitter led the desperate defense, even though painfully wounded in the face, arms, and chest by bursting hand grenades. The Marine lines were dented but soon restored with the assistance of reserves rushed forward, including a number of Royal Marines. The battle for East Hill ended in a stalemate at dawn.

Throughout the Hagaru-ri perimeter, hundreds of Chinese were heaped in the wire lanes and across the frozen ground in front of the Marine and Army parapets. Ten prisoners were taken, and they confirmed that their comrades were suffering from frostbite and hunger. At 6:45 A.M., the X Corps communications center reported that telephone and teletype links to the division at Hagaru-ri were out. At that point, the only communications to the Marine forward command post was by continuous wave (CW) mode.[3]

Marine stocks of essential items at Hagaru-ri were extremely limited, and reliance was placed on parachuted supplies until the engineers could complete the emergency airfield. There were also hundreds of wounded men awaiting evacuation. Heavy snow during the night impeded progress, and the engineers began clearing it away so that earth-moving equipment could get to work. By mid-afternoon, the airstrip was still less than half completed, but a C-47 pilot decided to make a trial landing and initiate medical evacuation.

The cargo plane landed successfully and took eighty-four patients to Y'onpo airfield, where all aerial-delivered casualties were received. The wounded troops were segregated according to the seriousness of their wounds and sent to either the 1st Marine hospital at Hungnam, the 121st Evacuation Hospital at Hamhung, the hospital ship USS *Consolation* in Hungnam harbor, or—in the most urgent cases—directly to Japan.[4]

The Marines requested an emergency airdrop of signal equipment to keep up communications and more mountain sleeping bags, but the delivery was cancelled because of adverse weather. Medical supplies were needed at once, but could not be parachuted either. Continued action created a tremendous influx of casualties, which would be increased shortly by the arrival of the battered 5th and 7th Marines. Shortages persisted in litters, blankets, whole blood, and special items such as tubocurare, oxy-cel, antibiotics, and spirits. At one point the supply of whole blood was down to a single pint.[5]

Koto-ri was a critical checkpoint on the corps logistical route on the other end of the plateau south of Hagaru-ri. The town was defended by Lt. Col. Allan Sutter's 2d Battalion of the 1st Marines reinforced by various Army troops, including the elements of the 185th Engineer Battalion. The garrison realized its perimeter was in imminent danger of attack. Aircraft observers reported Chinese columns moving in their direction, and the town defenders later heard enemy troops loudly digging all around them.

Koto-ri post was snowed in completely during most of the day. The enemy lashed the perimeter with sporadic rifle and automatic weapons fire, but chose not to mount a major assault against it. The defenders were joined by survivors of the 2d Battalion, 31st Infantry, after its attempted journey to reach Hagaru-ri was defeated by enemy action. The Chinese were in total possession of the overland supply route between these two Marine garrisons, and aircraft pilots saw enemy troops below looting ambushed resupply trucks along the road.

The corps logistical posture was critically low in almost every category. Supplies that had been plentiful just the week before were now

Changjin Reservoir

Map by Shelby L. Stanton

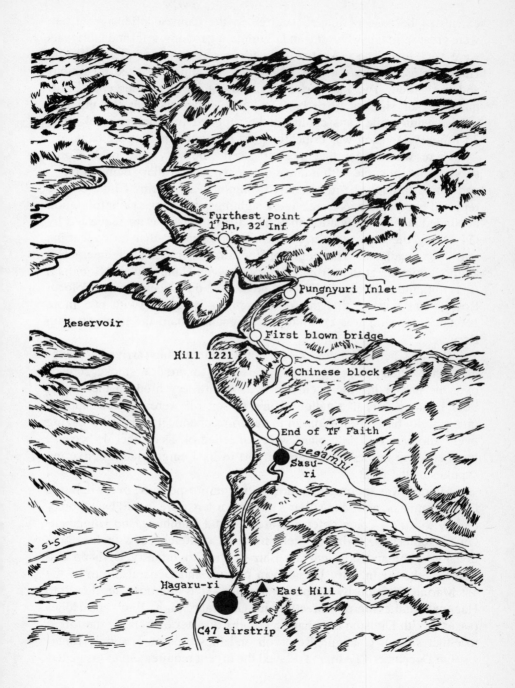

Furthest Point
1ˢᵗ Bn, 32ᵈ Inf.

Pungnyuri Inlet

Reservoir

First blown bridge

Hill 1221

Chinese block

End of TF Faith

Paegamni

Sasu-
ri

Hagaru-ri

East Hill

C47 airstrip

exhausted because of losses incurred in the Chinese offensive. There were great shortages of mortar and illuminating rounds. Fuel and lubricants were very low. The G4 office radioed for shipments of diesel oil into Hungnam as soon as possible. There was a compelling need for rations and fresh food. The 1st Marine Division obtained by emergency airlift quantities of shoe-pacs, parkas, and wool blankets, but the urgently needed winter pile caps could not be supplied for another week. The 3d Infantry Division was critically short of mountain sleeping bags.

There was danger that the port itself, the very core of X Corps survival, might come within range of enemy pack artillery being dragged and carted through the mountains. Columns of advancing Chinese were reported everywhere as exaggerated sightings and erroneous information abounded. Field fortification materials for Hungnam were requested by G4 during the day, but Far East Command replied that no concertina wire was available. The engineers began constructing an emergency ammo dump site at the carbide factory between Hamhung and Hungnam to get munitions out of the port area, and on December 1, Colonel Rowny was notified that the 79th Engineer Battalion (with 663 more combat engineers) was en route to Hungnam aboard the transport ship *Brewster*.

The 4th Chemical Smoke Generator Battalion, which arrived in Hungnam only fifteen days ago, was geared up to provide smoke screens over the harbor in case enemy mortars or artillery fired on the docks. Four hundred fifty-five-gallon drums of fog oil were ordered shipped on a priority basis from Wonsan to the corps chemical dump for "hazing over" the harbor. These plans were cancelled on December 4, because the men were needed at Y'onpo airport to load cargo planes delivering supplies to the front.

Almond was thoroughly alarmed by the prospects of overwhelming Chinese attacks, and MacArthur's explicit orders were to pull back immediately to a new corps defensive area around Hamhung and Hungnam. On November 30, Almond held morning conferences with his three division commanders, Generals Barr of the 7th Infantry Division and Soule of the 3d Infantry Division in person, and General Smith of the 1st Marine Division by telephone hookup. That afternoon he flew into Hagaru-ri and conferred directly with Generals Smith, Barr, and Hodes (assistant 7th Division commander) on the disaster overtaking the forces to either side of Changjin Reservoir and the corps main supply route.

On December 1, Almond relayed the urgent requirement to his generals that all forces must be concentrated in the newly established Hamhung-Hungnam defensive area. He stressed the need to fall back with all possible speed, and even authorized abandonment of all equipment that might delay retreat to the seacoast, stating that it could be destroyed by aircraft later. General Smith replied sternly, however, that his Marine Division would withdraw to Hamhung as rapidly as evacuation and movement of wounded permitted. He also stated he could not afford to discard equipment needed to fight his way out: "It was his intention, therefore to bring out the bulk of it."[6]

On December 2, snow flurries continued along the northeast coast and low clouds and overcast hampered air operations most of the day. Some cloud ceilings were as low as two hundred feet, but eighty-three sorties were conducted by the pilots of the Marine Air Wing as they strafed, rocketed, and napalmed targets around Changjin Reservoir. A Marine pilot reported to X Corps, "the enemy was dug in and difficult to see from the air at times, but the planes were directed from the ground and placed their ordnance in the desired areas."[7]

On the east side of Changjin Reservoir, the disastrous panorama of the end of Task Force Faith could be seen clearly from the air. At 11:12 A.M., Major Lynch of the 7th Infantry Division operations section located at Hagaru-ri relayed the picture to X Corps, "There are many bodies around the trucks. Apparently these bodies are the wounded who were left on the trucks and the people who stayed to protect the trucks. According to Maj. Jones, 3d Bn, 32d Inf, Col. Faith was hit yesterday morning and again severely late yesterday afternoon. He was put on a truck and the truck tried to make a run into Hagaru-ri. It did not get through." Marine Captain Pippin flew over the trucks and definitely saw wounded who tried to wave, but at 12:50 P.M. a heart-broken General Hodes reported to the corps that the "unit was completely overrun."[8]

At Hagaru-ri, the night of December 1–2 passed quietly, and aircraft streamed into the field despite the bad weather to evacuate more rows of wounded troops. General Almond made a short inspection of the proceedings in the afternoon. The defenders of Koto-ri also reported hardly any enemy activity, but pilots noted that large enemy buildups were taking place in both areas. The garrison spent the day bolstering their perimeter with a double circle of defensive positions to forestall enemy overruns of the compound.

By mid-morning on December 3, the snow flurries over Changjin Reservoir stopped and the highlands valley fog and haze started to disperse. There was negligible wind and Hamhung temperatures climbed from zero to twenty-eight degrees as the scattered low and middle clouds disappeared during the afternoon. The Marine Air Wing began to provide aerial support as soon as the weather cleared, at 10 A.M., and flew ninety-one daylight sorties. The main effort was aimed at neutralizing enemy blocking positions in front of the Marines approaching Hagaru-ri from Yudam-ni. Air support in other areas was restricted until noon.

The Chinese *60th, 76th,* and *77th PLA Divisions* moved closer to breaking the entire length of the main corps supply road. Lt. Col. Thomas O'Neil's 3d Battalion of the 7th Infantry was detached from the 3d Infantry Division and pushed up to occupy blocking positions at the key logistical site of Majon-dong, just south of the Funchilin Pass. The perimeter of Company I received a heavy attack from the north beginning at midnight that lasted for an hour, long enough for the Chinese to destroy the major bridge spanning Hungnim-ch'on River two miles north of town. About seventy-six dead enemy soldiers were found near the demolished bridge, but it was small consolation. A company from the 73d Engineer Battalion constructed a ford around the destroyed bridge site and put the main road back into operation, but traffic was held up for hours. Renewed enemy assaults forced the battalion to pull in its outlying positions along the roadway.

On December 4, as the battered 5th and 7th Marines slogged their way into temporary safety at Hagaru-ri, the scattered morning high clouds and valley haze gave way to a sparkling clear but windy day perfect for air strikes. A record-setting total of 232 bombing sorties were flown in close support of X Corps, including 136 by the 1st Marine Air Wing, 80 from aircraft carriers, and 37 by Air Force F-80 fighters and Douglas B-26 Invader bombers. The pilots rocketed, bombed, and strafed vehicles, houses, oxcarts, herds of horses, and even one column containing pack camels. The cargo airlift continued into Hagaru-ri as C-47 aircraft landed to deliver forty-eight tons of supplies. This effort was supplemented by another forty C-47 aircraft from Ashiya Air Base in Japan which parachuted two hundred tons of supplies into the Hagaru-ri perimeter.

These aerial missions were always attended by a degree of danger. A pair of fighters from Fighter Squadron 32, based on the aircraft carrier *Leyte* (CV-32), were strafing targets over Changjin Reservoir when one of the planes was hit by antiaircraft fire and forced down behind enemy lines. The other pilot, Lt. (j.g.) Thomas J. Hudner, Jr., circled over his injured squadron mate, who was trapped alive in the burning wreckage, and observed enemy troops approaching the area. Hudner executed a skillful wheels-up landing in the mountain wilderness and dashed over to the crippled aircraft. He used his bare hands in the subzero temperatures to pack snow into the fuselage in an effort to keep the flames away from the wounded flier, whom he then tried to pull out of the cockpit. Unable to free his comrade, Hudner raced back over to his own aircraft radio and called for a helicopter. He remained at the crash site and struggled to save his dying comrade despite the cold, flames, and Chinese rifle fire until rescued by helicopter.

While aircraft were sweeping the battlefield, General Almond was planning the final defense of the Hamhung-Hungnam area. He held a series of morning conferences with his chief of staff, General Ruffner, and other key personnel to discuss the corps reconsolidation. At 1 P.M., he departed the command post in an L-17 and flew to Hagaru-ri, observing the road and enemy dispositions. Upon landing at the Marine bastion, Almond spoke briefly with the evacuation officer at the airstrip who stated that over six hundred patients had already been evacuated.

Almond proceeded to the Marine division command post and pinned Distinguished Service Crosses on General Smith, Colonel Litzenberg of the 7th Marines, Lieutenant Colonel Murray of the 5th Marines, and Lt. Col. Olin L. Beall, the commander of the Marine 1st Motor Transport Battalion. There was no time for written citations, which were prepared much later.

General Smith viewed the clustered presentation as a belated and insincere attempt by Almond to ingratiate himself with Marine leadership. Smith, like Faith, found Almond's manner of dispensing decorations reprehensible. Instead of post-action recognitions of valor, medals in X Corps seemed to be "morale-boosting" tokens, and Smith viewed the whole process as irreparably cheapened by Almond's own acceptance of the same decoration under much less deserving circumstances.

Smith tolerated the ceremony and then pressed Almond about more immediate concerns, such as the availability of supporting firepower. Almond assured him that "every effort within the power of X Corps and the Air Force was being put to the task of assisting the withdrawal of the Marines and attached Army units from the Hagaru-ri and Ko-to-ri area to Hamhung."[9]

At 2:30 P.M. Almond flew into Koto-ri and conferred with Colonel Puller on artillery and air support during the Marine movement to his fortified locality, which would constitute the first stage of the general withdrawal. A plan was drafted by which the Marines moving from Hagaru-ri would pass through Koto-ri and continue down Funchilin Pass while the 1st Marines held the crest of the incline as the rear guard. At the conclusion of the briefing, Almond decorated Colonel Puller and Lieutenant Colonel Reidy with the Distinguished Service Cross and passed out a number of Silver Stars to other officers and men.

Returning to Hamhung late in the afternoon, General Almond conferred with Colonels McCaffrey and Forney who had returned from MacArthur's Japan headquarters with more directives. At 5:15 P.M., Almond briefed Col. John A. Gavin, the new commander of the decimated 31st Infantry who had also arrived fresh from Tokyo, to replace the missing Colonel MacLean.

A few scattered high clouds dotted the sky on December 5. Temperatures at Hamhung reached as high as thirty degrees, although occasional gusting winds created a lower wind chill and it was always colder in the mountains. The fighter and bomber pilots enjoyed another optimum day of flying weather as 220 sorties supported X Corps. Air Force B-26 Invaders bombed Sachang-ni and destroyed two-thirds of the town since it was a suspected Chinese command post. Fighters swooped low to destroy enemy troop columns and haystacks containing enemy supplies. In another devastating air raid, nearly three-fourths of Anbyon was leveled after it was reported that enemy troops were hidden inside the houses. Over Kanggye, the original corps objective area, four F-80 fighters were pounced on by two MIG-15s attacking from the rear and coming out of the sun at five hundred miles per hour. The F-80s dropped their ordnance and chased the enemy jets away, but one F-80 was hit by cannon fire in exchange.

The 1st Marine Division spent the generally quiet daylight hours at Hagaru-ri in preparation for its movement south, to be conducted in tactical offensive fashion over a Chinese-held roadway. The airlift of supplies and fresh troops into the isolated bastion continued. Over 537 Marine replacements were flown into Hagaru-ri and 4,312 casualties evacuated during the first five days of December.

Almond conducted a late-morning flight in his L-17 aircraft over the road south of Koto-ri to observe the artillery fire being registered on the line of march and against enemy targets. The effects of this shelling could not be determined from the air. Almond then directed the pilot to fly toward the Changjin Reservoir. As the plane flew over the main road near Koto-ri, he thought he saw numerous enemy groups on the ridges on each side of the road.

When his plane circled over Changjin Reservoir, Almond discerned a group of thirty individuals trailing two large sleds across the ice surface toward Hagaru-ri. This group appeared to have four fighters protecting its movement. During the day, a colonel and seven enlisted men also came into the Marine perimeter from the eastern side of the iced-over reservoir. The eight men, suffering from frostbite and wounds, were prisoners released by the Chinese. The former captives stated they were neither harmed nor interrogated. They were never fed by the Chinese, but allowed to get their own rations.

Almond returned to Hamhung and held an acrimonious conference on control of supporting air assets. He closed the discussion with the Air Force and Marine aviation commanders by insisting that he alone, as corps ground commander, should exercise total operational control over all supporting air units. The air control question remained unsettled, however, and following the X Corps' northeastern campaign, no Allied corps fighting in Korea was allowed its own "private air force" again.

In the meantime, the corps engineers hastily unloaded and issued field fortification material for construction of the final Hamhung-Hungnam defensive barriers. The Far East Command sent an urgent message to the Eighth Army, directing necessary action be taken immediately to expedite the shipment of ten M46 Patton tanks from depot stocks in Pusan to the defenders of Hungnam. X Corps was bracing for a major Chinese offensive against the port area as soon as the enemy moved into the coastal sector from their highland victories.[10]

2. Overtaxing the Supporting Arms

The Allied military situation in northeastern Korea deteriorated rapidly as the Chinese continued to apply heavy pressure against the scattered formations of X Corps. The entire *20th PLA Army* was now fully engaged along the corps front and redeploying to more advantageous positions. Although the *58th PLA Division* was stalemated at Hagaru-ri, the *59th PLA Division* side-stepped the Marines after winning Toktong Pass and drove forward against the corps main supply route. The *60th PLA Division* occupied the high ground on both sides of Funchilin Pass. The *89th PLA Division* marched into the Majon-dong vicinity on December 2.

The four divisions of *27th PLA Army* were also maneuvering farther south. The *79th* and *81st PLA Divisions,* having secured victory at Yudam-ni, were identified around and beyond Hagaru-ri. The *80th PLA Division* finished mopping up east of the Changjin Reservoir and was deploying for another pincer attack. The *90th PLA Division*, still in army reserve, was sending columns of fresh replacements to sustain other front-line divisions.

On December 5, the Chinese *26th PLA Army* suddenly appeared on the corps central front. The *76th* and *77th PLA Divisions* took up positions around Hagaru-ri and Koto-ri. The *78th* and *88th PLA Divisions* were close behind this leading vanguard, but not yet engaged.

Against this overwhelming numerical superiority, the X Corps soldiers and Marines relied on the technical capability of advanced communications, artillery firepower, and motorized response to even the odds. Unfortunately, the corps was dispersed beyond the supporting ability of these services, and geographical difficulties were compounded by weather, logistical, and supervisory problems. The modern technical mainstays could no longer insure American success over enemy numbers.

The first and most critical breakdown occurred in the corps communications network. Units without mutual ground contact depended on radio or wire transmissions for reinforcement or supply, but these often failed in Korea's mountainous terrain. Much of the radio apparatus was underpowered World War II surplus equipment hurriedly rebuilt in Japan for the Korean emergency, and often issued without necessary components. Wire communication was the trusted standby, but the available W-143 wire lacked tensile strength and its insulation snapped in cold weather. Stronger W-110 wire was in short supply because corps supervisors never ordered enough of it.

The most distressing signal deficiency was created not by substandard equipment, but by ineptitude associated with the corps Army-Marine rift, fostered to a large extent by the adverse relations between Generals Almond and Smith. This noncooperation was tragically exemplified by the fact that Army radios within X Corps were incompatible with Marine radios, and Army infantry-packed radios were incapable of netting with either Marine or Army tank radios.

Such elementary communication flaws required only the right circumstances to produce disaster. These occurred in the blizzard-swept highlands of the Changjin Reservoir, when the radio link connecting Colonel MacLean's 31st Regimental Combat Team simply evaporated. The trapped regiment was unable to reach either the Marine task force at Hagaru-ri or its own separated tank company south of the Chinese roadblock. Thus, news of this important enemy strong-point blocking Faith's escape route was never transmitted.

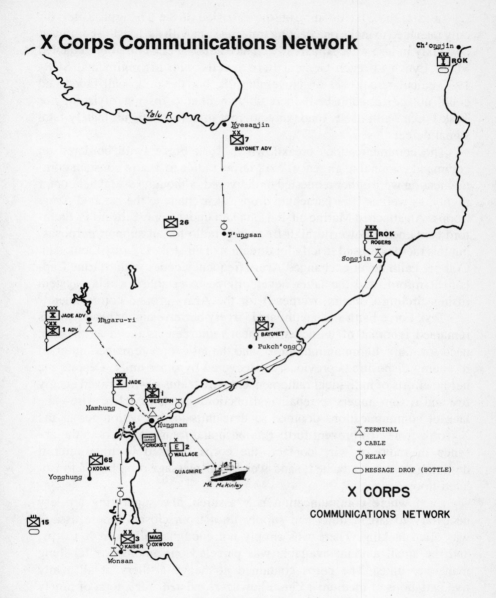

X Corps Communications Network

X CORPS

COMMUNICATIONS NETWORK

In fact, the 31st Infantry on the east side of the Changjin Reservoir only managed to make one fleeting transmission with its division command post sixty miles away. Apparently chance atmospheric conditions enabled Major Lynch to reach General Barr directly with his regimental SCR-193 vehicular radio set on November 28, but the radio call faded and could not be reestablished. Incredibly, neither corps nor division, nor Task Force Faith itself, made any attempt to correct this ultimately fatal signal defect.[11]

The communications breakdown in Task Force Faith bordered on command criminal negligence. No Marine radios to assure constant communication were either requested or delivered, although several helicopter flights, as well as later parachute drops, were made to the isolated Army troops. An attached Marine air-liaison team under Capt. Edward P. Stamford contained a powerful high-frequency radio for air support purposes, but this radio was used strictly for direction of air strikes. Army Lieutenant Colonel Faith never exchanged Army frequency codes with Marine Captain Stamford, and the latter never offered to establish a relay system (using circling Corsairs overhead) for the Army ground commander.[12]

Task Force Faith was annihilated largely because higher headquarters remained ignorant of its actual combat requirements (such as the dire need for more 40mm ammunition), and the task force remained ignorant of enemy dispositions previously discovered by other units. Despite the heroic efforts of individual radiomen and wire teams—who braved enemy fire and frozen fingers to repair malfunctioning sets or splice wire—the lack of communications doomed several units to destruction across the X Corps front. To prevent further ambush and transmit orders in the absence of radio or wire contact, the corps resorted to light aircraft dropping streamer-attached, sand-weighted "message drop bags" to isolated troops.

Even where communication was assured, the supporting artillery necessary to shield units and supply lines from close Chinese assault was often lacking. There was simply not enough artillery in X Corps, and the small amount available was parceled out among the far-flung maneuver units. The corps contained no heavy artillery at all. Only five battalions of medium 155mm howitzers existed, for a total of ninety tubes. The corps possessed 162 light 105mm howitzers assigned to its divisions, but these were scattered in battery increments throughout the zone. The corps lacked an artillery observation unit and could not perform sound and flash ranging. Artillery spotting aircraft were often diverted on medical evacuation or courier flights.

The corps artillery assets were further diminished by high losses in battle and vehicular mishaps on icy mountain roads. As the Chinese offensive gained momentum, many artillery pieces were overrun, abandoned in place for destruction by friendly air strikes, or limbered on withdrawing vehicles in a non-firing mode. Artillery losses became so heavy that a general X Corps retreat within range of protective naval gunfire was mandated. In the meantime, air strikes offered a temporary respite, if weather permitted, during daylight hours (the few night strikes were inconsequential as artillery substitution).

General Almond could hardly be faulted for a shortage of artillery pieces in Korea, but he failed to exercise good control over the scant resources on hand. Instead of artillery being massed on a combined corps frontage, firepower was diluted in direct support of fractionalized corps forces in separate areas. Almond also misused his two corps artillery battalions. Both units were transformed into non-tactical security forces from late November through the first part of December, making them unavailable for prompt response when needed.[13]

The soldiers and Marines of X Corps also counted on the American motorized mobility to shift reserves to threatened areas, but this resource also failed under General Almond's leadership. The X Corps Transportation Office did not even attempt to regulate traffic conditions on the main supply route until November 28. Only at this late date, when the urgency of the frontline situation around Changjin Reservoir demanded emergency measures, was any effort made to protect bridging against sabotage, safeguard wire lines, or establish truck pools. Before these deficiencies could be corrected, the Chinese cut the supply road between Koto-ri and Hagaru-ri and prevented reinforcements from reaching the forward battle area.[14]

The relief convoy to Hagaru-ri began filing out of Koto-ri at 9:30 A.M. on November 29, under an umbrella of close air strikes and artillery firing against the ridges on either side of the road. By mid-afternoon, trucks were still joining the elongated convoy, known as Task Force Drysdale, under the command of Lt. Col. Douglas B. Drysdale of the British Royal Marine 41st Independent Commando. In addition to this 225-man Royal Marine recon element, the column also included one Army company (Company B, 31st Infantry) and a Marine company (Company G, 1st Marines) escorting the trucks. A contingent of Marine tanks led the column.

Task Force Drysdale was forced to fight its way through scattered sniping and automatic weapons fire from the commencement of its journey, and this caused confusion in the truck serials as they departed Koto-ri. Marine and Army trucks were intermixed along the route of march and convoy tactical unity was lost. Each truck group maintained a fifty- or one hundred-yard interval and there were frequent unexplained halts. Only the leading elements had any knowledge of the enemy situation.

The vanguard of the convoy encountered entrenched Chinese on a commanding hill about a mile and a half north of the town. The hill was cleared of enemy troops after Marine MSgt. Rocco A. Zullo crawled forward with his 3.5-inch rocket launcher and destroyed a number of bunkers. This segment of vehicles moved slowly around roadblocks and huts, and the tempo of enemy fire increased as twilight faded into evening.

At Hell Fire Valley, a long alpine valley containing a partially frozen creek and flanked by sharply rising mountains about halfway to Hagaru-ri, the convoy was ambushed and splintered into three fragments. As darkness descended the column's forward elements, spearheaded by the tanks, fought their way into Hagaru-ri. A few tanks and trucks at the rear of the column turned around or backed up and reached Koto-ri, although that town was also under heavy Chinese attack. The rest of the convoy was stranded helplessly on the road and was subjected to piecemeal destruction. Each cluster of truck-mounted soldiers and drivers conducted its own battle for survival.

Lieutenant Catania of the 377th Transportation Truck Company was leading a convoy section that travelled only three miles before stopping after nightfall. He walked forward to determine the reason for the delay. Between fast-moving clouds the moonlight revealed a streambed to the left and a narrow-gauge railroad on the right, just in front of the steep mountain side. The light also glinted off the quilted uniforms of a squad of Chinese soldiers walking along the rail line, and Catania opened fire. The night was suddenly engulfed in a blazing display of tracers and grenade explosions as the Chinese on the slopes and beside the railroad opened fire on his section of vehicles.

There were large gaps between vehicles and no concentration of men at any one spot. The mixture of different units allowed no defensive cohesion. Catania tried to rally a few soldiers around him to make a stand in the field behind the trucks: "There was no cover, however, and it was impossible to dig into the frozen ground. Casualties were mounting, and I was wounded twice. I was hit once in the back by a shell fragment, and in the shoulder by a caliber .45 slug that broke my collar bone and lodged in my neck, and an infantryman even bandaged me there. He also gave me a shot of morphine to ease the pain. I had my head propped up on my helmet and continued to give what little control was possible in the situation."[15]

One truck in the middle of the valley field had a light machine gun strapped to its front fender and a box of ammunition under the seat, but it was clearly silhouetted by the moonlight where it had been abandoned by the driver who tried to outrun the ambushers. A transportation soldier braved direct enemy automatic weapons fire to untie the weapon and get its ammunition, although attempts to secure its tripod were unsuccessful. This man fired the machine gun from the hip until it ran out of ammunition, and then the band of soldiers around him made a break for the far mountains by wading across the ice-cold, fast-moving stream.

Catania, who was severely wounded, led his small contingent of soldiers across the same stream to escape the onrushing Chinese. Their boots were soaked in the icy crossing, and as soon as they were up in the mountains the troops used knives to cut off the lacings. The iced-over socks were frozen into the boots, and could not be removed. The men were forced to abandon their useless boots and jerry-rig footwear with pile-liner caps and blanket wrappings. These troops eventually hobbled into Koto-ri, and Catania was medically evacuated to Japan days later.

After the Chinese cut the convoy into pieces, separated groups kept trying to hold out—hoping to survive until daylight or until a rescue unit reached them. One Army jeep-mounted 75mm recoilless rifle crew kept firing at Chinese mortar flashes until every man was killed or wounded. Marine Warrant Officer Loyd V. Dirst, the officer-in-charge of the headquarters military police battalion, deployed the group nearest him along a ditch beside the road. He courageously moved up and down the road to encourage his hastily organized men in defending their precarious position, and personally repulsed several grenadiers before he was wounded by mortar shrapnel after a twelve-hour fire fight. Awarded the Navy Cross for his valor, Dirst died less than two years later from complications caused by his wounds during the encounter.[16]

Maj. Henry W. Seeley, Jr., the Marine division motor transport officer, was initially in the rear of the column but he fought his way forward and joined the main group (the original middle section of the convoy). Ammunition was running low and the Chinese were already looting the trucks. About 5 A.M., a shout was heard from the enemy ranks asking for a cease-fire so that terms of surrender could be discussed. Major Seeley went farther up the road and encountered an Army unit, out of ammunition and led by a sergeant, separated from the next element by two gullies. Major Seeley and the sergeant went over the crest of the hill and met two Chinese officers, who had Marine Maj. James K. Eagen with them (later declared missing in action).

While waiting for an interpreter, Majors Seeley and Eagen discussed the situation. Eagen stated that the Chinese had brought up many mortars and, for the sake of the many wounded, he should surrender. The interpreter finally showed up. He was a former South Korean soldier. A seven-minute truce was decided upon and surrender terms were discussed. The Chinese offered to take care of the wounded if the column would surrender. Major Seeley discussed the matter with the Army sergeant, who stated he would surrender his portion of the Army company and thus stall for time while Major Seeley reorganized the defense.

Major Seeley returned to his lines and said he decided to fight it out. He organized a fighting withdrawal with those who wanted to go and could walk. He rounded up people from scattered units, kept men awake and moving to prevent freezing, and directed the retreat into the hills. When his pistol was shot out of his hands, inflicting a painful wound, he grabbed a carbine and kept fighting.[17]

Within a halfhour, back in the main convoy, a cease-fire order was passed along and both sides stopped firing. There was no chance to destroy equipment and the Marines and Army survivors began blaming each other for the disaster. It was apparent that the lack of centralized, effective control contributed heavily to the tragedy of Task Force Drysdale. Company B, 31st Infantry, alone lost 119 men, 100 of them killed or missing. Marine Sgt. G. H. Tovar was one of numerous prisoners taken by the Chinese and recounted his experiences,

They brought us under fire mostly from the right side of the road. . . . We tried to get through they blew up one of our jeeps. We turned around and went back. The next morning we tried to run the blockade. They caught us again and we had to dig in down in a ditch on the opposite side of the road. Then we started to run out of ammo. People were asking, "Do you have any M1 ammo?" "Do you have any carbine ammo?" "Do you have an M1?". . . . They (Chinese) started to come at us with fire from the side. That is how I got hit behind the ear. It started to bleed and I was afraid I was going to bleed to death. They placed me under a truck and I remember Blas coming over and putting a blanket over me. I was dizzy and can't remember just what went on after then.

They (Chinese) treated us all good. They bandaged the wounded the first night and kept us in a room in a village about a mile and a half from where we were hit. They fed us mostly spuds and dried beans. They gave us an extra ration one night so we had a pretty good idea they would be leaving shortly. The next morning when we got up they were gone.[18]

Unfortunately, the destruction of Task Force Drysdale was just one of many adverse events along the main supply route. Patrols reported that two enemy companies were dug in on a ridge line astride the road south of Koto-ri. The bridge in that area was blown, and the nearby villages were occupied by Chinese troops. Corps engineers constructed turnabouts, truck parking areas, and bypasses around destroyed sections of the highway but their efforts were impeded by enemy action.

Lack of control over the corps transportation arrangements was largely responsible for the failure of the 2d Battalion, 31st Infantry, to join Colonel MacLean's command east of Changjin Reservoir. The addition of another rifle battalion in his sector might have enabled his regimental combat team to stave off the Chinese attacks long enough to escape safely. As it happened, however, the battalion spent precious days in limbo waiting for trucks and clearances, while their own trucks were diverted to ammunition hauls. When they finally boarded trucks, the vehicles were ordered off the road to let secondary convoys pass through.

Traffic delays and mix-ups in truck scheduling prevented Lt. Col. Richard R. Reidy's 2d Battalion of the 31st Infantry from moving through Funchilin Pass until the morning of November 30. After travelling a mile up the winding, cliff-edge road, the Chinese attacked and destroyed both leading jeeps and two medium cargo trucks. The motor convoy stopped while Reidy called in for air strikes and radioed back that the pass was not secure.

A Marine reconnaissance aircraft passing over Funchilin Pass later in the day reported to corps that the convoy was halted a mile from the top of the incline and making no effort to fight its way out. This report caused General Almond to become livid and "he reacted violently to the news."[19] A corps G3 staff officer, Maj. Joseph I. Gurfein, was dispatched to the scene by jeep and ordered the battalion to attack. The convoy started moving again about an hour before midnight as snow fell thickly across the road. Within a halfhour a booby trap exploded near the head of the convoy and a panicked rout ensued as trucks turned full circle and jeeps careened around to head back downhill. The soldiers simply pushed Reidy and his command group aside with screams that the Chinese were coming. Major Gurfein, exasperated by Reidy's inaction, finally rallied the troops by pointing out that no shots were fired by anyone.

About an hour past midnight on December 1, the rear of the 2d Battalion convoy was fired on by Chinese as it rolled across the top of Funchilin Pass toward Koto-ri. The entire battalion disintegrated under the desultory fire, although the leading company barrelled into the town. The rear company stopped and engaged the Chinese in a long-range small-arms duel, while one company scattered and another company simply got out of its vehicles and abandoned them on the road. When the battalion commander made no effort to regroup his forces, Major Gurfein went back down into the winding pass and reorganized the convoy, although many of the abandoned trucks were never recovered and later pushed off the road.

On December 5, the Corps Transportation Office was directed to make all its vehicles available for evacuation of the remaining forces around the Changjin Reservoir. On this date, every non-divisional truck was rounded up. The 2d Engineer Special Brigade had 42, the Marine 7th Motor Transport Battalion had 175, the 52d Transportation Truck Battalion had 60, and another 28 were pooled from hospitals and other sources. Only 305 transport vehicles could be mustered at corps level.[20]

3. Flank and Rear Security

Major General Soule's 3d Infantry Division was charged with securing the corps extended southern area of responsibility, as well as various lines of communication behind the front. This task included mopping up the Wonsan area, protecting the railroad and all its whistle stops, securing widely separated road junctions, patrolling rugged mountain hamlets, and guarding individual bridges in deep forested gorges. In order to cover these vast distances, the assets of the division were parceled out in a welter of isolated sentinel detachments scattered throughout the remote countryside. The division ceased to exist as such, and its headquarters was linked to subordinate commands primarily by the Wonsan airstrip—a concrete highway in front of the central command post.

Col. John S. Guthrie's 7th Infantry completed landing on November 17 except for its tank company and baggage. The regiment was an old regular Army outfit traditionally known as the "Cottonbalers" from its exploits at the Battle of New Orleans in 1815. Colonel Guthrie brought the regimental nickname more in reality with Korean war expectations when he gave it the signal codeword, "Killer." The 3d Battalion was dispatched to the city of Hamhung as a corps reserve. The 1st Battalion was given bridge and construction site security throughout the division sector. The 2d Battalion went to Kowon, midway between Wonsan and Hamhung on the main rail line.

Col. Dennis M. Moore's 15th Infantry, a regiment that had served over twenty years on China station and was most recently the training regiment for the infantry post of Fort Benning, Georgia (its motto "Can Do" was derived from the pidgin English used by the Old China Hands), was also dispersed after landing at Wonsan on November 11. The 1st Battalion was posted to the former Marine outpost of Majon-ni, the 2d Battalion guarded Wonsan, and the 3d Battalion was picketed on the road to Majon-ni at the "Halfway Point" village of Pakchon-ni.

The regiment discovered their area of operations was infested with enemy troops. Daily fire fights erupted between patrols and guerrilla skirmishers. Supply convoys forced to weave through the high mountain roads were harassed by ambushes and roadblock techniques used against the previous Marine occupiers of the region. On November 18, a patrol uncovered a huge ammunition dump tucked away in the hill fortress of Tap-kol (ten miles southwest of Wonsan), and the attached ROK Marines found an even larger cache containing enough munitions to sustain a division assault.

The regiment's 3d Battalion, led by Lt. Col. Milburn N. Huston, was one of several black units in the 3d Infantry Division. Other units included the 999th Field Artillery Battalion and the 64th Tank Battalion, as well as the attached 58th Field Artillery Battalion. Along with the Puerto Rican 65th Infantry (which Almond considered "black"), these elements, totalling seven battalions, constituted the prime reason why General Almond distrusted the military capability of the 3d Infantry Division.[21]

Lieutenant Colonel Huston's outfit had just settled into new positions taken over from the Marines west of Wonsan when an enemy force was observed concentrating near its perimeter. Company K conducted a reconnaissance-in-force mission to deter this buildup, but became embroiled in heavy fighting. One platoon led by 2d Lt. John W. Timmins, Jr., stumbled across a North Korean outpost and was pinned by enemy rifle and machine gun fire from well-entrenched hillside positions. Timmins disregarded the hail of enemy fire and organized two of his squads as a base of supporting fire. He then led the rest of the men in a flanking attack that forced the enemy back temporarily. Timmins was killed in the mountain assault, but his bravery was instrumental in enabling the company to disengage and reach safety back in the main lines. His valor was recognized by the posthumous award of the Silver Star.[22]

Shortly afterwards, Lieutenant Colonel Huston was relieved from battalion command and "kicked upstairs" to the X Corps G2 intelligence office. Many blamed this sudden trouble on a falling out between Huston and Brig. Gen. Armistead Mead, the assistant division commander, over the circumstances surrounding the death of Timmins, who formerly had served as Mead's aide-de-camp. Others suspected the main problem was Huston's incompatibility with the regimental colonel.[23] Whatever the real reason, the leadership of black units in Almond's corps was always subject to "head-chopping" that undercut confidence and any attempt to build performance continuity.

On November 21, the North Koreans smashed into Lt. Col. Robert M. Blanchard's 1st Battalion perimeter at Majon-ni. They were supported by three armored fighting vehicles and breached the perimeter before withdrawing around dawn. Despite the obvious danger, Colonel Moore insisted that Blanchard try to establish overland connections with an ROK Marine battalion even farther west at Tongyang. A mechanized patrol escorting a supply convoy was sent out, but eight miles into its fateful journey an overturned Japanese truck blocked the road where it curved through a narrow mountainous pass. The column was immediately struck by a scorching cross-fire from the canyon walls.

The North Koreans began closing in on the flaming trucks, but the patrol's wire chief, Sgt. Van E. Clagg, manned a vehicle-mounted machine gun and fired into the attackers until he was severely wounded in the head. He fell mortally wounded, but his action allowed three jeeps to escape. Several other members of the destroyed convoy staggered into Majon-ni during the night, but twenty-eight of the ninety-three-man expedition never returned.[24]

The following day, Lieutenant Colonel Blanchard dispatched a stronger patrol to secure the road, escorted by two tanks. The NKPA had cratered the road in numerous places, making it impassable to wheeled or tracked vehicles. On the way back, one of the tanks was disabled by a mine and towing efforts proved futile. The tank was stripped of all weapons, tools, and ammunition and abandoned on the winding mountain trail. Several other attempts to reach Tongyang by road also failed, and the ROK Marine garrison stationed there was forced to rely on parachuted supplies for sustenance until November 25.

Col. William W. Harris's Puerto Rican 65th Infantry moved entirely from railroad general security duty after its near-defeat at Yonghung, and joined the 1st Battalion deep in the mountain wilderness where it had been trying unsuccessfully to make ground contact with the Eighth Army. The regiment was expected to block North Koreans retreating northward and to use Kwangchon as a patrol base for expeditions into the Paek-san heights far to the west of Hamhung.

A fourth regimental task force, Col. Rhee Chi Suh's ROK 26th Regiment, was sent northwest to Huksu-ri to hold the belt of mountains below the Marine division zone. Attempts to establish contact between the South Koreans and the Puerto Ricans farther north along the Taebaek Range failed when a company of the latter regiment pushed toward 1724-meter-high Paek-san during the third week of November.

Hundreds of enemy soldiers jumped this 65th Infantry company in the early morning darkness of November 23, supported by mortars and machine guns. The company repulsed the attack but exhausted most of its ammunition and found it impossible to evacuate the wounded safely back down the mountain roads. At 6:30 A.M. the enemy increased their strength to nearly a half-thousand men for another overrun attempt, but the company received air-dropped ammunition just in time and discouraged this second attack. Fortunately, clear weather conditions allowed Navy helicopters to fly out numerous casualties from the remote alpine battlefield.

By this time, the enemy was severing supply lines throughout the expanse of territory in the division sector. Cumulative losses in men and equipment were high. The safety of logistical lines was a problem seldom encountered before by American combat units, and the division was not trained for this type of warfare. The South Korean KATUSA soldiers displayed their usual reluctance to participate in any action and expressed even more reluctance in black units (in Japan, the KATUSA recruits had revolted when paired with black soldiers). Apart from racial disharmony, the division was largely filled with combat-inexperienced troops. As the 3d Infantry Division history carefully worded it,

> In initial engagements, fire control posed the problem usually common to troops realizing for the first time that they were targets for an enemy bent on killing them. Momentarily stunned by the imminence of death or injury and by the violence of the battle scene of which they were a part, some men succumbed to the urge to fire wildly or not at all. In soldier's familiar terms, they were 'trigger-happy' and sought to find in the ineffective noise from their weapons a measure of relief from the fears which assail any normal, healthy man under such circumstances.[25]

4. The Breakdown of Civil Affairs

The soldiers of the 3d Infantry Division realized that enemy strength and determination in this desolate region had been gravely underestimated by Allied intelligence. Instead of shattered North Korean units content to lie low through the winter, the enemy was aggressive and battle-conditioned. Almost every unit was subjected to ambushes where heavy automatic weapons fire was delivered at close range, or hit by sudden raids from all directions. Patrols and outposts routinely received sniping and burp-gun fire in the darkness or from rocky terrain.

Clusters of farmers became targets of suspicion, and even women and children were found counting American soldiers or vehicles and sending this information to local partisan groups. Common woodpiles or huts sometimes contained enemy weapons and ammunition. Soldiers patrolling the roadways learned to probe rice stacks, culverts, and other likely cache sites. Communication wire being tapped by enemy agents was often traced to innocuous native dwellings near Allied perimeters.

The enemy infiltrated agents and saboteurs behind the lines with regularity. Korean police and Army military police manning checkpoints examined Korean travellers carefully, and in many cases concealed weapons or enemy uniforms were discovered underneath peasant clothing. Soldiers who once had disregarded the Korean's habitual baggy trousers and long outer garments as a pleasant curiosity, now viewed this dress style with open apprehension.

The communists kept organized resistance movements viable in the larger cities as well. On November 20, enemy agent Chun Song Kun arrived surreptitiously in Hamhung and secured two houses that he converted into the operational headquarters of the *NKLP* (Puk Chosun No Dong Dang). He obtained valuable information about X Corps activities in the city and spread a number of false rumors as instructed. After he completed his mission he returned to P'ungsan on foot. A more dangerous communist mission was discovered December 1, when the leader of a fifteen-man North Korean assassination group, Park Ke Wan, was reported at large in Hamhung.[26]

During late November, two young female espionage agents, Lee Chyun Za and Hwong Hai Do, were apprehended by local police at Chung Pong. After intense questioning, they stated the *NKPA* had dispatched them, with eight packages of poison powder each, to poison water wells used by UN forces. When the girls were asked to produce the poison, they claimed the bags were buried along the banks of the Chung Ri River. They refused to give further information and the female agents were turned over to the X Corps interrogators of the 210th Counter Intelligence Corps Detachment in Hamhung, who conducted more thorough investigations.[27]

Several sophisticated communist plots were suspected of having international overtones. On December 7, members of the 2d Engineer Special Brigade at Hungnam port caught a Japanese stevedore after he climbed a mast of the *Shinano Maru* and made a sketch of corps positions in the harbor. Corps intelligence analysts interrogated the stevedore, who finally revealed how he passed data on port facility operations to his North Korean contacts. The stevedore agent buried his information in a tin can at a designated spot for the North Korean agents to retrieve. Because this espionage ring had connections with the Japan Communist Party, the suspect was whisked to Tokyo for further questioning.[28]

Civil affairs teams tried to reopen trade between towns, institute public health to prevent epidemics, and form viable civil governments to effectively administrate the provinces. Although X Corps determined that the population was largely anti-communist, there was no central Korean government structure capable of contesting the highly organized communist cells. The communist underground was extremely ruthless and slaughtered any persons suspected of helping the Allied cause. Sometimes, this terror became indiscriminate and in one case near Hamhung nearly five hundred civilians were clubbed to death and thrown down the shaft of a mine.[29]

The most urgent civil affairs mission was the rationing and distribution of food, medicine, fuel, and other commodities necessary to prevent wide-scale starvation, disease, and public unrest. Although these supplies were available in quantity, the distribution channels were disorganized and the needed transport competed with corps tactical requirements.

The civil affairs teams were expected to assist in rear-area security through the recruitment and arming of Korean police, who would protect village sectors against marauding *NKPA* and partisan bands. The civil police effort left a lot to be desired. In Hungnam itself, the "model" city of this system, the police were actually a heavily armed vigilante group numbering 450 individuals, and contained numerous teenage boys. On November 21, this group shot an American soldier in the hills outside town, claiming that he was intoxicated and had failed to heed their challenge.

On the following day, Maj. Thomas J. Osekowski, the Provost Marshal of the 2d Engineer Special Brigade, demanded to meet with the police chief of Hungnam, Mr. Won Jang Seup. He recounted the meeting,

> When we entered the police station there was a room full of these policemen and I asked through the interpreter who was in charge. The group that I saw, I judged or estimated that about one-third were not more than 12 to 14 years of age. In fact, I remarked that the youngest member of this police force, I thought, was apparently standing guard outside the police station holding an automatic weapon with his finger on the trigger. He could not have been more than 12 years old. The entire street outside the police station seemed crowded with what I call armed boys, about 25 percent of them had automatic weapons. It is still a common sight to see civilians walking the streets of Hungnam carrying a weapon.
>
> I announced my intentions to disarm most or all of these people to Colonel [William T.] Campbell [the X Corps Provost Marshall] . . . and that this would take effect just as soon as I got an opinion of most of these people [Campbell and his staff] as to whether this action was proper or not. I also discussed this with the commanding officer and officers of Company I, 7th Infantry [port security force] who stated that this was a good idea because in case of an infiltration they would not know where to begin shooting.[30]

Later that day Major Osekowski summarily dismissed Mr. Won and installed a South Korean, Captain Park, "in order to provide the necessary security for the military port installation.'' Captain Park had served as the chief of police both at Inch'on and Iwon. The mayor of the city, Kim Gook Han, was sent from Seoul to be mayor of Hungnam and this change also caused resentment among the town citizens.

Mr. Won appealed his relief to the Hamhung Provincial Civil Affairs Team, and on November 25 he was restored to office. This change was made after the provincial chief of police Hang Dong Seuk, an elected official, insisted that Mr. Won was an elected official who could not be arbitrarily removed. Maj. Millard F. Dougherty of the Marine counter-intelligence corps at Hungnam described the police force: ''It is believed that the police, from a political viewpoint, are reliable. As a trained police force they are unreliable due to lack of supervision and training.''[31]

During the first week of December, the internal squabbles of Korean politics and police training were forgotten as the corps civil affairs section reoriented itself to meet the conditions of tactical retrograde movement, becoming involved almost exclusively with refugee control. As areas were abandoned by withdrawing troops, effective civil control was lost.[32] As part of the inevitable irony experienced by retreating conquerors, many native police joined North Korean units and turned their weapons against the UN forces who brought them the guns and permits originally.

Notes

1. X Corps headquarters and service units—6,153 (5,681 Army + 472 Koreans); corps combat units—4,978 (4,306 Army + 672 Koreans); 1st Marine Division—24,297 (24,117 Marines + 71 Army + 109 Koreans); Royal Marines—234; 2d Engineer Special Brigade—1,334; Marine Air Wing—2,414; Air Force 6150 Tactical Support Wing—1,668; 3d Infantry Division—22,167 (16,008 Army + 6,159 Koreans); 7th Infantry Division—22,500 (15,941 Army + 6,559 Koreans); 1st Korean Marine Regiment—2,228; ROK I Corps units—3,417; ROK Capital Division—11,392; ROK 3d Division—11,596. X Corps Periodic Operations Report No. 66, Pt. V-12.
2. X Corps G-3 Daily Summary, dtd 1 December 1950; Item J-118 contained Navy air termination; Item J-127 contained corps transmission.
3. X Corps G-3 Daily Summary, dtd 1 December 1950, Item J-29.
4. 1st Marine Division Special Action Report, Annexes Dog and Easy to Annex Howe Howe, pp. 3 and 7, respectively.
5. 1st Marine Division Special Action Report, Annex Queen, dtd January 1951, p. 6.
6. Montross and Canzona, III, p. 239.
7. Maj. C. P. Weiland transmission to X Corps G3, dtd 2 December 1950.
8. X Corps G-3 Daily Summary, dtd 2 December 1950, Item J-38 contained Major Lynch report; Item J-115 contained Captain Pippin's report; Item J-47 contained General Hodes's report.
9. X Corps CG Diary, dtd 4 December 1950.
10. X Corps G-3 Daily Summary, dtd 5 December 1950, Item J-107.
11. Appleman, *Chosin,* p. 87.
12. Appleman, *Chosin,* p. 177.
13. X Corps Artillery Summary, dtd 31 December 1950. The five medium artillery battalions totalled 90 authorized 155mm howitzers: 18 self-propelled (tracked) howitzers of the 92d Armored Field Artillery Battalion and 18 towed howitzers each from the 96th and 999th Field Artillery Battalions, 1st Marine Division, and 7th Infantry Division. The 3d Infantry Division utilized the 999th as its medium artillery battalion during this campaign. Each Marine and Army division also contained three battalions of light (105mm) howitzers, each with 18 tubes, or 54 light howitzers per division, giving the corps a total of 162 light howitzers.
14. X Corps, *Special Report on Chosin Reservoir,* 27 November–10 December 1950, Transportation Report, p. 67. One example of inadequate supervision was the mystery surrounding the constant interruption of corps telephone communications. During the height of the Chinese offensive, when the telephonic link became essential for coordination of withdrawal efforts, the corps finally investigated and resolved the problem. It was discovered

that friendly tanks were cutting the wires while turning into fields, and simple traffic precautions were instituted to safeguard the vital lines.

15. "Truck Platoon in Korea," Department of the Army, *Combat Support in Korea*, Combat Forces Press, 1955, p. 55.

16. Marine Corps Historical Center, Folder of Commissioned Warrant Officer Loyd V. Dirst, USMC. He died on July 22, 1952.

17. X Corps IG Ltr, Subj: Report of Inquiry into Alleged Surrender of American Personnel on 30 November 1950, dtd 13 December 1950.

18. X Corps Periodic Intelligence Report No. 44, Incl. 1.

19. Appleman, *Chosin*, p. 161.

20. X Corps, *Special Report on Chosin Reservoir*, 27 November–10 December 1950, Transportation Report, p. 70 (Item 15).

21. Blair, p. 411.

22. Far East Command General Orders No. 14, dtd 23 January 1951.

23. Blair, p. 413.

24. Sgt. Van E. Clagg received the Distinguished Service Cross. Far East Command General Orders No. 109, dtd 3 May 1951.

25. 3d Infantry Division in Korea, p. 76.

26. X Corps Periodic Intelligence Report No. 66, p. 2.

27. X Corps Periodic Intelligence Report No. 67, p. 2.

28. X Corps Periodic Intelligence Report No. 72, p. 4.

29. 3d Infantry Division in Korea, p. 80.

30. X Corps, IG Report, Subj: Report of Investigation Concerning Alleged Inefficiency in the Hungnam Civil Affairs Team, dtd 8 December 1950, Exhibit B-3.

31. Ibid., Exhibit B-4.

32. X Corps, *Command Report for December 1950*, "Summary of Major Activities," p. 3.

CHAPTER 12

RETREAT TO THE SEA

1. Retracting the Horns: The North

At the beginning of December, as the Chinese onslaught threatened to cave in the X Corps central front, General Almond desperately ordered his northern wing to fall back and reconcentrate for the final defense of the Hamhung-Hungnam area. The corps operations center dutifully issued orders for full retreat to both General Kim's ROK I Corps and General Barr's 7th Infantry Division, but it was uncertain whether these northern units could fall back without being destroyed themselves.

The 7th "Bayonet" Infantry Division had already taken heavy losses in the charnel of Changjin Reservoir, where a third of its combat power was annihilated. The largest concentration of the remaining division strength was Colonel Powell's 17th Infantry at Hyesanjin on the distant Yalu River. To reach relative safety near the coast at Pukch'ong, this regimental combat team would have to travel two hundred miles over dangerous mountain roads in temperatures ranging from freezing to forty degrees below zero. The trip, under ideal weather conditions without enemy contact, would take over seventy-two hours. Under present conditions, the regiment would have to be back-hauled by mechanically undependable vehicles across winter roads subject to potential attack by fresh Chinese formations crossing the Yalu onto the battlefield.

The adverse tactical situation, with virtually no choice in the manner of retreat for Powell's troops, however, presented an unpleasant dilemma for the corps. The unchecked main Chinese attack in the Marine sector mandated that the remainder of the corps be withdrawn as quickly as possible, by exposed motor march if necessary, in order to reach Hungnam while it was still in Allied hands.

Therefore, the plan for saving what was left of the 7th Infantry Division was fairly straightforward and without much maneuver finesse. Two battalions (one each from the 31st and 32d Infantry), beefed up by the ROK 26th Regiment north of the Ungi River, would screen Powell's departure from Hyesanjin. The division's 13th Engineer Battalion would attempt to maintain the main avenues of retreat from snow drifts or partisan ambush. The division recon company would act as an emergency reserve to secure endangered crossroads or counter enemy probes. Division support would be fully committed to the retreat. The only other available maneuver battalion of the division (the 2d Battalion, 32d Infantry) was kept by General Almond as a reserve for his own headquarters at Hamhung and not released for General Barr's use.

The first critical checkpoint in the Bayonet retreat was Kapsan. The 17th Infantry expended the "utmost effort to make all vehicles operable to drive out under [their] own power,"[1] and started its lone trek south. At 4:30 P.M., in the waning daylight hours of the first day's march, a corps courier plane soared over the wilderness south of the Yalu River. The pilot confirmed that the long column of trucks, jeeps, and armored vehicles was moving slowly but uneventfully over the barren white plains to Kapsan.

General Almond seized upon this news to draw an optimistic conclusion. If the Chinese were in the area, they would brush aside any thinly picketed screening force and jump such a large, unprotected motor convoy. Lack of action meant lack of Chinese forces to the north. He ordered General Barr to disengage the screen at an accelerated pace and get all his troops back to Hamhung as fast as possible. He wanted Barr to reform a regiment in Hamhung to help cover the Marine withdrawal to the coast. The pell-mell withdrawal of the 7th Infantry Division would leave the unfortunate ROK I Corps farther out on a limb without American flanking support.

By this time, General Kim's ROK I Corps—code name "Rogers"

(after Kim's KMAG advisor, Colonel Rogers)—was also attempting to execute a rapid retreat. Unlike the Bayonet retreat, however, the Rogers retreat was contested by strong enemy forces. When the corps order to retreat was received, Kim's corps was within fifty miles of the Soviet border. The ROK Capital Division under Brig. Gen. Song Yo Chan was engaged in a rolling see-saw battle with several cornered North Korean formations in the vicinity of Ch'ongjin. The other corps formation, the ROK 3d Division under Brig. Gen. Rhee Chong Chan, was slightly behind the Capital Division and holding the road from Kilchu to Hapsu. Although Colonel Powell's 17th Infantry was at the other end of the Kilchu-Hapsu road, at Hyesanjin, only evanescent contact was ever made between the two Allied commands, and the region between both towns remained essentially a no-man's land.

From the outset, the retreat of General Kim's corps was completely uncoordinated with Colonel Powell's retreat. The South Koreans thus faced the real danger of enemy forces infiltrating between both separately withdrawing Allied contingents and outflanking any rearward motion. At the tip of General Kim's front, the withdrawing Capital Division was counterattacked by the *4th NKPA Division*. Tactical problems were compounded by ten inches of fresh snow propelled by arctic winds falling across the corps zone, and covering the main supply road with man-high snow drifts.

The safety of the Rogers retreat hinged on a successful disengagement from its North Korean opponents, and this depended entirely on the offensive spirit of the enemy troops. The North Koreans did not offer serious interference, however, and the Capital Division was able to hold Ch'ongjin with only one regiment while the rest of the troops loaded trains south of the city for the rail journey back to Hungnam. Throughout the Rogers retreat, the North Koreans were content to follow the retreating South Koreans at a leisurely pace, and the only real opposition came from partisan attacks and sabotage incidents.

On December 3, the first troop trains from both ROK 3d and Capital Divisions began arriving at the Hamhung rail depot, and the smooth withdrawal of General Kim's ROK I Corps seemed assured. Almond's gamble of sacrificing flank security, in order to quickly relocate both the Rogers and Bayonet forces at Hamhung, appeared to be working. By evening, however, a series of mishaps threatened the cohesion of all retreating elements.

In the Rogers area, a large Capital Division train derailed in a tunnel on its way south, blocking two more trains and an undetermined number of cars behind the wreckage of the first. A plane was dispatched north along the coast to investigate the status of the withdrawing division. The pilot reported that large clusters of soldiers abandoned the train and were walking and riding an assortment of vehicles toward Kilchu. Advancing North Korean troops were following closely, but refrained from attacking.

In the Bayonet area, the division recon company was committed to hold a vital road junction, exhausting the reserve, and Colonel Powell's regiment became split along different roads. The road to the nearest railroad, near P'ungsan, proved impassable to vehicle traffic. Almond had planned to evacuate a large number of Bayonet soldiers by train shuttle, but these troops were forced to undergo a tortuously slow and exhausting foot march to reach the railhead. In the meantime, the main motor convoy (escorted by one company of tanks) lumbered closer to Pukch'ong, but vehicular road accidents and breakdowns seriously reduced the amount of salvageable equipment.

The Bayonet force was also having difficulty executing Almond's "scorched earth" orders as it abandoned the frozen wilderness between Pujon Reservoir and the Kaima Plateau. Road shelters, bridges, and many habitations were marked for demolition, but the rushed pace of withdrawal left little time for such details. In many cases, the Americans had to leave structures undamaged for the ROK 26th Regiment retreating behind them. This hapless South Korean "screening" regiment was left north of the Ungi River, out of communication, for days until an aircraft finally dropped a message bottle ordering it to pull back to Pukch'ong. The South Koreans quick-marched past Kapsan, leaving the critical bridge there intact, and later aircraft sorties failed to destroy this crucial span.

By mid-afternoon on December 4, the retreat was stalled. The Bayonet truck convoy entered Pukch'ong during mid-afternoon, but Major Dudley (from the 7th Infantry Division operations section) reported, "We must have these people [drivers stay] here for a few hours' rest as the trucks have been going for approximately 48 hours, and the drivers are beginning to go asleep and wrecking the vehicles while driving."[2] The Rogers retreat cleared Kilchu, but enemy saboteurs caused a third train wreck that halted further movement. Major Drew (the liaison officer with ROK I Corps) reported that vehicles could not detour around the smashed train because enemy partisans had placed obstructions in the adjacent mountain pass, and the South Koreans lacked engineer equipment and cranes to clear these road blocks.[3]

On the following day, the Rogers retreat terminated at the industrial port of Songjin. All surviving trucks in General Kim's corps were pooled into one convoy and the ROK Cavalry Regiment was selected to make a final road dash down the coast. The rest of the corps was ordered to evacuate Songjin by water and an assortment of vessels from LSTs to small fishing boats was used in this embarkation. Once again, the North Koreans were seemingly content to allow a peaceful departure. When the evacuation was finally completed, most of the ROK I Corps' larger transports were diverted to South Korean ports outside of X Corps control.

On December 6, General Almond declared the 7th Infantry Division reconsolidated at Hamhung, officially concluding the Bayonet retreat. The 7th Infantry Division managed to escape from the banks of the Yalu River largely because of a general absence of enemy opposition in its sector. Unfortunately, both men and equipment were forsaken in the mad scramble to reach safety.

At Pukch'ong, the KMAG officer with the ROK 26th Regiment reported that the 7th Infantry Division hastily burned fifty trucks, abandoned six boxcars of rations, and left hurried instructions with the ROK rear guard to finish destroying tons of abandoned equipment.[4] Even more distressing was the fact that several groups of 17th Infantry stragglers were left behind at Pukch'ong, and these men reported other troops left behind as far back as P'ungsan—including soldiers unable to move because of wounds or appendicitis.[5] These reports confirmed the rather disorderly nature of the Bayonet withdrawal.

On December 7, General Barr reoriented his formation toward assisting the Marine breakout to the coast. Infantry-escorted wrecker trucks continued to ply the northeastern roads, however, for the next few days in an attempt to rescue stranded vehicles and missing soldiers.

2. Retracting the Horns: The South

On December 1, General Almond also ordered the 3d Infantry Division on the X Corps southern front to pull back to Hamhung. Unlike the retreat of the northern wing, which was either unengaged or facing reluctant North Korean opposition, elements of the 3d Infantry Division, code name "Kaiser," were duelling with tough Chinese adversaries in scattered remote locations. The success of the Kaiser retreat depended on a carefully executed withdrawal program, but General Almond's indecision jeopardized the process.

The majority of the division's 7th Infantry was heavily engaged with the *89th PLA Division* near Sach'ang-ni. This activity precluded its immediate withdrawal from the front. General Soule decided to pull his division back by using the "Killer" 7th Regiment as a pinning force to safeguard the Wonsan-Hamhung coastal railway from immediate Chinese conquest. He also wanted to continue using the corps Special Activity Group, a commando force on loan to the division, as a screening force against the *126th PLA Division* in the Taebaek Range, but Almond insisted on having his commandoes redeploy promptly to Hamhung.

This complicated Kaiser retreat arrangements, as the 15th Infantry and attached South Korean Marine regiment suffered ambushes and probing attacks from advancing enemy forces in the Tongyang and Majon-ni areas. Tongyang was abandoned and Majon-ni was cut off. Ammunition had to be parachuted to the 1st Battalion, 15th Infantry, holding the latter town. In spite of these enemy advances, the 3d Infantry Division held most of its key mountain choke points and moved the Puerto Rican 65th Infantry ("Kodak") from Wonsan and Yonghung to Hamhung.

The Kodak retreat, although by rail, was very uncomfortable. The Puerto Ricans were forced to spend the bitterly cold journey cramped on board open gondola cars. At 10 P.M. in the freezing darkness, the 65th Infantry was just reaching the outskirts of Hamhung when General Almond ordered the Kodak force turned around and moved back south to defend Wonsan port and airfield. The X Corps operations planning manager, Lt. Col. Frank T. Mildren, conveyed Almond's instructions and stated that only the South Korean Marine Regiment would move into Hamhung.[6]

The 3d Division history records the consternation: "Wondering at the sudden reversal of orders, division elements executed a quick about face and moved back toward Wonsan. Troops with teeth still clattering from the cold ride northward in the open gondolas picked up their equipment and climbed back aboard for an equally cold ride to the south. Truck drivers who already spent hours behind the wheel on the twisting, icy roads also turned around and headed for Wonsan."[7]

For days, Kaiser retreat plans were kept in a state of flux by the many orders and countermands issued by corps. On December 3, X Corps ordered the division to assemble without delay and move again

to the Hamhung area. Colonel Harris's 65th Infantry received three different sets of orders, only to have each one abolished successively in the
space of three days.

On December 2, the 65th Infantry started back to Wonsan, and
corps was assured at 2:40 P.M. that the 64th Tank battalion would follow
as quickly as it completed refueling. The long trip south by the infantry
in open rail cars was mitigated somewhat by the gift of over five hundred
cases of free beer from the Cevaria India Company of Puerto Rico,
given to the 65th Infantry regimental special service officer.[8]

During the same day, the forward battalion of Colonel Guthrie's
7th Infantry, isolated at Sach'ang-ni, destroyed all the equipment that
could not be manhandled down the road and retreated under the guns
of a full Chinese regiment. The Chinese followed close behind and
delivered harassing fire. When Lt. Col. Charles T. Heinrich's 1st Battalion
was stopped by a badly cratered roadway midway to safety, the Americans
sensed ambush and a final showdown. Instead, the Chinese watched
from the high ridges and made no attempt to stop a battalion tank-dozer
from repairing the damage.

The battalion was able to reach Huksu-ri and joined Lt. Col. Robert
Besson's 2d Battalion of the same regiment. Throughout the night a
regiment of the *89th PLA Division* skirmished against American lines
west of the town. Using green and red flares as predesignated signals
for maneuvering, the enemy troops crawled from one firing position to
another under the cover of intense automatic weapons fire. By early
morning, the enemy succeeded in making limited penetrations through
the American lines.

With the sanctity of his position compromised, Lieutenant Colonel
Besson was forced to withdraw his unit southeast of Huksu-ri, where
he reorganized it on the commanding ridges. At 1 P.M., December 3,
Major Clark of the regiment contacted X Corps operations, "Four companies in fair shape. Believe we can hold high ground S [south] of
Huksu-ri providing we get air strike. Enemy going around both
flanks."[9] The enemy attacks tapered off, however, and the Chinese disengaged before nightfall.

During the afternoon of December 3, General Almond flew into
Wonsan and announced another change of direction to General Soule.
He wanted the Kaiser retreat fully implemented immediately and the
3d Infantry Division moved into the Hamhung area. The Kodak force
(Colonel Harris's 65th Infantry) was directed to reestablish guard posts

along the railroad to insure continued Allied use of the rail system. There was too little time, however, to move heavier division equipment and supply stocks by rail. Almond agreed to have the Navy divert all available LSTs to Wonsan for sea evacuation of this material.

General Almond departed Soule's command post shortly after 3 P.M. by plane and saw the southbound division convoys stopped, apparently preparing to turn around and go north. Satisfied that his new orders were being carried out, Almond conducted a quick recon flight over the Huksu-ri battlefield and returned to corps headquarters at Hamhung within two hours. That night, the town of Anbyon, defended by five hundred Allied Korean police, was overrun by enemy troops.

On December 4, the Kaiser retreat shifted into high gear as the 3d Infantry Division raced to reach Hamhung. Only two battalions of South Korean Marines were left at Wonsan to supervise the LST beach area. The Chinese pushed beyond the destroyed town of Huksu-ri and pilots reported seeing evidence of heavy night travel along the surrounding snow trails. Numerous company-sized groups of enemy soldiers, garbed in either white or dark-colored uniforms, were spotted moving relentlessly eastward from Huksu-ri toward Majon-dong and the corps main supply line.

On December 5, division Brigadier General Mead formed an ad hoc task force of infantry, artillery, and engineers to protect the Majon-dong vicinity for the Marine withdrawal. Artillery fire plans were hastily drafted to shell enemy approaches to the highway and engineers began repairing the critical bridges from Koto-ri south. Other elements of the division took up new positions in the wide defensive arc being built around the Hamhung-Hungnam complex.

Closely pursued by Chinese forces and under fire, the Kaiser rear guard was forced to abandon much of its equipment along the narrow icy roads. The 7th Infantry left behind five tanks and a tank-dozer in this hasty retreat. The division ditty was sung to the tune of the old hill-billy song, "Movin' On":

> Twenty thousand Chinks comin' thru the pass
> The Third Division is haulin' ass
> They're movin' out
> They're buggin' out
> They got us outnumbered
> Bug out while there is time

When you hear the pitter patter of GI feet
That's the Third Division in full retreat
They're movin' out
They're buggin' out
They got us surrounded
Bug out while there is time

Three Yak nines comin' thru the pass
Caucasian nine says haulin' ass
I'm movin' out
They're comin' in
They got us outnumbered
Bug out while there is time[10]

3. The Marines Strike Camp

December 6 was a clear day with only occasional scattered clouds and
coastal temperatures of thirty-five degrees, before low clouds and thicken-
ing overcast closed in during late afternoon. Allied aircraft ranged over
northeastern Korea in support of X Corps before their activity was curtailed
by adverse weather. Late in the morning, General Almond himself showed
up at Yonp'o airport, inspected the Cargo Command activities, and went
to the operations section of the airfield. He attended a pilot's briefing
and ordered the pilots to destroy any reservoir power plants if enemy
activity was suspected, giving the airmen complete license to bomb at
will.

The umbrella of air protection afforded X Corps was still highly
effective, but it was being challenged more frequently by new enemy
countermeasures. Some light bombers were strafed by "very aggressive
and very maneuverable" MIG jet fighters,[11] and these direct air confronta-
tions were supplemented by a host of clever "flak traps" being built
on the ground. Holes were dug into hill caves and appeared like railroad
tunnels from the air. Manufactured smoke was sent out, giving the impression that locomotives were hiding inside. Any planes making a run at
the suspected target were taken under heavy antiaircraft fire from the
nearby hills.

The news of jet attacks and flak traps caused increasing alarm at
Far East Air Force headquarters; it was obvious that air support to X
Corps would become more perilous with each passing day. On December

6, however, over 270 sorties were flown directly for X Corps ground troops, and an Airborne Tactical Air Direction Center was established in a C-54 aircraft to direct the multitude of ground support missions. Most of this intense air support was in direct support of the Marine division, which initiated its breakout to the coast on the same day.

At the Marine division command post at Hagaru-ri, reveille was held at 5 A.M. Immediately afterward, the Marines began striking camp as tents, stoves, and other gear were loaded on trucks for the long march south. Throughout the day, C-47 cargo planes flew into the base to take out wounded men and critical items. All excess materiel such as office equipment, extra clothing and baggage, unserviceable weapons, and apparatus that might hinder the retreat was burned or destroyed. At 3 P.M., General Smith flew the command group from Hagaru-ri to Koto-ri. His plane winged over Marine communications teams yanking out the wire lines, terminating field phone connections as one of the last steps in the dismantling process.

The Marine convoy, reinforced by a composite Army battalion under Lt. Col. Berry K. Anderson, commenced departure from Hagaru-ri at 6:30 A.M. The convoy was formed up with vehicles on the road and troops marching in single file on both sides of the vehicles. The only men riding were drivers, shotgun relief drivers, radio operators of mobile radio equipment, and the wounded. The convoy proceeded underneath a display of devastating aerial support. Air strikes raked the enemy-held ridges with cannon fire and bombs five hundred yards in front of the Marine vanguard.

Elements of six *PLA* divisions, occupying the high ground on both sides of the road, offered moderate to heavy resistance as the long column led by four tanks slowly fought its way forward. When the first roadblock was encountered, the lead tank was hit by three bazooka rounds from a 3.5-inch rocket launcher.

One of the spearhead units was led by Lt. Welton R. Abell, whose unit was composed of survivors of the five-day Hagaru-ri siege and many special services personnel unfamiliar with infantry tactics. The unit's ranks were decimated by casualties early in the action, but Abell dispatched runners to notify his platoons of an attempted enemy envelopment of their positions. Both dispatchers were struck down before completing the mission. Abell moved through the mortar bombardment and shifted his men to block the threat against his lines. By noon, two rifle companies supported by tanks had smashed through the enemy blockade.

The main column continued its advance, but the sharp fighting took its toll on remaining mobile Marine equipment. Each skirmish further diminished the motorized capability of the division to punch through. In this first day of the main retreat, a single engineer platoon reported pushing sixty damaged vehicles off the road to keep it passable for traffic following behind. By evening, with forward Marine elements still twenty-five hundred yards shy of linking up at Koto-ri, many doubted whether the Marines could get their heavier equipment to the coast.

While enemy action was concentrated against the main supply route, the Marines at Hagaru-ri were also fighting for possession of East Hill. At 7 A.M., the 2d Battalion of the 5th Marines began a savage twenty-two-hour battle for control of this key height. The Chinese fought with skill and determination, and counterattacked constantly during the night of December 6–7. Over eight hundred Chinese were killed in front of the Marine positions on the hill.

Farther south, the Chinese infiltrated around the main supply route between Sudong and Majon-dong. They slept in their foxholes during the day and moved only at night, utilizing many patrols, listening posts, and sentries to observe U.S. movements. There were a large number of English-speaking Chinese soldiers, who sometimes posed as American outpost members. On the morning of December 6, the Chinese attacked various outposts along the road. The enemy troops used chemical-type six- or ten-inch long "potato masher" grenades which produced low-order charge bursts and emitted yellow smoke, causing sneezing and coughing. After the Chinese determined positions in this fashion they showered the defenders with fragmentation and concussion grenades.

A ten-vehicle convoy was ambushed south of Sudong with machine guns and mortars, and the Chinese established a blocking position that cut a portion of the main road. This obstacle was cleared by soldiers from the 7th Infantry Division during the afternoon. That evening, the 3d Battalion of the 7th Infantry repulsed an attack on its Majon-dong perimeter. Northwest of the village, a reinforced patrol became involved in a brisk fire fight with a Chinese battalion. The enemy used molotov cocktails and satchel charges in the encounter before breaking contact. Corps operations officers worried that the Chinese might attempt to slice the corps' logistical lane along its entire length.

General Almond's activities during the day revolved around the visit of General Collins, the Army Chief of Staff, who had just finished visiting the Eighth Army as it withdrew to positions south of P'yongyang.

Walker informed Collins that further withdrawals to Seoul were mandated, but a rigid defense of the Inch'on-Seoul area would expose his army again to the possibility of Chinese encirclement. Collins and Walker agreed that orderly evacuation from Inch'on was nearly impossible because of the poor harbor facilities and tidal conditions, but that a retreat to Pusan would give the army access to a superb port with heavy cargo cranes and excellent docks, close to Japan. Walker stated that reinforcement of his command by X Corps would allow the Pusan perimeter to be held indefinitely.

General Collins landed at Yonp'o at 1:30 P.M. and Almond briefed him on the current X Corps situation. The 7th Infantry Division was already in the Hamhung-Hungnam area, and was providing security for the final stages of the 1st Marine Division's march to the coast. The 3d Infantry Division was consolidated in the Hamhung area, except for rear elements guarding Wonsan. The ROK I Corps was evacuating Songjin by sea and would reinforce the X Corps perimeter. Almond expressed confidence that his corps could defend the Hamhung-Hungnam area for a considerable time without serious losses.

After a working lunch, Generals Almond and Collins boarded an L-17 and flew over the main supply route as far north as Sudong. By 4 P.M., dense overcast precluded their plane from flying beyond Funchilin Pass, and the command party returned to Hamhung. Almond reassured Collins that in the event evacuation was required, X Corps could withdraw "successfully and cheaply when so ordered." Collins agreed with Almond's estimate and left Yonp'o for the return trip to Tokyo at 6 P.M. General Almond was confident he had made a good impression, "General Collins seemed completely satisfied with the operation of X Corps and apparently much relieved in finding the situation well in hand."[12]

As General Collins's plane disappeared into the night sky, the lights of Hamhung blinked out. The enemy had reached Hochon power plants Nos. 1 and 2 on the eastern coast, and cut off all commercial electric power into the city.

4. The Last Bridge

The ninth anniversary of Pearl Harbor Day, December 7, 1950, was ushered in with 120 high-explosive rounds of eight-inch naval gunfire from the heavy cruiser St. Paul (CA-73) covering the Wonsan beaches.

The sky was visible through the broken overcast and coastal temperatures again rose above freezing (to 35 degrees).

Aircraft supporting X Corps used the good flying weather to log a record 305 sorties, about half (146) from the Marine air wing. Among other targets, Marine pilots spotted about three hundred Chinese with fifty horses hiding in a ravine near the slaughtering ground of Task Force Faith, and annihilated the entire group—man and beast—with a few well-aimed rocket volleys.

Some enemy targets had to be repeatedly bombed. An early morning overflight disclosed a tunnel entrance at Sunamo (about two and a half miles south of Koto-ri) being used by many enemy soldiers. Two direct hits were scored against the enemy assembly area at 1:40 P.M., followed by another direct hit with a five hundred-pound bomb. According to a Corps Special Activities Group agent sent to assess damage in the area, the Chinese suffered severe casualties from the triple hits. The agent also confirmed that the tunnel was put back in use as a major enemy base the very next day.[13]

One of the most critical air missions of the entire Korean war was flown on the same day. The Marine division faced an impassable chasm in its projected line of march three and a half miles below Koto-ri, where a critical concrete one-way bridge was dropped by enemy saboteurs. The bridge had crossed over four large pipes (penstocks) carrying rushing water from the Changjin Reservoir out of a tunnel down the sharp incline into the power plant turbines in the valley below. A long concrete gate house covered the upper penstocks and was situated just uphill from the missing bridge. Below the gate house was a sheer one thousand five hundred-foot cliff that terminated in the gorge below. There was no possibility of a bypass and the gap, if left unbridged, would prevent the division from bringing out any wheeled or tracked vehicles, or their towed or loaded cargo (the men could cross using rope slings).

A solution to the dilemma was possible if an M2 treadway bridge could be parachuted to the Marine column. The accompanying Army 58th Engineer Treadway Bridge Company, fortuitously at Koto-ri, possessed two working six-ton Brockway bridge trucks suitable for mounting treadway bridge sections. No complete M2 treadway bridge had ever been airdropped before, and no one knew whether it could be delivered by air without excessive bending or damage to the sections.[14]

Eight C-119 aircraft were allocated to the delicate task. Each cumbersome steel span weighing 2,350 pounds required its own Flying Boxcar.

Although four spans composed a full bridge, eight spans were dropped. The eleven men of the forward detachment from the 2348th Quartermaster Airborne Air Supply and Packaging Company at Yonp'o carefully rigged two large G5 cargo parachutes on opposite ends of each span, doubling the assurance that the forty-eight-foot canopies of these monstrous parachutes would hold up to their advertised three thousand-pound load capabilities. Ideally, it was hoped that the parachutes would bring the spans down nicely, but one parachute failure would still leave enough canopy to land the piece safely. The spans were tied to wooden pallets and loaded aboard. Their parachute static lines were fastened to the plane's anchor cables and the mission commenced.

As the planes approached the drop zone the cargo masters loosened the rope tie-downs and pushed the spans rearward. Upon a signal from the pilot, the remaining rope sling was cut and the span rolled free, clearing each aircraft in two or three seconds. Most spans drifted down beneath two chutes as intended but there were two mishaps. One span fell with only one G5 parachute supporting its descent. Although this span landed on one end, rather than flat as the others, it was reported serviceable by the engineer officer at the drop zone. Another span fell into the hands of Chinese surrounding Koto-ri. Enough necessary M2 bridge components, however, were delivered successfully to the ground troops.[15]

The withdrawing 1st Marine Division fought through fierce enemy resistance on the night of December 6–7. Six miles south of Hagaru-ri, in the midst of the infamous Hell Fire Valley, the enemy opened fire on the division column a half hour before midnight. Light machine gun fire caused the convoy to stop and become fragmented as the bullets ripped into six vehicles and a contingent of 150 Chinese prisoners being herded down the road. The senior convoy section commander tried to get his segment moving again, but his own jeep was hit and set afire.

The enemy rifle and machine-gun fire intensified from the high steep ridges on the left and the parallel railroad embankment. The convoy trucks and jeeps were struck by concentrated enemy mortar fire, and Chinese submachine gunners and grenadiers dug into the slopes and railroad culverts opened fire at close range. One 2.36-inch rocket launcher crew behind sandbags in one culvert scored numerous hits on the stalled vehicles within range. The Marines were pinned by this heavy fusillade and the numerous fires from exploding gas tanks silhouetted their efforts to move forward.

Two Marine machine gun squads managed to move into position on both sides of the road and joined the fire fight. Marine riflemen were able to move through the fairly deep drainage ditches alongside the road. By now, the leading group vehicle was dead in the road with a bullet-riddled motor, and five trucks and vans behind it were burning. The key vehicle used for air control purposes was knocked out and its radio destroyed. During this confusion, the Chinese prisoners—who were caught in the cross-fire—tried to make a break for the open fields beyond the road and were gunned down by the Marines.

A Marine rocket launcher team tried to silence the nearby enemy bunkers, but their bazookas failed to fire. Both were reloaded but still refused to fire. The next morning a careful examination revealed that snow had become lodged in the trigger mechanism and shorted the magneto. A tank finally clambered into action, but by the time it reached the battle zone the Chinese were withdrawing. The fire fight simmered as the overcast lifted sufficiently to permit some night air strikes on enemy mortar and machine gun emplacements. With the approach of daylight, enemy soldiers scrambled away from further aerial retaliation. At dawn, the engineer dozers pushed the blazing vehicles off the road.[16]

The enemy, however, continued to direct light intermittent fire against other convoy sections until just before daybreak. At that time, a group of two hundred Chinese stormed down the hills and reached positions within yards of the convoy as a lively fire fight erupted. Lt. James C. Barnes, Jr., of Battery A, 48th Field Artillery Battalion, was one of the composite Army battalion members. When his segment of the convoy was hit by a well-emplaced enemy machine gun on the high ridge, he ordered a platoon to follow him in a rapid charge against the enemy. His men were soon pinned down by enemy fire and unable to advance, but Lieutenant Barnes raced across the fire-swept open ground and destroyed the machine gun nest with grenades and carbine fire. He was later awarded the Distinguished Service Cross.[17]

Close air support was brought in by the convoy officer-in-charge and the intelligence officer acting as forward air controllers from radio jeeps. Their action broke the enemy attack and forced the Chinese to break and run. As the enemy retreated, they were taken under fire by the convoy and the road block was cleared. Although a 6x6 truck received a bullet in the engine block, it continued to run and the vehicle was able to remain in the convoy.

Approximately three hundred yards down the road, the convoy was again brought to a halt as another group of Chinese charged down the slope. The enemy assault troops reached the railroad embankment about fifty yards from the road, but well-directed convoy firepower stopped the Chinese at that point. At 8:30 A.M., Chinese snipers and automatic weapons crews opened up on the convoy from houses just off the road. Aircraft were called in promptly and the enemy troops broke and ran under the searing napalm and rocket attack. Unfortunately, the commander of the 3d Battalion, 7th Marines, Lt. Col. William F. Harris, was declared missing in action at 5:30 A.M. and was later declared killed by enemy fire.[18]

By 7 A.M., the point of the column was in Koto-ri but its rear was still at Hagaru-ri eleven miles distant. At 10:30 A.M., General Almond overflew the entire length of the Marine convoy and saw the rear of the truck convoy of the 5th and 11th Marines just south of Hagaru-ri. He directed the plane lower and noted that the convoy was stopped but did not appear to be engaged by enemy fire. Infuriated, he landed at Koto-ri at noon and proceeded to lecture General Smith on more rapid movement procedures. Smith reported that the 7th Marines had suffered over two hundred casualties in their move from Hagaru-ri to Koto-ri, but that he expected the 5th and 11th Marines would fare better. General Smith was concerned about securing artillery priority for his Marines once they entered the valley, and Almond assured him that General Soule's 3d Infantry Division and the artillery would provide maximum protection for the final Marine movement from Chinhung-ni down the valley to Hamhung.

Throughout the day, the Marine convoy filed into Koto-ri and by midnight, December 7, all units were at the town except the rear guard. Along the road, the column rescued a group of British Marine commandos that had been isolated since November 30. There were twelve litter cases and thirty to forty walking wounded among the British survivors. The tail of the huge convoy was followed by nearly five thousand refugees about two hundred yards behind the Marines, and another refugee column was walking along the side of the column about five hundred yards off the road. The Marines were wary of both groups because of the possibility of infiltrators.

On December 8, a blinding snowstorm driven by eight-knot winds developed in the morning and dominated the day's activity. No fighters were able to take off at Yonp'o because of freezing rain (coast temperatures reached a high of thirty-seven degrees), and a severe snowstorm at sea prevented aircraft carriers from launching their planes. Only one C-47 transport landed at Koto-ri, and it evacuated twenty emergency patients despite the heavy snowfall. Its valiant mercy mission represented the sole corps air support for the day.

The Chinese applied heavy pressure against the corps forces forging a link-up south of Koto-ri. At 8 A.M., the mixed Army-Marine column struggled through the snowstorm to negotiate the most difficult terrain of the journey—a winding road twisting sharply downhill through the dreaded incline of the Funchilin Pass. The enemy launched attacks against both ends of the column, but were repulsed after bitter fighting.

The convoy was reinforced by two more battalions of Army troops, Lieutenant Colonel Reidy's 2d Battalion of the 31st Infantry, and another composite tactical battalion formed in Koto-ri from Army service troops under the command of Lt. Col. John U. D. Page from the X Corps Artillery staff. Page had already demonstrated his combat prowess during the past several days around Koto-ri, in acts ranging from manning tank turret machine guns against close assaults on the airstrip to dropping hand grenades on top of startled Chinese in foxholes outside the perimeter from a light liaison airplane.

The Army and Marine spearhead units seized the commanding ridges along the route of march from deeply entrenched enemy forces. Lieutenant Colonel Page accompanied the rear elements, which included the vital Army treadway bridge trucks which needed to be kept safe from Chinese mortar barrages. The Chinese mounted strong attacks from both sides, however, as the rear guard neared the entrance to the narrow pass. Page climbed on top of an abandoned tank and manned its machine gun despite intense enemy fire. He delivered effective counterfire while the column passed through the ambuscade. Lieutenant Colonel Page was killed at the head of his troops near the bottom of the pass two days later, and his courage was later recognized by a posthumous Medal of Honor.

One of the most difficult aspects of the march was the triage of the frostbite cases. Nearly every Marine wanted to stay in the column and assist in combat, but Marine and Navy medical teams had to determine who was capable of actually helping and who might be a hindrance despite their good intentions. All frostbite cases were screened three times: once by local unit surgeons, again by the medical companies, and finally by a team of division and regimental surgeons with a senior line officer from each regiment. As a rough guide, those with large blisters or excessive discolored areas were considered candidates for evacuation. Many men with toes and parts of toes completely blackened, however, never turned themselves in. Much to the later amazement of medical authorities, these Marines somehow completed the winter march all the way to the coast.[19]

On December 9, the clouds broke apart after 2 A.M. and the skies cleared as temperatures dropped. The temperature along the Marine route of march was six below zero. The good flying weather brought a total of 322 sorties to aid the Marine breakout although enemy antiaircraft fire was becoming deadlier. A Navy fighter-bomber was shot down four miles north of Hagaru-ri. Corsairs drove off several hundred Chinese attempting to capture the two airmen while a helicopter rescued them under fire. Thirteen C-119 flights parachuted petroleum barrels into Koto-ri as fifteen C-47s landed on the short runway bringing in more petrol and carrying out the wounded. The last airdrop of the day was made just before the rear-guard element vacated the town and its airfield.

The Chinese tried to block the main road through Funchilin Pass with strongly organized hillside positions, and Marine division assault units spent much of the day clearing the ridges overlooking the road before the convoy could move southward. Many enemy field fortifications were built of sandbagged log revetments, and resisted general air strikes. The Marines suffered more casualties trying to neutralize these bunkers by ground attack.

The most important event of the day was the installation of the treadway bridge at the gate-house by Marine and Army engineers. The new bridge was painstakingly erected under fire and featured a sandbag and timber crib bent and four sections of the M2 steel treadway bridge. Traffic proceeded across the structure gingerly, but a tractor towing earth-moving machinery broke through the plywood center panel and threatened to block further movement across the bridge. The hero of the hour was driver T/Sgt. Wilfred H. Prosser, who managed to drive the machine expertly in reverse and get it off the bridge.

The loss of the wooden center was a severe blow, because the spacing of the treadway sections closed them to wheeled traffic without the plywood board. The engineers, however, did some quick calculating and realigned the bridge so that it could both support tanks and jeeps, but there was no margin for error. The wheeled vehicles had to ride the inside rims in the darkness. Using flashlights and raw courage, the drivers passed over the bridge in slow procession as the Marine column cleared the hurdle of this last bridge to safety.

5. The Link-up

On December 7, while the Marines continued their trek southward, Task Force Dog of the 3d Infantry Division moved forward to relieve the 1st Battalion, 1st Marines, at Chinhung-ni. The 92d Armored Field Artillery Battalion positioned its tracked self-propelled howitzers on the plain just outside Chinhung-ni. The 999th Armored Field Artillery Battalion moved into firing positions near Majon-dong. Both battalions pummelled the enemy-occupied ridges with sustained artillery barrages, and the task force met the Marines at the town during mid-afternoon.

General Almond arrived at the 3d Infantry Division command post at 3:30 P.M., where General Soule briefed him that enemy pressure in the Majon-dong area had let up. Soule stated the situation was now well in hand along the main supply route. Almond then advised Soule that the Marine division was taking over control of all artillery firing in the valley, to support their main march, and Soule complied with this arrangement.

On the afternoon of December 8, General Almond remained secluded in his van quarters. The reason became apparent at 6:30 P.M., when he angrily directed his public information officer to arrange a top-level telecon with Tokyo. Almond was enraged about a *Stars and Stripes* story about his "loose" awarding of high medals to Army and Marine personnel, and insisted on clearing up the "inaccuracies." He also warned the press that, in compliance with a request from Far East Command, he was taking severe measures against "premature disclosure of movements of Marines south of Koto-ri."[20] Incensed by press coverage of his impact awards, General Almond was now clamping down on all news stories from the front.

While Almond fumed over the press, the Marines were fighting their way through the snowstorm. The Marine battalion, along with engineer and artillery support from Task Force Dog, advanced northward through Funchilin Pass to meet the Marine column moving south. The combined task force advanced up the sharply winding road against "unexpectedly light resistance,"[21] and cleared the road to the huge defile six miles south of Koto-ri. There the 1st Marines waited for the main convoy to cross over the emergency treadway bridge. The link-up was accomplished.

While the Marines solidified their junction, elements of 65th Infantry and Task Force Dog continued to secure the corps main supply route between Hamhung and Chinhung-ni. Company G of the 65th Infantry was hit by a strong enemy assault against its covering positions. This Chinese contingent was repulsed and retreated northward to slash into the Marine column, where the enemy was destroyed in close-quarters fighting.

In front of Hamhung, the X Corps special missions group (8227th Army Unit) was operating on outpost security for the 7th Infantry Division. Lt. Col. Wallace M. Hanes's unique unit consisted of Royal Marine commandos, the provisional raider company, a Marine provisional raider company, and a Royal Navy volunteer group. Originally formed for ship-launched night shore raids, the group was now involved in mountain warfare screening the approaches north of Hamhung. The raiders slipped into Sinhung, screened the undefended valley to the east of the withdrawing Marines, and performed other crucial missions.

The goat-trails buried in two feet of snow hampered their operations, and the freezing cold weather penetrated the layers of winter clothing and endangered the small patrol actions that typified their style of warfare. The shoe pacs, while warm in static defensive positions, were too heavy and gave insufficient ankle support for marching, and the combat boots preferred in hiking gave too little protection against the cold whenever the troops stopped. The group was forced to rely on Korean HID agents for surveillance throughout the critical valleys and villages within its large sector.[22]

At 9:15 on the morning of December 9, with the safety of the Marine column almost assured, General Almond held a major conference on outloading and naval support at Hungnam. Admirals Struble, Turner Joy, and Doyle as well as Marine Generals Shepherd and Harris attended. When the conference was over, General Almond held his first major press conference in weeks. Admiral Joy, Admiral Struble, and General Shepherd made brief statements and General Almond summarized the activities of X Corps since November 24, praising the "magnificent manner in which the Marines and 7th Division elements with the Marines have conducted this operation."[23]

At the conclusion of the press conference, Almond boarded his L-17 and made an aerial reconnaissance of the defensive positions northeast of Hungnam and the Marine column. As he flew over the snowy terrain shortly after 12:00 noon, he noted that the Marine units appeared to have met at the power station near the crest of the mountain, and that sections of the treadway bridge were being moved rapidly to the breach in the platform bridge. 7th Infantry Division and ROK Corps troops were well disposed and digging in on the commanding high ground along the main line of resistance.

Privately, General Almond was not so pleased with the Marine withdrawal. He would later reply to a question asking him to judge the Marine division at that point, and whether it was greatly reduced as an effective fighting force, "Well, more mentally were they reduced than they were physically. While there were a number of casualties and disorder during the Changjin Reservoir operation, when the Marines got back in hand in the Hungnam area, and readjusted themselves to the conditions, they were considered combat effective."[24]

The great fortitude and courage displayed by the Marine withdrawal—which succeeded despite strong enemy pressure and adverse weather—ranked as one of the great accomplishments of American arms, but it found little real favor with General Almond. He did not favor retrograde movements under any circumstances, and his clashes with General Smith created a corps chasm far deeper mentally than the physical gorges that could be connected by treadway bridges.

Notes

1. 7th Infantry Division, *Action Report: From Hyesanjin to Hungnam Outloading,* p. 5.
2. X Corps G-3 Daily Summary, dtd 4 December 1950, Item J-72.
3. X Corps G-3 Daily Summary, dtd 4 December 1950, Item J-34.
4. X Corps G-3 Daily Summary, dtd 7 December 1950, Item J-32.
5. X Corps G-3 Daily Summary, dtd 7 December 1950, Item J-91.
6. X Corps G-3 Daily Summary, dtd 1 December 1950, Item J-138.
7. 3d Infantry Division in Korea, p. 88.
8. X Corps Command Report Annex for 2 December 1950.
9. X Corps G-3 Daily Summary, dtd 3 December 1950, Item J-62.
10. Song supplied by Col. Benjamin S. Silver, a division officer who recorded the music during the retreat, in correspondence to the author, 28 March 1987.
11. X Corps Periodic Intelligence Report No. 72, III-2(a).
12. Quotes from Schnabel, p. 283, and X Corps CG Diary, dtd 6 December 1950.
13. X Corps G-3 Daily Summary, dtd 8 December 1950, Item J-29.
14. X Corps, *Special Report on Chosin Reservoir,* p. 55.
15. U.S. Air Force 315th Air Wing Report, Subj; Report, 10 September 1950–24 January 1951.
16. 1st Marine Division Special Action Report, Annex Easy Easy, dtd 15 January 1951, p. 26.
17. Far East Command General Orders No. 118, dtd 12 May 1951.
18. 1st Marine Special Action Report, Annex Charlie Charlie, Appendix 2, p. 11.
19. 1st Marine Special Action Report, Annex Queen, dtd January 1951, p. 5.
20. X Corps Commander's Diary, 8 December 1950.
21. 3d Infantry Division in Korea, p. 92.
22. 8227th Army Unit, *Command Report,* December 1950, pp. 1,4.
23. X Corps CG Diary, dtd 9 December 1950.
24. USAMHI Interview, p. V-17.

CHAPTER 13

CONCLUSION OF A CAMPAIGN

1. MacArthur's Strategic Appraisal

The Chinese offensive against X Corps forced General Almond to conduct a full-scale retreat to the Korean coast. In the northern area, where there was no Chinese contact, a portion of the 7th Infantry Division and ROK I Corps averted disaster and managed to extricate themselves with relatively light casualties. The 3d Infantry Division withdrew from the southern front under more direct pressure (complicated by conflicting corps orders), but escaped largely intact. On the central corps front in the Changjin Reservoir area, however, the Chinese multi-army assault wiped out an Army regimental equivalent and threatened the 1st Marine Division with extinction. The Marines fought successfully through the gauntlet of Chinese fire by fusing collective bravery with considerable tactical skill, and reached the coast despite enemy intentions. The overall impact of the Chinese offensive, however, caused the Allied front to collapse across Korea.

The military defeat suffered by both Eighth Army and X Corps created a crisis at the highest national level. President Truman faced not only the prospect of catastrophic UN military failure in Korea, but a third world war if unchecked Chinese advances continued. He called an emergency session of the National Security Council, where both Secretary of Defense George C. Marshall and the Joint Chiefs of Staff advised, in the strongest terms, that the United States avoid war with China.

This top-level strategic decision led to major restrictions being placed on Far East Command in its use of air and naval power against China. General MacArthur was incensed because "he was being forced to fight the Chinese with his hands tied,"[1] and he used both military communiques and press briefings to argue for swift retaliation against China. On December 9, the Joint Chiefs of Staff issued MacArthur a stern warning to refrain from publicly discussing political or foreign policy matters beyond the scope of his command.

In early December, MacArthur was still opposed to withdrawing X Corps from northeastern Korea and consolidating it with Eighth Army. He not only wanted to avoid the specter of an American Dunkirk, but he believed Almond's corps, as presently situated, hindered the freedom of Chinese movement through central Korea. He remained convinced that the added strength gained by joining Eighth Army with X Corps was less beneficial than the "freedom of maneuver deriving from their separate lines of supply by sea."[2]

General Collins, the Army chief of staff, returned to Washington after his field visit to the Far East Command with a gloomy report. He briefed the Joint Chiefs of Staff, "If the United Nations decision is not to continue an all-out attack in Korea and if the Chinese communists continue to attack, MacArthur should be directed to take the necessary steps to prevent the destruction of his forces pending final evacuation from Korea."[3]

United States leaders were considering several courses of action in Korea. In the hope of arranging an armistice with China while remaining militarily viable, the first scheme envisioned a withdrawal of UN forces to the 38th Parallel. MacArthur believed this option represented the best option available to the UN if certain military measures were precluded, such as battlefield use of the atomic bomb or naval and air blockade against China. He argued that his command must be reinforced (he recommended Nationalist Chinese troops from Formosa) in order to hold the front and provide incentive for armistice negotiations. In this scheme X Corps would be pulled back to Pusan and the Eighth Army would hold positions controlling the Inch'on-Seoul corridor.

The second course of action involved the holding of three beachheads on Korean soil as long as militarily feasible. These would include two Eighth Army enclaves at Seoul-Inch'on and Pusan, and the X Corps enclave at Hungnam. MacArthur now saw little use in holding out in defensive pockets, even if these offered the chance of prolonged resistance. He favored a line of defense to be held until additional reinforcements permitted a renewed offensive against the Chinese invaders. In this scenario, MacArthur wanted X Corps to withdraw overland, in a series of defensive lines coordinated with the Eighth Army, until the two commands could be joined and stabilized along a cross-peninsula front.

The third course of action involved evacuating all UN forces from Korea, a military necessity if China intensified its commitment to the conflict. Under these circumstances, X Corps would be removed to Japan at once, and the rest of the UN command would follow. This option was the least desirable from the United States strategic standpoint because it would entail abandonment of Korea to enemy forces. Any political solution to the conflict would lack the military leverage necessary to compel Chinese compromise on negotiated terms of settlement.

On December 7, General Wright presented MacArthur with a frank assessment on Allied disengagement from Korea. Wright recommended X Corps be sea-lifted from Hungnam as soon as possible and sent south to join the Eighth Army. The Joint Chiefs of Staff no longer felt northeastern Korea should be defended, and relegated MacArthur's and Almond's reasons for holding this slice of territory to secondary importance. The primary purpose of the Far East Command, MacArthur was informed, was to safeguard the Eighth Army by strengthening it with all forces available on a united front. MacArthur approved Wright's recommendations and notified Almond to prepare for the speedy evacuation of Hungnam.

2. Almond's Tactical Appraisal

X Corps was divided between units fighting to break through the Chinese entrapment and other units digging in around the Hamhung-Hungnam defensive enclave to safeguard the port area. The corps had suffered heavy losses in both personnel and equipment. The tremendous quantities of materiel lost during the retreat to Hamhung covered all categories, from bedding and tentage to construction and signal materiel. Enough supplies were lost through enemy action, abandonment, and voluntary destruction in two weeks to refit, according to conservative corps estimates, one-half a division.[4]

As the full extent of the Chinese offensive was realized, the intact withdrawal of X Corps became paramount. The speed of its retrograde movement was not dictated by corps tactical planning, but by the threat of overwhelming enemy attack. Long columns of enemy troops intermixed with red-paneled vehicles and weapon-loaded oxcarts, all streaming rapidly toward the corps' shrunken perimeter, were sighted daily by aircraft flying over the Korean hinterland. These reconnaissance flights also reported signs of heavy troop concentrations building along the web of snow-covered trails and mountain roads just beyond the corps lines. To Almond, the Chinese were clearly massing for their final offensive against his corps.

The first corps conference on evacuation was held December 8, in compliance with General MacArthur's directives. The corps planners anticipated a sea evacuation operation simply reversed from the normal amphibious landing process. Almond rejected the initial proposal for exclusive sea movement because he was still aware that MacArthur favored an overland corps withdrawal in conjunction with phased contractions of the Eighth Army front. Almond instructed his corps planners to consider every alternative, even cross-country escape, in case sufficient shipping became unavailable.

Overland and aerial movement plans were drafted, but their unreality became evident quickly. The roads leading south consisted of a poorly surfaced highway and a few trails twisting through mountain spurs along the coast. To traverse this distance, the corps would have to fight its way through Chinese roadblocks while traveling in a vehicular procession reliant on seaborne and air-delivered supplies along the route of march. The lack of trucks would also force the destruction or abandonment of most corps gear before the journey began. Airlift was not viable because of the scale of the enterprise. There were also questions about how long K27, the modern Yonp'o airport south of Hungnam, could be held within the collapsing Allied perimeter.

On Sunday morning, December 10, Almond drove to the Hungnam airstrip for a quick aerial surveillance of the corps front. At 11:15 A.M., his L-17 command plane soared into ten-knot winds under a brilliant blue winter sky broken only by scattered high clouds. The ground temperature had risen from a frigid twelve degrees to twenty-seven, but gusting snow was being driven over the rocky landscape below. The wind-driven snowdrifts reaffirmed the wind chill factors belying all thermometer readings.

Almond directed his aircraft over the main route as far as Koto-ri. He could see the entire Marine column snaking in a seemingly endless procession through Funchilin Pass and over the emergency treadway bridge. The cliff-ledge roadway's abrupt alpine descent stopped at Chin-hung-ni, at the foot of the mile-high mountains, and leveled out into a two-lane road that crossed the rolling foothills and disappeared into the valley leading to Hamhung in the distance.

Hours earlier in the early morning darkness, the vanguard of the withdrawing Allied column had reached Chinhung-ni, following a bitter cold night spent negotiating the treacherous incline. During the night a mud-clogged bypass over an icy stream had mired traffic temporarily near the cable car underpass, but engineers working in the bone-numbing cold repaired the roadway.

The scrubby village of Chinhung-ni was now full of Marine and Army vehicles. Almond glanced down at the town as the returning troops clambered into trucks for the last segment of their journey to Hungnam port. As his aircraft circled over Chinhung-ni, Almond could see Army self-propelled howitzers of the 92d Armored Field Artillery Battalion below. The battalion guns were already zeroed in on Koto-ri and prepared to level the former Marine stronghold as soon as it was abandoned in the afternoon.

Action still flared along the Marine route of march. Rising smoke smudged the top of a hill adjacent to the main road south of Koto-ri where a company of the 1st Marines repulsed a Chinese assault. Several Chinese company-sized elements were decimated after they were spotted in the open fields east of Hill 1081, moving on a course parallel to the Marine column. Army mobile 40mm guns of the 50th Antiaircraft Artillery Automatic Weapons Battalion pumped devastating air-burst fire over the enemy ranks. The Marine official history recorded: "The slaughter continued for an hour as the Chinese kept on moving southward [across the field of fire] with that fatalism which never failed to astonish the Marines."[5]

Almond's command plane flew east over the 1670-meter heights of Taebau-san as he reconnoitered the solitary northeastern market road leading to Sinhung. The town was still smoking from an earlier morning bombing. Almond spotted small ten or fifteen-member groups moving south, but could not determine their status. He noted their tight banding was indicative of split military maneuvering rather than civilian refugee mobs. At 12:30 P.M. Almond's aircraft landed at Hamhung and he drove to General Soule's 3d Infantry Division command post.

The 3d Infantry Division prepared defensive positions along the western portion of the corps' arc-shaped perimeter as it covered the 1st Marine Division's withdrawal from Koto-ri. Almond informed Soule and his division artillery commander, General Shugg, about the possible enemy infiltration parties he had seen nearing the divisional zone. Almond wanted motorized jeep patrols, supported by artillery, pushed vigorously up the valley road as far north as Sinhung. Soule assured him that a patrol from the 15th Infantry had been dispatched to scout the Sinhung area, but noted all division artillery was supporting the Marines. Almond personally ordered some artillery shifted to patrol support.

Almond checked the 3d Infantry Division's mapped-out positions and technical assets. He was angered that some divisional equipment was being removed to Hungnam port for future loading. Almond was fearful over the impact of premature measures, as they might trigger a wave of defeatism. He sharply rebuked General Soule and directed him instead, to "coil and concentrate his units for effective action," especially along the main supply route held open for the Marines. Almond emphasized, "We must maintain our strength intact to provide the capability of launching an effective attack in any direction." He departed after Soule agreed to adhere strictly to this principle.[6]

Just after 2 P.M., Almond arrived at the 7th Infantry Division command center for a quick fifteen-minute visit. The division consolidated positions guarding the northeastern arc of the Hamhung-Hungnam area perimeter and prepared demolitions on key structures. General Barr briefly described defensive and loading plans, while Almond emphasized the necessity for concentrated strength during the out-loading stages. The division strength was sapped, however, by the near destruction of one-third of its effective fighting force in the Changjin Reservoir debacle. Almond's exhortations to mass remaining military power rang hollow in the somber division headquarters.

The next stop on Almond's Sunday tour was at the Hungnam dockside. Corps deputy chief of staff Marine Col. Edward H. Forney was the control group officer-in-charge who coordinated final ship loading. The evacuation system was predicated on maintaining a fine balance between tactical and service elements on the beachhead. If too few tactical units were present, the corps perimeter would be jeopardized by military weakness, but if too few service units were available, the tactical troops would be stranded with insufficient logistic support. Col. Aubrey D. Smith determined the delicate sequence in which technical support units were displaced to the rear. He insured the orderly phasing out of service facilities, leaving enough critical support for the remaining combat forces at all times. As units displaced to the port for embarkation, Colonel Forney took charge of the actual evacuation and ship movements. His office was located in the central port complex.

In a previous conference, Admiral Doyle had expressed optimism that turn-around shipping would be unnecessary, but Forney disagreed with this prediction as he briefed Almond on December 10. Forney discussed the tremendous amount of tonnage that had to be moved (perhaps a half-million measurement tons of bulk cargo) and the shipping required for such transport. He also recommended the corps be allocated a reserve of shipping for unforeseen purposes. His concern turned out to be a wise precaution.

Almond toured Hungnam's actual port operations with the commander of the 2d Engineer Special Brigade, Col. Joseph J. Twitty. This brigade served as the operating agency for Forney's control group. The engineer formation organized and supervised all personnel boarding and cargo handling for the port. As the military situation deteriorated, Korean workers became scarce. The engineers employed up to five thousand laborers at any one time, but this number proved inadequate as shipping activity peaked. The absence of manpower curtailed loading operations and made it imperative to use every shortcut possible.

General Almond and Colonel Twitty weaved their jeep through the congested docking area while discussing engineer shortfalls and other pressing matters. They observed long lines of chained vehicles being hoisted aboard ocean-going freighters by booms and heavy pier-side cranes. The muddied docks were crammed with cargo stacked between buildings, and the cranes had to work carefully around the maze of telephone poles and wires. The two commanders also inspected jumbled storage areas and troop staging points. Almond promised to supplement the engineers with a quartermaster battalion, a tank company, and an ordnance ammunition company. On the same day, the latter unit underscored the imminence of the evacuation—all ammunition off-loading was discontinued.

During late afternoon a X Corps staff officer flew over the Marine column just after the rear units moved out of Koto-ri. The town was smothered in haze and smoke as the 92d Armored Field Artillery Battalion pounded the upland community with barrages fired from the flats at Chinhung-ni. The officer radioed that the Marine column was being followed by thousands of refugees. Slightly less than half the vehicles were south of the tramway bottleneck, and the column was still jammed along the steep-graded road stretching from Koto-ri to Chinhung-ni. Vehicles clearing Chinhung-ni were speeding down the highway to Majon-dong, where the Marines transferred to narrow-gauge trains. By dusk, the first hospital train carrying Marine casualties reached the Hamhung railroad station. At 7 P.M., the first troop train, with 750 Marines aboard, pulled into the Hamhung railyard.[7]

At Almond's evening conference on December 10, he was presented a major staff appraisal of the corps posture and estimated time remaining for evacuation. The report concluded that X Corps had only ten days to evacuate its 105,797 troops and 17,500 vehicles before a renewed Chinese onslaught would crush the organization at water's edge.[8]

3. A Visit from MacArthur

General MacArthur was most reluctant to place Almond under Walker's command, but yielded to the Joint Chiefs of Staff dictates to consolidate Allied power in Korea. He departed Japan and flew into Yonp'o to convey his decision to Almond personally and review the corps plans for evacuating northeastern Korea. At 11:30 A.M. on December 11, MacArthur's command plane landed through partially overcast clouds at the Korean airport and taxied past the smoldering wreckage of a C-47 Skytrain that had crashed two hours earlier. The supreme commander stepped out of the plane with Generals Hickey and Wright and Colonel Canada. The stiff seven-knot southwesterly wind kept the thirty-five degree temperature at colder wind chill factors.

The conference between MacArthur and Almond was held in the pilot's briefing room of Yonp'o air base. Almond summarized the current corps dispositions. The ROK 3d Division, having completed its sea embarkation from Songjin, was proceeding south in transports to Pusan. The Capital Division had arrived in the Hungnam area, along with other ROK I Corps forces, by a combination of LST, rail, and motorized movement and was defending the eastern side of the corps perimeter. Wonsan had been abandoned to the enemy.

The 1st Marine Division continued to close into the Hungnam area, after brushing past a final Chinese night ambush that claimed seven tanks (the crews were forced to ditch them after running out of ammunition, and the armor was later destroyed by air) and some other vehicles. The 3d Infantry Division's Task Force Dog was withdrawing back to the main corps perimeter, having successfully held the road open from Chinhung-ni to Hamhung for Marine passage. The 7th Infantry Division was engaged in patrolling and demolition activity as it guarded the final corps defensive area.

Almond finished the briefing by discussing corps plans for embarkation from Hungnam port. He stated that X Corps would be able to clear Hungnam by Christmas day, December 25, with arrival in Pusan projected two days later. He thus expected X Corps to be ready for employment under the Eighth Army by the end of the month. Almond outlined his requirements: almost four hundred thousand tons needed to be out-loaded from Hungnam, requiring 75 cargo transports, 15 troop vessels, and 40 Landing Ships, Tank (LSTs). He also wanted five hundred tons of equipment airlifted each day for five days during this process. Almond closed by promising that no serviceable supplies or equipment would be destroyed or left behind for the enemy.

MacArthur questioned Almond and his staff on their estimate of enemy action and its effects on corps evacuation. Almond replied that the withdrawal would be orderly, and enemy forces in his area were too decimated by the cold and effects of battle to interfere effectively with the planned movement.

At the conclusion of this briefing, MacArthur and Almond held a private conference. MacArthur stressed the fact that the juncture of X Corps and Eighth Army would place the corps commander under the direct authority of the Eighth Army. The former independence Almond had enjoyed with his separate reporting channels to Far East Command would be terminated. MacArthur emphasized that Almond would be placed under Walker's command, and subjected to Walker's will. MacArthur would no longer be able to intervene on Almond's behalf if he remained corps commander.

As Almond recounts, "General MacArthur explained that I could come back to Tokyo as [his] chief of staff in an active capacity, because I was still chief of staff in name at the time. Here I made a major personal decision. I chose to remain as commanding general of the X Corps in its assignment to the Eighth Army. I chose command in the field instead of the easier staff job back in Tokyo."[9]

After their private session, General MacArthur went to his aircraft. He saluted the assembled field leaders with the highest tributes on the corps' performance in breaking contact with the enemy and assembling intact for evacuation from Hungnam. At 12:40 P.M., the supreme commander's plane left the runway at Yonp'o and turned in the air as it headed for Kimpo field across the Korean peninsula. This brief, hour-long stopover was MacArthur's only visit to northeastern Korea.

4. Evacuating the Marines

Almond enjoyed a subdued birthday party at his corps headquarters at 8 P.M., December 12. The city of Hungnam was a bleak collection of concrete buildings ringed by pits for artillery howitzers, their muzzles aimed at the dark skyline of jagged hills. Almond's forthcoming task was without U.S. Army precedent: complete abandonment of a strategic battlefield under enemy pressure, with maximum emphasis on retrieving fighting forces and their equipment by sea.

He faced the delicate mission of evacuating the corps through a steadily contracting perimeter, under constant enemy observation and possible attack, as units departed on naval shipping in programmed phases. These phases were finely tuned toward retaining a balanced defense force on shore until the final day of departure. There were no manuals covering the evacuation of such a large military organization, complete with equipment, from an area under continual enemy surveillance.

One of Almond's major problems concerned the multitude of Korean refugees streaming into the corps perimeter. Effective civil control was lost as withdrawing corps troops abandoned forward areas, but now firm control had to be regained in the port area. Otherwise, large and potentially unruly civilian mobs could hamper or even overwhelm the military out-loading process. The mass exodus of refugees surpassed the wildest estimates of evacuation planners, and the cities of Hamhung and Hungnam buzzed constantly with the whining of gasoline-powered DDT dusting apparatus. Despite these precautions, four new cases of typhus were reported in the port as early as December 3.

The civil affairs office instructed the governor of Hamyong-Namdo Province and other selected officials to calm the populace. The crowds were informed of preventive measures being taken to eradicate the disease. The officials told the refugee assemblies to disregard false rumors, and that all civilians would be fed and evacuated if they abided by UN directives.

General Almond's policy to evacuate all civil government officials and their families, along with other pro-UN citizens who faced certain death at the hands of the conquering communists was only partially a humanitarian gesture. The policy was promulgated to lessen the sense of fear pervading the swarms of refugees. Almond also ordered his corps counter intelligence detachment to screen and release as many political and civilian prisoners as possible, permitting both ROK and Army military police to concentrate on crowd control duties.

The civil control situation suddenly worsened on December 6, after it was ascertained that Miss Mo Yun Suk, Korean delegate to the UN, had made an unauthorized flight into Hamhung and returned to Seoul with several dignitaries, including Rhee Ku Ha, the provincial governor, her uncle Mo Hak Bok, and Rhee Un Chun, the vice-mayor of Hamhung. The corps staff reported euphemistically, "this action has left a feeling of uncertainty among the remaining civil officials."[10]

Almond was enraged by the flight of these senior officials. He remembered vividly the disastrous scene of panic-stricken Korean hordes outside Seoul during the first weeks of the war. The very next day, X Corps published an ordinance prohibiting the congregation and circulation of civilians, as well as their possession of weapons, ammunition, and explosives. As the refugees continued to mob the defense perimeter, it finally became necessary to turn new arrivals away. Within the defense perimeter, civilians were restricted to their own areas to enhance control measures, prevent congestion of the limited road network, and discourage sabotage activity.

No enemy contact was reported on December 12, even though motorized patrols from the 7th Infantry Division ranged as far as ten miles inland. Corps intelligence analysts guessed that the Chinese were using this lull to regroup battered units and give their troops an opportunity to recuperate from the incapacitating effects of the recent frigid weather. The temperatures were above freezing throughout the day, rising as high as forty-three degrees under the clear sky. At Hungnam docks, the 1st Marine Division managed to load half of its bulk cargo and most of the 7th Marines. The valiant 7th Marines earned the right to be the first major American corps unit to depart this frozen wasteland. Of the fourteen medals of honor awarded to Marines in November and December, ten were earned by troops of the 7th Marines.

The refugee situation continued to threaten orderly evacuation. During the day, Colonel Williamson of the corps operations section called 7th Infantry Division officers about the thousands of new refugees swarming into the Hamhung area. Williamson reemphasized Almond's directives that the division was charged with keeping refugees out of its defensive area. He concluded the phone call by stating the refugee problem must be brought under control, because all civilians entering Hamhung ended up crowding the port at Hungnam.

At 9:20 P.M., corps was alerted that 150 freight cars in the Hamhung rail yard were being looted by starving civilians. A corps staff officer called 3d Infantry Division and told them to put guards on the rail cars. On the following day, however, flour was distributed to civilians at several points throughout Hungnam. Almond was keenly aware that starving people could not be controlled, and the foodstuffs were designed to forestall further incidents threatening the embarkation schedule.

On December 13, patrols from both the 3d and 7th Infantry Divisions fought small fire fights with enemy forces venturing toward the corps perimeter. Interrogation of the few prisoners revealed that an independent *NKPA* unit was trying to infiltrate the main perimeter disguised as stragglers, and a new Chinese division, the *81st PLA Division,* was reported in the vicinity. The only other action resulted from an accidental strafing of four jeeps by Navy aircraft. The mishap caused Lieutenant Colonel Besson, the hero of the Huksu-ri battle, to be evacuated after he shattered his ankle while dismounting from his jeep during the air strike.[11]

During the day, General Almond drove along the main highway to Hungnam, which was jammed with vehicles and mobs of Koreans moving toward the port. He stopped to inspect the MP guard post at the bridge and found no interpreter present; the officer-in-charge was not manning his station at all hours, and the guards were confused about their duties. Almond became infuriated at the prospect of enemy infiltrators slipping through this vital checkpoint, and insisted that General Soule relieve the military police of further responsibility for the bridge.

Almond expressed his displeasure in the strongest terms to Soule. The corps commander became more aggravated when his counter intelligence detachment reported the existence of a direct telephone line extending from Hungnam north into enemy-held territory, on which daily calls were being placed by local civilians. Almond was informed that the Hungnam terminal was located in the 2d Engineer Special Brigade compound and the northern terminal was at Huchiryong. He ordered the military intelligence staff to monitor the circuit to determine both the nature of information being transmitted and the sources involved.[12]

On the morning of December 14, Almond held an angry morning conference with Lieutenant Colonel Barsanti, his assistant G1, regarding rebuttal of the "grossly exaggerated press reports of losses in Chosin area and Dunkirk-type evacuation for X Corps." He also complained about United Press reports disclosing classified schedules for evacuating the Hamhung-Hungnam perimeter.[13]

The corps commander departed by jeep and inspected the port activities. All ships at the docks were being loaded, and trucks, supplies, and troops were assembled and being moved in an orderly fashion to the loading areas. Civilian relief flour and barley were being placed aboard trucks for distribution. One ROK LST and several barges were being loaded with refugees for movement south. At noon Almond stepped into Colonel Forney's control office and was briefed that the Marine division would be fully loaded by nightfall. Forney stated there was a good chance that the corps evacuation schedule would be completed earlier than expected. The good news tempered Almond's acrid mood, although a cold light rain started falling over the port.

The Marines division departed Hungnam port as Forney had promised. General Smith's command post was transferred to the attack transport (APA-33) *Bayfield* as the afternoon rain turned to snow flurries at night. The first elements of the 7th Infantry Division had already started boarding ships. The honor was reserved for the survivors of the Changjin Reservoir battle and the march with the Marine column from Hagaru-ri. During the day, the enemy conducted several light probing attacks against the northwestern sector of the 3d Infantry Division perimeter.

5. Destruction Along the Perimeter

On December 15, enemy activity along the corps perimeter increased sharply as the thirty-eight-degree temperatures dropped and the persistent drizzle turned to snow. Lowering clouds decreased visibility until air support was grounded by mid-afternoon. There were five separate attacks against positions of the 7th Infantry west of Hamhung, and one against the 65th Infantry north of the city. The enemy also assaulted the lines of the 15th Infantry at Chipyong.

These skirmishes were typified by the experience of Company B,

7th Infantry, under Capt. John J. Powers. The enemy surrounded one of the company's platoons and ambushed his relief force, even though it was escorted by three medium tanks. Captain Powers led his unit through an intense mortar barrage while directing tank fire against the enemy machine gun nests on either side of the road. He was seriously wounded in the encounter, and the relief force suffered numerous casualties. Powers regrouped his men and pressed forward in a vain attempt to reach the isolated platoon. The enemy forced his unit to retreat, and the column returned to its initial assembly area with the wounded crammed on the decks of their armored vehicles. As forward strong points became untenable, the 3d Infantry Division withdrew to prepared positions along the main perimeter.

Almond traveled by jeep to the 7th Infantry Division command post and presented General Barr with the Distinguished Service Cross. At noon, Almond drove to the Hungnam docks and viewed rows of Army tanks and trucks being hoisted aboard cargo vessels. The 44th Engineer Construction Battalion was operating floodlights in the LST loading area for round-the-clock operations. Almond visited Colonel Forney's control office, where he was briefed that ROK loading was being kept segregated from X Corps dockside activity. Forney had South Korean vehicles carried on lighters and small harbor craft directly to ships in the harbor.

The 8224th Engineer Construction Group completed two C-47-capable airfields near Hungnam. The airstrip beside the 121st Evacuation Hospital was finished, and the strip along the beach was ready for emergency landings. The group was also engaged in a multitude of other activities, from clearing the crash site at Yonp'o after a Curtiss C-46 Commando transport belly-landed and crashed into the terminal facilities, to sending dump trucks with shovel-laden engineers to repair the road in front of Almond's quarters.

The group commander reported that morale was dampened by "the uncertainty of the situation, long working hours, abnormal [cold] working conditions, continual attendant confusion, and the knowledge that our forces were in retreat throughout the [Korean] theater and that evacuation was made advisable as a result of enemy action." Although his engineers did not mind hard work, they were frustrated by the fact that their projects were destined for quick demolition soon after being completed.[14]

Each installation was demolished as soon as it was no longer needed. The first phase of railroad demolition was put into effect on the previous day when the engineers commenced destroying the highway and railroad bridges outside Hamhung. X Corps Transportation Officer Col. Loren A. Ayers instructed Company B of the 185th Engineer Combat Battalion to begin the eighteen-hour process of rolling locomotives and freight cars off the railroad bridge at Hamhung, during which time the structure itself would be destroyed.[15]

The 2,100-foot railroad bridge consisted of twenty-nine spans, eight having wooden-tie cribbings up to deck level. When the engineer company received orders to destroy this bridge and all rolling stock in the Hungnam area, it was decided that the spans of the bridge could be dropped individually and as many cars and engines as possible would be pushed into the void before blowing up the next span. About fifteen locomotives and 275 cars were assembled for mass destruction. The Korean railroad men helped shuttle the railroad cars from Hungnam to the bridge, but they hesitated after learning of the planned demolition. The Korean laborers and rail crews had to be "prodded" to do the job, but the engineers were able to release a lot of pent-up emotion. Lt. Erwin C. Hamm stated, "They had a helluva time. It was a good chance for the men to release their destructive characteristics."[16]

At 3:45 p.m., December 15, the southernmost span was blown. Ten cars and several engines were pushed into the gap until it was filled. Some of the cars were loaded with gasoline and the engines had steam up. As they were pushed into the defile the wreckage caught fire, and this process was repeated on each span. When the section of wood cribbing was reached, several carloads of petroleum and an engine were situated on top of it and the cribbings were ignited. The flame and heat was so intense that the locomotive became cherry-red and its whistle started blowing. In a few minutes the whole section crumbled into the river bed. As the rolling stock was pushed into the gaps, the rails sometimes spread or ripped, and prevented other cars from being pushed off. The blocked spans were blown with cars still on them. The only mishap occurred when a boxcar loaded with demolitions was pushed onto some flaming wreckage by mistake, and the resulting blast wounded two engineers.

Unknown to the engineers, Almond made one quick pass over the area in his L-17 command aircraft at 4:45 p.m. He jotted in his journal simply, "observed from air the burning of bridge with railway engine on bridge near Hamhung."[17] After Almond returned to Yonp'o he toured the airport with the base commander, Colonel Batterton, and discussed the removal of bombs and other equipment.

The corps commander concluded the day by holding a sentimental farewell dinner for fellow veteran officers of his former 92d Division. There was little time for reflection, however, and the assembled officers solemnly discussed the evacuation. They agreed that the most serious enemy threats to the final X Corps defensive pocket could be mauled by naval gunfire and air strikes. At this point, they decided, logistical considerations governed the rate of evacuation. The final evacuation process would become a simple matter of how rapidly the ships at Hungnam could be loaded.[18]

Notes

1. Schnabel, p. 284.
2. Schnabel, p. 281.
3. Schnabel, p. 285.
4. Schnabel, p. 297.
5. Montross and Canzona, Vol. III, pp. 324–325.
6. X Corps Commanding General's Diary extracts, dtd 10 December 1950.
7. X Corps, *G3 Operations Journal,* dtd 10 December 1950, Item J-60 and J-78.
8. The X Corps actual strength was as follows: Corps Hq and service units— 5,745 (5,273 Army + 472 Koreans); corps misc. combat units—5,714 (5,045 Army + 669 Koreans); 1st Marine Division—21,936 (21,755 Marines + 75 Army + 106 Koreans); Royal Marines—157; Marine Air Wing— 2,420; 2d Engineer Special Brigade—1,344; 3d Infantry Division—21,716 (15,726 Army + 5,990 Koreans); 7th Infantry Division—18,211 (13,335 Army + 4,876 Koreans); 1st Korean Marine Regiment—2,228; ROK I Corps troops—3,423; ROK Capital Division—11,498; ROK 3d Division— 11,403. X Corps, *Periodic Operations Report No. 75,* Pt. V-12. Ten-day estimate from X Corps, *Special Report on Hungnam Evacuation,* p. 2.
9. USAMHI, p. V-20.
10. X Corps Periodic Intelligence Report No. 71, Part V (19).
11. X Corps G-3 Daily Summary, dtd 13 December 1950, Item J-58.
12. X Corps Periodic Intelligence Report No. 78, II-6.
13. X Corps CG Diary, dtd 14 December 1950.
14. 8224th Engineer Construction Group, Dec 50 *Command Report,* Part IV, Remarks, p. 9.
15. X Corps G-3 Daily Summary, dtd 14 December 1950, Item J-81.
16. Eighth Army Military History Section, *Destruction in Hamhung and Hungnam,* p. 4.
17. X Corps CG Diary, dtd 15 December 1950.
18. The 7 P.M. dinner on 15 December 1950 was reserved for Almond's fellow officers from the 92d Division. These were Lieutenant Colonels McCaffrey, Rowny, Dobbs, Campbell, and Majors Sieminski and O'Connor.

CHAPTER 14

THE HUNGNAM EVACUATION

1. Covering the Evacuation

On December 16, X Corps forces withdrew from Hamhung and occupied a tighter defensive arc around the fog-enshrouded Yonp'o airfield and Hungnam port. Late in the morning, as a moderate snowfall blanketed the Allied coastal positions, Almond conferred with both Generals Barr and Soule on further withdrawals. Although enemy action against the perimeter had slackened, there were reports of a substantial buildup in the hills north of the city. As the number of X Corps troops guarding the perimeter dwindled in accordance with the scheduled constriction of the beachhead, intelligence officers warned about an increasing likelihood of a major enemy attack. Almond felt this risk was mitigated by the shrunken size of the perimeter, which allowed a smaller force to hold it and still cover weak spots and provide defense in depth.

The division generals reiterated their beliefs that the pace of retrograde movement was too fast. The job of defending the final perimeter was more difficult if premature withdrawals gave enemy troops unopposed approaches within striking distance of the beach. If the formations lost their maneuvering space too quickly, military units would be unable to respond effectively to a major enemy attack. Almond approved a new plan that established a strong picket line, controlled by outposts, in front of the main Hungnam line of resistance.

In the meantime, the South Korean units were departing Hungnam as scheduled, and by the end of the day most ROK troops (70 percent) were aboard shipping in the harbor. Almond instructed Barr to supervise the rapid movement of his 7th Infantry Division to the dock area for expeditious boarding as soon as transport ships arrived.[1]

The 3d Infantry Division was chosen as the final defending force for the Hungnam beachhead, based on its late arrival in Korea compared to the 7th Infantry Division. This scheduling, however, caused the final—and most dangerous—stand outside the harbor to be conducted by a disproportionate number of "colored troops." Maneuver elements manning the final ring around Hungnam included the Puerto Rican 65th Infantry, the black 3d Battalion of the 15th Infantry, and the black 64th Tank Battalion, or five of the ten battalions guarding the front line. There were also several black artillery battalions. The mettle of these contingents would be tested during the final phases of the X Corps evacuation.

The fortitude of the black 999th Armored Field Artillery Battalion was demonstrated during the morning snow squalls that grounded all carrier-based aircraft. Adverse weather conditions prevented aerial observers from directing artillery support for the Hungnam beachhead. The corps artillery staff feared that the Chinese might be tempted to launch an attack if they detected a diminishing amount of spotted artillery fire.

First Lt. James C. Isabell of the 999th volunteered to fly his unarmed aircraft between the low overcast and the jagged mountains, despite high velocity winds and subzero temperatures, to reconnoiter and direct artillery fire against enemy emplacements. When he returned from this mission, Lieutenant Isabell learned that naval guns needed to be used against enemy forces concentrating beyond the range of shore artillery. He voluntarily flew again into the extremely strong wind and directed accurate naval shellfire that neutralized several hostile strong-points.[2]

On December 17, the enemy still refrained from launching a coordinated assault against Hungnam. The Chinese and North Koreans concentrated instead on light and scattered thrusts against the 3d Infantry Division perimeter. Some observers believed these tactics suggested a reconnaissance of X Corps lines preparatory to a large offensive operation. The only corps-level command elements left at Hungnam were those essential to the actual supervision of the evacuation.

Air operations ceased at Yonp'o airport during the morning. In the final analysis, airlift played only a small part in the X Corps evacuation. Flights from Yonp'o were reserved for this purpose from December 10–15, and totalled 3,600 soldiers, 1,300 tons of cargo, and 196 vehicles—with most of this load being carried out in the last three days of that period.[3]

Capt. James B. Reed was in charge of corps transportation operations and remembered, ''We just loaded and moved cargo and passengers as fast as we could outload them. We forgot about safety limits and carried maximum loads. Still, in the midst of the confusion and evacuation, the Air Force did a peculiar thing. While we were trying to get rid of supplies, planes coming from rear areas brought us drums of gasoline we did not want. It took a lot of time to unload those 55-gallon drums, and then we had to haul the gasoline to Hungnam to get it evacuated. We got the Air Force to stop once, but then the shipments began again. Don't ask me what it was all about. I never figured it out.''[4]

On December 18, the weather turned noticeably colder, and the day's high of twenty-six degrees contrasted sharply with the forty averages of the previous warm spell. Stronger attacks were launched against the Hungnam beachhead, but the enemy only committed a minor portion of his available forces. The Chinese displayed their usual reluctance to assault strongly fortified compounds directly, and the net of naval gunfire and air support around the corps' final perimeter served as major insurance against an all-out enemy advance.

Arrangements were completed for relief of the 7th Infantry Division by the 3d Infantry Division. Two heavy cruisers, the *Rochester* (CA-124) and *St. Paul* (CA-73), as well as three destroyers, were offshore providing eight-inch and five-inch gunfire for General Soule's formations. These warships were assigned direct support missions covering the perimeter and received instructions from Navy gunfire spotting teams assigned to each regiment. The naval weapons were used for long-distance shelling and battlefield illumination, and became increasingly active in a short-range capacity as the field artillery was embarked. Carrier-launched aircraft also supported the defenders during daylight hours while B-26 bombers from the Fifth Air Force maintained night coverage.

During the morning, Colonel Moore's 15th Infantry sustained the brunt of the enemy attacks directed against the corps outpost line. The *79th PLA Division* was identified in action on the left flank, while the *227th NKPA Brigade* was reported attacking within three miles of Hungnam. During the early morning hours, five hundred enemy troops charged into the final defensive wire barriers.

First Lt. Douglas C. Wilson, a mortar platoon leader of Company H, 15th Infantry, was positioned at an observation post in front of the main line of resistance. Wilson learned that the observer at his first outpost was having difficulty adjusting his rounds, and moved across the fire-swept ground to reach the forward position. Soon after his arrival, the observer was wounded in his foxhole and the lieutenant tried to secure medical aid for the wounded soldier. Wilson was mortally wounded as he raced across the open ground under heavy automatic weapons fire.[5]

The increased enemy pressure on the perimeter caused the corps to accelerate destruction of the main airport of Yonp'o, about five miles south of the port. When the engineers arrived to "finish demolition" they found every building left intact and large quantities of gasoline, food, and other materiel abandoned. Five tons of bombs, rockets, and other munitions littered the area. Even pup tents were still standing. Maj. Robert A. Atkins of the X Corps engineer section remarked, "It looked as if someone in the Air Force had blown a whistle, and they all loaded planes and took off."[6]

The Yonp'o field offered a virtual treasure trove of ordnance and other materiel if seized by the enemy. X Corps was forced to divert its engineers from booby-trap and mine-laying details to destroy the abandoned gear at the airport.

During the first six hours of December 19, the enemy conducted his heaviest attacks yet on the final corps perimeter. Most of these were methodical assaults by the reconstituted *3d NKPA Division*, designed to locate the dividing points between units and detect weak spots along the perimeter. At 3 A.M. in the cold darkness, elements of Company F, 17th Infantry, were deployed in a series of bunkers approximately five hundred yards apart just north of Hungnam. Corp. James Hensley, a squad leader, observed a large hostile force approaching his strongpoint through a mountain pass. He awakened the members of his squad and alerted them to the enemy threat. Hensley manned a machine gun and waited until the North Korean soldiers advanced almost to his weapon before opening up with point-blank fire that shattered their lead ranks.

Both strong-points on either side of his position were overrun in the ensuing fire fight and the *NKPA* troops aimed recoilless rifles directly at Hensley's squad bunker. He refused to abandon his vantage point and turned his machine gun around to deliver accurate fire on North Korean infiltration groups behind him. Hensley was wounded after enemy grenadiers crawled forward and pitched hand grenades into the squad position at close range. After an hour, Hensley's machine gun became defective and failed to fire automatically. The corporal continued to fire single rounds manually until the weapon became totally inoperable. With his machine gun out of action, and carbine ammunition dwindling, Hensley led his squad in a charge through the North Korean attackers to reach the nearest surviving friendly bunker. During this battle, he lugged the heavy machine gun with him to prevent it falling into enemy hands.[7]

By this time, the X Corps command post was located in a cave along the beach. There were ten thousand refugees in the dock area and fourteen thousand more refugees in a village two miles north of the port. Almond drove to the northern refugee area and found no guards among the throngs of people. He was appalled at the danger posed by this situation, but lack of manpower forced him to insist on a single hourly patrol. He visited the black battalion lines and was briefed on their eleven-hour battle. Almond's entry reflected his opinion of the action, "1340: Visited CP 3rd Battalion, 15th Infantry, and Major Farrell briefed CG on previous night's activities in which his troops repelled a small enemy attack. The enemy had infiltrated one OP [observation post] and killed a man in his sleep."[8]

At 3:40 P.M. on the overcast afternoon of December 19, as temperatures hovered at twenty degrees, General Almond boarded a small boat and proceeded to the command ship (AGC-7) *Mount McKinley*, where his staff had already prepared his cabin suite. From this date forward, Almond directed the evacuation from his floating headquarters.

2. The Final Evacuation

On December 20, the enemy remained relatively inactive as the 7th Infantry Division completed out-loading at the port. Constant naval bombardment against shore targets kept enemy troops at a respectful distance, and the "overhead rustle of outgoing shells was a source of great comfort to the men on the line."[9]

At Hungnam dockside, Lt. Col. Wayne G. Higgins of the X Corps ordnance section supervised the 69th Ordnance Company and a wrecker crew from the 1st Ordnance Medium Maintenance Company as they loaded over nine thousand tons of ammunition and four hundred unserviceable vehicles and tanks aboard transport vessels. This work continued through the morning of the final evacuation.

General Almond enjoyed breakfast aboard the *Mount McKinley* in the Admiral's mess and his briefing was conducted in the ship's stateroom. He went ashore for only three hours and saw thousands of fuel barrels on the beach. He was chagrined at Navy directives to salvage everything possible, including the barrels. Almond recalled, "When the great number of barrels of fifty[-five]-gallon drums of petroleum products which we were evacuating instead of destroying were put aboard ship, two refugees would roll the fifty[-five]-gallon drum of petroleum or gasoline to the water's edge and place it aboard the small vessels available, really rowboats, and from there they would be moved to the ship's side and brought up by a derrick. This was a wonderful way to salvage [relatively unimportant] material that we would have otherwise left to the enemy or blown up!"[10]

Almond told Colonel Twitty, the engineer special brigade commander, to double the force of Korean laborers trying to manhandle the petrol drums at the water's edge into rowboats. At 1:43 P.M., a message was received from the Eighth Army informing Almond that General Smith's 1st Marine Division, now in South Korea, was relieved from further attachment to X Corps.

On December 21, the North Koreans made a substantial attack against all-black Company L of the 15th Infantry about four miles east of the Hungnam docks. The fighting continued for over three hours, and diaries and prisoner interrogations revealed that a regiment of the reconstituted *1st NKPA Division* was involved.

High winds, which reached gale-force gusts up to twenty-seven knots, buffeted loading procedures during the day. The frantic pace of out-loading continued as remaining corps service elements neared the completion of their out-loading. Just before midnight, the radio and cable section at Hungnam was destroyed by fire, injuring a number of soldiers and ruining most communications equipment.

On December 22, as Almond issued his Christmas message to his troops, small enemy patrols conducted probing attacks under the cover of darkness against the perimeter outskirts. All corps artillery units were loaded on ships and the perimeter was largely dependent on naval gunfire support during the night hours.

On the following day, the outpost line was abandoned and the 3d Infantry Division withdrew to its final defensive perimeter. Almond stepped ashore on the crowded beach to briefly pin the Distinguished Service Cross on General Soule. The high decoration completed Almond's round of similar awards given almost every commander with the rank of colonel or above in X Corps, with the notable exception of silver stars handed out to Colonels Guthrie, Harris, and Moore of the 3d Infantry Division on the final beachhead.

Planned demolitions of bridges and installations were executed by members of the 10th Engineer Battalion and Navy underwater demolition teams. While the X Corps Engineer office completed rigging the city and adjoining facilities for demolition, the Provost Marshal handled numerous criminal cases ranging from felonies to misdemeanors. The section was also heavily involved in many phases of the Hungnam evacuation including traffic control, security, and implementing the necessary measures to expedite civilian control and evacuation.

The personal conduct of X Corps members during the Hungnam evacuation was outstanding. For the month of December, there were only seven murders, thirteen aggravated assaults, six rapes, and two robberies. Unfortunately, the record was marred by numerous fatal traffic accidents, but X Corps was not alone in this unfortunate statistic. During the day, Almond received a priority message that General Walker, the commander of the Eighth Army, had died in a jeep accident earlier that morning.[11]

On December 24, there was no enemy activity and the last units of the 3d Infantry Division left Hungnam. The covering forces consisted of a battalion from each infantry regiment, which departed the beach in amphibious tractors and landing craft under the guns of LSTs and destroyer escorts.

Large amounts of explosives remained on the beach, including four hundred tons of frozen dynamite, five hundred 1,000-pound bombs, and two hundred gasoline drums.[12] These items were rigged for demolition at the last minute, and fuses detonated the explosives while the last battalion was just leaving shore. Two or three boats carrying troops were overturned by the blast waves as the tremendous series of explosions leveled the Hungnam waterfront. Even this destruction did not totally consume all the munitions on the beach, however, and destroyers were forced to close in and fire rounds directly into the stacks of intermixed gear and ammunition.[13]

The success of the evacuation was primarily a Navy triumph. Without warships and merchant vessels, the greater portion of X Corps would have been annihilated in an overland march. Over 90,000 troops were transported by sea from Hungnam, and smaller ferrying operations took out 16,500 ROK soldiers safely from Songjin and 1,100 South Korean Marines from Wonsan beach. The use of turn-around shipping enabled the entire corps to be evacuated in 103 large transport vessel loads and 89 LST loads.

Most refugees evacuated from the Hungnam area were loaded at Sohojin, a suburb of Hungnam. A total of 98,100 refugees were evacuated, not including babies carried on their mother's backs. This achievement was possible because as many people as possible were crammed on the ships. For example, two large cargo carriers, the *Meredith Victory* and *Virginia Victory* each sailed with 14,500 people aboard. The next largest number was carried by LST 668, filled to overflowing with 10,500 civilians and their baggage. Outside of Hungnam, the *Lane Victory* carried 7,000 civilians from Wonsan, and a South Korean transport, *BM 501*, carried 4,300 people from Songjin.

X Corps was extremely fortunate that the enemy never seriously challenged the evacuation process. Hungnam was neither bombarded nor attacked by sizeable Chinese or North Korean forces, and the corps was able to maintain a perimeter large enough to permit uninterrupted dockside activity throughout the out-loading process. Twenty years later, the Army's official history on policy and direction of the war still reflected bafflement over enemy intentions, "Fortunately, and for reasons best known to themselves, the Chinese made no concerted effort to overrun the beachhead, although light scattered thrusts suggesting reconnaissance in preparation for larger operations were made by them throughout the evacuation operation."[14]

The United Nations forces in northeast Korea were completely evacuated from Hungnam by 2 P.M. on December 24, 1950. As the troops reached the ships and were evacuated, they came under control of the amphibious force commander, Rear Admiral Doyle. General Almond observed the destruction with Admirals Doyle and Struble (Seventh Fleet commander) aboard the *Mount McKinley* which then departed for the open sea.

Almond explained his sentiments, "The fact that we had successfully made an evacuation and had an experience like Dunkirk in some respects, was a great relief to my mental and physical well-being that I well remember. As I remember, the night of Christmas Eve, instead of waiting up for Santa Claus, I went into a dead sleep right after dinner and woke up about mid-morning the next morning—several hours, however, before the ship arrived at Ulsan [South Korea]. My notes show that I had breakfast with the admiral on the 25th of December at 8 A.M. I hope I made the breakfast, but I don't remember any detail what happened.''[15]

The X Corps campaign in northeast Korea was over and its 1951 campaign as part of Eighth Army in southern Korea was about to begin.

3. Conclusion

The last battle of the X Corps 1950 campaign was fought on Sinbul-san, a mountain over 350 miles south of Hungnam, on the main Eighth Army front. General Almond's personal commando group, the 8227th Army Unit (Special Activities Group), was flown from Yonp'o airport south to Pusan on December 14. Lt. Col. Wallace M. Hanes's unit had escaped relatively unscathed from its northeastern Korean ordeal and was re-deployed immediately to Kyongju. From this location, the group began patrolling and reconnoitering the future corps sector of the Allied battle line.

On December 23, the Special Activities Group was ordered to capture Sinbul-san, the main North Korean mountain stronghold in the region, although little was known about the extent of defenses or enemy strength on the objective. The group's Special Attack Battalion, composed of South Koreans advised by U.S. Army and Marine volunteers as well as British Royal Marine commandoes, was chosen for this task and reinforced by the 8245th Army Unit Raider Company. The long approach march was conducted in the midst of a raging snowstorm which prevented detection of the assault force from Sinbul-san's commanding heights.

The boulder-strewn slopes of the mountain were glazed over with thick ice, forcing the commando force to utilize existing goat trails to reach the summit. The advance was painfully slow and difficult. Blizzard conditions forced the raiders to move up the narrow pathways on their hands and knees. As they climbed higher, the special mission group members encountered increasing resistance from snipers and machine gunners nestled among boulders littering the craggy hillside. The approaches up the sharp ridges were cleared in hand-to-hand combat before the main battle commenced.

The North Koreans were entrenched on the summit's four knolls and ringed by five lines of bunker complexes. As the Special Attack Battalion charged forward over the broken ground, enemy marksmen targeted key officers and sergeants waving hand signals during the assault. The battle disintegrated into a series of bitter skirmishes in the swirling snow, and offensive spirit waned as casualties mounted and the battalion leader was killed.

The group seized three hilltops and four bunker rows, but the last line of fortifications on the strategic mountain continued to resist. In a final effort to gain victory, the military advisors attempted to take direct command of the battalion and its companies. These changes were impossible to implement because of language difficulties, and many advisors became casualties trying to lead by example. The battalion was finally withdrawn because of worsening weather, survivor exhaustion, and plunging night temperatures.[16]

The North Koreans abandoned Sinbul-san peak shortly afterwards, but Lieutenant Colonel Hanes's decimated Special Activities Group never recovered from its heavy losses (being disbanded in March 1951). General Almond's hand-picked commando group had eluded the slaughtering ground of north Korea, but like all other X Corps combat formations— the 1st Marine, 3d Infantry, 7th Infantry, ROK Capital, and ROK 3d Divisions—it suffered a very costly setback before the year ended.

The X Corps campaign in northeastern Korea, whether at Wonsan, near the Changjin Reservoir, in the Taebaek Range, or around Ch'ongjin, shared much in common with the final corps engagement of 1950 at Sinbul-san. The majority of combat operations were dominated by bitterly frigid weather. The height of battle activity was often coincident with wind-driven, intense subzero cold, during which normal shelter or warming methods became impossible.

Frozen temperatures and high winds created a lethal combination that numbed the brain, jammed weapons, split engine blocks, froze limbs, and cracked artillery ammunition. Soldiers were forced to redouble their fortitude to fight both the enemy and the weather. The retention of personal willpower became as important as tactical prowess in combating the twin assailants. The severity of these wintry conditions forced the

X Corps soldier and marine to undergo an arduous winter campaign unequalled in American history with the possible exceptions of the Siberian expedition and the Revolutionary Trenton-Princeton engagements.

Under these adverse conditions, General Almond exhibited a forceful presence as X Corps commander. His constant frontline visitation to various headquarters, bridge sites, and even patrol bases reflected an unflagging, intense dynamism that drove fatigued commanders, insured subordinate response, and maintained a high level of activity throughout corps operations. Without this energetic measure of Almond's authority, the functional effectiveness of the corps might have been crippled by the Korean winter.

In addition to weather, the Allied combatants on Sinbul-san were also endangered by inaccurate knowledge of enemy dispositions, a problem that had plagued the entire corps venture into northern Korea. The colossal failure of Allied military intelligence to produce either sound strategic or tactical information was perhaps the most striking deficiency of the campaign.

Enemy mines were an unpleasant, and potentially disastrous, surprise when detected off the Wonsan invasion beaches. No accurate maps or terrain analysis existed of the entire region, and weather information was marginal. The size and capability of the enemy "guerrilla" movement—in actuality composed of well-armed but fragmented North Korean regular units—was never assessed correctly. There was a complete inability to predict properly or even recognize the magnitude of Chinese military participation on the battlefield—up to the very hour that forward Chinese divisions were storming Marine and Army lines on both sides of the Changjin Reservoir.

This inadequacy of military intelligence was primarily the fault of Far East Command and not X Corps. The small corps intelligence section gathered information and sent observations to higher headquarters for review and analysis. In the case of the first Chinese prisoners, General Almond may not have understood their significance, but he never interfered with the objective appraisal of his intelligence officers. In fact, he expedited their report to MacArthur's personal attention.

Almond cannot be blamed for the fact that MacArthur's staff misread its accumulated evidence, or tampered with it for political purposes. In the final analysis, X Corps was completely dependent on Far East Command for its military intelligence picture. The surprise Chinese offensive caught both X Corps and the Eighth Army equally unprepared, and many formations under the latter command were also ambushed and forced to execute precipitous retreats.

General Almond, however, was guilty of several serious errors in administering the tactical business of his corps. Most of these can be traced directly to either his intense loyalty to MacArthur, or his unfortunate racial prejudice. In the first category, his total MacArthurian allegiance robbed him of independent judgment and caused confusion in corps priorities.

A clear example of misplaced priorities was demonstrated by Almond's premature role as ad hoc United Nations representative for northeastern Korea during October and November. In a conventional warfare situation like Korea, corps leadership was strained by the need to monitor both civil and combat aspects in divergent areas. Almond's role as civil administrator interfered seriously with his corps command responsibilities, and should have been delegated to his chief of staff or other personnel. At the same time, it is clear that Almond assumed this mantle in deference to MacArthur's vision of early victory, and probably at MacArthur's own insistence.

General Almond was a corps commander subordinated to Far East Command, and was compelled to follow General MacArthur's orders. Although the dispersed maneuvering of X Corps may have appeared foolish in retrospect, it was dictated by superior orders which Almond was obligated to follow or else face charges of insubordination. Throughout all offensive stages of the corps' Korean campaign, its direction was actually decreed in Tokyo. During the retreat stages, the corps withdrawal was determined more by Chinese activity than by Allied plans, but even at this stage Almond was given little operational latitude. X Corps stratagem was formulated, approved, and ordered by General MacArthur himself.

Almond was directly responsible, however, for the internal mis-utilization of corps assets based on his rigid Southern convictions regarding the inferiority of non-white races. Almond's lack of confidence in many of his units caused him to openly question their performance value, undermine their morale, and shun their effectiveness. His distrust of non-white soldiering ability, aggravated by his frustrating World War II command experience, cancelled much of the corps' operating effectiveness. In a wartime situation, improper employment of such a large portion of total available resources inevitably courted disaster.

The X Corps was a unique polyglot, multi-racial assemblage in a segregated Army. One division (the 7th) was practically one-third Korean, and relations between the American and Korean soldiers deteriorated to the point that Medal of Honor recipient Lieutenant Colonel Faith resorted to summary pistol executions of Korean division members in the heat of battle.[17] Another division (the 3d) was nearly one-third Puerto Rican and one-third Korean, with a black infantry, tank, and artillery battalion as well. Marine Major General Smith personally integrated the 1st Marine Division by distributing a thousand black Marines throughout his command, rather than keep them in a separate service outfit, an act that incensed Almond. The corps itself contained mostly black service units, including both its medical ambulance companies, engineer dump truck companies, and ordnance ammunition companies, as well as its signal construction company, salvage company, bakery company, petroleum support company, and laundry company. Of the six corps truck transport companies, four were black.[18]

Almond's prejudices resulted in poor command coordination and supervision that hampered available support. Corps artillery, for instance, was badly mishandled. Almond was initially too impatient to get this artillery into action, resulting in the early November disaster at Yonghung when a black artillery battalion was hurried into exposed positions and decimated without proper infantry support. Almond blamed black incompetence instead, and relegated the battalion to non-artillery assignments. During the Chinese offensive it became imperative to use this firepower—whether black or not—but precious time was lost reorienting the unit toward its primary mission. Other areas of corps technical support also faltered, most noticeably in the crucial communications and transport services required to link the widely scattered corps units.

The main culprit in this case was actually the United States Army. Almond was simply a product of Virginia at the turn of the century, and cannot be chastised for a lack of modern sensitivity toward human equality. His racial views were formulated in his Virginia youth and molded by his narrow regional background and service experience. The Army, however, deliberately anchored his career advancement on the foundation of these innate prejudices.

Almond was promoted to star rank—by both his own and the Army's admission—for the express purpose of commanding a black division because he was perceived as "understanding Negroes." Given Almond's lack of fundamental military unit experience before World War II, it is doubtful he would have been promoted to general officer for any other reason. The Army later excused his abysmal record of division command by blaming the quality of his black troops. Despite Almond's pronounced sentiments against racial integration and non-white capability, the Army ultimately allowed MacArthur to appoint him to command the most racially diverse field command in Korea.

The Army, which at the time reflected the national policy of separate but equal treatment for its citizens, ultimately paid a high price for promoting Almond under these standards. The long shadow of the American Civil War, which shaped Almond's philosophy, fell across an Army institution painfully adjusting to global responsibilities, and stabbed dangerously into the frozen Korean wasteland as a modern manifestation of racial disharmony. The combat trial of X Corps reflected the Army's archaic perpetuation of regionalism at the expense of national heritage, as well as high command inability to grasp the limitations of human nature when personal loyalty was considered the greater virtue.

When X Corps returned to Pusan in late December 1950 it was placed under Eighth Army control and most of its constituent components were sent to other commands. At the insistence of Marine authorities, the 1st Marine Division was separated immediately from X Corps for utilization on another sector of the front. The 3d Infantry Division was reorganized and withdrawn from X Corps to an area south of Seoul. The 7th Infantry Division was only retained by X Corps until May 1951, although Major General Barr left the command on January 25. Less than a month later, on February 13, MacArthur rewarded Almond with his third star.

In April 1951 President Truman dismissed MacArthur from the Far East Command. The Army community was severely shaken by this action. For purposes of officer corps morale, General Collins decided against initiating any action that could be construed as retaliatory toward MacArthur adherents still in positions of authority. Thus, Lt. Gen. Edward M. Almond continued to serve as X Corps commander until relieved by Eighth Army commander General Matthew B. Ridgway, in concert with normal rotation policy, on July 15, 1951. Almond returned to the United States as Commandant of the Army War College, and retired in 1953.

The conflict in Korea was terminated that same year, and X Corps was withdrawn south of the newly created Demilitarized Zone. Once envisioned by MacArthur as the postwar U.S. headquarters for South Korea, the X Corps reputation was now too tarnished by defeat at the hands of the Chinese and evacuation from Hungnam to be seriously considered for this role. The Department of the Army selected I Corps for the task once reserved for X Corps, and the latter corps flag was quietly flown to Fort Riley, Kansas, for inactivation on April 27, 1955.

Devoid of any unit citations for its Korean service, the corps distinguishing flag remains cased in perpetual solitude. Underneath the cloth covering, two 1950 service streamers—inscribed simply with "UN Offensive" and "CCF Intervention"—are suspended from the wooden flagpole. The narrow blue pennants, each banded with white along the center and edges, bear mute testimony to the most crucial period of X Corps history.

The first "offensive" streamer honors the victorious commencement of the corps' Korean campaign as MacArthur's spearhead for the invasion of Inchon and liberation of Seoul. The blue and white cloth exemplifies the mix of rain and sea as waves of amphibious tractors churned toward the seawall of Inchon harbor. The second "defensive" streamer, in the same blue and white colors, represents the bleaker months of November and December, when soldiers in winter parkas shivered on the snowy banks of the Yalu River under a blue winter sky.

Both streamers were manufactured long after machine guns ceased clattering in the flare-lit darkness near the frozen Changjin Reservoir, and the last vehicle crossed the air-dropped "miracle bridge" spanning the canyon near Koto-ri. All those details are woven into the fabric of history underpinning both streamers. The pieces of cloth, like the "Big X" flag itself, are currently shrouded in darkness and no longer unfurled. Like the Roman Imperial X Legion, remembered primarily for its fidelity to two emperors, America's Tenth Legion, MacArthur's loyal instrument in two world wars, ultimately shared the glory and demise of its creator.

Notes

1. X Corps Command Report Annex for 16 December 1950.
2. Far East Command General Orders No. 192, dtd 24 July 1951. Lieutenant Isabell received the Distinguished Flying Cross.
3. X Corps, *Special Report on Hungnam Evacuation,* p. 3.
4. Dept. of the Army, *Combat Support in Korea,* p. 67.
5. Far East Command General Orders No. 145, dtd 31 May 1951.
6. Eighth Army Military History Section, *Destruction in Hamhung and Hungnam,* p. 6.
7. Far East Command General Orders No. 196, dtd 29 July 1951. Corp. Hensley was awarded the Distinguished Service Cross.
8. X Corps CG Diary, dtd 19 December 1951.
9. 3d Infantry Division in Korea, p. 103.
10. USAMHI interview, pp. V-29, 30.
11. X Corps Provost Marshal Report for December 1950.
12. Blair, p. 545.
13. USAMHI, Mildren Interview, p. 124.
14. Schnabel, p. 303.
15. USAMHI interview, p. V-31.
16. Hq Special Activities Group, 8227 Army Unit, *Command Report,* December 1950, Section III: Operations, with daily chronology.
17. For Lieutenant Colonel Faith's murder of Korean KATUSA troops, see Appleman, *East of Chosin.*
18. Black units in X Corps during 1950 were the 96th Field Artillery Battalion; 999th Armored Field Artillery Battalion; 3d Battalion, 15th Infantry; 64th Tank Battalion; 73d Engineer Combat Battalion; 76th and 512th Engineer Dump Truck Companies; 573d Engineer Pontoon Bridge Company; 559th and 560th Medical Ambulance Companies; 65th and 69th Ordnance Ammunition Companies; 58th Quartermaster Salvage Company; 130th Quartermaster Bakery Company; 506th Quartermaster Petroleum Supply Company; 549th Quartermaster Laundry Company; 272d Signal Construction Company; and the 377th, 396th, 514th, and 558th Transportation Truck Companies.

Appendix I
KEY PERSONNEL OF X CORPS AND SUPPORTING ORGANIZATIONS
(With Communications Codes)

Forward Command Party, United Nations Command [1]
Under General of the Army Douglas MacArthur

Naval Forces, Far East	Vice Admiral Charles Turner Joy USN
Fleet Marine Force, UNC [2]	Lt Gen Lemuel C. Shepherd, Jr. USMC
Deputy Chief of Staff, UNC	Maj Gen Alonzo P. Fox
Antiaircraft Officer, UNC	Maj Gen William F. Marquat
Engineer Officer, UNC	Maj Gen James G. Christiansen
Assistant Operations, UNC	Brig Gen Edwin K. Wright
Ordnance Officer, UNC [3]	Brig Gen Urban Niblo
Military Secretary	Brig Gen Courtney Whitney
Personal Staff	Col Charles C. Canada
Aid-de-camp and Pilot	Lt Col Anthony F. Story, USAF

President Truman's Personal Observer
Frank Lowe (Maj Gen, National Guard, Retired)

X Corps ("Jade")

Commanding General	Maj Gen Edward M. Almond
Aide-de-Camp	Capt (Maj) Jonathan F. Ladd
Aide-de-Camp	Capt Lloyd E. Jones, Jr.
Aide-de-Camp	1Lt (Capt) Alexander M. Haig

Corps Chief of Staff

Chief of Staff	Maj Gen Clark L. Ruffner
Deputy Chief of Staff [4]	Col Edward H. Forney, USMC
Deputy Chief of Staff	Col Esher C. Burkhart
Deputy Chief of Staff [5]	Lt Col William J. McCaffrey
1st Marine Div Liaison	Lt Col George F. Waters, USMC

Corps G1 Section, Administration/Personnel

G1 Personnel	Col Richard H. Harrison
Assistant G1 Personnel	Lt Col Olinto M. Barsanti
Adjutant General	Lt Col Frank W. Roberts
Chaplain	Col Frank A. Tobey
Civil Affairs Officer	Lt Col James A. Moore
Finance Officer	Lt Col Joseph H. Wiechmann
Inspector General [6]	Lt Col George G. Boram
Judge Advocate	Lt Col Russell T. Boyle
Occupation Court Officer [7]	Lt Col Lewis J. Raemon
Postal Officer	Lt Col Samuel W. Horner II
Provost Marshal	Lt Col William T. Campbell

Public Information Officer   Lt Col Kenneth E. Lay
U.N. Public Health & Welfare   Col Cecil S. Mollohan

Corps G2 Section, Intelligence

G2 Intelligence Officer   Lt Col William W. Quinn
G2 Executive Officer   Lt Col Robert R. Glass
Assistant G2 Intelligence   Lt Col Volkman
Assistant G2 Intelligence   Lt Col Mildren N. Huston (Dec)

Corps G3 Section, Operations

G3 Operations   Lt Col John H. Chiles
G3 Executive Officer   Lt Col William T. Ryder
Operations War Room   Lt Col Roy Lutes
Operations Coordination   Lt Col Ellis W. Williamson
Operations Planning   Lt Col Frank T. Mildren
Embarkation Officer   Lt Col Charles E. Warren, USMC

Corps G4 Section, Logistics

G4 Logistics   Col Aubrey D. Smith
Logistical Operations   Lt Col J. McCormick
Assistant G4 Logistics   Lt Col Dews
Amphibious Logistics   Lt Col Ray J. Laux

Corps Air Support Section

Tactical Air Support Officer   Col Edward C. Dyer, USMC
Combat Cargo Air Officer   Lt Col Bert M. Carleton, USAF

Corps Artillery

Corps Artillery Commander   Col William P. Ennis, Jr.
Assistant Artillery Cdr [8]   Col James K. Wilson, Jr.
Artillery Executive Officer   Lt Col Neil M. Wallace
Artillery Operations   Lt Col Avery W. Masters
Artillery Operations   Lt Col John U. D. Page [9]
Artillery Intelligence   Lt Col Oren Swain

Corps Engineer Section

Corps Engineer   Lt Col Edward L. Rowny
Engineer Operations   Lt Col Ernest W. Chapman

Corps Medical Section

Corps Surgeon   Col Alvin L. Gorby
Medical Executive Officer   Lt Col David Perlow
Medical Operations   Lt Col Hubert L. Binkley

Medical Sanitation | Lt Col Stanley J. Weidenkopf
Medical Supply | Lt Col R. V. Rivenbark

Corps Ordnance Section

Ordnance Chief | Col John D. Billingsley
Executive Officer | Lt Col Wayne G. Higgins

Corps Quartermaster Section

Corps Quartermaster | Col J. R. Ranck
Deputy Quartermaster | Lt Col Hugh Kevin

Corps Signal Section

Corps Signal Chief | Col Alvin R. Marcy
Assistant Signal Chief | Lt Col Edward N. Dahlstrom

Corps Transportation Section

Corps Transportation | Col Loren A. Ayers
Executive Officer | Lt Col Tucker

Corps Headquarters Commandant

Headquarters Commandant | Maj John W. Medusky (until Dec 8)
| Lt Col Watson [10] (Dec 9 only)
| Lt Col Hines
Troops Staging Area [11] | Lt Col Walsh

Tactical Air Command, X Corps
(1st Marine Aircraft Wing)

Command General | Maj Gen Field Harris, USMC
Assistant Commanding General | Brig Gen Thomas J. Cushman, USMC
Chief of Staff | Col Kenneth H. Weir, USMC
| (to 1 Nov)
| Col Caleb T. Bailey, USMC
Marine Aircraft Group 12 | Col Boeker C. Batterton, USMC [12]
Marine Aircraft Group 33 | Col Frank C. Dailey, USMC

1st Marine Divison ("Western")

Commanding General | Maj Gen Oliver P. Smith, USMC
Assistant Div Commander | Brig Gen Edward A. Craig, USMC
Division Artillery | Col James H. Brower, USMC
| (to 30 Nov)
| Lt Col Carl A. Youngdale, USMC
Division Chief of Staff | Col Gregon A. Williams, USMC

1st Marines	Col Lewis B. Puller, USMC
5th Marines	Col Raymond L. Murray, USMC
7th Marines	Col Homer L. Litzenberg, Jr., USMC

3d Infantry Division ("Kaiser")

Commanding General	Maj Gen Robert H. Soule
Assistant Div Commander	Brig Gen Armistead D. Mead
Division Artillery	Brig Gen Roland P. Shugg
Division Chief of Staff	Col Oliver P. Newman
7th Infantry	Col John S. Guthrie
15th Infantry	Col Dennis M. Moore
65th Infantry	Col William W. Harris

7th Infantry Division ("Bayonet")

Commanding General	Maj Gen David G. Barr
Assistant Div Commander	Brig Gen Henry I. Hodes
Division Artillery	Brig Gen Homer W. Kiefer
Division Chief of Staff	Col Louis T. Heath
17th Infantry	Col Herbert B. Powell
31st Infantry	Col Richard P. Ovenshine (to 5 Oct)
	Col Allan D. MacLean (to Nov 29)
	Col John A. Gavin
32d Infantry	Col Charles E. Beauchamp

2d Engineer Special Brigade ("Wallace")

| Brigade Commander | Col Joseph J. Twitty |

8224th Army Unit, Engineer Construction Group

| Group Commander | Col Leigh C. Fairbank, Jr. |

Republic of Korea I Corps ("Rogers")

I Corps, Commanding General	Maj Gen Kim Paik Il
Deputy Corps Commander	Brig Gen Rhee Jun Sik
Capital Infantry Division	Brig Gen Song Yo Chan
3d Infantry Division	Brig Gen Rhee Chong Chan
26th ROK Infantry Regiment	Col Rhee Chi Suh (to 3 Nov)
	Col Seo Jung Chil
1st ROK Marines (KMC)	Col Jun Hyun Shin, KMC

Navy Joint Task Force 7 [13]
Seventh Fleet, Vice Adm Arthur D. Struble

Task Force 90, Attack Force [14]
Task Force Commander, Rear Adm James H. Doyle

Support Elements

Flagship Element	Rear Adm Lyman A. Thackery
Tactical Air Control	Cdr Theophilus H. Moore
	Cdr R. W. Arndt**
Naval Beach Group	Capt Watson T. Singer
Service Unit	Capt Charles M. Ryan
	Lt Cdr J. D. Johnston*
Repair and Salvage Unit	Cdr Emmanuel T. Goyette
	Capt P. W. Mothersill*
	Cdr L. C. Conwell**
ROK Naval Operations Chief	Rear Adm Won-Yil Sohn, ROKN

Transport Elements

Advance Attack Group***	Capt Norman W. Sears
Transport Recon Group***	Cdr Selden C. Small
Transport Group	Capt Virginius R. Roane
	Capt Samuel G. Kelly**
First Transport Echelon	Capt Samuel G. Kelly
	Capt Albert E. Jarrell**
Second Transport Echelon	Capt Louis D. Sharp, Jr.
Third Transport Echelon***	Capt Albert E. Jarrell
LST Tractor Group	Capt Robert C. Peden

Fire Support Elements

Screening & Protective Group	Capt Richard T. Spofford
Blockade and Covering Force	Rear Adm William G. Andrewes, KBE, CB, DSO, Royal Navy
	Rear Adm John M. Higgins**
Air Support Group	Rear Adm Richard W. Ruble
Gunfire Support Group	Rear Adm John M. Higgins
	Rear Adm C. C. Hartman*
	Rear Adm R. Hillenkoetter**

Task Force 77, Fast Carrier Group
Task Force Commander, Rear Adm Edward C. Ewen

Task Force 79, Logistic Support Group
Task Force Commander, Capt Bernard L. Austin

*   during Wonsan landing only
**   during Hungnam evacuation only
***   not present at Hungnam

Notes

1. Present at invasion of Inch'on-Seoul, 15–21 September 1950.
2. During the Inch'on operation General Shepherd was assigned to MacArthur's staff for temporary duty as amphibious adviser and personal liaison officer to the 1st Marine Division.
3. Present at Wonsan landing only.
4. During the Hungnam evacuation, Col. Forney was in charge of embarkation shipping coordination.
5. Lieutenant Colonel McCaffrey was in charge of establishing the X Corps Advance Command Post at various stages of the campaign.
6. Lieutenant Colonel Boram served as X Corps Embarkation Officer at Pusan during October 1950.
7. The X Corps Occupation (Provost) Court Officer-President ensured public safety in the Hamhung-Hungnam area commencing December 3, 1950. Lt. Col. Raemon served in a dual capacity, also being the Chief of Civil Affairs for the City of Hungnam.
8. The staff members of X Corps Artillery and 5th Field Artillery Group served in a dual capacity except that Colonel Ennis was the X Corps artillery chief and his assistant, Colonel Wilson, was also the commander of the 5th Field Artillery Group.
9. Lt. Col. John U. D. Page was detached from X Corps Artillery with the mission of establishing traffic control on the corps main supply route. He was killed in action 10 Dec 50 and received the Medal of Honor.
10. Previously Corps Rear Area Security Officer.
11. Established for Hungnam during Dec 50.
12. Col. Batterton was also commander of Yonpo Air Base in Dec 50.
13. Joint Task Force 7 was discontinued after the Wonsan landing, and the Hungnam evacuation was carried out by the same components under direct Seventh Fleet control.
14. Task Force 90 Attack Force was known as the Amphibious Force during the Hungnam evacuation.

Appendix II
X CORPS UNITS

3 infantry divisions (1st Marine, 3d Infantry, 7th Infantry)

1 field artillery group (5th)
> with 2 separate field artillery battalions (92d, 96th)
> > 1 separate antiaircraft artillery battalion (50th)

1 amphibious tank and tractor company (Co A, 56th AT&T Bn)

1 base post office (1st)

1 chemical smoke generator battalion (4th)
> with 1 decontamination company (21st)
> > 1 smoke generator company (69th)
> > 1 chemical service detachment (504th)

3 counter intelligence corps detachments (7th, 181st, 210th)

1 engineer special brigade (2d)

1 engineer combat group (19th)
> with 2 engineer combat battalions (73d, 185th)
> > 3 bridge companies (58th, 526th*, 573d*)

1 engineer construction group (8224th)
> with 3 engineer construction battalions (44th, 62d*, 79th)
> > 1 port construction company (50th*)
> > 2 dump truck companies (76th*, 512th)

other engineer assets to include:
> 1 base depot company (712th*)
> 1 petroleum distribution company (82d)
> 1 water supply company (91st)
> 1 maintenance company (538th*)
> 1 light equipment company (630th)
> 1 topographic detachment (Det A, 64th Bn)
> 1 map reproduction detachment (8218th)
> 1 map distribution detachment (8223d)

1 finance disbursing section (106th)

3 hospitals (1st Surgical, 4th Field*, 121st Evacuation)

1 medical battalion (163d)
> with 2 ambulance companies (559th, 560th)
> > 1 collection company (421st)
> > 1 clearing company (618th)

other medical assets to include:
> 1 medical mobile laboratory (8216th)
> 1 blood distribution section (from 6th Medical Depot)
> 1 veterinary food inspection detachment (150th*)

3 military intelligence service detachments (163d**, 521st, 522d)

1 military police battalion (772d**)
> with 4 military police companies (58th, 59th, 88th, X Prov)
> > 1 criminal investigation detachment (19th)

1 ordnance group (60th*)
    with 2 ordnance battalions (74th*, 328th)
        3 ammunition companies (58th**, 65th*, 69th)
        1 heavy maintenance company (82d*)
        3 medium maintenance companies (1st, 2nd**, 7th*)
        1 automotive maintenance company (538th*)
        1 artillery and vehicle park company (13th*)
        1 base depot company (833d*)
        1 technical intelligence detachment (508th)
        3 explosive disposal squads (14th**, 15th*, 17th**)

1 quartermaster group (6th*)
    with 1 quartermaster battalion (142d)
        1 salvage company (58th)
        1 bakery company (130th*)
        1 bath company (821st**)
        2 laundry companies (537th*, 549th*)
        1 petroleum supply company (506th*)
        2 service companies (527th*, 580th**)
        1 subsistence supply company (20th*)
        1 clothing supply platoon (1st Plat, 564th Co)
        1 graves registration platoon (1st Plat, 565th Co)
        1 petroleum products laboratory (6th*)

2 replacement companies (52d, 369th)

1 signal battalion (4th)
    with 1 radio relay company (561st)
        1 construction company (272d)
        2 service companies (226th, 507th*)
        1 depot company (181st*)
        1 signal repair platoon (from 205th Co)
        5 radio-teletype teams (from GHQ, UN Command)

1 special activities group (8227th)

2 transportation port battalions (14th*, 21st**)
    with 1 port company (155th*)

2 transportation battalions (52d, 55th*)
    with 7 truck companies (377th, 396th*, 505th*, 513th**, 514th*, 515th**,
        534th*)
        1 amphibian truck company (558th*)

---

*   relieved from X Corps from 10 October–5 November 1950.
**   added to X Corps during either late October or early November and remained
    under corps control through December 1950.

BIBLIOGRAPHY

Primary Sources

This book was based primarily on official documentary sources stored in two locations. The General Almond papers and oral histories of other senior officers are housed in the U.S. Army Military History Institute, Carlisle Barracks, Pennsylvania. The Far East Command and X Corps records are contained in the Modern Military Field Branch of the Washington National Records Center, Suitland, Maryland.

Specific X Corps records utilized for this research included the following (all 1950): Periodic Intelligence Reports issued from September 19–December 31; G–3 Journal Files of September 15–December 31; Periodic Operations Reports Numbers 1–19; Operations Orders 1–10 covering the period August 28–December 31; War Diary Monthly Summaries and enclosures; Command Reports for October, November and December with daily annexes; Engineer Staff Study, August–December; IG Section Investigations and Complaint File; and Decorations Files.

X Corps also prepared a summary report, "Big X—Korea" (dated 1 May 54) and three special reports which were very helpful: "Operation *Chromite:* 15 Aug–30 Nov 50"; "Hungnam Evacuation: 9–24 Dec 50";

and "Chosin Reservoir: 27 Nov–10 Dec 50." Numerous other official wartime documents were also used, such as the Eighth Army monograph "Special Problems in the Korean Conflict." These sources are cited within the notes at the end of each chapter.

Published Works

Alexander, Bevin R., *Korea: The First War We Lost,* Hippocrene Books, 1986.

Appleman, Roy E., *U.S. Army in the Korean War: South to the Naktong, North to the Yalu,* Dept. of the Army, 1961.

Appleman, Roy E., *East of Chosin,* Texas A & M University Press, 1987.

Blair, Clay, *The Forgotten War,* Times Books: New York, 1987.

Dept. of the Army Office, Assistant Chief of Staff, G-2, *Korean Handbook,* dtd Sep 50.

Donnelly, Ralph W. et al, *A Chronology of the United States Marine Corps, 1947–1964,* Volume III, U.S. Marine Corps Historical Division, 1971.

Fehrenbach, T. R., *This Kind of War,* Macmillan Company: New York, 1963.

Goulden, Joseph C., *Korea: The Untold Story of the War,* Times Books: New York, 1982.

Gugeler, Russell A., *Army Historical Series: Combat Actions in Korea,* Dept. of the Army, 1970.

Hastings, Max, *The Korean War,* Simon & Schuster: New York, 1987.

Hopkins, William B., *One Bugle, No Drums,* Algonquin Books of Chapel Hill, 1986.

Knox, Donald, *The Korean War: An Oral History,* Harcourt, Brace, Jovanovich: New York, 1985.

Leckie, Robert, *Conflict,* G. P. Putnam's Sons, 1962.

MacGregor, Morris J. Jr., *Integration of the Armed Forces,* Dept. of Defense, 1980.

Manchester, William, *American Caesar,* Little, Brown, & Company: Boston, 1978.

Ridgway, Matthew B., *The Korean War,* Doubleday & Company: New York, 1967.

Santelli, James S., *A Brief History of the 7th Marines,* U.S. Marine Corps History and Museums Division, 1980.

Sawyer, Maj. Robert K., *Military Advisors in Korea: KMAG in Peace and War,* Dept. of the Army, 1962.

Schnabel, James F., *U.S. Army in the Korean War: Policy and Direction: the First Year,* Dept. of the Army, 1972.

Sharp and Dunnigan, *The Congressional Medal of Honor: The Names, The Deeds,* Sharp & Dunnigan Publications: Forest Ranch, California, 1984.

U.S. Marine Corps G-3 Division Historical Branch, *A Brief History of the First Marines,* Marine Corps, Reprinted 1968.

U.S. Marine Corps, *The 1st Marine Division and Its Regiments,* Marine Corps History and Museums Division, 1981.

Westover, John G., *U.S. Army in Action Series: Combat Support in Korea,* Dept. of the Army, reprinted 1987.

INDEX